Remembering *Brown* at Fifty

Remembering

Brown at Fifty

THE UNIVERSITY OF ILLINOIS COMMEMORATES

BROWN V. BOARD OF EDUCATION

EDITED BY
ORVILLE VERNON BURTON
AND
DAVID O'BRIEN

UNIVERSITY OF ILLINOIS PRESS
Urbana and Chicago

A generous grant from Agnes Gund
made the color reproduction
of the art possible.

Library of Congress Cataloging-in-Publication Data
Remembering Brown at fifty : the University of Illinois
commemorates Brown v. Board of Education /
edited by Orville Vernon Burton and David O'Brien.
p.   cm.
Includes bibliographical references and index.
ISBN 978-0-252-03477-0 (cloth : alk. paper)
ISBN 978-0-252-07665-7 (pbk. : alk. paper)
1. Discrimination in education—Law and legislation—
United States—History. 2. Segregation in education—
Law and legislation—United States—History.
3. African Americans—Civil rights. 4. Civil rights—
United States. 5. Brown, Oliver, 1918–1961—Trials,
litigation, etc. 6. Topeka (Kan.). Board of Education—
Trials, litigation, etc. I. Burton, Orville Vernon.
II. O'Brien, David, 1962–
KF4155.R45   2009
344.73'0798—dc22   2009026685

CONTENTS

ACKNOWLEDGMENTS

We wish to thank a number of individuals whose work and support made this volume possible. A generous grant from Agnes Gund made the color reproduction of the artwork possible. Simon Appleford, Beatrice Burton, Nick Gaffney, Victor Martinez, and Mary Beth Zundo were excellent research assistants. At the University of Illinois Press, we wish to thank Joan Catapano, Rebecca Mc-Nulty, Jennifer Reichlin, and Sue Breckenridge. A grant from the Center for Democracy in a Multiracial Society allowed David O'Brien to devote his time more fully to the *Brown* commemoration.

Two individuals must receive our deepest gratitude. The idea of devoting a year's worth of programming to the *Brown* decision was that of Nancy Cantor, who was Chancellor of the University of Illinois at Urbana-Champaign from 2001 to 2004 and is now President and Chancellor at Syracuse University. The many stimulating, moving, and enriching events commemorating *Brown* at Illinois during the 2003–4 academic year were first and foremost the result of her vision. Richard Herman, the current Chancellor of Illinois, has been immensely supportive of our efforts, and in his leadership at the university he has admirably promoted the ideals that stand behind *Brown*. We dedicate this volume to them.

Remembering *Brown* at Fifty

Introduction

Orville Vernon Burton
and David O'Brien

The year 2004 marked the fiftieth anniversary of the landmark decision of *Brown v. the Board of Education of Topeka, Kansas,* perhaps the most significant decision in American constitutional law and one that speaks eloquently to our vision of equality and justice for all. In a unanimous ruling, the Supreme Court declared that racially segregated public schooling is inherently unjust and therefore a violation of the constitutional rights of American citizens. Arguably, this decision set in motion the single most comprehensive and far reaching campaign of civil rights reforms the United States has known. Despite the uneven success of efforts to desegregate American education and achieve integrated schooling, the *Brown* decision is notable because it established the fundamental principle of equal access to public goods for all Americans and the responsibility and obligation of the state to protect those rights for its residents. *Brown,* more than just addressing public education, is a profound response to the 1896 *Plessy v. Ferguson* decision, which set forth the doctrine of separate but equal. As such it addresses core issues of citizenship and equal access and has had far-reaching consequences well beyond the confines of public education.

At its most basic level, *Brown* promised equal educational opportunity for all Americans, recognizing that racially segregated schools simply cannot make good on such a guarantee. More than just a decision about schools, *Brown* ended centuries of official state-sponsored discrimination against African Americans, articulating a principle of integration that proposed to sweep away Jim Crow laws in the South and to end de facto segregation in the North. More than simply a case about race, *Brown* promised equality of opportunity to all people, rich and poor, male and female, straight and gay, abled and disabled, urban, suburban, and rural. Perhaps no single decision has meant so much to so many (both in the United States and around the world) and to their dreams for a better life.

During the University of Illinois's commemoration of *Brown* in 2003 and 2004, no one, to our knowledge, expressed the expectation that a black person would be elected President of the United States in 2008. It seems fair to say that even the most optimistic among us would have considered this a slim possibility, even in Illinois, where we were well aware of the abilities of our then state senator

Barack Obama. (There is one possible exception: Obama himself, who attended a conference at the law school that was part of the commemoration.) And this despite the fact that none other than Martin Luther King Jr. had voiced the dream in 1964 that there might be a black president "in less than forty years."[1] The nation is rightly proud of the election of President Obama, which alone speaks volumes about the possibilities for progress in race relations in the United States. Yet fifty years after the decision, *Brown*'s promises seem unfulfilled to many. Expectations for a radical change in politics, which appeared abundantly in the press even before Obama was elected, need to be balanced against persistent problems that have hardly changed at all, or changed for the worse.

Poor children living in urban centers overwhelmingly attend resegregated schools as more affluent white families have departed for the suburbs. Methods of school funding virtually ensure that wealthy districts will offer superior educational opportunities. As a result, educational opportunity for many now means the chance to attend a private school, as voucher programs and school choice further threaten the funding of many financially strapped school districts. Studies continue to reveal persistent gaps in rates of punishment for school misconduct and in gifted program enrollments. White students have increasingly challenged race-based affirmative action programs, arguing that such programs interfere with their own right to equal educational opportunity. The Supreme Court's decision in the 2003 case *Grutter v. Bollinger,* which questioned the University of Michigan's use of affirmative action in its admissions policies, raises important questions about the future of such programs and about the ability of the educational system to eliminate achievement gaps in the next twenty-five years.

· · ·

To commemorate the anniversary of *Brown v. Board,* the University of Illinois devoted a year of academic and artistic programming to the issues addressed in the decision. From hosting the Brown sisters (and their mother) to an original production by choreographer Ralph Lemon, the year's activities acknowledged the broad and deep impact of *Brown* on the theory and practice of equal opportunity, while at the same time engaging in a debate about the success of *Brown* in ending racial discrimination. The centerpiece of this commemoration was a major conference held between April 1 and 3, 2004—fifty years after the decision came down—that explored the past, present, and future of the decision, bringing together a distinguished group of judges, policy makers, public intellectuals, and academics to discuss the challenges the nation faces in delivering on the promises of *Brown.* This volume gathers together many of the papers that were presented at this conference, along with others that prominent artists, scholars, and activists delivered at other events organized by the university throughout the year. Apart from an assessment of *Brown*'s specific successes and failures, these essays examine a second generation of school desegregation litigation, the challenges posed by school voucher and charter programs, the prospects for achieving parity in educational funding between urban and suburban schools, and the challenges of integration in the current environment.

Section I: *Brown*: Its History and Legacy

The first section of this book seeks to place the *Brown* decision in its historical context. Following the brief experiment of interracial democracy during Reconstruction in the nineteenth century, southern states began a program of discrimination that served to deny African Americans the guarantees of political and social equality provided by the Fourteenth and Fifteenth Amendments. To ensure white hegemony, whites kept African American citizens separated from them in every aspect of life: they established hospitals, parks, schools, even cemeteries and other forms of public accommodation to ensure that whites need never come into contact with African Americans. What quickly became common practice, accepted as a societal norm, soon found legitimacy during the nadir of race relations in the 1890s through the adoption of state constitutions that explicitly excluded African Americans from the political process and Supreme Court decisions that reaffirmed white supremacy. In a paper delivered at the Illinois conference commemorating *Brown*, historian Darlene Clark Hine argues, however, this very separation helped create a professional cadre of African American lawyers, pastors, doctors, and teachers who worked unnoticed by southern whites in fostering their resistance to the existing racial hierarchy.

Hine demonstrates in "The *Briggs v. Elliott* Legacy: Black Culture, Consciousness, and Community before *Brown*, 1930–1954," that a new "oppositional consciousness" emerged in the first half of the twentieth century. This consciousness succeeded in creating community-based support networks capable of challenging the "endless cycle of poverty and powerlessness" within which rural African Americans invariably found themselves trapped. Although white southerners increasingly sought—and, for the most part, received—assurances that African American communities were locked in their dependency, they overlooked the growing development of a system of core values that succeeded in channeling African American disaffection and resentment into the emergence of leaders with the resilience necessary to challenge segregation.

Almost as soon as the Supreme Court handed down its decision in *Brown v. Board,* white authorities made efforts to undermine its effectiveness and to ensure the continued dominance of white interests within U.S. society. In "Getting Around *Brown*: The Social Warrant of the New Racism," George Lipsitz outlines the "deliberate, collective, and organized white resistance" to desegregation that "remains pervasive, powerful, and predominant in every region of the country." Lipsitz sees every level of local, state, and national government as culpable in transforming the civil rights movement's "social warrant"—those unwritten, but generally accepted, rules for what a society does and does not permit its citizens to do—from one that promotes the equality of all citizens to one that embraces selfishness and individual advancement, favoring the already wealthy and advantaged over the poor and disfranchised.

Lipsitz sees the roots of this new racism in the very triumph that seemed to mark a new beginning for racial equality. By ambiguously declaring that desegregation should proceed with "all deliberate speed" rather than immediately, the Supreme Court allowed groups with a vested interest in preserving white supremacy to delay the implementation of desegregation policies. These groups have furthermore succeeded in subverting the language of *Brown* from an impassioned denunciation of de jure segregation into a rationale for the preservation of de facto segregation.

Although the Supreme Court's 1954 ruling in *Brown* dealt specifically with ending the formal segregation of public schools, its consequences have extended far beyond this. Margaret L. Andersen discusses the way in which the Courts broadened the reach of *Brown* to change perceptions of race and social equality throughout the United States. In "From *Brown* to *Grutter:* The Diverse Beneficiaries of *Brown v. Board of Education*," she shows how many groups—from other ethnicities to gays and lesbians to the aged and those with disabilities—have taken advantage of the legal framework that the Supreme Court opened to improve their own social, political, and moral standing in United States society. Public opinion polls now show an overwhelming level of support for integrated education and equal access to jobs. As the majority of Americans have shown a greater level of support for racial equality, so they have supported other social groups that have relied on *Brown*'s expanded interpretation of the Fourteenth Amendment to extend the guarantee of equal protection to all citizens, regardless of race, gender, age, or sexual orientation.

Although equal opportunity is legally in place, actual equality remains elusive, as *Brown* failed to eliminate the institutional basis of race, gender, and class privilege that underlies discriminatory and racist practices. Furthermore, Andersen argues that *Brown* inadvertently provided a framework in which the increasing conservatism of the judicial, legislative, and executive branches of government could dismiss considerations of race, gender, age, and sexual orientation ostensibly in pursuit of a society that is blind to any consideration of identity. The standard for determining discrimination now appears to rest on the concept of "intent" rather than "effect" and favors concerns about the "harm" done through such programs as affirmative action by "favoring" racial and social minorities over white males. Ironically, the success of *Brown* and the civil rights movement in ending Jim Crow segregation and overt racism has made it more difficult for activists to mobilize public opinion against the institutionalized forms of racism and privilege that still exist in the United States.

Segregation in schools was just one of numerous forms of discrimination that white southerners used to minimize contact between the races; segregated public accommodations in southern states included parks, hospitals, beaches, courthouses, golf courses, prisons, and even bookmobiles. In his essay, "Beyond School Desegregation: The Impact of *Brown*," Laughlin McDonald discusses the transition of *Brown* from a narrowly interpreted decision, severely limited in its reach as a result of the Supreme Court's edict that desegregation should be carried out "with all deliberate speed," to the reassertion of *Brown* by the civil rights movement and the courts as a means of facilitating the dismantling of this all-encompassing system of racial dominance.

Jason Chambers's "A Mind Is a Terrible Thing to Waste" examines another effort to build on the achievement of *Brown*: the advertising campaign of the United Negro College Fund. His work addresses African American students' limited access to college education due to a lack of funding as well as the financial struggles of historically black institutions of higher learning. He looks to the UNCF's extremely successfully advertisement slogan, "A Mind Is a Terrible Thing to Waste," as a turning point for African American students and colleges. Chambers tells of Tuskegee Institute president Dr. Frederick Patterson and the far-reaching impact he had when he created the UNCF. Chambers writes, "while the *Brown* decision opened the door to educational opportunity, it was the UNCF that was part of the action mechanism that allowed blacks to step through and to broaden educational access within America."

Chambers recounts the initial challenge of the advertising campaign: the UNCF did not want to portray African Americans as charity cases. With the help of the Advertising Council, they launched a campaign that showed the potential among African Americans that had gone unrealized due to discrimination. The goal was to see the UNCF as a human issue, not a race issue. Chambers examines themes in the campaign throughout the years, such as great achievers from historically black institutions and African American celebrities supporting the UNCF, and he concludes, "The advertising campaign for the UNCF not only brought more positive images of blacks to the nation's advertising landscape, it also helped initiate a national conversation about race and opportunity." Although the campaign began a decade before the *Brown* ruling, Chambers demonstrates that in many ways the Supreme Court decision and the UNCF campaign needed each other to bring equal access to the African American community.

In "Success *and* Failure: How Systemic Racism Trumped the *Brown v. Board of Education* Decision," Joe R. Feagin, who inspired the Illinois Center for Democracy in a Multiracial Society, and Bernice McNair Barnett, who organized a symposium in honor of Feagin, take a wide-ranging look at the history of *Brown v. Board*. They explain the development of "systemic racism"—which they define as the "racialized exploitation and subordination of Americans of color by white Americans"—and how segregation of the public school system continues to form an integral part of it. The authors then examine the efforts of the NAACP to challenge this institutionalized racism through legal strategies that culminated in the *Brown v. Board of Education*. Although Feagin and Barnett outline the numerous positive effects of *Brown* in education and other areas, they explore the impact that desegregation had on the lives of children affected by it. They argue that legal desegregation failed as a result of continued discrimination within integrated schools and conclude that this deliberate failure results from white policymakers and politicians undermining the ideals that lie at the heart of the *Brown* decision.

In "From Racial Liberalism to Racial Literacy: *Brown v. Board of Education* and the Interest–Divergence Dilemma," Lani Guinier, the 2004 University of Illinois at Urbana-Champaign Commencement speaker, also argues that the basis upon which NAACP counsel argued *Brown v. Board* and the Supreme Court decided the case inadvertently helped to create a ruling that redefined "equality, not as a fair and just distribution of resources, but as the absence of [the] formal, legal barriers that separated the races." According to Guinier, the arguments at the heart of *Brown* derived from a form of "racial liberalism" that was specifically tailored to highlight the "effects of racial discrimination without fear of disrupting society as a whole," while protecting the interests of middle- and upper-class whites that would remain largely unaffected by desegregation. As Guinier shows, however, the cause of racism in the United States was not segregation but white supremacy.

Guinier argues that the failing of *Brown v. Board* is that its authors framed the problem as a "psychological and interpersonal challenge rather than a structural problem routed in our economic and political system." Furthermore, their analysis failed to acknowledge the importance of race to working-class whites, who were able to look at themselves as being more advantaged than their African American neighbors. By doing so, they failed to anticipate how quickly and easily the attitudes that underpinned segregation would reappear in new forms; they especially underestimated the vehemence with which working-class whites would oppose desegregation. To confront this new understanding of the nature of racism, Guinier proposes a paradigm shift away from the racial liberalism that has dominated political thought for the last fifty years to a new way of thinking that she terms "racial literacy," which presents race as "epiphenomenal" and recognizes its interplay with class and geography. As long as Americans fail to acknowledge that racism is fundamentally a question of the distribution of power in society, it will continue to emerge as the principal form of division within the United States.

Scholars' interpretations of *Brown*'s effects remain mixed. Despite the initial success that efforts at desegregation had, white resistance did not go away, and today many schools have once again segregated. Some parents who can afford to are now sending their children to private schools that are essentially all white. White-flight to the suburbs of major cities is creating schools that are as racially segregated as before the *Brown* decision. Furthermore, whereas the Supreme Court had previously shown itself willing to tackle segregation, its philosophy has now changed so that in rulings such as 1995's *Missouri v. Jenkins,* which terminated Kansas City's desegregation plan, justices have supported actions designed to ensure white students' access to better funded and equipped schools. In 2007 the Supreme Court struck down integration plans championed by school boards in Louisville, Kentucky, and Seattle, Washington, and the opinion exuded hostility toward any race-based solution to integration.

This resegregation of America's schools and the corresponding failure of support to education for African Americans and other minority groups have correlated with a staggering increase in the number of people incarcerated in America's prisons and on parole—up from 1,842,100 in 1980 to 6,934,200 in 2003. An estimated 9.3 percent of African American males aged between twenty-five and twenty-nine were in prison in 2003, compared to 2.6 percent of Latino males and only 1.1 percent of white males in the same demographic.[2] Given that the majority of states prevent those with criminal convictions from participating in elections, the disparity in incarceration rates between the different races that this statistic reveals has startling implications for African American representation in the political system. Perhaps by rechanneling some government funding away from prisons and toward programs that ensure minorities truly have an equal education, it will be possible to correct this injustice.

Section II: *Brown* and Lived Experience

In 1947 the Reverend Joseph A. De Laine, a pastor in Clarendon County, South Carolina, was attending classes at Allen University, where he was a trustee. He heard the president of the South Carolina NAACP complain that they had been unable to find anyone brave enough to become a plaintiff in a school bus discrimination case against the state, even though the Palmetto Teachers Association had the funds necessary to take the suit to trial. De Laine immediately vowed that he would find someone among his parishioners who was willing to stand up against white supremacy. Although the first suit De Laine organized had to be dropped, in December 1950 the residents of Clarendon County filed

Briggs v. Elliot in Federal Court, seeking the abolition of legal segregation in the state on the basis that the separately maintained schools did not provide equal facilities for their students. This case was the earliest of the five separate suits that came before the Supreme Court as *Brown v. Board* and was the only one originating in the Deep South, which required segregation by law. Although more people know about the Kansas case, which originated with the Brown sisters, one could date the beginning of the modern civil rights movement from the valiant efforts of Reverend De Laine and his troop of rural heroes.

So overwhelming was the evidence in *Briggs v. Elliott* that, when the case was originally argued, South Carolina officials made no effort to defend the inequality between the schools, instead announcing plans to "equalize" the segregated schools through a massive spending program funded by a new $75 million sales tax. At the same time, however, the white residents of Clarendon County embarked on a sustained effort of intimidation against the African American plaintiffs, many of whom lost their jobs and homes and faced threats of violence. Even though De Laine was not himself one of the plaintiffs, the community recognized him as leader of the desegregation effort, and white supremacists singled him out as a target. After the *Brown* ruling, whites burned his church to the ground and fired at his home; ultimately he fled the state after he tried to protect his family by returning gunfire.

In two essays, "*Briggs*: South Carolina's Bold Step That Led to *Brown*" and "About Integration: In Memory of the Reverend J. A. De Laine," two of De Laine's children, Joseph A. De Laine Jr. and Ophelia De Laine Gona, recall the origins and challenges of *Briggs* and remember how difficult these times were both for their father and for the African American community in Clarendon County. What emerges from their stories is their father's strength and dignity in the face of overwhelming obstacles and his faith that whites and African Americans would one day live together in peace and equality. John Hope Franklin, who served as an expert witness for the series of *Brown* cases, recounts his experiences in working with the legendary civil rights attorney Thurgood Marshall. In his compelling story of working on the landmark case, Franklin reveals much about Thurgood Marshall as well as about Franklin himself, and race relations in America.

One of the most common means by which whites in communities such as Clarendon County attempted to avoid desegregation was through so-called "freedom-of-choice" plans in which parents were theoretically able to pick the school that their children attended. In practice, however, freedom-of-choice plans merely served to reinforce segregated patterns: schools that had been all-white generally remained overwhelmingly white; schools that were all–African American remained exclusively African American. In New Kent County, Virginia, for example, although 115 African American students chose to attend mostly white New Kent High School, 85 percent of all school-age

African Americans in the county—and no whites—attended the traditionally all–African American George W. Watkins School. Constance Curry's essay "The Intolerable Burden" tells the story of the Carter family—one of the few African American families in rural Mississippi who utilized a freedom-of-choice plan to send their children to a previously all-white school.

As the only African American children in these schools, the Carter children faced years of torment from their fellow students, and the white community harassed and threatened the family. The Carters were not unusual in facing such retribution: African American families whose children went to previously white schools faced the loss of their jobs and lines of credit, had their livelihoods destroyed, and endured burning crosses and physical intimidation. Two Supreme Court rulings—*Green v. County School Board* in 1968 and *Alexander v. Holmes County Board of Education* in 1969—ended this overt resistance by declaring that freedom-of-choice plans were ineffective and ending Mississippi's operation of dual school systems, finally allowing African Americans to attend integrated schools without fear of retribution. Seven of the Carter children, for example, graduated from the University of Mississippi, a former bastion of white elitism.

In the wake of *Brown v. Board,* the Supreme Court heard several other challenges to segregation, including the 1960 case *Boynton v. Virginia,* which supported an African American law student's challenge against his conviction by the State of Virginia for trespassing after refusing to move to the "colored" section of a restaurant at a bus station. Although the Court did not touch on any constitutional questions, it ruled that segregation in interstate public facilities violated the Interstate Commerce Act, which made it illegal "to subject any particular person . . . to any unjust discrimination" while engaged in interstate commerce. In order to test compliance of this ruling, the Congress of Racial Equality (CORE) and the Student Non-Violent Coordinating Committee (SNCC) organized a series of "freedom rides," integrated buses from northern cities to locations in the Deep South, where they met intimidation and violence from white mobs determined to prevent desegregation.

In 1961 thirteen brave souls from across the country came together to test the Supreme Court's rulings on desegregated public facilities in interstate travel in the South. Both blacks and whites participated in this "Freedom Ride." In "The Freedom Riders: Two Personal Perspectives," James Onderdonk uses portions of talks delivered in Champaign-Urbana by the Reverend Ben Cox and Henry "Hank" Thomas, two of the original thirteen riders, as part of the university's commemoration of *Brown v. Board of Education.* Following Onderdonk's essay, Ed Blankenheim, a white Chicagoan and another original Freedom Rider, explains in a brief biographical sketch his own awakening to the racial intolerance of the South. As a Marine stationed in North Carolina, he could not understand the indifference displayed by his commanding officers when two military policemen essentially escorted a fellow Marine off a bus when he refused to sit in the back. This incident later motivated him to join the Freedom Riders, whom he portrays as a group of people fully aware of the dangers confronting them but determined to do what was necessary to help end segregation.

In "The Middle Generation after *Brown*," Kal Alston speaks directly to a young audience. She writes to a generation born after the 1960s, and her essay "is meant to be a bridging story, one story about what it meant to be too young to march but too old ever to believe in racism as simply an historical artifact." In a very personal account, Alston relates her experiences with her family's move from Greensboro, North Carolina (where her neighbor had been a participant in the Woolworth sit-ins), to suburban Lawrence Park, Pennsylvania. They moved into an all-white neighborhood because her parents, both educated African Americans, "knew the direct connection of educational opportunity to life chances." Therefore, they chose the location with the best school and broke the color-barrier of the Pennsylvania town.

Alston and her siblings made friends in Lawrence Park, but at the time she did not see her life in terms of race. She explains, "I enjoyed the benefits of my parents' racial struggles without having to engage in very many battles on my own behalf." Alston's story is one of triumph: "we were taught to see ourselves as the *beneficiaries* of an ongoing struggle, as *entitled* to be participants in the next phase of America's attempts to include all her sons and daughters." Her essay serves as call to action for the younger generation. Reminding them of the doors *Brown* opened for all people, she encourages her audience to "take up the legacy of *Brown*," to "experience as fully as you can your fellow students and your faculty in all the forms of their diversity. Learn from their different backgrounds, experiences, and worldviews."

Section III: The Arts and *Brown*

In recent years, the University of Illinois at Urbana-Champaign has demonstrated a strong commitment to the arts, seeing in them forms of knowledge and understanding that must stand alongside other fields of academic inquiry. The *Brown* commemoration was unique in the prominent role it gave to the arts as a means for remembering the landmark decision and exploring its ramifications. The events at Illinois included a student production of Lorraine Hansberry's *A Raisin in the Sun;* visits by dancers and choreographers Karen Love, Reggie Wilson, and Ralph Lemon; teaching residencies for film director Frederick Marx, choreographer Dianne McIntyre, and Amaniyea Payne of the Muntu African Dance Company; a number of film series; a lecture by theater producer and director Woodie King Jr.; and a visit from book artist Amos Paul Kennedy Jr.

In this volume, the poet Sekou Sundiata, who also visited campus in 2004, addresses the important role that the arts have to play in achieving the democratic and diverse society envisioned in *Brown*. Sundiata writes of "imagination as a necessary and sacred space, a space in which 'if not probable, all is possible.' And although the imagination exists within material borders and is shaped, to a large degree, by the material world, it can transcend those borders and conjure infinite possibilities of being. . . . [Art] can facilitate and compel the imagination in irresistible ways. We know that Imagination alone cannot solve real world problems, but real world problems cannot be solved without it." For Sundiata, the failure of the United States to fully deliver on the promises of *Brown* is in part a failure of the imagination: "For People of Whiteness the problem is twofold: one, a failure to imagine anything other than itself as the defining reality; and two, a willingness to see the Other in terms that erases the humanity of the Other." Art has a clear role to play here, for it "works on our consciousness in special ways that compel us and enable us to imagine the Other."

During the *Brown* commemoration, the arts fulfilled again and again the special role Sundiata envisions for them. One particularly spectacular example was dancer and choreographer Ralph Lemon's *Come Home Charlie Patton,* which had its world premiere at the university's Krannert Center for the Performing Arts and then toured to venues in Chicago, Dallas, Minneapolis, Newark, New York City, and Pittsburgh. The performance used the arts of dance, music, video, and digital imaging to conjure up images of African American cultural history, racial oppression, and the civil rights struggle. Lemon spent four years traveling in the Deep South, where he visited, among other places and people, unmarked lynching sites and the descendants of legendary blues musicians. In his essay in this volume, entitled "What Was Always There," Lemon reflects on his efforts to connect with the local societies there and his feelings of both identity and difference. Lemon was especially interested to find traces of a disappearing world where the great achievements of bluesmen sprang forth in the midst of racial oppression. For Lemon, the arts function as a repository of African American memory, a testament to endurance, and a means to imagine new possibilities by building on and reacting to the experiences of the past.

Other essays in the volume document projects funded as part of the commemoration. John Jennings describes "The Chance Project," a national collegiate poster-design competition that used the phrase "A Chance to . . ." as a starting point for entrants to create a slogan and poster design addressing the implications of the *Brown* decision. Jennings, a prominent artist working primarily in comic books and graphic novels and a professor and former graduate student at the University of Illinois at Urbana-Champaign, reflects not only on the results of the competition, but also on his own experiences in the field of graphic design at the University of Illinois and at historically African American colleges and universities.

David O'Brien partially recreates here another project funded by the *Brown* commemoration, an art exhibition entitled "Social Studies: Eight Artists Address *Brown*," using reproductions of the work in the show. Many of these artworks help us to imagine the current significance of the issues at the heart of the *Brown* decision. Some of the artists explore the role of education and integration in their own lives or the lives of young people still in school. Others force us to recognize that various groups, such as homosexuals and the disabled, still endure the discrimination and bigotry that *Brown* addressed. Even for the racial and ethnic groups that the *Brown* decision had in mind, the promises of the ruling have remained unfulfilled. One of the artists in the exhibition, Carrie Mae Weems, contributes an interview here in which she reflects on the special difficulties faced by African American artists in the United States and the curious ways in which the work of African American artists "is always reduced to an expression of race and a question of class [which, in turn] becomes an easy, quick shorthand for dismissing it or not engaging with it as serious art." Weems speaks eloquently of the double-bind faced by African American artists who wish to take on racial issues but who do not want to limit their work to these issues. Referring of her recent efforts "to push the conversation to another arena," Weems notes that "it doesn't mean I am not interested in these questions [of race], but it does mean that I am endlessly limited in the ways in which the work is discussed."

Section IV: Illinois and *Brown*

The *Brown* commemoration offered an opportunity for reflection not just on the national historical significance of the decision, but also on its significance for the state of Illinois, Champaign-Urbana, and the university itself. This volume preserves that aspect. Kathryn H. Anthony and Nicholas Watkins's essay, "A Legacy of Firsts," documents the history of African Americans in the School of Architecture at the University of Illinois at Urbana-Champaign, as well as the achievements of notable African American alumni. Their research reveals that while the field of architecture "has been all too slow to diversify its ranks. . . , the University of Illinois at Urbana-Champaign has contributed significantly to the education of African American architects around the United States, perhaps more so than any other public university with the exception of historically African American schools with accredited architecture programs." Nathaniel Banks also focuses on the local context, though in his case it is the public and private schools of Champaign that occupy his attention. Banks's essay, "Reflections on the *Brown* Commemoration from a Champaign Native," offers a personal, candid, and critical assessment of the effects of efforts at integration in the Champaign schools from the point of view of a former student in those schools, an administrator in local schools, both public and private, and a member of the school board.

Joy Ann Williamson Lott, a former Illinois PhD student currently at the University of Washington, examines the impact of the *Brown* decision on the overwhelmingly white University of Illinois at Urbana-Champaign and its attempts in the late 1960s to attract a higher proportion of African American students to its campus. Like many small northern cities, Champaign "maintained a firm pattern of residential and educational segregation," while the university endorsed several racist policies, creating an inhospitable environment for African American students and townsfolk alike.

Spurred on by liberal administrators, faculty, and students, as well as federal incentives, however, the university adopted a series of affirmative action plans designed to achieve racial diversity, but as late as 1967 only 223 African American undergraduates attended Illinois. In response, a more radicalized group of African American students formed the Black Students Association and, especially after the assassination of Martin Luther King Jr. in April 1968, more aggressively sought to increase African American enrollment at the university, successfully enrolling over 500 African Americans in the freshman class of fall 1968. Their arrival, however, prompted a series of peaceful protests that culminated in the arrest of over 200 of these new students in an event that the media declared was the first student riot of the 1968–69 academic year. Focusing her analysis on the climate within which African American students and university administrators discussed and often clashed over reform of the university's policies, Williamson Lott emphasizes both the achievements of black students and the price they paid to bring about reform.

Chancellor Richard Herman personalizes the issue of immigration to America by telling the story through the lens of his immigrant grandparents. In looking to the global economy and the flattening world today, he relates how immigrants over the latter half of the last century contributed to American innovation and to the greatness of the nation's universities. Herman's commitment to welcoming the world to the University of Illinois and preparing all students to participate on the global stage resonates with the best legacy of *Brown v. Board* and demonstrates that Illinois is moving in the right direction.

The final essay in this section addresses a much-neglected aspect of race relations in Illinois as well as the nation, especially outside the South. *Brown v. Board* tackled the problem of the segregation of schools in areas where different races lived in some proximity, but what if communities were racially homogeneous by design and far apart from one another? In "Enforcing *Brown* in Sundown Towns," sociologist James W. Loewen, a native Illinoisan who frequently visits to speak and lead workshops at the University of Illinois, explores a little-recognized phenomenon that still pervades the United States—the existence of communities, whether towns or suburbs, that actively deny the right of African Americans, and other ethnic groups, to buy or rent properties or even spend the night there. According to Loewen, these "sundown" communities began to appear in every state outside of the "traditional South" in the last decade of the nineteenth century until, by the 1930s, they were the rule rather than the exception. As late as 1970 in Illinois, for example, 70 percent of towns with a population greater than a thousand were essentially all-white. They came about through a combination of local ordinances, covenants, intimidation, and violence, tactics that school districts also employed as a means of enforcing segregation.

It is an unfortunate truth that the power of the judiciary lies in the willingness of the federal government to enforce its rulings. There is no Supreme Court ruling better fitted to illustrate this than in the efforts of such states as Mississippi and South Carolina to avoid implementing *Brown*. Almost as soon as the Supreme Court announced its decision, southern states implemented a program of massive resistance to integration, and it was only with the threat, or even presence, of National Guardsmen that they finally bowed to the inevitable and integrated their school systems. Had African American activists not continually challenged the defiance of these states by attempting to integrate these schools with their own children, it is not inconceivable that *Brown* would have gone down in history as a largely symbolic, and ultimately fruitless, gesture. Since sundown communities by definition have no African American populations to dispute their legality, they have remained largely ignored by the judiciary, legislature, and civil rights activists alike.

Furthermore, the courts have generally supported the existence of sundown communities in the few instances where the phenomenon has been challenged. In *Milliken v. Bradley* (1974), for example, the Supreme Court effectively ruled that so long as communities did not openly declare themselves to be all-white, it was lawful for them to be so. The Court came to this decision despite numerous incidents of violence against African American families that attempted to move into the Detroit suburbs at the center of the case. Such rulings have severely undermined the impact of *Brown* in ensuring the integration of public schools, particularly in northern communities where hostility toward African Americans has always been less explicit than in the South.

Section V: Public Intellectuals and *Brown* and Its Legacy

As part of its commemoration, the University of Illinois invited to campus a number of individuals who have played key roles as public figures in pursuing the goals of *Brown* or in communicating its ideals to a broad audience. In addition to some of the authors already mentioned, these included Julian Bond, the civil rights leader and former chair of the National Association for the Advancement of Colored People, Freeman Hrabowski III, the prominent educator and chancellor of the University of Maryland, Baltimore County, and the writers and journalists Juan Williams and Chris Benson.

Benson's essay in this volume addresses a shockingly brutal but all too typical episode of racial violence from the years following the *Brown* decision. White supremacists in the South reacted to the Supreme Court's order to end segregation predictably enough: by organizing a massive program of officially sanctioned resistance to desegregation efforts and a marked increase in the number of race crimes designed to remind African Americans of their place in Jim Crow society. One such incident occurred on August 28, 1955—just three months after the Supreme Court's second ruling on *Brown v. Board*—when two men burst into a small home in Money, Mississippi, and spirited away a fourteen-year-old Chicago boy who was visiting relatives. They proceeded to beat and torture the boy before finally murdering him and dumping his naked body in the Tallahatchie River, where he was discovered, almost unrecognizable, three days later. The men had singled out Till for this punishment for two reasons: first, he reportedly had the audacity to whistle at the white wife of one of his murderers, and second, he was African American.

In many ways, Emmett Till's death was anything but unusual, just one more racially motivated hate-crime designed to keep the South's African American population firmly in check. Mississippi was the country's poorest state and also the state with the largest African American population. Racism and violence against African Americans was an everyday fact of life. What ensured that Till's death did not become another forgotten statistic, just one of the more than five thousand recorded lynchings since Reconstruction, was his mother's insistence, over the objections of Mississippi authorities anxious to prevent the truth from being revealed, that his body be sent home to Chicago, where she buried him after an open-casket funeral.

Chris Benson was Illinois's Martin Luther King Jr. Day speaker in 2005, and his essay "Just Because of the Color of His Skin: The 1955 Lynching of Emmett Till," recounts the story of Mamie Till-Mobley, a woman who lost her son to the evil of the Jim Crow South but whose bravery and dignity inspired a generation of activists to demand equality and civil liberties for all Americans. One hundred thousand mourners viewed Till's body as it lay in state in Chicago; the *Chicago Defender* and *JET* magazine printed photographs that people across the country and throughout the world saw. That a jury acquitted the two men identified as Till's killers after little more than an hour of deliberations and that a month later they admitted everything in a magazine interview only made the need for the Supreme Court's intervention all the more apparent.

Emmett Till's death brought home to many, especially nonsoutherners, the reality of the terrorism facing African Americans living in the South, in a way that an abstract declaration from the Supreme Court could not. It certainly had far greater resonance and impact than *Brown* for many African American children who were at school at the time, a significant number of whom went on to be prominent members of the civil rights movement, and showed that the race problem was not the South's problem alone, but America's. Before Till's death there had been few efforts to carry out the Supreme Court's order to end segregation; three months after his murderers' acquittal, Rosa Parks drew inspiration from his death when she refused to give up her bus seat to a white man. Although *Brown v. Board* provided the legal and judicial backing necessary to fight segregation, Emmett Till and his mother made that fight possible.

Benson, who is currently an associate professor at his alma mater, the University of Illinois, worked with Till-Mobley writing her memoir, which they finished shortly before her death in 2003. As Benson makes clear, Till-Mobley did not collapse with despair or hatred at the death of her son, but instead used the tragedy as opportunity for activism. After her son's death, she went on to lead an enormously productive life as a teacher and activist. In his moving address, Benson uses Till-Mobley's example to encourage today's students not simply to pursue the ideals for which she lived, but also to live their lives as richly as she did.

In "Reflections on America's Academic Achievement Gap: A Fifty-Year Perspective," Freeman A. Hrabowski III, another University of Illinois alumnus and the recipient of an honorary degree from his alma mater in 2004, explores the impact that the *Brown* decision has had on every level of America's education program. Hrabowski grew up in segregated Birmingham, Alabama, and as a ninth-grader participated in the nonviolent protest marches that so dramatically demonstrated to the country the brutal methods employed by white southerners to maintain their white supremacist society. For their participation, authorities barred Hrabowski, a straight-A student, and the other school-age demonstrators from returning to their classrooms. A court order soon reversed this blatant act of discrimination, however, and three years later Hrabowski was able to attend Hampton University in Virginia. He later became a graduate student at the University of Illinois, where he worked with some of the same students recruited to the school in the programs discussed in Williamson Lott's essay.

Working at the University of Illinois, Hrabowski found that many of these African American students were unprepared for the academic rigors of college life and became discouraged and isolated, helping create a significant academic achievement gap between minority and white students that still exists on many university campuses today. Hrabowski argues that the cause of the problem lies in America's high schools, where resegregation and even "hypersegregation" are combining with the ineffective policies of *No Child Left Behind* to continue to leave minority students unready for the transition from high school to university. He goes on to explain how, as vice-provost and then chancellor, he confronted this very situation at the University of Maryland, Baltimore County, and implemented policies to eliminate any such achievement gap on his campus. By creating an increasing number of academically high-achieving minorities and demonstrating that it is possible to overcome any so-called "deficiencies," Hrabowski argues that minority children will begin to see that it can be "'cool' to be smart," and will become motivated to break this devastating cycle.

In the keynote speech to the University of Illinois's commemoration of *Brown v. Board,* Julian Bond, former chair of SNCC, former state legislator from Georgia, political activist, and historian, discusses the state of race and racial discrimination in today's United States. Fifty years after the Supreme Court declared that segregation violated the equal protection provisions of the Constitution, Bond finds the races still divided. Nevertheless, "Civil Rights: Then and Now" reminds us that we must not underestimate the importance of *Brown,* which facilitated the passage of the civil rights movement's greatest legislative achievements—the Civil Rights Act of 1964 and the Voting Rights Act of 1965.

During the ten-year gap between *Brown* and passage of the Civil Rights Act, the United States awoke to the realities of the Jim Crow system in the South, allowing the mobilization of a "nonviolent army" that transcended race, gender, and class to fight against the evils of discrimination and seek social justice for those long without. This was a time in which parts of our nation denied millions of Americans, whose only "fault" was the color of their skin, the most basic of civil liberties—from the right to vote to a university education. Bond dubs this system of white supremacy "a vast affirmative action plan for whites" that had but one aim: "to crush the human development of a whole population." By ending segregation in schools, the Supreme Court set in motion a movement that created the political willpower to try to end such inequalities. Nevertheless, Martin Luther King's dream of a fully integrated America remains elusive today, in particular for the millions of African Americans who have found themselves disenfranchised politically and economically.

Although the civil rights movement's victories made the outward signs of discrimination a thing of the past, they also, perhaps paradoxically, created a more pervasive and insidious form of discrimination that permeates contemporary American society. The Republican Party in the South played upon white southern prejudices and resentments when Lyndon Johnson signed the Civil Rights Act into law and gained control of southern politics. With the ascendance of the Republicans' so-called southern strategy, Bond argues that the gains made by minorities have increasingly come under attack from individuals and organizations purporting to believe in a form of "color-blind" equality that has usurped the language of the civil rights movement in an effort to reverse the progress of the last decades. African Americans remain more likely to have a lower income, lower educational attainments, and lower self-worth than whites. They have fewer savings and are far more likely to live in substandard housing, and yet many Americans believe that race is no longer an impediment—that these inequities are somehow the fault of the individual and not society.

Bond compares the great struggles of America's past with these challenges of today and finds our current leaders—from both sides of the political spectrum— lacking. Race has become a political tool of both parties, hauled out at election time to garner votes. According to Bond, in the mid-2000s the majority of Republicans and Democrats stood placidly aside, content to appease the sensibilities of white voters, even as an administration more interested in protecting the interests of the rich rather than those in need eroded the civil liberties of all Americans.

Bond's assessment of the state of the nation's leadership in 2004 is grim, yet Juan Williams and Christopher Teal's essay provides us with a heroic counterexample in the person of Thurgood Marshall. With the possible exception of the plaintiffs, no figure is more associated with the *Brown* decision than Marshall. The grandson of a slave, Marshall attended Howard University Law School after the University of Maryland Law School denied him admittance. In 1934 he began working for the NAACP, where he eventually became chief counsel. He had great success arguing cases before the Supreme Court, but none of his victories is more famous than *Brown*. In 1967 Lyndon Johnson appointed Marshall to the Supreme Court, where he served for twenty-four years as the first African American to hold this position.

In their essay, "Thurgood Marshall's Vision," Juan Williams and Christopher Teal reflect on Williams's highly acclaimed biography *Thurgood Marshall: American Revolutionary,* for which Teal served as a research assistant.[3] Recalling the many people who have contacted them since the appearance of the biography, all of whom Marshall's life and work deeply affected, they write: "Their stories vary in the details, but they all circle that one critical moment in American history like planets orbiting the sun—the momentous ruling in *Brown*. It was *Brown* that raised the possibility of integration becoming a reality in their minds, whether they were for it or against it; it was *Brown*, in a single ruling, that put the power of the federal government's judges, FBI agents, and even the U.S. military's force on the side of equal rights for all; it was *Brown* that made segregation not only immoral, but a crime."

Thurgood Marshall: American Revolutionary concludes that "Marshall was right that full integration is a necessary precondition for equal rights,"[4] but Williams and Teal's essay here stresses how controversial such a conclusion is today, when new forms of segregation affect education at all levels, when many seek to end affirmative actions programs, and when Marshall's replacement on the Supreme Court and currently its only African American member, Justice Clarence Thomas, has become Marshall's "most visible opponent."

Williams and Teal point to the many court cases and public debates that revolve around Marshall's work and legal legacy to argue for his continued importance. For them he was a "visionary" insofar as he recognized that integration was key to curing the ills of American society. Marshall is first and foremost the "architect" of the *Brown* decision and of a way forward for American race relations, and, thus, "*Brown* still ranks as one of the most significant legal decisions in U.S. history."

Mary Dudziak's concluding essay provides a fitting epilogue to the volume because it moves us beyond the national context to the ramifications of the decision around the globe. *Brown*'s significance abroad was not simply a matter of the United States setting a positive example. As Dudziak writes, "*Brown* stemmed damage done to the nation's image around the world, which for years had been negatively affected by racial segregation." In the midst of the cold war, the United States needed to contradict charges of racism and to affirm the value of American democracy and the rights it accorded to every citizen. Dudziak demonstrates that officials in both the State Department and the Justice Department saw the *Brown* case in part as a matter of contradicting assertions, particularly those emanating from communists, that racial discrimination crippled American democracy. The reception of the decision in 1954 by foreign newspapers suggests that they were right to ascribe this role to the case. Dudziak's article reminds us that, in our increasingly transnational world, "the most enduring way to improve the U.S. image is to live up to the nation's ideals."

Taken together, the essays in this volume demonstrate how much the issues and injustices at the root of the *Brown* decision are still unfortunately with us today. Yet if the recalcitrance of racism in America is cause for a sober reconsideration of *Brown* and its legacy, the heroic efforts of those who have fought for racial equality and the concrete successes that have come in the name of *Brown* are cause for celebration. Both responses were amply present in Illinois's commemoration, which was a model of how academic programming can be both critical and inspiring, socially relevant and all-inclusive. In addition to its contribution to our understanding of *Brown* and its legacy, this volume serves as documentation of a highpoint in one university's intellectual and creative life.

Notes

1. BBC interview with Bob McKenzie, available at http://news.bbc.co.uk/2/hi/programmes/world_news_america/7838851.stm (accessed March 9, 2009).

2. Bureau of Justice, "Correctional Facilities, 1980–2000," summary document, available online at http://www.ojp.usdoj.gov/bjs/glance/tables/corr2tab.htm (ac-

cessed March 9, 2009) and Paige M. Harrison and Allen J. Beck, "Prisoners in 2003," *Bureau of Justice Statistics Bulletin*, NCJ 205335 (November 2004), http://www.ojp .usdoj.gov/bjs/pub/pdf/p03.pdf.

3. Juan Williams, *Thurgood Marshall: American Revolutionary* (New York: Times Books, 1998).

4. Ibid., 404.

Section I

Brown: Its History and Legacy

Brown v. the Board of Education overturned the "separate but equal" doctrine as established in the 1896 U.S. Supreme Court ruling of *Plessy v. Ferguson.* But *Brown* was only one of several cases attacking school segregation, and the only case not from one of the former Confederate states. Although *Brown* went on to have further-reaching implications, in the years prior to the decision the Supreme Court had ruled against segregation in graduate schools, law schools, and other institutions of higher learning. In 1950, both *Sweatt v. Painter* and *McLaurin v. Oklahoma State Regents for Higher Education* upheld desegregation of such institutions, and the NAACP lawyers relied on these cases as precedence for *Brown.*

The legacy of school desegregation began before *Brown,* and the legacy of *Brown* reached far beyond the 1954 decision. In this section, scholars examine the implications of *Brown.* Darlene Clark Hine looks at Clarendon County, South Carolina, the location of one of the court cases combined into *Brown,* to show the tradition of African American consciousness and institutions. George Lipsitz examines the implications of the phrase "all deliberate speed" for recalcitrant southern whites following the *Brown* decision, and Margaret L. Andersen and Laughlin McDonald both present essays demonstrating *Brown's* expansion from African Americans to other groups and from schools to other institutions. Jason Chambers looks to the UNCF's advertising campaign and the impact of their slogan,

"A mind is a terrible thing to waste," in gaining equal access to colleges for African American students. Joe R. Feagin and Bernice McNair Barnett analyze Brown and its aftermath from the perspective of sociologists to explain "systemic racism." And attorney and social critic Lani Guinier argues that it was white supremacy, not segregation, that caused and fosters racism.

The *Briggs v. Elliott* Legacy

Black Culture, Consciousness, and Community before *Brown*, 1930–1954

Darlene Clark Hine

How do we use the occasion of the fiftieth anniversary of the 1954 *Brown v. Board of Education* U.S. Supreme Court decision, which overturned the judicial foundation of separate but equal in public education, to open up new ways of understanding its significance for the world we live in today? The question suggests the need to place the decision in long historical context. Constitutional issues and the strategies of NAACP lawyers have dominated recent scholarly discourse on this landmark case.[1] It may be instructive, therefore, to examine anew the lives and experiences of the rural southern black people in South Carolina who launched *Briggs v. Elliott,*[2] the first of the five cases that together formed *Brown v. Board of Education.* In the first half of the twentieth century, African Americans composed 43 percent of the population of South Carolina. Although burdened by white oppression and the ravages of the Great Depression, even in the bleak 1930s black South Carolinians struggled to regain political and social citizenship rights. In their local communities, they agitated for equitable distribution of health and welfare resources, and for better schools for their children.[3]

An examination of *Brown*'s origins in rural Clarendon County, South Carolina, illustrates how local people and their leaders waged a long, multifaceted struggle to overthrow Jim Crow. This essay has two parts. The first part recapitulates the evolution of *Briggs v. Elliott* and the deplorable state of rural southern black schools in the 1930s and 1940s, which gave rise to the education reform movement that unfolded in the courts. Rural southern black professionals, especially ministers, teachers, and nurses, found the deteriorating health status of black people as alarming as the overwhelming inequalities in physical plant, teachers, and equipment that burdened black schools. These two overlapping concerns, education and health care, were structurally intertwined in *Briggs* and implicit in *Brown.* The second part of this essay concentrates on the sociohistorical context from the 1890s through the 1940s that witnessed the simultaneous emergence of racial segregation codified in law and the development of a black professional class that would pursue various strategies to destroy Jim Crow, especially in the educational arena.

The educational arena became a political and emotional battlefield after Reconstruction collapsed in 1877. During the ensuing two decades, court decisions combined with southern states' disenfranchising constitutions to nullify the Fourteenth and Fifteenth Amendments, which guaranteed equal protection for black citizens' civil, social, and political rights.[4] Black peoples' loss of the rights to vote, serve on juries, testify in court, and have access to places of public accommodation and transportation systematized racial hierarchy and supported white hegemony. The fate of black education was hotly contested, and black people fared badly. According to historian James D. Anderson, between 1860 and 1935 most black children in the South did not have access to public elementary schools: "High schools were virtually nonexistent, and the general unavailability of secondary education precluded even the opportunity to prepare for college."[5] Still, black southerners held fast to "a fundamental belief in learning and self-improvement and a shared belief in universal education as a necessary basis for freedom and citizenship."[6]

These convictions led rural black southerners to practice a form of double taxation to achieve racial uplift. Communities of parents and teachers built their own school buildings and supplied their own transportation, equipment, books, and supplies, while most of their tax revenues went to support the white schools. Teachers used their meager salaries, as well as funds solicited from white philanthropic foundations, to provide supplies and services. For example, Nannie L. Craighead asked the Rosenwald Fund for money to defray expenses to take her students to a health clinic in Richmond, Virginia.[7] Seventy-three of her seventy-six pupils suffered from enlarged tonsils, poor vision, or bad teeth.[8] These were, by no means, the worst, or the least, health problems black students and adults faced. All of these forces—double taxation, meager resources, and illness—operated in Clarendon County, and they weighed heavily on Joseph Armstrong De Laine.[9]

The Evolution of *Briggs*

Every black community had individuals who, as historian V. P. Franklin put it, possessed a passion for education and believed that through its acquisition they could achieve self-possession, determination, preservation, sufficiency, and improvement.[10] Between 1930 and 1954 the creative agency and courage of the second generation "New Negro" teachers, ministers, and nurses in rural South Carolina were skillfully deployed. These rural black professionals were just as significant in their communities—perhaps even more so because they were in short supply—as were those who practiced in the large metropolises. Joseph Armstrong De Laine, an African Methodist Episcopal (AME) minister and teacher of great personal dignity and self-possession, was one of these rural southern black professionals. Born in 1898 in Manning, South Carolina, De Laine earned a teaching license and, in 1931, a Bachelor of Theology degree from Allen University in Columbia, South Carolina. He married Marie Belten, a schoolteacher, and together they had three children. During the week, De Laine and Belten taught at Scott's Branch School, and on the weekends Reverend De Laine served as a pastor on a rural AME circuit.[11]

In 1947, with the full support of the black citizens of Clarendon County, De Laine approached the chair of the District 22 Board of Trustees, Roderick W. Elliott, with a simple request for a school bus for black children. It was a reasonable and just entreaty given the grossly inequitable distribution of tax revenues and material resources that black residents received. Approximately 70 percent of Clarendon County's 32,000 residents were African American. Most of the black population earned less than a thousand dollars a year, and the average number of years they attended school was four. In the opinion of many, "[t]he black schools of South Carolina were a disgrace." The average white teacher in Clarendon County earned two-thirds more than the average black teacher, and black parents had to pay not only for supplies, but also for coal to heat ramshackle one-room school buildings. "[T]he county previously had charged each black pupil $7 a year for coal and other sundries that the white got free." Black children had sixty-one schools while white students had twelve; however, the county provided thirty buses for white students and none whatsoever for black children.[12]

Elliott was well aware of the distributional inequities. Indeed, as the longtime head of the District 22 School Board, he had approved virtually every unequal expenditure during the previous twenty-five years.[13] Black citizens in South Carolina had few, if any, social, civil, or political liberties that the state's justice system protected. Thus, Elliott responded to De Laine's request with all of the unquestioning arrogance of a white supremacist: "We ain't got no money to buy a bus for your nigger children."[14] Elliott's coldly dismissive response to the simple request for a school bus set in motion forces that neither he, nor De Laine, could have foreseen would signal the doom of the separate but equal doctrine.

De Laine quietly began mobilizing the black community, its ministers, teachers, farmers, parents, and veterans to take legal action to force the government to address their grievances. He engaged a Columbia black attorney, Harold R. Boulware, to fashion the petition against the Clarendon School District for a bus. They filed *Pearson v. County Board of Education* in the U.S. District Court in Florence County. The court threw out the petition on the grounds that Levi Pearson, the named plaintiff, was not a resident of the appropriate school district.[15]

In March of 1949 De Laine and Pearson went to Columbia for a meeting with Thurgood Marshall. By November, De Laine, following the plan he had worked out with Marshall at their March meeting, had persuaded twenty black farmers to sign an NAACP petition. The first name listed on the petition was Harry Briggs. Briggs, a thirty-four-year-old Navy veteran, was the father of five children and worked at the Carrigan service station in Summerton. His wife, Liza, worked as a maid at a Summerton motel. Both would lose their jobs when the case of *Briggs v. Elliott* was filed. Indeed, most of the petitioners suffered similar experiences of white terrorism, violence, and economic retaliation for exercising their rights as U.S. citizens.[16]

The rage of white South Carolinians strengthened black resolve to invest everything they had and to launch an all-out quest to achieve both freedom of opportunity and equality of condition. For Reverend De Laine, there was no equivocation, but a grim determination to persevere. In 1950, in an open letter widely distributed throughout the Clarendon County black community, De Laine rallied his people: "Shall we suffer endless persecution just because we want our children reared in a wholesome atmosphere? What some of us have suffered is nothing short of Nazi persecution."[17]

The hearings before the U.S. District Court in Charleston revealed the deplorable status of black education. On the stand, Matthew Whitehead, a Howard University professor of education, reported on the survey he had conducted of the Clarendon County schools. In response to the skillful questioning of NAACP attorney Robert Carter, Whitehead testified:

> There was no running water at all, nor any urinals in any of these places for boys. At Scott's Branch School, the same situation prevailed, only to a greater degree of disgust . . . 694 students serviced by two toilets for boys and two toilet seats for girls, of the same out-of-door type construction, no running water, no urinals.[18]

Whitehead also described the inadequate instructional equipment:

> The lady who taught the first grade at the school showed me three chairs which she had just received that had been sent over from the white school, that were dilapidated and the children could not sit in them. Other chairs had spokes and rounds out in them and the bottoms were out in many of them.[19]

As far as the writing tables were concerned, he noted that "there were actually holes in the tables." He later recalled, "[i]t was all now down there on the record, and I could see it multiplied throughout the South. And you could see it on the faces of the people in the courtroom—a sort of sigh of relief that it had finally all come out."[20]

On June 23, 1951, the district court ruled against the black plaintiffs' plea to end racial segregation in South Carolina's schools. However, in a twenty-page dissent, Judge J. Waties Waring, a native white South Carolinian, declared: "[S]egregation in education can never produce equality and . . . is an evil that must be eradicated."[21] He wrote:

> This case presents the matter clearly for adjudication, and I am of the opinion that all of the legal guideposts, expert testimony, common sense and reason point unerringly to the conclusion that the system of segregation in education adopted and practiced in the State of South Carolina must go and must go now.[22]

Waring concluded emphatically, "[s]egregation is per se inequality."[23] The *Briggs* case was consolidated with the four other cases from Kansas, the District of Columbia, Delaware, and Virginia that, on appeal to the Supreme Court, became collectively known as *Brown v. Board of Education.*[24]

Briggs's Historical Context: Destroying Jim Crow

Comprehending the revolutionary significance of *Briggs* and *Brown* requires a return to the late nineteenth century. As historian Howard Rabinowitz noted, "It is now clear that something highly significant happened in southern race relations during the 1890s."[25] Scholars have speculated greatly about this mysterious and dangerous "nadir" decade. Even before the 1890s, white southerners had already inaugurated practices that separated them from African Americans in schools, churches, hospitals, and places of public accommodation. Why, then, did the 1890s witness new segregation laws and judicial decrees that merely reinforced customary practice? In an incisive critique of the many editions of C. Vann Woodward's *The Strange Career of Jim Crow*, Rabinowitz speculated that, perhaps, black "resistance to de facto segregation may have helped move white southerners in the direction of additional laws."[26] Recent scholars have similarly targeted black attitudes and refusal to acknowledge white supremacy. An increase in racial violence, disfranchisement, and lynching seems to correlate with the rising tide of black land ownership.[27]

African American communities turned inward as white southerners codified Jim Crow.[28] Black southerners searched for creative ways to ensure that black needs for health care, education, and social services were met, and, as historian Elsa Barkley Brown posits, "to construct communities of struggle."[29] Eventually, black communities established their own network of medical, nursing, legal training institutions, and normal schools, resulting in a professional class.[30] White philanthropic foundations often provided welcome assistance in this institution-building process of community formation. The Rosenwald Fund helped black communities build hundreds of one-teacher elementary school houses that amounted to a "great transformation of the overall structure of black elementary schooling." As Anderson observes, "there were school build- ings, teachers, desks, and seats throughout the black South in 1940 that had not been available in 1900."[31] Embedded cultural values augmented an insurgent consciousness among black rural southerners that strengthened their resolve to maintain control over their education.

Fettered by inadequate economic resources, and dogged by the ever-present specter of white violence and terror, the marginal and precarious status of most African Americans severely restricted the space in which they could fashion resistance. Therefore, they improvised a nuanced and multifaceted compound of resistance strategies, uplift institutions, and oppositional consciousness.[32] Few southern whites discerned the radical potential of black life behind "the veil." The erection of parallel institutions—that is, the creation, maintenance, and sustenance of an institutional infrastructure boasting a rich variety of religious denominations, colleges and universities, social service clubs, newspapers and businesses, fraternal organizations and professional associations, and hospitals and clinics combined with fluid family structures—offered effective bulwarks against hopelessness and despair.[33] This black parallelism allowed the requisite nurturing in safe spaces that southern rural African Americans needed to dis- cuss public and private concerns.[34] Psychologically and metaphorically relatively secure behind the veil, black southerners crafted their own meaning of race and shared memories of the rights that had been wrested from their grasp. They knew that no period of "Negro Domination" had existed, and they also knew that they were outnumbered and outgunned.[35] They had to amass other resources for the long struggle. During the nadir of the 1890s, they constructed an oppositional consciousness that illuminated the complications of being poor, rural, black, and southern with, as yet, unfulfilled dreams of American citizenship.[36]

It is as important to unravel the dynamics of black resistance to white politics and law as it is to understand the social construction of whiteness. The tacit collusion of the interests of northern industrialists, southern demagogues, and planter elites to create a permanent subordinate labor force confined African Americans into an endless cycle of poverty and powerlessness. Interlocking sys- tems of economic exploitation and electoral disfranchisement adversely affected the status, shape, and substance of black education, health, and welfare. As W. E. B. Du Bois declared, "a disfranchised working class in a modern industrial civilization . . . will be diseased, it will be criminal, it will be ignorant, it will be the plaything of mobs and it will be insulted by caste restrictions."[37]

Writing in 1914, a white Georgian physician underscored Du Bois's assess- ment, but he blamed black people themselves for their deteriorating health while asserting that "the negro health problem is one of the 'white man's burdens.'" He opined that "there was no more healthy race of people to be found anywhere in the world than the slaves of the South before the Civil War." After enumerating the morbidity and mortality statistics of black southerners from tuberculosis, smallpox, typhoid fever, whooping cough, rheumatism, influenza, and heart disease, he concluded that "the kind of education we have been trying to give the negro has been a disappointment." He elaborated: "Millions of dollars have been spent, and thousands of teachers and others have devoted many years of earnest labor to the education of the negro, and as a result of it all we find the negro race as a whole in worse condition than they were in slavery times."[38] The physician suggested the kind of education that African Americans should receive:

> In addition to improved methods of farming, stock raising, poultry raising, etc. . . . [t]he women should be instructed in cooking, and the care of infants. . . . They should be made to know that typhoid fever is an infectious disease, and instructed in methods of disinfection and cleanliness, and informed of the benefits of typhoid vaccination. They should be told how the mosquito spreads malaria, and instructed in methods of prevention. They should be told of sanitary privies, and that houseflies are as dangerous as mad dogs. They should be especially instructed concerning the two twin enemies of the negro race—gonorrhea and syphilis. . . . Divest their minds of the vague superstitions which most of them harbor concerning the causation of disease, and make them understand that disease is caused from uncleanliness, alcohol, germs, bad habits and bad morals."[39]

His opinions represented white southern conventional wisdom about the impending destruction or disappearance of the black race. The education whites advocated for black people would have prepared them to return to servitude.

As the material conditions of black citizens worsened, many white southerners not only denied culpability, but also embraced a fictitious scientific theory dubbed "survival of the fittest" or "social Darwinism." They deployed the rhetoric of the white man's burden to rationalize consolidation of a Jim Crow society. At the outset of the 1890s, white southerners smothered their fear, anxiety, and ambivalence about the prospect of black self-sufficiency and landownership. They concealed their anxiety under deep loathing and disdain for their alleged "racial inferiors." The tension arising from fear of inferiors forged the core of what historian Grace Elizabeth Hale has dubbed the "culture of segregation."[40]

Southern landowners sought proof of black dependency and servility, and demanded reassurance that black people accepted economic subordination and resigned themselves to the reality of white power. Any overt expression of black resistance to "utter demoralization" alarmed whites, who were otherwise outwardly complacent.[41] Booker T. Washington's 1895 address at the Cotton States Exhibition in Atlanta, Georgia, accommodated white desire for acknowledgment of black unreadiness for political citizenship. Washington placated white people with assurances that, in all things social, the two groups could be as separate as fingers on the hand.[42] In the *Atlanta Compromise Address of 1895,* Washington seemed to privilege racial uplift over social equality as the prerequisite for social citizenship.[43] But Washington did not earn the title "Wizard of Tuskegee" without justification. He sponsored annual conferences for black farmers to help them become more skilled and efficient.[44] At the same time that he preached servility, the wily Washington taught self-sufficiency and autonomy and created opportunities for black rural southerners to come together, exchange information, and build communities.[45]

Washington, like many rural southern African Americans, proved adept at wearing a mask and engaging in other forms of dissemblance. Many African Americans wore the mask of deference and abided the customary laws of racial etiquette without betraying their disaffection and resentment. The strategy of black parallelism emerged from, and reflected back upon, the core values that black people transmitted to one another across time and place. The core value system proved to be especially resilient in the rural South with its relatively isolated, widely dispersed small black communities.

To understand the full dynamics of black resiliency during the years between 1890 and the 1920s, and to chart the process of constructing, revising, and transforming communities of struggle, requires a wider lens. Despite its solidarity under shared oppression, the black community was never monolithic. Internal fissures, factions, disputes, and battles raged. Indeed, between 1930 and 1954, prominent New Negro professionals and activists generated considerable discord.[46] Professors, physicians, nurses, and lawyers heatedly debated the efficacy of black institutions. One group of activists and elite professionals argued for the complete overthrow of racial segregation and the separate but equal doctrine.[47] Others insisted that black people should pursue the goal of equality of condition to preserve educational institutions and maintain control of their schools.[48]

In the early 1940s, South Carolina native Gordon Blaine Hancock posed the questions that consumed so much black attention:

> What proportion of our moral and material energies shall we use fighting segregation and what proportion shall we employ making the most of it, to gain strength with which further to fight it? Shall we adopt the same type of education current among the whites or shall we seek a type of education that meets the needs of the millions of Negroes who must live by the labors of their hands rather than a type that meets the needs of the few Negroes in the higher brackets of life? In the first case we too often satisfy merely our pride; in the second we satisfy the demands of an inexorable situation.[49]

The *Brown* decision and the earlier *Briggs* case answered Hancock's questions and represented a triumph for the integrationist stance.[50]

By the dawn of the twentieth century, the social construction of race appeared to be complete. A chasm of silence, absence, and mystery divided the white and black communities. In historian Charles Wesley's rueful contention, black Americans "developed the mask which grinned through shinning teeth and the lips which hid behind the soul of protest. Many a shuffling, smiling, bowing and bending body of a servant and worker carried within a violence of opposition which the suppression of speech alone prevented."[51] Perhaps it was this tradition of black people shielding their inner thoughts and beliefs that made Roderick Elliott feel free to insult Reverend De Laine. Times had changed one man, but not the other.

By the 1940s a transformed black consciousness was readily apparent to anyone who cared to look. De Laine could not turn his back and shuffle away from Elliott's humiliating words. He had to fight. In the most remote regions of the rural South, national and global events that began during the World War I emergency and continued through the devastation of the Great Depression and the limitations and frustrations of the New Deal affected black consciousness. When combined with the Great Migration, the New Negro renaissance, the spread of Marcus Garvey's nationalist ideas about race pride and black solidarity,[52] and the "Double V" campaign against Nazism and fascism abroad and Jim Crow discrimination at home during World War II, there existed a fertile environment for a heightened race consciousness and militant advocacy to flourish.[53]

Three distinct national victories by second generation New Negro professionals and activists composed the success of a New Reconstruction. First, beginning in the 1930s and early 1940s African Americans overthrew one of the most effective disfranchisement devices, the Democratic Party white primary.[54] The 1944 decision in *Smith v. Allwright* opened the door to participation in the electoral process that white southerners had denied black citizens since the first Reconstruction had collapsed in 1877.[55] Second, during World War II African Americans led a Double V campaign to fight Nazism and fascism abroad, and racism at home. Activists set in motion forces that spurred the desegregation of the U.S. military.[56] These forces inspired the third victory. In 1949 local rural black men and women in Clarendon County, South Carolina, under the leadership of De Laine launched a suit for equality of educational resources that would culminate in the 1954 *Brown* decision, overthrowing the separate-but-equal doctrine promulgated by *Plessy v. Ferguson*.[57] Thus, the 1940s witnessed a multifaceted black struggle against the entire edifice of segregation. The momentum of the previous two decades peaked with the victory in *Brown*.

• • •

In his argument before the U.S. Supreme Court, Thurgood Marshall asked the Court to declare *Plessy v. Ferguson* unconstitutional. He recounted the high-points of the long struggle of African Americans to secure equal justice under the law. He declared that race ideology undermined the fabric of American democratic values. The problem of the twentieth century had indeed been that of the color line, as W. E. B. Du Bois had prophesized.[58] By the time Marshall made this argument, black intellectuals, scholars, and activists, together with their progressive white allies, had closed ranks to support integration. To suggest alternatives as the goal for African Americans at this juncture was unthinkable. On May 17, 1954, the Supreme Court ruled unanimously that a classification based solely on race violated the Fourteenth Amendment to the U.S. Constitution. Chief Justice Earl Warren emphatically declared, "[I]n the field of public education the doctrine of 'separate but equal' has no place. Separate education facilities are inherently unequal."[59]

The *Brown* decision reverberated deeply in black people's political consciousness because it represented more than an end to segregation in public school education. The decision also concerned the dismantling of distributional inequalities in health care and social welfare services. *Brown* was a culmination of the African American struggle for freedom of opportunity that began in the post-Emancipation era. *Brown* was about the emergence of a militant second-generation New Negro consciousness and the evolution of aggressive demands for equality of condition and social justice. The outcome of this New Reconstruction differed significantly from the one that had collapsed in 1877. A series of precedent-setting U.S. Supreme Court decisions in the 1940s and early 1950s marked the successful onslaught against the all-white primary disfranchisement laws, white-only restrictive housing covenants, and separate and unequal education. On July 26, 1948, President Harry Truman issued Executive Order 9981, initiating the desegregation of the U.S. military.[60]

The *Brown* decision ended a major phase in black educational, social, and political history, but it simultaneously ignited another more encompassing phase in the long struggle that would have national and international consequence. *Brown* unleashed a powerful demonstration of massive white violence and intolerance that met an even stronger black position in the social revolution known as Civil Rights Movement. Eventually this movement destroyed the segregation laws and public policies that had regulated vital aspects of black life including education, health care, and social welfare.

A long perspective on *Brown* provides a clearer understanding of the connections between local struggles such as that led by Reverend De Laine in Clarendon County, South Carolina, and the national NAACP-orchestrated legal cases for social justice and freedom of opportunity. The social revolution was one of the unforeseen consequences of local and national collective black resistance to those actions of late nineteenth- and early twentieth-century white southerners who had erected the legal, political, and social edifice of Jim Crow, and the efforts of their grandchildren who massively resisted demolition of separate but equal in the aftermath of *Brown*.

Notes

1. *Brown v. Board of Education*, 349 U.S. 294, 301 (1955) (*Brown* II); *Brown v. Board of Education*, 347 U.S. 483 (1954). See generally Jack Greenberg, *Crusaders in the Courts: How a Dedicated Band of Lawyers Fought for the Civil Rights Revolution* (New York: Basic Books, 1994); Waldo E. Martin Jr., *Brown v. Board of Education: A Brief History with Documents* (Boston: Bedford/St. Martin's, 1998); Mark V. Tushnet, *Making Civil Rights Law: Thurgood Marshall and the Supreme Court, 1936–1961* (New York: Oxford University Press, 1994); Mark V. Tushnet, *The NAACP's Legal Strategy against Segregated Education, 1925–1950* (Chapel Hill: University of North Carolina Press, 1987).

2. *Briggs v. Elliott*, 98 F. Supp. 529 (E.D.S.C. 1951).

3. Patricia Sullivan, *Days of Hope: Race and Democracy in the New Deal Era* (Chapel Hill: University of North Carolina Press, 1996), 143–50. Sullivan provides a cogent analysis of the interaction between a diverse local leadership of South Carolinians and the national leaders of the National Association for the Advancement of Colored People (NAACP) during the 1930s and 1940s. She argues that "voting was the major impetus for the expansion of civil rights activities during the late 1930s and early 1940s" (143).

4. See, e.g., *Cumming v. Richmond Board of Education*, 175 U.S. 528 (1899); cf. *Yick Wo v. Hopkins*, 118 U.S. 356 (1886).

5. James D. Anderson, *The Education of Blacks in the South, 1860–1935* (Chapel Hill: University of North Carolina Press, 1988), 285.

6. Ibid., 281.

7. Ibid., 177.

8. Ibid.

9. Ibid., 179; Richard Kluger, *Simple Justice: The History of Brown v. Board of Education and Black America's Struggle for Equality* (New York: Vintage Books 1977 [1975]), 3–26.

10. See, e.g., V. P. Franklin, *Black Self-Determination: A Cultural History of the Faith of the Fathers* (Westport, Conn.: L. Hill, 1984), 147–85.

11. Kluger, *Simple Justice*, 8–10, 11–15.

12. Ibid., 4, 6, 8, 13–14, 22.

13. Ibid., 349.

14. Ibid., 4.

15. Ibid., 17.

16. Ibid., 23, 24–25.

17. Ibid., 25.

18. Ibid., 350.

19. Ibid., 351.

20. Ibid.

21. *Briggs v. Elliott,* 98 F. Supp. at 547–48.

22. Ibid., at 548.

23. Ibid.

24. For a discussion of the Justice Department's amicus brief supporting the end of school segregation, see Mary L. Dudziak, *Cold War Civil Rights: Race and the Image of American Democracy* (Princeton: Princeton University Press, 2000), 99–102. The brief ended with a quote from President Harry Truman, "If we wish to inspire the people of the world whose freedom is in jeopardy, if we wish to restore hope to those who have already lost their civil liberties, if we wish to fulfill the promise that is ours, we must correct the remaining imperfections in our practice of democracy" (101–2).

25. Howard N. Rabinowitz, "More Than the Woodward Thesis: Assessing the Strange Career of Jim Crow," *Journal of American History* 75 (1988): 842, 848.

26. Ibid., 850.

27. See Terence Finnegan, "Lynching and Political Power in Mississippi and South Carolina," in *Under Sentence of Death: Lynching in the South,* ed. W. Fitzhugh Brundage (Chapel Hill: University of North Carolina Press, 1997), 189–218. Finnegan noted that, in South Carolina "[f]rom 1896 to 1910 the Republican regions had about the same percentage of the black population (43.5 percent of the black population, but had only 26.8 percent of black lynching incidents) but black lynching incidents increased to 34.3 percent of the state's total" (216 n.12). Finnegan concluded that "[w]hites disfranchised African Americans because of their supposed inferiority, but they lynched when African Americans challenged the myths that sustained white supremacy and refused to accept the social, economic, and political constraints that white racism demanded" (215).

28. See generally Jack M. Bloom, *Class, Race, and the Civil Rights Movement* (Bloomington: Indiana University Press, 1987), 18–46. Bloom argues that "[t]he oft-besieged black population was forced into a solidarity that transcended class and status lines and helped to forge a black consciousness. The black movement of the 1950s was very much a product of the whole black community" (145). This analysis is an accurate description of the Clarendon County black community that came together to launch the *Briggs v. Elliott* case. See also Steven Hahn, *A Nation under Our Feet: Black Political Struggles in the Rural South from Slavery to the Great Migration* (Cambridge, Mass.: Belknap Press of Harvard University Press, 2003), 451–52, 463. For insightful discussions of the community mobilization process in the modern civil rights movement era, see Aldon D. Morris, *The Origins of the Civil Rights Movement: Black Communities Organizing for Change* (New York: Free Press, 1984); and John Dittmer, *Local People: The Struggle for Civil Rights in Mississippi* (Urbana: University of Illinois Press, 1994).

29. Elsa Barkley Brown, "Negotiating and Transforming the Public Sphere: African American Political Life in the Transition from Slavery to Freedom," in *The*

Black Public Sphere: A Public Culture Book (Chicago: University of Chicago Press 1995), 111, 113.

30. For a discussion of the development of black nursing training facilities and hospitals see Darlene Clark Hine, *Black Women in White: Racial Conflict and Co-operation in the Nursing Profession, 1890–1950* (Bloomington: Indiana University Press, 1989), 94–107; and Darlene Clark Hine, "Black Professionals and Race Consciousness: Origins of the Civil Rights Movement, 1890–1950," *Journal of American History* 89 (2003): 1279, 1289.

31. Anderson, *The Education of Blacks in the South*, 181.

32. Cynthia Neverdon-Morton, *Afro-American Women of the South and the Advancement of the Race, 1895–1925* (Knoxville: University of Tennessee Press, 1989), 78–103. Neverdon-Morton documents the uplift activism of several urban southern black women health professionals. See especially her discussion of nurse Millie E. Hale and the establishment of the Millie E. Hale Hospital and Auxiliary in Nashville, Tennessee on July 1, 1916. Hale and her husband, physician John H. Hale, transformed their fourteen-room home into a community center replete with pre- and postnatal care, a free drug dispensary, and adult clinics. In summarizing the extent and breadth of services provided in 1923, Neverdon-Morton notes that, "1,155 people received food, money, bedding, and coal; 400 sick people were provided with meals; nurses visited 7,687 homes to provide bedside care; and nurses were assigned to two medical dispensaries" (173).

33. David T. Beito, *From Mutual Aid to the Welfare State: Fraternal Societies And Social Services, 1890–1967* (Chapel Hill: University of North Carolina Press, 2000), 2–3. Beito notes that "the movement to build hospitals thrived especially in the South. By 1931 black fraternal societies had founded nine fraternal hospitals in the South" (181). But the threat of white offense remained. As Beito declared, black hospitals "stood as visible reminders of the wider potential for black organizational talent and assertiveness" (190).

34. For a discussion of the role the church played in providing safe spaces, see Evelyn Brooks Higginbotham, *Righteous Discontent: The Women's Movement in the Black Baptist Church, 1880–1920* (Cambridge, Mass.: Harvard University Press, 1993), 10. See also Kevin Gaines, "Rethinking Race and Class in African-American Struggles for Equality, 1855–1941," *American History Review* 102 (1997), 378–87.

35. See, e.g., Eric Foner, *Reconstruction: America's Unfinished Revolution, 1863–1877* (New York: Harper and Row, 1988), 88–95.

36. Thavolia Glymph thoughtfully suggests that "[t]he white South continued to control much of black people's world but black people's memories of the Civil War and emancipation pressed against that control in ways that are only beginning to be explored and understood" (Thavolia Glymph, "'Liberty Dearly Bought': The Making of Civil War Memory in Afro-American Communities in the South," in *Time Longer Than Rope: A Century of African American Activism, 1850–1950*, ed. Charles M. Payne and Adam Green [New York: New York University Press, 2003],

111, 130). Elsa Barkley Brown insightfully identifies the places where political ideas and consciousness raising took place beyond the white gaze: "Forums for political discussions were literary societies, ward meetings, mutual benefit society and fraternal society meetings, women's clubs, labor organizations, newspapers, street corners, kitchens, washtubs, and saloons" (Brown, "Negotiating and Transforming the Public Sphere," 111, 142).

37. W. E. B. Du Bois, quoted in Charles H. Wesley, "The Negro Has Always Wanted the Four Freedoms," in *What the Negro Wants*, ed. Rayford W. Logan (Chapel Hill: University of North Carolina Press, 1944), 90, 99–100.

38. L. C. Allen, "The Negro Health Problem," *American Journal of Public Health* 5 (1915): 194, 195, 199.

39. Ibid., 252–53.

40. Grace Elizabeth Hale, *Making Whiteness: The Culture of Segregation in the South, 1890–1940* (New York: Vintage Books, 1999), xii. Hale writes: "Southerners created a common whiteness to solve the problems of the post–Civil War era and built their collectivity on not just a convention or a policy but on segregation as a culture" (xi).

41. Hahn, *A Nation under Our Feet*, 428–29. Hahn maintains that "[w]here blacks had constructed a substantial basis of community life and continued to wield measures of local power—the coasts of South Carolina and Georgia leap out as examples—lynchings were rare and the threat of them could arouse an armed and militant defense" (428).

42. See Louis R. Harlan, *Booker T. Washington: the Making of a Black Leader, 1856–1901* (New York: Oxford University Press, 1972), 218.

43. See Louis R. Harlan, *Booker T. Washington: The Wizard of Tuskegee, 1901–1915* (New York: Oxford University Press, 1983), 205.

44. Allen W. Jones, "The Role of Tuskegee Institute in the Education of Black Farmers," *Journal of Negro History* 60 (1975): 252, 254–67.

45. See Anderson, *The Education of Blacks in the South*, 51–52; Jones, "The Role of Tuskegee Institute," 252–67.

46. See generally Jonathan Scott Halloway, *Confronting the Veil: Abram Harris Jr., E. Franklin Frazier, and Ralph Bunche, 1919–1941* (Chapel Hill: University of North Carolina Press, 2002).

47. In 1944 historian Rayford Logan enumerated the six "irreducible fundamentals of first-class citizenship" for black Americans. "1. Equality of opportunity, 2. Equal pay for equal work, 3. Equal protection of the laws, 4. Equality of suffrage, 5. Equal recognition of the dignity of the human being, 6. Abolition of public segregation" (Rayford W. Logan, "The Negro Wants First-Class Citizenship," in Logan, *What the Negro Wants*, 1, 14). While historian Charles H. Wesley conceded that advances had been made through black institutions, he rejected "the fallacies in this argument that the Negro's status can be advanced by in-group progress along one path of material development and delay in other paths of life" by comparing black Americans to German Jews (Wesley, "The Negro Has Always Wanted," 99).

48. Richard Robbins, *Sidelines Activist: Charles S. Johnson and the Struggle for Civil Rights* (Jackson: University Press of Mississippi, 1996), 130–34.

49. Gordon B. Hancock, "Race Relations in the United States: A Summary," in Logan, *What the Negro Wants*, 217, 242–43. Gordon Blaine Hancock was born in 1884 in Ninety-Six, South Carolina. He received an A.B. degree from Benedict College in Columbia, South Carolina, in 1911 and A.B., B.D, and A.M. degrees from Harvard University in 1919, 1920, and 1921, respectively ("Who's Who," in Logan, *What the Negro Wants*, 345, 347).

50. Fifty years later the debate continues as scholars explore the social and economic costs of desegregation that included the threat to historically black institutions. See Albert L. Samuels, *Is Separate Unequal? Black Colleges and the Challenge to Desegregation* (Lawrence: University Press of Kansas, 2004).

51. Wesley, "The Negro Has Always Wanted," 91.

52. Robbins, *Sidelines Activist*, 93. Robbins observed that "Garvey's black nationalism with its Africanist cultural overtones . . . had a profound, astonishing appeal to the consciousness of black masses" (93). Hahn asserts that Garveyism was more prevalent in the South than in the North: "For although Garvey's movement is generally understood to have taken hold largely in the black urban North, its most extensive bases were in fact to be found in the rural and small-town South" (Hahn, *A Nation under Our Feet*, 471). According to Hahn, there were twenty-five divisions of Garvey's Universal Negro Improvement Association in South Carolina (471, 472).

53. Nan Elizabeth Woodruff, *American Congo: The African American Freedom Struggle in the Delta* (Cambridge, Mass.: Harvard University Press, 2003), 6. Woodruff examines the struggles of black sharecroppers in Mississippi and Arkansas for social and economic justice during the first half of the twentieth century.

54. See Darlene Clark Hine, *Black Victory: The Rise and Fall of the White Primary in Texas* (Columbia: University of Missouri Press, 2003).

55. Ibid., 231–48; see also Charles Zelden, *The Battle for the Black Ballot: Smith v. Allwright and the Defeat of the Texas All-White Primary* (Lawrence: University Press of Kansas, 2004).

56. Executive Order No. 9981, *Code of Federal Regulations*, title 3, sec. 722 (1943–48).

57. *Plessy v. Ferguson*, 163 U.S. 537 (1896); Robert J. Cottrol et al., *Brown v. Board of Education: Caste, Culture, and the Constitution* (Lawrence: University Press of Kansas, 2003), 119–32.

58. W. E. B. Du Bois, "The Souls of Black Folk," in *Three Negro Classics* (New York: Avon Books, 1965), 221.

59. *Brown v. Board of Education*, 347 U.S. at 495.

60. For an analysis of President Truman's Executive Order 9981, see Dudziak, *Cold War Civil Rights*, 83–86.

2

Getting Around *Brown*

The Social Warrant of the New Racism

George Lipsitz

The dominant group is not concerned with the subordinate
group as such, but it is deeply concerned with its position
vis-à-vis the subordinate group.
—HERBERT BLUMER,
  "Race Prejudice as a Sense of Group Position"

Change is not slow; it is resistance to change that
makes it take a long time.
—CATHERINE A. MACKINNON,
  "MacKinnon J., concurring with the judgment"

Getting Around Brown is the name of a fine book by Gregory Jacobs about
school desegregation in Columbus, Ohio, but it is also the best way to describe
the most powerful force within the political culture of the United States during
the past half-century.[1] Contrary to the celebratory stories occasioned by the
fiftieth anniversary of the Supreme Court's 1954 decision in *Brown v. Board,*
deliberate, collective, and organized white resistance to the desegregation of
opportunities and life chances in U.S. society remains pervasive, powerful, and
predominant in every region of the country. Getting around *Brown* has been the
main mechanism for mobilizing a sense of group position among whites, for
protecting and augmenting the value of past and present discrimination, and
for enabling elite individuals and interests to build a conservative consensus
within national political life.

Evading the desegregation mandate of the *Brown* decision has been the
single most important dynamic within the U.S. political system, a practice
encouraged and legitimated by both political parties, protected by the judiciary,
subsidized by the tax code, and sustained by a complex combination of public
and private policies. In their efforts to "get around *Brown,*" whites enact powerful identity politics based on assertions of group rights, while condemning
communities of color for "playing the race card" and shunning individualism.
Getting around *Brown* entails evasions of moral and legal responsibility in order
to protect the unfair gains and unjust enrichments that accrue to whites as a

consequence of systematic and illegal housing discrimination and widespread and intentional educational inequality.

Less than two years after the Supreme Court issued the *Brown* decision, sociologist Herbert Blumer offered an analysis of race prejudice that would prove extraordinarily prescient. Speaking at the dedication of the Robert E. Park building on the campus of Fisk University in Nashville, Blumer explained that race prejudice was not primarily a matter of private, personal, and individual attitudes, but rather a matter of group position, a fusing of public, political, and institutional actions designed to protect privileges and advantages. He granted that members of dominant groups often express personal disdain for those they view as inferior, alien, and intrinsically different. Yet they do, Blumer argued, largely out of fear that the subordinated group threatens their entitlement to important privileges and prerogatives.

Blumer made no prediction about the implementation of *Brown v. Board,* but he did note that individuals with standing, prestige, authority, and influence within the dominant group had the power to "manufacture events to attract public attention and to set lines of issue in such a way as to predetermine interpretations favorable to their interests."[2] Resistance to school desegregation and busing—and later, resistance to affirmative action—became precisely those kinds of events. Elite whites with standing, prestige, authority, and power chose to portray judicial efforts to implement desegregation mandates as cataclysmic occurrences, as events more threatening to the nation than the segregation and discrimination that caused the courts to act in the first place.

The ferocious opposition to desegregation led by southern demagogues has been well chronicled.[3] Ninety southern members of the U.S. House of Representatives and all but three of the region's twenty-two United States Senators signed the March 1956 "Southern Manifesto" declaring the *Brown* ruling illegitimate and urging "massive resistance" to it by citizens.[4] In order to resist desegregation Senator Harry Byrd and Governor Lindsay Almond, both from Virginia, worked together to make operation of public schools a local option for the state's counties and cities. As a result of their efforts, the Prince Edward County Board of Supervisors evaded a federal court order to desegregate by abolishing the county's entire public school system in 1959, creating a foundation to run all-white private schools paid for by tax credits from the county and tuition grants by the state. Seventeen hundred black students in the county went without any education at all for five years, until the U.S. Supreme Court ruled Prince Edward County's scheme unconstitutional.[5]

Arkansas governor Orville Faubus called out the National Guard to prevent nine black students from enrolling in Little Rock's Central High School in 1957. When President Eisenhower placed the guard under federal control to carry out the orders of the Supreme Court, Faubus closed all four high schools in Little

Rock for the 1958–59 academic year to prevent them from becoming integrated.[6] Political leaders in Alabama championed a successful effort to amend the state constitution in 1956, authorizing the legislature to abolish public education and to allocate state funds and authorize the use of state facilities for segregated private schools for whites in order to frustrate the implementation of *Brown v. Board*.[7] In Georgia, the legislature made it a crime for state or local officials to disburse public funds for desegregated schools. South Carolina repealed its laws making school attendance mandatory, while Louisiana and Mississippi passed laws forbidding children from attending integrated schools.[8]

Less well chronicled, however, have been the actions of white elites from all regions of the country aimed at frustrating the most effective measures likely to implement the mandate of *Brown*. President Eisenhower refused to endorse *Brown v. Board* openly, contenting himself with a condemnation of "the extremists on both sides." As Vincent Harding, Robin D. G. Kelley, and Earl Lewis point out, with that comment the president equated "courageous children and their communities who were working for democratic change with men and women who defied the Supreme Court, dynamited buildings, and assassinated leaders."[9] In the justice departments of the Eisenhower and Kennedy administrations, timid approaches to enforcing *Brown v. Board* raised the percentage of black students attending schools with whites in the states of the Old Confederacy only from 0 percent in 1955 to 2 percent in 1964. Peter Irons notes that this pace would have postponed full integration for an additional five centuries.[10] Despite this incremental pace, in 1966 52 percent of northern whites told pollsters that they felt that the government was pushing integration "too fast."[11]

Richard Nixon secured the endorsement of segregationist ex-Democrat and ex-Dixiecrat Senator Strom Thurmond in the 1968 presidential campaign in return for a pledge to reduce federal action on behalf of school desegregation.[12] He campaigned against "extremists" whom he described as those in favor of "instant integration."[13] After his election, Nixon disregarded the school desegregation guidelines issued in the 1964 Civil Rights Act, nominated resolute opponents of busing to the Supreme Court, and in his 1972 reelection campaign urged Congress to pass legislation overturning court-ordered busing for purposes of desegregation.[14]

Most community and political leaders in the North proved to be as resolute as their southern counterparts in their defense of school segregation. In the Columbus, Ohio, desegregation case in 1978, *Penick v. Columbus Board of Education*, federal district court judge Robert M. Duncan outlined the many methods used by the local school board over the years to create and maintain segregated schools. Duncan delineated a clear and consistent pattern of gerrymandering pupil assignment areas, building new schools only in sites where their neighborhood populations would be all-white or all-black, creating noncontiguous and optional attendance zones, and making racially based hiring and appointment decisions. A Republican appointed to the bench by Richard M. Nixon, Duncan concluded that "the real reason the courts are in the school desegregation business is the failure of other government entities to confront and produce answers to the many problems in this area pursuant to the law of the United States."[15]

In Los Angeles, segregated schools were mandatory by law in the nineteenth century. De facto segregation persisted in the twentieth century to such a degree that the California Supreme Court in 1976 declared the local school district as "among the most segregated in the entire country."[16] In 1963 black students filed a class action lawsuit, *Crawford v. Board of Education of the City of Los Angeles,* to end policies that established South Gate High School as nearly all white and Jordan High School as nearly all black, even though the two schools were located less than two miles apart. White parents and political leaders in South Gate claimed they opposed the merger for nonracial reasons. They contended that they did not want their children to have to walk across "dangerous" Alameda Street, even while the segregated set-up required black children to cross the equally busy and equally "dangerous" Firestone Boulevard.[17] When California judge Alfred Gitelson ruled on the case in 1970 he concluded that the Los Angeles School board "knowingly, affirmatively, and in bad faith . . . segregated, de jure, its students to create and perpetuate segregated schools."[18] He ordered the school board to adopt a plan to desegregate as the remedy for the injury done to minority students for decades of mistreatment.

Governor Ronald Reagan immediately called the order "utterly ridiculous" and a decision that "goes beyond sound reasoning and common sense." President Nixon condemned Judge Gitelson's order as "probably the most extreme judicial decree so far."[19] In the Supreme Court's decision upholding desegregation and the legality of the judge's decision, Justice William Rehnquist coached antibusing opponents about how they could amend the state constitution in order to invalidate busing mandated by state, but not federal judges. Armed with that suggestion, white political leaders in California placed a proposition on the ballot to prevent state judges from ordering busing. The proposition passed with nearly 70 percent of the vote.[20]

School desegregation efforts faced massive resistance in the North and the South. Yet even with clear evidence of massive refusal to comply with the *Brown* decision, the courts did not begin to evaluate proposed remedies for segregation critically until the 1968 case *Green v. County School Board of New Kent County, Virginia.*[21] Federal courts did not direct school districts to adopt specific remedies like busing until 1971 with the *Swann v. Charlotte-Mecklenburg Board of Education* case, and the Supreme Court did not announce that the time for "all deliberate speed" had run out until the 1974 and 1977 *Milliken v. Bradley* cases I and II.

By inviting and condoning more than two decades of delay, the Supreme Court enabled the systematic denial of black children's constitutional rights. The Court elevated the comfort of white parents and their representatives into a constitutionally protected right, simply because they argued that remediation inconvenienced them and interfered with their expected privileges.[22] Yet when the courts finally ran out of patience with two decades of "getting around *Brown*," elite white leaders responded by characterizing the resort to busing to achieve desegregation as an epochal event. They represented busing as an injury to whites to be treated more seriously than the original injury done by segregation's systematic denial of the constitutional rights of black and Latino children.

Busing had been a standard practice during the era of segregation, but it was viewed differently when used for purposes of school desegregation. No white leaders had opposed busing when it served as the primary mechanism for segregating schools. None argued that the concept of the neighborhood school should override the imperatives of segregation. In the 1971 *Swann* decision, Supreme Court chief justice Warren Burger noted that eighteen million children—39 percent of the total population of K–12 students—already rode buses to school during the 1969–70 academic year.[23]

Yet when the Supreme Court endorsed busing for purposes of racial desegregation, white elites from all sections of the country joined together to condemn busing. Liberal Democrats Edith Green from Oregon and James O'Hara from Michigan joined Michigan Republican William Broomfield to encourage the House of Representatives to vote overwhelmingly (235–126) in 1971 for a resolution delaying the implementation of any court order mandating busing until all appeals had been exhausted.[24]

In the 1974 *Milliken v. Bradley* desegregation case, Federal District judge Stephen A. Roth ruled that the city schools in Detroit had been deliberately segregated by school board decisions to build new schools in either all-white or all-black neighborhoods and to allow white students to escape from largely black schools while forbidding black students from transferring to predominately white schools. Moreover, because the Michigan Supreme Court had ruled repeatedly that education in the state "is not a matter of local concern, but belongs to the state at large," Roth ordered an interdistrict busing program between the city of Detroit and its suburbs. Although nearly three hundred thousand children in the three county area covered by Judge Roth's ruling already rode buses to school, politicians from both major political parties condemned Roth's resort to busing for the purposes of desegregation.[25] None of the many vocal and visible opponents of Judge Roth's decision addressed the extensive evidence cited by the judge that private sector actions in real estate and home lending followed school segregation patterns or that whites had come to expect the schools their children attended would be better funded and better equipped than schools with a majority of black students in them.[26]

In *Milliken v. Bradley,* the Supreme Court overruled Judge Roth, citing the sanctity of the principle of "local autonomy of school districts" and the value that citizens rightly place on neighborhood schools. Yet as Justice Thurgood Marshall pointed out in his dissenting opinion, school district lines in Michigan were not based on neighborhoods or even municipalities. The state drew district lines in such a way that the Detroit metropolitan area included eighty-five districts. Some suburbs contained as many as six different school districts, while one school district served five different cities. Two districts spread over three counties, and seventeen districts stretched across two counties.

The Court majority also evaded the violations of federal and state fair housing laws that produced black cities surrounded by white suburbs. Speaking for the majority in a 5–4 decision, Justice Potter Stewart ignored the voluminous evidence that Judge Roth cited connecting residential racial segregation in Detroit and its suburbs to a plethora of actions by city, county, and state agencies. Instead, Stewart offered a stupefyingly disingenuous suggestion—that segregation in Detroit and its suburbs stemmed from "unknown or unknowable causes."[27]

Jamin Raskin notes that the Supreme Court's ruling in *Milliken v. Bradley* gave "judicial impetus and imprimatur to white flight."[28] It rewarded suburban areas for segregation, granting those that had successfully excluded blacks from residence an exemption from desegregation remedies. It advised white parents— including those who became party to the *Milliken* case because they objected to the state of Michigan denying their children a desegregated education—that the only way to secure optimal educational resources for their children was to move away from areas where blacks lived.

The Court's decision in *Milliken v. Bradley* drew widespread support and emboldened the opponents of desegregation. During the administration of President Carter, Congress voted to prohibit the executive branch from cutting off federal funds to school districts resisting desegregation (as mandated in the 1964 Civil Rights Act) if those cases entailed mandatory busing as a feasible remedy.[29] In *Milliken v. Bradley II* the Court permitted educational enrichment in segregated inner city schools as an allowable remedy for past discrimination, but opposed these "sweeteners" in the 1995 *Missouri v. Jenkins* case. The Court argued that such remedies made central city schools too attractive to voluntary transfers by suburban whites, therefore violating the ban against interdistrict remedies enunciated in *Milliken v. Bradley.* The federal Emergency School Aid Act of 1975 allocated funds for schools under desegregation decrees to retrain staff, hire race relations counselors, and develop curricular materials sensitive to the needs of minority students. The Reagan administration, however, eliminated the program in 1981, effectively terminating federal investment in integrated schools.[30]

Presidents Carter and George W. Bush validated the politics of group position and the possessive investment in whiteness by appointing to the office of attorney general men who led resistance to court ordered desegregation. Carter assigned the role of the nation's chief law enforcement officer to Griffin Bell, a man who had improperly interfered with court ordered desegregation in Atlanta. While serving as a sitting judge on the federal Fifth Circuit Court in 1973, Bell secretly represented a group of white civic and business leaders in closed door negotiations with middle-class African American leaders to settle the pending *Calhoun v. Cook* case before the circuit court. He did so to help them circumvent an earlier decision by the circuit court that concluded that busing remedies like those applied in *Swann* should be considered in Atlanta. Bell knew from his role as part of the three-judge panel that issued a stay stopping the proceedings in *Armour v. Nix*, another school desegregation case in the city that posed the possibility that Atlanta would be confronted with orders to desegregate housing and schooling in the city. By stopping the proceedings in *Armour v. Nix* temporarily, Bell helped buy time for the litigants in the *Calhoun* case to reach a settlement. But he extended additional aid to them through his direct and distinctly inappropriate actions as a participant in negotiations that helped end the case. Thus, a sitting Fifth Circuit judge advised participants in pending litigation about the best ways to settle the case to impede the Fifth Circuit's decision that busing be considered as a remedy in Atlanta. Rather than facing disbarment for improper intervention in a pending case, Bell was rewarded with appointment as attorney general, a position that entails responsibility for protecting the Fourteenth Amendment rights of all citizens.[31]

Slightly more than two decades later, President George W. Bush appointed another stalwart protector of the group position of whites to the post of attorney general, John Ashcroft. While serving as the junior United States senator from Missouri, Ashcroft praised the *Southern Partisan* magazine, a racist right-wing journal that once argued that blacks benefited greatly from being enslaved. Ashcroft granted an interview to the publication in which he characterized the treasonous and slaveholding Confederacy as an honorable cause.[32] Earlier, when Missouri's attorney general and then governor, Ashcroft played a key role in impeding court-ordered desegregation in St. Louis and Kansas City, securing nearly four million dollars from the state legislature for the express purpose of fighting against the legitimate orders of the federal courts.

Ashcroft opposed every measure proposed by the courts, challenging even voluntary interdistrict busing programs and magnet schools. He lost every appeal to the U.S. Supreme Court, but secured political popularity in his home state by portraying himself as a resolute defender of the settled expectations and group position of its white citizens. Ashcroft declared the modest and voluntary interdistrict transfer plan that emerged from the *Liddell* case in St. Louis to be "an outrage against human decency," and boasted in his 1984 campaign for governor that he had done everything within his power to fight against the orders of the federal courts.[33]

Ashcroft claimed repeatedly that the state of Missouri had never been found guilty of violating the constitutional rights of black children by assigning them to segregated schools. Yet Missouri was one of the states that had mandated Jim Crow schools before *Brown*. In direct violation of the first *Brown* ruling in 1954, the state's attorney general announced that individual school districts could decide whether they wanted to comply with the decision or not. In both *Adams v. United States* and *United States v. Missouri,* the federal courts found the state guilty of supporting segregation. In the St. Louis desegregation case, the court cited the wording of the *Adams* case: "In sum, the State defendants stand before the Court as primary constitutional wrongdoers who have abdicated their affirmative remedial duty. Their efforts to pass the buck among themselves and to other state instrumentalities must be rejected."[34] Yet Ashcroft continued to claim the state had never been found guilty of wrongdoing. In reward for this pattern of lying, Ashcroft received appointment as attorney general of the United States.

At his confirmation hearings, Ashcroft lied four different times under oath. He claimed that the state of Missouri had been made a party to the St. Louis school desegregation case before he became attorney general. In fact, as the court of appeals noted, the state of Missouri was added as a defendant during the summer of 1977 when Ashcroft was already attorney general. Nominee Ashcroft swore under oath that the state of Missouri "had done nothing wrong" and was "found guilty of no wrong." In fact, the district court decisions explained that Missouri's liability in the case went back to 1954. Ashcroft had appealed this ruling three times and was rejected all three times. The presiding judge in the case characterized Ashcroft's stance as one of politically motivated "total opposition."[35]

Nominee Ashcroft also testified that he carried out all the orders of the federal courts as attorney general and as governor. In fact, Ashcroft resisted every order. The federal district court threatened to hold him in contempt of court for refusing to submit a plan for voluntary desegregation. His administration never asked municipalities to come up with fair housing proposals as the court mandated. Ashcroft's obstructionism caused the court to complain about the state's "continual delay and failure to comply," and to draw the conclusion that "the state has, as a matter of deliberate policy, decided to defy the authority of the court." Finally, Ashcroft announced at his confirmation hearings that "nothing could be farther from the truth" than the allegation that he opposed voluntary desegregation. In fact, as the district court noted in *Missouri v. Jenkins*: "during the course of this lawsuit the Court has not been informed of one affirmative act voluntarily taken by the Executive Department of the state of Missouri or the Missouri General Assembly to aid a school district that is involved in a desegregation program."[36]

The same John Ashcroft who condemned the St. Louis voluntary desegregation plan as "an outrage against human decency" had also opposed a 1981 plan by the Reagan administration for voluntary desegregation.[37] Yet despite this perjured testimony, no charges were brought against Ashcroft for his falsifications of his record, and no senator from either party attempted a filibuster to prevent Ashcroft's nomination.

• • •

The pattern and practice of getting around *Brown* stem, in part, from the limits of the original decision. Constitutional rights in the U.S. system are generally "personal and present"; their violation is a matter of the greatest importance, requiring immediate redress and remedy. The *Brown* decision, however, undermined its mandate for desegregation by specifying that corrective actions were to be taken with "all deliberate speed," rather than immediately. This left both the pace and the parameters of desegregation up to the comfort and convenience of those doing the discriminating.[38] Thus, the Court's own ruling incited defiance and invited delay.

Recent rulings have used the very success of those delaying tactics as a rationale for ending longstanding court orders. In the Kansas City case, city and state officials did nothing to implement *Brown*'s mandates until they were successfully sued in 1977. They did not come up with a plan until the courts mandated one in 1985, and the plan was not implemented until 1988. A mere seven years later, however, the Supreme Court ruled in *Missouri v. Jenkins* that racial inequality in education in the Kansas City area no longer stemmed from segregation, but from "voluntary" and "natural" decisions about where people live.

The Court claimed, in all seriousness, that residential choices in Kansas City had nothing to do with the legacy of segregation, even though these decisions concentrated white people in affluent suburbs with well-funded schools while relegating blacks to poverty-stricken inner city neighborhoods where schools were literally falling apart.[39] As soon as the majority of the school population became black, the white majority of the electorate failed to pass a single bond issue or tax levy to support the schools.[40] In her dissenting opinion, Justice Ruth Bader Ginsburg pointed out that the Court majority had decided that remedial programs had effectively countered in seven years the legacy of discrimination that started in Kansas City with the proclamation of the Code Noir by King Louis XV of France in 1724, followed by slavery, state laws prohibiting public education for blacks, mandatory Jim Crow segregation, and thirty years of inaction after the *Brown* decision.[41]

It should be remembered that the ingenious strategy followed by Charles Houston, Thurgood Marshall, and the other attorneys for the plaintiffs in *Brown v. Board* and related cases was not to overturn the "separate but equal" doctrine in *Plessy*, but to raise its costs: to make it too expensive for whites to endure by compelling cities, counties, and states to make "equal" expenditures on schools for blacks. The state of Texas allocated one hundred thousand dollars to build an entirely new law school for blacks rather than admit a fully qualified black applicant into the state-supported, all-white University of Texas Law School that admitted only whites. The Supreme Court ruled in that case, *Sweatt v. Painter*, that even if the new black law school built for Sweatt equaled the UT Law School in the quality of its physical plant and equipment (itself a doubtful assumption), that Sweatt would still be deprived of the learning environment of the white law school, its alumni contacts, and its reputation.[42]

In *Brown v. Board*, the Court unanimously overturned *Plessy* as the law of the land. Yet as Derrick Bell reminds us, *Plessy* "is only fortuitously a legal precedent. In actuality, it is a judicial affirmation of an unwritten but no less clearly understood social compact that is older than the Constitution, was incorporated into that document, and has continually been affirmed."[43] That compact entails a possessive investment in whiteness and protections for the group position of whites in perpetuity, a systematic and structured advantage.[44] In her brilliant analysis of whiteness as property, Cheryl I. Harris explains that both before and after the passage of comprehensive civil rights laws, the U.S. judiciary has honored this compact, recognizing "implicitly or explicitly, the settled expectations of whites built on the privileges and benefits produced by white supremacy."[45]

Even though the Supreme Court disavowed *Plessy* in 1954, getting around *Brown* has produced a situation that is even worse: constitutional legitimacy for schools to be *both* separate *and* unequal. The wording of the *Brown* decision and its interpretation by subsequent judges has allowed school boards and state governments to substitute declarations of nondiscrimination for actual desegregation, sparing them the costs of operating dual school systems while continuing to reserve superior educational settings and resources for white children. Schools now have federal permission to do what even *Plessy* could not advise openly, to be both separate and unequal.

As a law clerk to Justice Robert H. Jackson, William Rehnquist wrote a memo on the occasion of the *Brown* deliberations that advised upholding the separate but equal doctrine in *Plessy*. He later claimed under oath that the memo did not reflect his actual views, but was merely prepared for Jackson as an intellectual exercise, a claim that is both disingenuous and implausible. Yet whatever Rehnquist's true feelings about *Plessy* might have been or might be, his actions on the Court as associate justice and chief justice played a major role in producing results that have reversed the gains of desegregation in order to advance the group position of whites.

Rehnquist and his colleagues produced an astounding range of rationales for getting around *Brown*. Their reasoning evidenced what philosopher Charles Mills describes as an "epistemology of ignorance"—a way of knowing dependent upon distortion, erasure, and occlusion.[46] It is not so much that they did not know, but rather that they devoted enormous energy to refusing to know. Their rulings contained inconsistencies and contradictions that would be unfathomable except for their underlying consistent fidelity to the possessive investment in whiteness.

When the drawing of school district boundaries has benefited whites (as in the access it supplied them to superior schools in suburban Detroit in *Milliken v. Bradley* and suburban Kansas City in *Missouri v. Jenkins*), the Supreme Court declared that democracy itself depends on keeping school district lines sacrosanct. They advanced the fiction that the boundaries were created by autonomous local decisions rather than by state action. But this was not a fiction to be sustained in all cases. In 1973, when Mexican American parents in San Antonio in *San Antonio Independent School District v. Rodriguez* demonstrated that their children received inferior educations because the state-drawn district lines and state-mandated reliance on the property tax left them isolated in a district with inadequate resources, the Court declared that "any scheme of local taxation—indeed the very existence of identifiable local governmental units—requires the establishment of jurisdictional boundaries that are inevitably arbitrary."[47] Thus, local boundaries are essential building blocks of democracy when they work to the advantage of whites, but inevitably arbitrary constructions when they disadvantage communities of color.

The Court conceded in *Rodriguez* that the educational opportunities available to Mexican American children in San Antonio were not equal to those routinely secured by white children in that city. Yet the Court ruled that San Antonio's Mexican American children and parents did not qualify for Fourteenth Amendment protection: it held that education is not important enough in society to make its unequal provision a constitutional injury. Yet five years later, in 1978, the same court decided that education was so important that it should adjudicate the case of Allan Bakke, a thirty-six-year-old white man denied admission to the medical school at University of California, Davis. The Court agreed with Bakke's claim that he had been rejected from the school because its special minority admissions program admitted sixteen students the year he applied. Bakke had a higher undergraduate grade point average than the cumulative GPA of the candidates accepted in the special admissions program. Yet he did not challenge the legitimacy of the thirty-six white students with GPAs lower than his who also secured admission that year, he did not challenge the credentials of the five students who were admitted to the school that year because their parents had attended the school or given money to it, nor did he challenge his rejection by other medical schools to which he applied that did not have minority admissions programs but preferred younger applicants. Even though at least one of the minority admits had a much higher GPA than did Bakke, and even though he had been the beneficiary of superior educational opportunities in the illegally segregated elementary schools of Dade County, Florida, the Court granted Bakke the protection of strict scrutiny, a level of review traditionally reserved only for complaints by "discrete and insular minorities."

Justice Lewis F. Powell conceded that white males were not a discrete and insular minority group, but argued successfully that Bakke should receive that protection because the special admissions policy made him think that he was being discriminated against. On the basis of this strict scrutiny, the Court ordered the medical school to admit Bakke, and to base its affirmative action admissions program on the benefits that white students get by being exposed to diverse classmates, rather than on the need to redress the injuries done to minority applicants by pervasive and systematic discrimination. The opportunity to get a quality education—not important enough for the Court to give to Mexican American children in San Antonio—suddenly became a matter of the greatest Constitutional urgency when Allan Bakke argued that he should never be disfavored in competition with black candidates for admission to professional school.[48]

The Rehnquist court argued for the necessity of reining in federal power and respecting traditions of local governance when it terminated the Kansas City school desegregation plan in *Missouri v. Jenkins.* This reversed the position, however, of freely deploying the power of the federal courts to overturn the minority set-aside program for city contracts approved by the Richmond, Virginia, city council in the 1989 *Croson* case, and in 1993 to void the North Carolina legislature's decision to create a congressional district with a slight majority of black residents in *Shaw v. Reno.* Justice Sandra Day O'Connor argued that the creation of one of the most integrated congressional districts in the nation by the North Carolina legislature was a form of racial apartheid that directly contradicted the constitutional obligation to meld different groups together into a unified totality. Yet O'Connor did not object to districts drawn to ensure the election of white candidates, with all white districts created by residential racial segregation, or with the hypersegregation of black and Latino students in underfunded ghetto schools.

The Rehnquist court ruled in *Shaw v. Reno* and *Miller v. Johnson* (1995) that whites are protected by the Fourteenth Amendment from dwelling in districts with irregular boundaries and African American or Latino majorities; African

Americans and Latinos have no corresponding freedom from living in districts with irregular boundaries and white majorities.[49] Justice Clarence Thomas supported the dismantling of the majority black congressional district in North Carolina because of the "stigma" it purportedly attached to the district, but argued that majority black schools in impoverished areas are a good thing, so good in fact, that the lower courts who tried to desegregate the Kansas City schools must have acted out of the belief that blacks are inferior.[50]

Over the years the Rehnquist court fashioned a narrative about itself as a defender of federalism, a respecter of local government, and a counterweight to unwarranted judicial activism by liberal judges. Yet its fidelity to federalism (a word that does not appear in the Constitution) did not consistently manifest itself: not when white contractors objected to the set-aside plan crafted by the democratically elected but predominately black city council in Richmond in the *Croson* case, not when white firefighters protested against a court-approved affirmative action hiring program in Birmingham, Alabama, in *Martin v. Wilks,* not when white teachers litigated against a voluntary collective bargaining agreement between the teachers union and the school board in Jackson, Michigan, in the *Wygant* case. The Michigan agreement had called for the protection of new black teachers from budget-related layoffs because seniority-based layoffs would unfairly harm minority teachers who had less seniority because of the district's history of discriminatory hiring.[51]

Rather than reducing judicial activism, the Rehnquist court was eager to expand it to defend white privileges. As Justice David Souter pointed out in his dissenting opinion in *Missouri v. Jenkins,* the Court was so eager to end Kansas City's seven-year-old desegregation program that it overruled "a unanimous constitutional precedent of 20 year standing, which was not even addressed in argument, was mentioned merely in passing by one of the parties, and discussed by another of them only in a misleading way." Souter concluded that "the Court's failure to provide adequate notice of the issue to be decided (or to limit the decision to issues on which certiorari was clearly granted) rules out any confidence that today's result is sound, either in fact or in law."[52]

The Rehnquist court displayed a double standard in defense of white privilege when it came to questions of legal standing as well. In the 1984 *Allen v. Wright* case, the Supreme Court decided against black parents suing to force the Internal Revenue Service to enforce the law by withdrawing tax exemptions from private schools with racially discriminatory policies. Speaking for the majority, Justice O'Connor ruled that citizens do not have the right to require the government to obey the law, and that the plaintiffs were not personally harmed by the actions they protested. She stated that to have standing to sue in the courts, the plaintiffs would have to prove that they suffered a concrete personal injury, not just an "Abstract stigmatic injury."[53] Yet in *Shaw v. Reno,*

O'Connor ruled that white plaintiffs had the right to have the North Carolina congressional district boundaries redrawn because living in a majority black district "reinforces racial stereotypes and threatens to undermine our system of representative democracy by signaling to elected officials that they represent a particular racial group rather than their constituency as a whole."[54] Moreover, in *Bush v. Gore,* the Court did not ask how Texas resident George W. Bush had standing to contest alleged denials of equal protection to an unidentified group of Florida voters. Justice Antonin Scalia and Justice Thomas joined the majority upholding Bush's claims without recusing themselves, even though one of the law firms representing Bush employed Scalia's son, and even though Justice Thomas's wife had been charged by her employer, the Heritage Foundation, to begin collecting curricula vitae to advise an incoming Bush administration on potential appointees.[55]

Perhaps the most egregious demonstration of the Court's epistemology of ignorance appears in its refusal to acknowledge the link between housing discrimination and school segregation. Although the Burger court recognized in the 1971 *Swann* case that segregated and unequal schools shape housing choices, subsequent rulings have denied that link.[56] While holding the Denver school system responsible for policies that intentionally segregated black and Latino students in the 1973 *Keyes* decision, Justice Powell absolved the district of responsibility to remedy "geographical separation of the races" that "resulted from purely natural and neutral non-state causes." In a 1976 decision on segregation in Austin, Texas, Justice Rehnquist asserted (without proof) that "economic pressures and voluntary preferences are the primary determinants of residential patterns." He waxed poetic on that theme in reviewing the Columbus, Ohio, case in 1977, claiming that residential segregation in the region resulted from a "mélange of past happenings prompted by economic considerations, private discrimination, discriminatory school assignments or a desire to reside near people of one's own race or ethnic background."[57]

In attributing residential segregation to "natural," "neutral," "voluntary" desires, the Court accepted the fictions of defendants in desegregation cases. Attorney James P. Gorton, who represented school districts in suburban St. Louis and Atlanta against desegregation orders, boasted to a reporter that he and his colleagues had established that "people live in specific school districts and urban areas based on job needs, personal preferences, and other factors—not because of race."[58] Yet an enormous body of unchallenged and uncontradicted evidence demonstrates the contrary. Researchers have found consistently that the racial composition of a neighborhood is more important to whites than housing quality, crime, environmental amenities, and location.[59] Even putatively nonracial considerations like the reputation of local schools often contain perceptions about the racial identities of the student body.[60] In the early years of school desegregation cases, judges drew on overwhelming evidence that residential segregation stemmed from a combination of private discriminatory acts including mortgage redlining, real estate steering, and blockbusting, along with public policies such as urban renewal, the allocation of Section 235 funds to only certain areas of cities, and placement decisions about public housing projects, subsidized developments, and schools.[61] As late as 1987 a circuit court established a mutually constitutive relationship between housing and school segregation in Yonkers, New York, fashioning a remedy that required integrated housing as well as integrated schools.[62] Yet the Rehnquist court consistently distorted the facts in order to excuse and erase this systematic discrimination. According to its reasoning, the existence of segregation in housing is attributed to nonracial causes. The Court pretended to believe that no whites move away from municipalities to secure the benefits they gain from neighborhoods and schools that are prohibited to blacks. Actually existing segregation is attributed to race neutral causes, beyond the concern of the courts. But school desegregation plans are rejected because they might cause white flight. Thus, whites are not now race conscious in their selections of neighborhoods and schools, but they might become so, the Court complains, if faced with desegregation.[63]

Perhaps the most honest expression of the judiciary's current attitude toward school desegregation came in the resolution of the *Armour v. Nix* case. This litigation was filed by the ACLU on behalf of a group of impoverished black women from Atlanta as a rival to the *Calhoun* case, which was settled in private with the help of Griffin Bell. The plaintiffs assembled an enormous compendium of evidence proving that repeated actions by the city, state, county, and federal governments about housing, transportation, and neighborhood development had led to permanent and seemingly intractable residential segregation in the Atlanta area. Judge William O'Kelly conceded that the region's residential segregation had been "caused in part by the actions of government officials," acknowledging eighteen separate actions including racial zoning laws, racially based selection of public housing sites, racial designation of schools, and segregated relocation from neighborhoods cleared for urban renewal. Yet he ruled that because the schools had not *caused* residential segregation, they should not be desegregated *because* of it. Nor would O'Kelly consider systematic violations of fair housing laws a proper matter for adjudication in the courts, declaring that "to change the residential patterns which exist it would be necessary to rip up the very fabric of society in a manner that is not within the province of the federal courts."[64] O'Kelly's ruling at least had the virtue of a certain honesty. Apparently the injury done to blacks in Atlanta was so systematic and so successful that remedy was now seen as beyond the power of the federal courts: to challenge the group position that whites secured from segregated housing would be to challenge the very fabric of society. Yet O'Kelly's honesty was short-lived. In a phrase reminiscent of Justice Stewart's ruling in *Milliken v. Bradley,* the Atlanta judge cited the testimony of David Armour, later an official in the Reagan administration, that "why people live where they do can never be fully explained."[65]

What *can* be fully explained is the result achieved by fifty years of "getting around *Brown.*" Black and Latino students find themselves segregated by race and by class in schools with fewer resources, less-experienced teachers, and more undiagnosed and untreated disabilities. School segregation today has reverted to levels not seen since the 1960s. After declining to around 62 percent in the early 1980s because of court ordered desegregation, the proportion of black students in segregated schools has reverted back to the numbers of the 1960s. Seventy percent of black students attended segregated schools in 1999, compared with 77 percent in 1968.[66] None of the twenty-five largest cities in the United States has a majority of white students in its school system.[67] The proportion of black students in "majority white" schools declined by 13 percent during the 1990s.[68]

The schools that serve minority and high poverty populations lack key science and math courses, offer fewer advanced placement courses, and have inferior equipment and supplies. Capital investments in schools located in high poverty areas are 31 percent lower than similar investments in middle class areas. The wealthiest school districts spend 56 percent more per student than the poorest ones.[69] Residential racial segregation, however, compounds the problems of poverty even more. Over 80 percent of hypersegregated black and Latino schools are located in areas of concentrated poverty, compared to only 5 percent of schools with an overwhelmingly white population.[70] Hypersegregated schools with black or Latino enrollments of 90 percent or more are fourteen times more likely to have a majority of impoverished students. Poor neighborhoods have high incidences of lead poisoning and asthma among residents, and schools serving these neighborhoods encounter high percentages of students who are hungry, have undiagnosed and untreated developmental disabilities, and whose families move so often because of scarce housing opportunities that they never develop relationships with school personnel.[71] Pervasive housing segregation means that middle-class black students are much more likely to have higher percentages of poor classmates than white students do.

Education is more important to blacks and Latinos than to whites because members of those groups are much less likely to receive inheritances from parents, have less access to family business networks, and tend to live farther away from employment centers. Yet school inequality and segregation leave them with inferior educational opportunities. Unfair impediments to education and asset accumulation for some people, however, translate into unfair gains and unjust enrichments for others. Opposition to school desegregation has enabled whites to preserve and augment advantages initially secured as a result of overt de jure segregation in an earlier era. As Gary Orfield argues, the superiority of suburban schools is taken for granted as a right attendant to home ownership, while desegregation is viewed as a threat to a system that passes racial advantages from one generation to the next. In Orfield's words, "Whites tell pollsters that they believe that blacks are offered equal opportunities, but fiercely resist any efforts to make them send their children to the schools they insist are good enough for blacks." At the same time, "the people who oppose busing minority students to the suburbs also tend to oppose sending suburban dollars to city schools."[72]

Yet "getting around *Brown*" does not only work to the disadvantage of aggrieved communities of color. By rendering racial inequality in the United States as natural, necessary, and inevitable, "getting around *Brown*" forms the basis for a broader social warrant rooted in inequality, hostile privatism, defensive localism, and a notion of citizenship as the consumption of city services and the hoarding of scarce resources. By transforming the meaning of the Fourteenth Amendment from the prohibition of subjugation into a measure that prevents government agencies from recognizing and remedying racial inequality, "getting around *Brown*" severs all citizens from the traditions most responsible for fairness, equity, and justice in the national life. It replaces the freedom dreams of aggrieved people with a social warrant for selfishness.

A social warrant is a widely shared and generally understood definition of what is permitted and forbidden in society. It is rarely written down, but draws its power from the diffuse authority of collective ideas and actions. It functions as a de facto Bill of Rights, articulating foundational principles about obligations and entitlements, about exclusion and inclusion. Social warrants author and authorize new ways of knowing and new ways of being. They are products of political mobilization, part of what social movements can win when they battle for rights, resources, and recognition. Every social warrant has to displace another social warrant that it hopes to surpass and supersede, and struggles over social warrants reveal history as dialogic, as collective, continuing, and cumulative.

The civil rights movement drew on the traditions of the labor movement and abolition democracy to fashion a new social warrant during the 1950s and 1960s. The movement helped democratize U.S. society through practices like consensus decision making, challenges to elite knowledge, insistence on direct democracy, and the cultivation of new grassroots leaders. This civil rights warrant found succinct expression in Dr. Martin Luther King Jr.'s 1968 sermon "The Drum Major Instinct," in the curriculum of the Mississippi Freedom Summer Project in 1964, and in a variety of legal decisions, most notably Justice William O. Douglas's condemnation of "slavery unwilling to die" in his ruling in the 1968 *Jones v. Mayer* case.

This social warrant of the civil rights movement was so powerful that even its opponents have tried to drape themselves in it. "Getting around *Brown*" proceeds by embracing both the *Brown* decision and the Fourteenth Amendment, but distorting them. In fashioning a new social warrant, the defenders of the group position of whites and the possessive investment in whiteness transform *Brown* from a mandate for desegregation into a requirement that state actions never openly favor anyone on racial grounds, even when that "favoritism" comes in the form of providing race-based remedies for race-based injuries. They pretend that the courageous black children and parents who fought for desegregation in the *Brown* case merely wanted to make sure that blacks received second-class schools on a de facto rather than a de jure basis.

By similar means, "getting around *Brown*" transforms the Fourteenth Amendment from an antisubjugation law into an antidiscrimination law.[73] Following the precedent that betrayed the first Reconstruction in the nineteenth century, this maneuver offers zealous protection and even extension of the Fourteenth Amendment rights of whites, but for all practical purposes denies them to members of aggrieved minority groups. In *Shaw v. Reno,* and subsequent cases, the Court majority held that while people of color have to prove both injury and intent in equal protection cases, whites merely need to show that government actions make racial distinctions, whether they are personally injured by them or not.[74]

"Getting around *Brown*" originated in the counterrevolution against the social warrant of the civil rights movement. Its premises and principles emerged from collective social mobilization by white activists and elites, especially in campaigns against busing and for limitations on taxes. It has succeeded because it developed a counter social warrant, one based on elevating the settled expectations and group position of whites over the demands for justice by members of aggrieved racial groups. There are several main mechanisms that make it possible to turn antisubjugation laws into antidiscrimination laws: require injured nonwhite plaintiffs to prove explicit racial *intent* not just racial *injury*; position harm done to white interests and expectations by enforcement of civil rights laws as a "reverse racism"; and take that "reverse racism" much more seriously than the millions of directly racist actions by public and private actors in society every day. The social warrant of "getting around *Brown*" is aimed not only at the specific gains secured by aggrieved minorities through the civil rights movement, but more broadly at the general egalitarianism and democratization of society that increased in the wake of civil rights struggles. For that reason, it contains not only a reactive backlash against desegregation, but also a distinct notion of citizenship based on increasing one's own private property and securing advantages in consumption of government services.

In his excellent study of the origins and evolution of the social movement for tax limitation that emerged visibly during the 1970s, Clarence Lo notes how antitax and antibusing activists developed a common notion of consumer citizenship. "Whites joined antibusing movements," Lo observes, "because they sought to maintain advantages for their racial or ethnic group in the consumption of government services."[75] The use of the term "forced busing" by white activists as the way to describe desegregation plans copied the example of opponents of fair housing laws, who in the 1964 campaign to repeal California's Rumford Act declared themselves opponents of "forced housing."[76] The defenders of segregated housing became the defenders of segregated schools. The segregated neighborhoods and social circles that resulted served as the main sources of mobilization for tax-limitation, budget cuts on social services, and the denial of social services to immigrants. Philip J. Ethington's empirically rich and theoretically sophisticated studies of race and space in Los Angeles show that the white neighborhoods most physically isolated from black communities provided the most enthusiastic support for California's unconstitutional 1964 repeal of fair housing legislation, 1978's Proposition 13 tax limitation initiative, and 1994's unconstitutional Proposition 187 denying state supported education and health care to undocumented immigrants.[77]

Just as the pursuit of immediate goals by civil rights activists eventually generated a broader social warrant aimed at reforming all of U.S. society, the antitax and antibusing activism of the 1970s eventually flowered into an effective and affective social warrant rooted in what Jürgen Habermas calls "civil-familial vocational privatism,"[78] a political ideology that succeeds as politics precisely because it disavows political aims and interests.

The social warrant at the heart of "getting around *Brown*" encourages well-off communities to hoard their advantages, seek to have their tax base used to fund only themselves and their interests, and displace the costs of remedying complex social problems onto less powerful and less wealthy populations. This stance places every subunit of government in competition with every other unit, strengthening the hand of wealthy individuals and corporations while defunding the institutions established to regulate them. By emphasizing the insulation and isolation of local taxing units from the broader needs of the city, county, state, or national entities, antitax activists can be fiscal liberals at home, enjoying high spending on services they consume directly, while acting as fiscal conservatives elsewhere, demanding cuts in services that go to others. These practices serve their self-interests twice over: increasing public spending in well-off districts increases their property values; reducing spending in poorer communities makes residences in them worth even less to their inhabitants. The effect of this social warrant is to add to white competitive and comparative advantage.

When the social warrant of the civil rights movement secured widespread credibility, support for education increased. If one thinks as a citizen or as a community member, then the more better-educated people there are, the better it is for everyone. But if one thinks as an accumulator and a consumer, educating other people's children might place your own at a competitive disadvantage. This creates massive inefficiency and misallocation of resources at the societal level. Direct discrimination costs the gross national product from 2 to 4 percent a year in lost productivity and waste. Yet what is disastrous at the societal level can be advantageous at the level of the household, at least in the short run.

The economic and political practices of consumer citizenship require a cultural corollary. Defining the public good as the preservation of private privilege and elevating private desires over public needs is not a winning argument, at least not yet. But portraying elites as oppressed victims, as producers oppressed by parasites such as government bureaucrats on the one hand and aggrieved minorities on the other, legitimates aggressive and predatory social policies by presenting them as simple self-defense and a return to "common sense."

This social warrant asks people to place their identities as accumulators and consumers above their responsibilities as workers and citizens. It builds a countersubversive consensus around the idea that economic stagnation and social disintegration stem from the excessive concessions made to subordinated groups as a result of the civil rights movement. It claims drops in real wages, declines in public services, and increased user fees and taxes on sales and payroll are the result of expensive experiments in social engineering like school busing for the purpose of desegregation, rather than the result of the power and greed of corporations and the regressive nature of the U.S. tax code. For special emotional effect, it portrays efforts to stop discrimination against communities of color as reverse discrimination against whites.

Promising wealth, stability, and security to "taxpayers," the social warrant of "getting around *Brown*," actually creates a speculative economy, severs the relationship between work and reward, plunders public resources for private gain, and promotes economic insecurity and social antagonisms. "Tax limitation" campaigns and cuts in capital gains, income, property, and inheritance taxes for the wealthy actually end up raising payroll taxes, sales taxes, and user fees. Cuts in social welfare spending undermine real wages and allow businesses to increase profits by raising the costs of medicine, food, and other staples.

Yet even failure has its uses. Budget cuts, deregulation, and racial polarization make everyday life worse for most people. The worse things get, however, the more receptive some parts of the populace are to demagogic moral panics that blame inner city dwellers, immigrants, or sexual minorities for society's problems. The more public debate swirls around "tax relief," the less likely public attention will be focused on decisions about production, investment, outsourcing, and profiteering in the private sector.

Getting around "getting around *Brown*" is a difficult task. It requires not only victories in individual cases and arenas, but the development of a social movement capable of generating a new social warrant. It necessitates restoring the antisubjugation dimensions of the Fourteenth Amendment and distinguishing them from their antidiscrimination applications. It entails establishing disparate and unfavorable racial impact as the basis for judging civil rights violations, even if the discriminators have been intelligent enough to avoid articulating their racist intent openly. It compels us to confront the evasions of "getting around *Brown*" directly by demanding full enforcement of fair housing laws, by filing suit against the perpetrators of home loan discrimination, real estate steering, insurance redlining, predatory lending, and the myriad other means used to keep the nation's neighborhoods separate and unequal. Most important, it forces us to relearn the lessons of the past by producing the kinds of collective learning that come from collective action, and to engage in struggles for rights, resources, and recognition that can generate new ways of knowing and new ways of being.

The social warrant of consumer citizenship contains internal contradictions that it cannot resolve. It produces the opposite of what it promises. Elevating the avarice and calculation of the consumer over the conscience and responsibility of the citizen leads to a war of all against all, leaving society fractured, spiteful, and angry. Competition for scarce services and amenities promote anxiety, envy, and disrespect. The privileging of property rights over human rights leaves capital free to fly to the sites of greatest return, but when social security pensions turn into private investment accounts and schools become sites for returning profits to investors, the quality of life for young and old diminishes.

Social movement struggles against the social warrant of consumer citizenship are already underway. Just as the successes of the civil rights movement forced its enemies to fashion a dialogic response, the victories secured by the proponents of "getting around *Brown*" leave the communities and individuals damaged by present policies with no choice but to fight back.

One particularly promising response to "getting around *Brown*" has been concentrated in the effort to repeal the Supreme Court's decision in *San Antonio Independent School District v. Rodriguez* by means of a constitutional amendment that reads "All children in the United States have a right to receive an equal public education for democratic citizenship."[79] This campaign shrewdly restores some of the radical possibilities embedded in the original *Brown* decision, while at the same time exposing the hypocrisy of the equal protection language used in *Milliken v. Bradley, Regents of the University of California v. Bakke,* and *Missouri v. Jenkins.* Yet as important as legal actions have been in determining the fate of desegregation, nothing can be won in court if a social warrant for it has not already been established in the broader society through collective mobilization. The process of social change is as important as the product. As Tomiko Brown-Nagin sagely advises, "The proper question is not whether courts alone can produce significant social changes, but rather, how lawyers and advocates can create the sociopolitical conditions that give rise to social movements whose momentum the Supreme Court cannot stop when movement lawyers bring test cases before it."[80]

Notes

Parts of this essay appear in "Racially Writing the Republic and Racially Righting the Republic" in *Racially Writing the Republic,* ed. Bruce Baum and Duchess Harris (Durham: Duke University Press, 2009). All rights reserved. Used by permission of the publisher.

1. Gregory S. Jacobs, *Getting Around* Brown: *Desegregation, Development, and the Columbus Public Schools* (Columbus: Ohio State University Press, 1998).

2. Herbert Blumer, "Race Prejudice as a Sense of Group Position," *Pacific Sociological Review* 1, no. 1 (1958): 6.

3. See, for example, Curtis M. Vaughan, *Faubus's Folly: The Story of Segregation* (New York: Vantage, 1959); Roy Reed, *Faubus: The Life and Times of an Arkansas Prodigal* (Fayetteville: University of Arkansas Press, 1997); Numan Bartley, *The Rise of Massive Resistance: Race and Politics in the South During the 1950s* (Baton Rouge: Louisiana State University Press, 1969); Robbins Gates, *The Making of Massive Resistance: Virginia's Politics of Public School Desegregation, 1954–1956* (Chapel Hill: University of North Carolina Press, 1964); Dan T. Carter, *The Politics of Rage* (New York: Simon and Schuster, 1995).

4. Vincent Harding, Robin D. G. Kelley, and Earl Lewis, "We Changed the World, 1945–1970," in *To Make Our World Anew: A History of African Americans,* ed. Robin D. G. Kelley and Earl Lewis (New York: Oxford University Press, 2000), 473.

5. Peter Irons, *Jim Crow's Children: The Broken Promise of the Brown Decision* (New York: Penguin Books, 2002), 80–94.

6. James T. Patterson, *Brown v. Board of Education: A Civil Rights Milestone and Its Troubled Legacy* (New York: Oxford, 2001), 109–13.

7. Richard A. Pride, *The Political Use of Racial Narratives: School Desegregation in Mobile, Alabama, 1954–1992* (Urbana: University of Illinois Press, 2002), 26.

8. Patterson, *Brown v. Board of Education,* 99.

9. Harding, Kelley, and Lewis, "We Changed the World," 473.

10. Irons, *Jim Crow's Children,* 190.

11. Jill Quadagno, *The Color of Welfare: How Racism Undermined the War on Poverty* (New York: Oxford University Press, 1994), 30.

12. Ibid., 127.

13. Irons, *Jim Crow's Children,* 241.

14. Gary Orfield, "School Desegregation after Two Generations: Race, Schools, and Opportunity in Urban Society," in *Race in America: The Struggle for Equality,*

ed. Herbert Hill and James E. Jones Jr. (Madison: University of Wisconsin Press, 1993), 240.

15. Jacobs, *Getting Around Brown,* 57, 62.

16. *Crawford v. Board of Education of the City of Los Angeles,* 17 CAL 3d 280 287 n.2 (1976).

17. Becky M. Nicolaides, *My Blue Heaven: Life and Politics in the Working Class Suburbs of Los Angeles, 1920–1965* (Chicago: University of Chicago Press, 2002), 301–2.

18. Joseph S. Ettinger, "The Quest to Desegregate Los Angeles Schools," *Los Angeles Lawyer,* March 2003, 57.

19. Ibid.

20. Clayborne Carson, "Two Cheers for *Brown v. Board of Education,*" *Journal of American History* 91, no. 1 (2004): 27; Ettinger, "The Quest to Desegregate Los Angeles Schools," 62.

21. Nathaniel R. Jones, "Civil Rights After *Brown*: 'Stormy the Road We Trod,'" in Hill and Jones, *Race in America,* 100.

22. Wiley A. Branton, "Race, the Courts, and Constitutional Change in Twentieth-Century School Desegregation Cases after *Brown,*" in *African Americans and the Living Constitution,* ed. John Hope Franklin and Genna Rae McNeil (Washington, D.C.: Smithsonian Institution Press, 1995), 86. Cheryl I. Harris, "Whiteness as Property," *Harvard Law Review* 106, no. 8 (1993): 1756.

23. Irons, *Jim Crow's Children,* 221.

24. Ibid., 227.

25. Ibid., 238.

26. Jones, "Civil Rights after Brown," 103; Cheryl I. Harris, "Whiteness as Property," *Harvard Law Review* 106, no. 8 (1993): 1756.

27. Patterson, *Brown v. Board of Education,* 178–81; Gary Orfield, "Segregated Housing and School Resegregation," in *Dismantling Desegregation: The Quiet Reversal of Brown v. Board of Education,* ed. Gary Orfield, Susan Eaton, and the Harvard Desegregation Project (New York: New Press, 1996), 296.

28. Jamin B. Raskin, *Overruling Democracy: The Supreme Court vs. the American People* (New York: Routledge, 2003), 160.

29. Gary Orfield, "Turning Back to Segregation," in Orfield et al., *Dismantling Desegregation,* 16.

30. J. B. Wellish et al., *An In-Depth Study of Emergency School Aid Act (ESAA) Schools: 1975–1976* (Santa Monica, Calif.: Systems Development Corporation, 1977); R. P. Nathan et al., *The Consequence of Cuts: The Effects of the Reagan Domestic Program on State and Local Governments* (Princeton: Princeton University Press, 1983).

31. Tomiko Brown-Nagin, "Race as Identity Caricature: A Local Legal History Lesson in the Salience of Interracial Conflict," *University of Pennsylvania Law Review* 151 (2003): 1925, 1934–36, 1938.

32. Ray Hartmann, "Is John Ashcroft a Racist or Does He Just Play One on TV?" _Riverfront Times,_ October 13, 1999. See also People for the American Way, "Ashcroft's Record Too Extreme for Justice," (2001), http://67.192.238.59/multimedia/pdf/Reports/thecaseagainstashcroft_part1.pdf and http://67.192.238.59/multimedia/pdf/Reports/thecaseagainstashcroft_part2.pdf (accessed January 28, 2009).

33. Amy Stuart Wells and Robert L. Crain, _Stepping Over the Color Line: African American Students in White Suburban Schools_ (New Haven: Yale University Press, 1997), 312; People for the American Way, "Ashcroft Further Undermines Integrity Claims by Misrepresenting Facts on Desegregation Case," Common Dreams Progressive Newswire, press release (2001), available at http://www.commondreams.org/news2001/0117-06.htm (accessed December 7, 2008), quoting _St. Louis Post-Dispatch_ June 15, 1984.

34. _Craton Liddell, et al., v. State of Missouri, et al.,_ 731 F.2nd 1294 (8th Cir. 1984).

35. Allison Morantz, "Money and Choice in Kansas City: Major Investments with Modest Returns," in Orfield et al., _Dismantling Desegregation,_ 249.

36. _Missouri v. Jenkins,_ 515 U.S. 70, 41 (1995) (Justice Souter, dissenting).

37. People for the American Way, "Ashcroft Further Undermines Integrity Claims," citing _St. Louis Post-Dispatch,_ March 5, 1981, November 7, 1982, June 15, 1984, UPI, February 12, 1984, and _Newsweek,_ May 18, 1981.

38. Patterson, _Brown v. Board of Education,_ 113; Charles Ogletree, _All Deliberate Speed: Reflections on the First Half Century of Brown v. Board of Education_ (New York: Norton, 2004), 25, 33, 44, 128, 143, 256, 294; Harris, "Whiteness as Property," 1735.

39. Morantz, "Money and Choice in Kansas City," 241–63.

40. Theodore M. Shaw, "Equality and Educational Excellence: Legal Challenges in the 1990s," in _In Pursuit of a Dream Deferred: Linking Housing and Education Policy,_ ed. John A. Powell, Gavin Kearney, and Vina Kay (New York: Peter Lang, 2001), 263.

41. _Missouri v. Jenkins,_ 515 U.S., at 53 (Justice Ginsburg, dissenting).

42. Patterson, _Brown v. Board of Education,_ 16–19. Patterson notes that even though the court ordered the University of Texas Law School to admit Sweatt, it could not protect him once he enrolled. Sweatt had his car tires slashed, was confronted with a burning cross next to his car, and subsequently became ill and flunked out of school. See Ogletree, _All Deliberate Speed,_ 122.

43. Derrick Bell, "Bell, J., dissenting," in _What "Brown v. Board of Education" Should Have Said,_ ed. Jack M. Balkin (New York: New York University Press, 2002), 185.

44. See George Lipsitz, _The Possessive Investment in Whiteness: How White People Profit From Identity Politics_ (Philadelphia: Temple University Press, 1998).

45. Harris, "Whiteness as Property," 1731.

46. Charles Mills, _The Racial Contract_ (Ithaca: Cornell University Press, 1997), 96–97.

47. Laurence H. Tribe, *American Constitutional Law* (Mineola, N.Y.: Foundation Press, 1978), 53–54, quoted in Richard Thompson Ford, "The Boundaries of Race: Political Geography in Legal Analysis," in Powell, Kearney, and Kay, *In Pursuit of a Dream Deferred*, 244.

48. Charles Lawrence III and Mari J. Matsuda, *We Won't Go Back: Making the Case for Affirmative Action* (New York: Houghton Mifflin, 1997), 45; Carter A, Wilson, "Exploding the Myths of a Slandered Policy," *Black Scholar*, May/June 1986, 20; Harris "Whiteness as Property," 1770.

49. Raskin, *Overruling Democracy*, 3, 167; Morantz, "Money and Choice in Kansas City," 241–63; Robert L. Carter, "Thirty-five Years Later: New Perspectives on Brown," in *Race in America: The Struggle for Equality*, ed. Herbert Hill and James E. Jones Jr. (Madison: University of Wisconsin Press, 1993), 86, 88.

50. *Missouri v. Jenkins*, 515 U.S., at 23.

51. See Lipsitz, *Possessive Investment in Whiteness*, 43–45.

52. *Missouri v. Jenkins*, 515 U.S., at 35.

53. Raskin, *Overruling Democracy*, 14.

54. J. Morgan Kousser, *Colorblind Injustice: Minority Voting Rights and the Undoing of the Second Reconstruction* (Chapel Hill: University of North Carolina Press, 1999), 242; Raskin, *Overruling Democracy*, 81.

55. Raskin, *Overruling Democracy*, 14, 27.

56. Drew S. Days III, "The Current State of School Desegregation Law: Why Isn't Anybody Laughing?" in Powell, Kearney, and Kay, *In Pursuit of a Dream Deferred*, 163.

57. Ibid., 175.

58. C. Verspereny, "Desegregation Case Defense Outlined," *St. Louis Post-Dispatch*, July 18, 1982, quoted in Wells and Crain, *Stepping Over the Color Line*, 259.

59. R. D. Taub, D. G. Taylor, and J. A. Dunham, *Paths of Neighborhood Change: Race and Crime in Urban America* (Chicago: University of Chicago Press, 1984); Craig St. John and Nancy A. Bates, "Racial Composition and Neighborhood Evaluation," *Social Science Research* 19 (1990): 47–61.

60. Thomas M. Shapiro, *The Hidden Cost of Being African American: How Wealth Perpetuates Inequality* (New York: Oxford, 2004), 271.

61. Meredith Lee Bryant, "Combating School Resegregation through Housing: A Need for a Reconceptualization of American Democracy and the Rights it Protects," in Powell, Kearney, and Kay, *In Pursuit of a Dream Deferred*, 56–58.

62. Bryant, "Combating School Resegregation through Housing," 58.

63. Gary Orfield, "Unexpected Costs and Uncertain Gains of Dismantling Desegregation," in Orfield et al., *Dismantling Desegregation*, 96.

64. Orfield, "Segregated Housing and School Resegregation," 301.

65. Ibid.

66. Shapiro, *The Hidden Cost of Being African American*, 143.

67. Irons, *Jim Crow's Children*, 289.

68. Chungmei Lee, "Is Resegregation Real?" (Cambridge, Mass.: Harvard Civil Rights Project Report, 2004), 6.

69. Shapiro, *The Hidden Cost of Being African American,* 145.

70. Jack M. Balkin, *What "Brown v. Board of Education" Should Have Said* (New York: New York University Press, 2002), 6.

71. Orfield, "Unexpected Costs and Uncertain Gains," 83.

72. Gary Orfield, "School Desegregation after Two Generations: Race, Schools, and Opportunity in Urban Society," in Hill and Jones, *Race in America,* 245, 240.

73. Theodore M. Shaw, "Equality and Educational Excellence," in Powell, Kearney, and Kay, *In Pursuit of a Dream Deferred,* 261. Shaw cites Justice William Brennan's concurring opinion in the 1978 Bakke case to show how widespread this interpretation was as late as 1978.

74. Kousser, *Colorblind Injustice,* 385.

75. Clarence Lo, *Small Property Versus Big Government: Social Origins of the Property Tax Revolt* (Berkeley: University of California Press, 1990), 58.

76. Philip J. Ethington, "Segregated Diversity: Race-Ethnicity, Space, and Political Fragmentation in Los Angeles County, 1940–1994," Final Report to the John Randolph Haynes and Dora Haynes Foundation, July 17, 2000, 25.

77. Ibid., 25–27.

78. Jürgen Habermas, *Legitimation Crisis* (Boston: Beacon Press, 1975), 71.

79. Raskin, *Overruling Democracy,* 165.

80. Brown-Nagin, "Race as Identity Caricature," 1973.

3

From *Brown* to *Grutter*

The Diverse Beneficiaries of *Brown v. Board of Education*

Margaret L. Andersen

The fiftieth anniversary of the landmark case *Brown v. Board of Education* provides an opportunity not only to reflect on the demise of formal, legal segregation in the United States, but also to think about the consequences of *Brown* for the advancement of different groups in U.S. society. Women (including African American, white, Latina, Native, and Asian American) are beneficiaries of the *Brown* decision, as are gays, lesbians, other racial and ethnic groups, and disabled people, to name a few. *Brown* provided a foundation—judicial, political, social, and moral—for opening social institutions to various social groups, the benefits to whom were not envisioned in the *Brown* decision per se. As we think about the impact of the *Brown* decision, we can consider not only its impact on race in America, but also on the experiences of all those who have benefited from this historic decision.

To understand the impact of *Brown,* we must first examine the context in which *Brown* was decided and the consequences it has had for race relations in the United States. As we will see, the implications of *Brown* extend beyond the law into the social and political arena. Although there is considerable debate about the difference *Brown* made and what changes would have resulted even without it, *Brown* is nonetheless a touchstone for assessing how far we have come and what remains to be done.

The Context of *Brown*

The social-historical context of the *Brown* decision is one in which vast changes were underway for many groups in U.S. society. In the early 1950s when the *Brown* decision was made, the United States had recently emerged victorious in World War II. The military had been desegregated by presidential order in 1948. The nation was in the midst of the cold war, having declared itself the leader of the world in fighting for democracy and against communism. Many have noted the impact that U.S. declarations of itself as the symbol of democracy had on thinking about the persistence of segregation. Black veterans returned home hopeful about seeing change in U.S. race relations, as they had witnessed the fall of Nazism in Europe. Having claimed to have defeated the forces of group hatred and oppression found in Nazism and anti-Semitism, the United States was hardly in a position to maintain overt racial oppression at home.

At the same time, massive changes were underway in the labor market affecting the social organization of gender and race within the United States. During the war, white women had entered the labor force in unprecedented numbers, and black women had substantially improved their status in the labor market. Many black women who prior to the war had been domestic workers moved into jobs during the war that were formerly closed to them. (Historian Alice Kessler-Harris estimates that about 20 percent of black women who had been domestic workers were able to move into factory-based jobs during the war.) Although black women never received the best jobs, the number working in factories doubled; clerical, sales, professional jobs also opened for black women. Although the vast majority of black women who were working at the war's end had in fact been doing so prior to the war, both black and white women found expanded opportunities for work during the war—many of which they lost at the war's end.[1] Still, by 1950 the gap in white and black women's labor force participation rates had significantly closed and reached near parity by 1970 (see figure 3.1).[2]

Not only were women of both races in the 1950s more likely to be in the public labor force, but the employment status of married women of both races was also changing, thereby affecting family structure. In 1954, 28 percent of all married women were in the labor force. By 1960 the labor force of all married women had grown to 32.3 percent, although black women were still more likely to be working when they had young children.[3]

Meanwhile, employment for black men was changing as well. Between 1948 and 1955 the percentage of nonwhite workers employed as farmers and farm operators dropped from 8.5 percent of the work force to 5 percent; the percent among farm laborers declined from 12.5 percent to 9.5 percent. At the same time, the percentage of nonwhite men working in professional or technical work increased from 2.4 to 3.5 percent.[4]

Despite the increased employment rates for black men and women, there was a substantial income gap between white and black families. In 1954 national median income was $2,410 for nonwhites; $4,339 for whites—a 56 percent gap. (The gap is 63 percent today.) Only 22 percent of nonwhite families had median incomes above the national median income, compared to 39.8 percent of whites.[5]

Changes in educational attainment for women and men were also afoot at the time of the *Brown* decision and were certainly spurred as the result of this

FIGURE 3.1

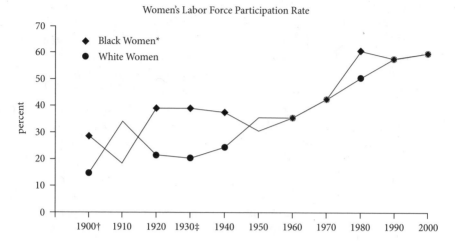

Women's Labor Force Participation Rate

* Defined as "Negro" in earliest data; "non-white" in other periods; now, as "Black."

† Women identified in data for this year as "employed as breadwinner." White women defined as both parents being white and "native."

‡ White women identified in data for this year as "native White."

Sources: U.S. Census Bureau, *Statistical Abstract of the United States (1910, 1920, 1930, 1940, 1950).* Washington, D.C.: U.S. Department of Commerce; Bureau of Labor Statistics. 2009. Data from the Current Population Survey, *Labor Force Statistics,* http:www.bls.gov.

decision. Educational attainment for both blacks and whites was increasing in the 1950s with no difference in the percentages of younger white and black men (between the ages of 5 and 34) enrolled in school (54 percent for each group in 1950). Women were somewhat less likely to be enrolled in school: 46.9 percent of white women and 47.4 percent of nonwhite women were in school. There were, however, significant gaps between white and black Americans in the median years of school completed, explained by the lower levels of education among older people in both populations. White men in 1950 had completed an average of 9.3 years of education; white women, 10.0 years. Nonwhite men had completed 6.4 years; nonwhite women, 7.2 years.[6]

Brown had a tremendous impact on closing the racial gap in educational attainment, although it was not the sole force doing so (see figure 3.2). By 1960, 41.8 percent of white men and 44.7 percent of white women had at least a high school diploma, compared to 18.2 percent of black men and 21.8 percent of black women—a 23 percent racial gap (and 3 percent by gender within each racial group). Twenty years later (twenty-six years after the *Brown* decision), the racial gap had closed to 18 percentage points between white and black men and 17 percentage points between white and black women. By 2000 the racial difference was down to 6.1 percent for men and 6.7 percent for women (see table).[7] College enrollment in the post-*Brown* years was increasing both among white and black women and men. In 1960, 2.8 percent of black men and 3.3 percent of black women held college degrees; this had increased to 8.4 percent and 8.3 percent respectively by 1980 and to 16.3 and 16.7 percent by 2000.[8]

These data reflect significant changes underway in American society at the time the *Brown* decision was made. Greater employment of women in general and increased educational attainment for all groups are important because they change people's expectations about their opportunities. Wartime work gave women a sense of accomplishment such that they could think of themselves in new terms, including, as we will see, demanding the rights associated with full citizenship. As the trends toward more education and a greater engagement in the public sphere accelerated in the period following *Brown*, people's expectations for their life chances also swelled.

The quantitative data provide one picture of a changing society, but many of us also recall what these times were like. As a young white student myself in the 1950s, I attended racially segregated schools in three quite different public school systems (Oakland, California; Rome, Georgia; and Boston, Massachusetts). The Rome schools were officially segregated—until my senior year of high school—when *Brown* was finally implemented, although minimally. As I recall it, in 1966 3 black students entered the senior class of my public high school—a class of about 120 students total. Not until later were the separate black schools in Rome closed. I had little political awareness at the time, but I remember thinking that the segregationist system in the South was wrong. But I also know that I assumed—indeed, expected—that my education would get me somewhere (though exactly where, I did not know). Looking back on it, I am sure that those three black students had similar expectations and that their parents had sacrificed mightily in the hope that a good education would lead them to a better future.

Table 1. Educational attainment by race, 1960 to 2000 (percentages)

| | White | | Black | |
	High school graduate or more	College graduate or more	High school graduate or more	College graduate or more
1960	43.2	8.1	20.1	3.1
1970	54.5	11.3	31.4	4.4
1980	68.8	17.1	51.2	8.4
1990	79.1	22.0	66.2	11.3
2000	84.9	26.1	78.5	16.5

Source: U.S. Census Bureau, *Statistical Abstract of the United States 2002* (Washington, D.C.: U.S. Government Printing Office, 2002), 139.

FIGURE 3.2

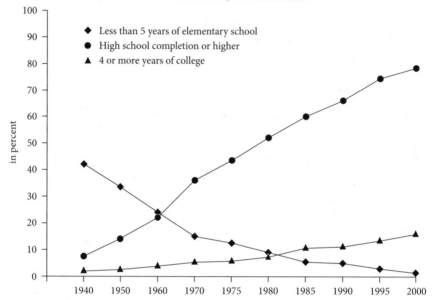

Educational Attainment, 1940–2001: Blacks

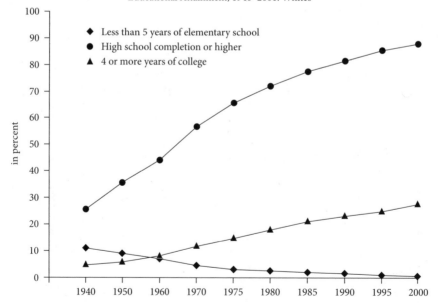

Educational Attainment, 1940–2001: Whites

Source: National Center for Educational Statistics, *Digest of Educational Statistics 2002* (Washington, D.C.: U.S. Department of Education, 2002).

Not all white people in my town shared these positive feelings about change. In the years following the *Brown* decision, new private schools were established in this and other southern towns; white families with the resources and will to do so avoided racial desegregation. For example, a private school for girls opened in 1958 in the town where I lived, which described itself as follows: "A Noble Legacy: Thornwood School for Girls opened its doors in 1958. Resting high on a hill, nestled in a quaint ante-bellum home, it was a world set apart."[9] A world set apart, indeed. At the time this school was established, the schools in this and other Georgia counties were still completely segregated.[10] Indeed, one of the consequences of *Brown* was fierce white resistance to desegregation, measured by the legal maneuvering that followed, a spike in white attitudes opposing the *Brown* decision,[11] and the white flight to suburbs that continues to plague the process of school desegregation.

But for many, these were optimistic times. Looking back, we can see multiple changes unfolding, not the least of which was the impact of the *Brown* decision. Schooling was increasing; the United States was not at war; women were entering the public sphere. For both white and black Americans, the old regime was changing. As Lewis Killian has written, "A revolution does not begin with a declaration of war and frontal assault on the Old Regime. It begins with incidents that, although noteworthy, are not fully appreciated for their long-run significance."[12] One of those incidents was the *Brown v. Board* decision on May 17, 1954.

The Consequences of *Brown*

It is impossible to gauge the specific consequences of any given court decision, given that such decisions occur within a larger social context. The impact of *Brown* is so intertwined with the incipient civil rights movement on which it was based and which it further inspired that it is hard to untangle the effects of the two. Nonetheless, understanding that connection, we can see numerous consequences of *Brown,* not the least of which was the inspiration for social movements that it provided.

The "Detonating Spark"

Perhaps the most immediate consequence of the *Brown* decision was the optimism that it generated and, thus, the platform it created for the mobilization of the civil rights movement. *Brown* did not, however, come out of the blue. It followed a long period of mobilization and organization by groups like the NAACP, the Brotherhood of Sleeping Car Porters, Congress of Racial Equality (CORE), the National Council of Churches of Christ, and other organizations working to eliminate Jim Crow segregation.[13] Years of legal work (including various court challenges), community organizing, and wrangling with school officials preceded this momentous decision. After all, it was not *Brown* per se that overthrew the social order of Jim Crow segregation, but the mass mobilization of black people and their white allies. But because of *Brown*, "hope was added to the discontent" that black people had long felt.[14] *Brown* provided a "detonating spark" to a long campaign by the NAACP and others to end segregation.[15]

In retrospect, we can see that *Brown* provides a necessary, but not sufficient, condition for abolishing Jim Crow. We cannot dissect the impact of *Brown* without simultaneously recalling the social action that was the civil rights movement. As sociologist Aldon Morris has argued, overthrowing the social order of Jim Crow through disruptive civil disobedience was "the genius of the Civil Rights Movement."[16] Let us briefly recall what happened in the years immediately following *Brown v. Board of Education*:

> 1955: Emmett Till murdered for purportedly whistling or speaking disrespectfully to a white woman; his mother showcases his brutally disfigured body in the national media;
>
> 1955: the Montgomery bus boycott and the subsequent rise of Martin Luther King Jr. as the leader of the civil rights movement;
>
> 1956: the Tallahassee bus boycott, inspired by the success in Montgomery;
>
> 1957: black students enroll in Little Rock Central High School, but are withdrawn after whites rioted;
>
> 1958: Little Rock schools remain closed, although the U.S. Court of Appeals orders the school board to carry out integration;
>
> 1959: sit-ins in Nashville department stores;
>
> 1960: student sit-ins in Greensboro, North Carolina, and other cities throughout the South; nationwide boycott of Woolworth's;
>
> 1961: Freedom Rides begin; first phases of the Albany, Georgia, movement with mass meetings and marches;
>
> 1962: Court of Appeals supports James Meredith's right to admission at University of Mississippi;
>
> 1963: Birmingham campaign; national media coverage of Sheriff Bull Connor using dogs and fire hoses against black demonstrators, including children; the assassination of Medgar Evers; one-quarter million people participate in March on Washington; four black girls killed in bombing of Birmingham church;
>
> 1964: Passage of the Civil Rights Act

This is but a brief list of the mass mobilization characterizing the civil rights movement in only the ten years following the *Brown* decision. But it shows the massive mobilization that took place in the aftermath of *Brown*, leading up to the passage of the Civil Rights Act of 1964. Thus, one of the major consequences of the *Brown* decision was that it was a catalyst for hope and mobilization, rousing the most vigorous and sustained movement for change ever mounted in the United States. The *Brown* decision generated the optimism that laid the path for subsequent mobilization—mobilization that was to benefit black Americans as well as groups as diverse as white women, gays and lesbians, the aged, and disabled people, as we will later see.

"God Has Spoken from Washington, D.C."

The *Brown* decision also declared that the highest authority of the nation was on the side of change, rather than in defense of the status quo.[17] Before *Brown*, Jim Crow segregation had been sustained via state power—power that accrued from the practices and beliefs of white supremacy. By pronouncing Jim Crow segregation unconstitutional, the Supreme Court brought the moral and judicial authority of the U.S. government to the incipient struggle for change. As recalled by one young black man, serving in the Marine Corps at the time, "On this momentous night of May 17, 1954, I felt that at last the government was willing to assert itself on behalf of first-class citizenship even for Negroes. I experienced a sense of loyalty that I had never felt before. I was sure that this was the beginning of a new era of American democracy."[18]

Many groups before had used the courts to seek racial justice. Often these rested on claims of citizenship, such as in the case of Takao Ozawa. Ozawa had arrived in California from Japan in 1894, graduated from high school there, and attended the University of California, Berkeley. After that, he worked for an American company, living with his family in the U.S. territory of Honolulu. In 1922 the U.S. Supreme Court denied his eligibility for citizenship based on the claim that he was not white.[19] As with Ozawa's case, appeals to the courts by racial or ethnic groups were typically unsuccessful and never resulted in the overthrow of a state-sponsored system of segregation, as did the case of *Brown v. Board of Education*. This may have been one of the greatest achievements of *Brown*: telling multiple groups that the government—in the form of the law—could be used to pursue social justice.

Trust that the federal government would be an ally in dismantling segregation was soon eroded, however. As civil rights leaders and others were soon to learn, the federal government entered only reluctantly and only under intense pressure from movement activists. Even then the government acted modestly and only when it seemed absolutely necessary to maintain social order. Still the faith that the federal government would enforce equal rights led many groups to seek redress through appeals to various governmental institutions.

Groups who followed in the footsteps of *Brown* similarly relied, as did civil rights activists, on a strategy of legal reform, appealing to the federal government through the courts, public policy, and Congress to redress social wrongs.

Thus, the National Organization for Women, the National Gay and Lesbian Task Force, the Older Women's League, and multiple other groups have used similar legal strategies to challenge various modes of segregation that denied groups full and equal benefits in educational and other social institutions.

Undoing Harm Done to "Hearts and Minds"

The framework of *Brown* rested on the argument that racial segregation harmed black children. Stemming from the model of social pathology that dominated social science thinking at the time, this argument saw segregation as detrimental to the psychological and social development of children. The model of pathology defined black culture and communities as inferior to white society, *because of* racial segregation. Eliminating segregation, the Supreme Court stated, would eliminate the "harm done" to those victimized by segregation. As Chief Justice Warren wrote in the decision, "To separate them [i.e., black children] from others of similar age and qualifications solely because of their race generates a feeling of inferiority as to their status in the community that may affect their *hearts and minds* [emphasis mine] in a way unlikely ever to be undone."[20]

The Court's concern was solely on the impact of segregation on the hearts and minds of black children. As many have shown, the Court never pointed out the harm done by the deprivation of rights. Also, the decision includes nothing about the hearts and minds of white Americans. Yet, the social scientists whose work was used in the *Brown* decision thought that racial integration would lessen racial prejudice. Changing minds—believed to follow from eliminating segregation—was thought to be the key to transforming race relations, based in part on the influence of Myrdal's *An American Dilemma*, which concluded that that race prejudice was a problem in the "hearts and minds" of white Americans.[21] Although no one was so naïve as to believe that you could legislate a change in attitudes, the idea was that increased interracial contact would reduce racial prejudice—an idea supported by at least some social science evidence.

In the short run, this was wrong, but a longer term examination of public opinion data shows that there has been a massive change in public attitudes since the *Brown* decision. Thus, although surely not solely the result of *Brown*, there has subsequently been a dramatic transformation in public consciousness about race.

This was no easy path, given the counterreaction to *Brown*, as we will see below. But in 1954 when the case was decided, 55 percent of Americans approved of the decision and 40 percent disapproved. (Seven in ten southerners disapproved.) Immediately following *Brown* there was a spike of disapproval of the Court decision—44 percent of the nation and 83 percent of southerners disapproved three years later. Disapproval leveled off by 1959, however, to levels similar to 1954. And, in 1994, the last time the question was asked, 87 percent of Americans approved of the Court's ruling and only 11 percent disapproved.[22] A 1948 survey used in the Court briefs found that 90 percent of the public thought that enforced segregation harmed blacks; 83 percent thought it harmed whites.[23]

Other opinion polls also show the impact of change in the years since *Brown,* the South having changed the most. A 2003 survey of regional attitudes about U.S. race relations finds little difference in southerners' opinions about race relations compared to people in the east and west. Moreover, by 2003, blacks living in the South did not differ in their perceptions of experiencing discrimination, compared to blacks in other regions of the country.[24] One would be hard pressed to attribute such attitude changes directly to the Supreme Court's action, but possibly one of the greatest impacts of *Brown* and subsequent movements has been the reduction of overtly expressed prejudice. Reduced racial prejudice can spill over to greater acceptance of equal rights for many groups. Thus, public opinion data show a much greater willingness for the public to support equal rights for gays and lesbians, women, the aged, and others since the 1950s. Though *Brown* is not singly responsible for such change, it is a watershed event in the transformation of public thinking.

The Counterreaction

The optimism spawned by *Brown* was nonetheless tempered by the fierce resistance that it also sparked. The *Brown* decision energized white resistance that had previously been cloaked under white paternalism. Sociologist Aldon Morris writes that the *Brown* decision "thrust the NAACP into the limelight and crystallized the emerging massive resistance movement dedicated to systematically destroying the NAACP across the South."[25] Whites mounted direct and indirect opposition to integration through violence, through legal maneuvering to thwart the implementation of *Brown,* and through withdrawal from public educational institutions. In many southern communities, whites who could afford to do so enrolled children in private schools; some also founded new private schools, promising a "quality" education but in reality avoiding having their children in school with black students.

Resistance took many forms, including the creation of White Citizens' Councils, but also in more subtle ways, the move toward suburbanization and greater use of private education (see figure 3.3). In the years since *Brown,* white resistance to desegregation has flared up in opposition to busing and to other plans for desegregating the schools. But, for the most part, resistance has now become more passive, cloaked in behaviors that seem on the face of it to be benign (such as seeking a "quality education" for one's children or maintaining one's property values). In the years following Brown, old forms of southern racial paternalism

FIGURE 3.3

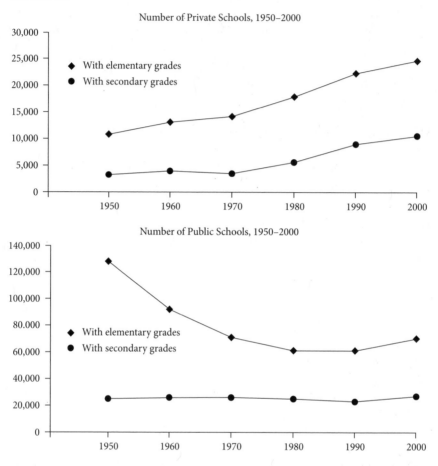

Number of Private Schools, 1950–2000

◆ With elementary grades
● With secondary grades

Number of Public Schools, 1950–2000

◆ With elementary grades
● With secondary grades

Source: National Center for Educational Statistics, *Digest of Educational Statistics 2002* (Washington, D.C.: U.S. Department of Education, 2002).

have now been replaced with new style forms of colorblind racism—racism that claims no prejudice but nonetheless protects white race and class privilege.

"A Right Which Must Be Available to All on Equal Terms"

Brown never went so far as to guarantee equal rights to all citizens. Stopping only with decrying the pathology segregation presumably creates, the *Brown* decision only addressed equal educational opportunities. Still, it provided the legal roots from which later forms of equal opportunity could grow.

Brown has its basis in liberal, democratic philosophy. Such a framework assumes that equality of opportunity is fundamental to the rights of all citizens. Furthermore, as stated in *Brown* and later echoed in Sandra Day O'Connor's majority opinion in *Grutter v. Bollinger,* the foundation of citizenship is education. The removal of formal obstacles to equal opportunity is a fundamental requirement in democratic societies. Where *Brown* stopped short of promising full equal opportunity, the Civil Rights Act of 1964 picked up—and herein lies the strong legal foundation for other group benefits. Numerous other groups have benefited from the equal rights foundation that *Brown* and related laws have established.

In sum, the *Brown v. Board* decision:

kindled the hope and optimism that fueled a mass movement for racial change;

generated faith in the power of federal institutions to conquer racial oppression;

acknowledged the harm done by racial segregation and legitimated the use of social science evidence in social change;

signaled the change in public attitude that was to come, while also rousing a strong white supremacist counterreaction;

helped reestablish equality before the law as a major principle of American society.

"What Can *Brown* Do for You?": The Extended Implications of *Brown*

Given the consequences and assumptions of the *Brown* decision, what can we conclude about its implications for diverse groups? Although it is impossible to separate the impact of *Brown* from the other events that surround and follow it, it is hard to imagine the history that would have unfolded had *Brown* not been in place. Despite its limitations, both the direct and indirect effects of *Brown* resulted in substantial change for African Americans *and* other groups.

One direct effect was for Mexican Americans, who, like African Americans, prior to *Brown* were relegated to segregated schools in many areas of the country. The practice varied in different school districts, and in Texas, Mexican Americans (now called Chicanos) were often forced into separate schools. They had presented numerous challenges to segregationist practices, arguing that they were "other whites," but the courts generally upheld a strict black/white color line with those labeled as "brown" or "yellow" being excluded from the category of white.[26] On the very day that *Brown v. Board* was decided, the U.S. Supreme Court ruled in *Hernandez v. Texas* that Mexican Americans constituted a separate group subject to the full protection of the Fourteenth Amendment.[27] In addition to dismantling de jure school segregation for Mexican Americans, this decision also stopped the heretofore legal practice of excluding Mexican Americans from juries in Texas—a practice that had previously been upheld via the Texas Supreme Court.[28]

Other effects of *Brown v. Board* for diverse groups may not be so direct, but show, nonetheless, the wide-ranging implications of this decision. These implications fall into three arenas: legal, political, and social.

The Legal Implications of *Brown*

Legally, the implications of *Brown* may be more narrow than the social revolution it inspired. Although legal scholars debate how effective *Brown* has been[29]—and it is not my intent here to engage a constitutional argument—the *Brown* decision is linked to the emergence of claims to equal rights by numerous groups who followed in the wake of *Brown v. Board of Education.*

Legal scholars have pointed out that, other than overturning legal racial segregation, the profound legal implications of *Brown* lie in its expanded interpretation of the Fourteenth Amendment. A central question in *Brown* was historic intent and the context of the Fourteenth Amendment. The written opinion rejected the argument that the historical circumstances surrounding passage of the Fourteenth Amendment were pertinent to the present time. Furthermore, the Court concluded that one could not determine with any certainty what the framers of the Fourteenth Amendment had in mind. As Warren wrote, "We cannot turn the clock back." As a result, *Brown* defined black children as citizens with the full and equal protection of the Fourteenth Amendment.

This reading allowed multiple groups to construct themselves as citizens with equal rights based on constitutional claims to equal protection under the law—a social construction that was also encouraged by the social changes underway at the time, as we have seen. Seen in this light, *Brown* did more than eliminate de jure segregation. It allowed the construction of diverse political communities who could appeal to the Constitution to protect their rights. *Brown* signaled that the Constitution need no longer be narrowly read, thus putting the federal courts on the side of groups identified as social "minorities."

In this sense, legal analysts suggest that *Brown* is a precursor to various legal decisions, including decisions as diverse as *Griswold v. Connecticut* (providing rights to women for the use of birth control), *Roe v. Wade,* and the Americans with Disabilities Act, among others.[30] The aged, for example, could now be defined as a minority group with rights that, although certainly not directly promised by *Brown,* result from the expanded interpretation of the Fourteenth Amendment on which *Brown* rested.

Paul Gewirtz, a professor of law, argues that *Brown* was a "triumph of the anti-discrimination model."[31] He claims that *Brown* helped to create a new world in which various groups could demand equal treatment. He posits that a variety of precedent-setting cases for diverse groups come as the result of *Brown's* reading of the Fourteenth Amendment. For example, the Age Discrimination in Employment Act of 1967 grants older adults rights of equal protection; the Supreme Court case *General Electric Company v. Gilbert* accepted pregnancy as a form of disability, thus allowing pregnant women to claim disability benefits when they leave work because of pregnancy; sexual harassment law stems explicitly from Title VII of the Civil Rights Act of 1964 (buttressed by the Supreme Court decision *Meritor Savings Bank v. Vinson*), giving constitutional authority to the argument that sexual harassment constitutes sex discrimination. Each, according to Gewirtz, stems from the "nondiscrimination model" initiated by *Brown* and later supported by the Civil Rights Act of 1964.

In sum, *Brown* changed how we think about citizenship in the United States. Diverse groups could now define themselves as citizens with equal rights. This resulted in a new assertiveness fueling social and political change in the years to come.

The Political Implications of *Brown*

In addition to legal and social changes, *Brown* provided a model of politics for many groups, most of whom probably do not trace their political origins to *Brown* per se, but who nonetheless were influenced by the strategy and tactics of the *Brown* case. We have already discussed the mobilization of the civil rights movement that *Brown* ignited—and the counterreaction that it also inflamed. But beyond these immediate actions, *Brown* and the social context in which it emerged mobilized many groups to seek equal protection before the law. Although it is difficult—probably impossible—to separate the impact of *Brown* from the impact of the civil rights movement, *Brown* and the civil rights movement provided a model for political organizing in the subsequent years.

As a result, common events now such as "Take Back the Night" demonstrations and marches on Washington owe a debt to the mobilization of civil rights leaders. Sociologist Aldon Morris argues that the "brilliance of the Civil Rights Movement" was its strategy of organized, sustained, and disruptive action.[32] This spawned numerous other social movements throughout the 1960s and beyond. The feminist movement, La Raza, the United Farm Workers, the American Indian resistance movement, the gay and lesbian movement, and the more recent disability rights movement have all used some of the same tactics and strategies of civil action that characterized the strategies used in the *Brown* campaign and the civil rights movement that followed.

Each of these movements is more complex in organization, ideology, and strategy than any singular focus on equal rights. But equal rights is now a common theme, derived from the framework of *Brown*. Furthermore, some groups, such as the NOW Legal Defense Fund, take their name directly from the NAACP Legal Defense Fund.[33] In addition, we can trace the emergence of parts of these movements directly to the civil rights movement following the *Brown* decision. The feminist movement, as well as other movements, was partially inspired by the work of women in civil rights.[34] The new leadership that emerged following the *Brown* decision changed the course of history for many.

The Social Implications of *Brown*

The legal implications of *Brown* are important, but from a sociological point of view what matters is not just what *Brown* says, but what people do and expect in its wake. By declaring segregation legally and morally wrong, *Brown* opened the door for many more groups to claim equal rights—in addition to the black citizens directly protected by the *Brown* decision. Though surely Earl Warren did not envision the identity politics that emerged, the legal and social benefits of *Brown* extend to many.

Following *Brown*, various groups used the courts and the law to seek group rights—based on such diverse group identities as age, gender, sexual orientation, disability, and religion, to name some. This happens not only in the legal arena, but also in the social identities created when a group identifies as a protected class. After all, as Gewirtz has put it, "Legal rights are empowering even if one never goes to court."[35] But *Brown* and the social movements that followed made group rights a matter of social justice; the implications of this extend to multiple and diverse social groups.

There was also a large and dramatic transformation of public attitudes about race, segregation, and equal opportunity. This cannot be attributed solely to *Brown* because it was also generated by the social changes underway in U.S. society. Nonetheless, *Brown* is a benchmark for the sea change in attitudes that has occurred since.

Consider the following: Since the *Brown* decision, support for racial segregation has dramatically declined. In 1942, 68 percent of the American public supported racially segregated schools; by 1985 that number had dropped to 7 percent. By the 1980s so few people were willing to endorse racial segregation that the question was dropped from national surveys.[36] In the time period since *Brown*, the public has expressed very high levels of support for school integration and equal access to jobs—attitudes that have affected all groups, not just African Americans. As one sociologist puts it, these changes have been "large, steady, and sweeping."[37] Yet, these are expressed attitudes. When it comes to actual practice and policy changes, public opinion is less encouraging. For example, 64 percent of whites in 1964 supported integrated schooling, but only 38 percent thought the federal government had a role to play in achieving this. By 1986, 93 percent supported school integration, but only 26 supported government efforts to increase it.[38] Now data show a very large gap in black and white perceptions of race in America. To illustrate, 81 percent of whites, but only 50 percent of blacks, think black children have as a good a chance as white children to get a good education in their community. Moreover, blacks are as pessimistic about their children being able to get a good education as they were forty years ago. Only 50 percent believe so, compared to 53 percent in 1962 and 68 percent at the beginning of the 1980s.[39]

Though events subsequent to *Brown* have reduced overt prejudice in America, now other forms of racism, variously labeled as "laissez-faire racism," "colorblind racism," "systemic racism,"[40] permeate American society, revealing a changed consciousness about race, but still a trenchant hold on whites' unwillingness to change systems of racial privilege.

One irony of the *Brown v. Board* decision is that it and other acts of equal rights legislation have created a fundamental contradiction: Multiple groups now vie for rights based on their particular identities even while the law establishes blindness to these identities as its fundamental principle. The implications for this contradiction are enormous, as we will see in the final section.

The Current Conundrum: From *Brown* to *Grutter*

The implications of *Brown* are so vast that it has been labeled "the case of the century."[41] Few doubt the far-reaching implications of this decision, even when they debate its specific effects. How can we evaluate the state of affairs for different groups in the post-*Brown* world? We have seen that the aftermath of *Brown* was marked by increased optimism, faith in the federal government to be an ally in reducing inequality, acknowledgement of the harm done by racial segregation, change in public consciousness about equal rights, the reestablishment of equality before the law and in major social institutions, and the legitimacy of social science evidence to direct progressive social change. Where do we now stand in these regards?

> Whereas *Brown* elevated optimism about the possibilities for change, now there is widespread pessimism about such possibilities and deep political cynicism about the effectiveness of mainstream politics to address problems for disadvantaged groups. The optimism that characterized the time of *Brown* is hard to find when young people worry they will not do as well as their parents, when downward socioeconomic mobil-

ity is as likely as upward mobility, when media framing of political news actually encourages political cynicism,[42] and when people feel that their votes do not matter. The increasing political alienation that people feel has been demonstrated to affect voter turnout, including among African Americans whose political alienation results from thinking that political institutions and public policies are not responsive to their needs.[43]

The faith in federal institutions that *Brown* promised has dissipated. Surveys find that few Americans have confidence in many of the major social institutions, particularly Congress and the Supreme Court. Confidence in Congress declined from 42 percent in 1973 to 29 percent in 2003; only 47 percent have a lot of confidence in the Supreme Court—a figure that has been quite steady since 1973.[44] While *Brown* had a "profound effect on the way Americans think about law's role in promoting social justice,"[45] now there is less sense that federal government and courts are on the side of racial justice. Although certainly many organizations that work on behalf of diverse groups continue to use the courts to address various inequities—and though there is progress in some regards (witness the Massachusetts Supreme Court's ruling on gay marriage for example)—progressive groups are struggling against a massive conservative turn in the courts, the executive branch, and the congressional branches of government.

Brown rested on the argument that segregation did harm, but harm in and of itself seems no longer to stand as a viable argument for legal redress. Instead, showing intent to discriminate seems to be the standard, something that is hard to do given the more covert way that institutional racism operates. Furthermore, as evidenced in the *Grutter* decision, concerns about "harm" have shifted to the harm done to whites by such measures as affirmative action. Thus, even though the *Grutter* case upheld affirmative action (within narrowly tailored means), Justice Sandra Day O'Connor speculated in the majority decision that "even remedial race-based governmental action generally 'remains subject to continuing oversight to assure that it will work the least harm possible to other innocent persons competing for the benefit.'"[46] Citing an earlier dissenting opinion in *Metro Broadcasting Inc. v. FCC*, she also writes that a race-conscious admissions program must not "unduly burden individuals who are not members of the favored racial and ethnic groups."[47] How ironic that, whereas in *Brown* the harmed were seen to be black children, now dominant groups think that the "harmed" are "innocent" white people, and racial minorities are perceived as "favored." Moreover, the *Grutter* decision shifts the benefits of programs like affirmative action to dominant institutions instead of specifically to minorities, as the argument in *Grutter* about the compelling state interest in achieving diversity in the student body makes clear.

The *Brown* decision rested on the use of social science evidence. No matter how flawed that evidence may have been, its use legitimated the application of social science in the pursuit of social justice. The Supreme Court has continued to use such expertise, as, for example, in the pivotal role that social science played in the more recent *Grutter* decision. However, in other arenas, most notably federal policy, social science evidence is routinely ignored. Conservative groups show no regard for social science evidence, relying instead on long disproved assumptions about the cultural inferiority of racial groups, such as in claims that welfare dependency results from the absence of work values, not the absence of work.

Brown helped put a legal framework in place promising equal rights and equal opportunity. Now, any failure to do so is viewed by the dominant group as the fault of groups who fare poorly. Whereas in years past, failure would have been seen as proof of biological inferiority or "the natural order" of things, it is now seen as evidence of the cultural inferiority or poor values of oppressed groups—despite the fact that *social science evidence consistently shows this not to be the case.*

In the years surrounding the *Brown* decision, Jim Crow segregation and racial prejudice were seen as the matters of greatest concern. Now colorblind racism has neutralized efforts to address persistent gender, race, and class inequality. Many whites now claim that race no longer matters, leading analysts to conclude that "new racism practices are subtle, institutional, and apparently nonracial."[48] Although there is nothing "new" about the "new racism"—in that racism has always been embedded in the structure of dominant social institutions—the ascendance of colorblind racism and gender-blind sexism show the reluctance of powerful groups to take measures that would alter systems of privilege and disadvantage.[49]

From "Hearts and Minds" to Colorblind Racism

The original premises of *Brown* are now not so clear. There is no longer a visible, single target such as Jim Crow segregation to finger as the major source of racial oppression. Overtly expressed prejudice no longer fuels the operation of racial oppression. The obstacles to change are now more abstract, making the mobilization of a mass movement for change far more challenging. Moreover, the complexities of organizing on behalf of multiple groups is difficult in a context where ideological frames contend that race, gender, and class do not matter—even when inequality along multiple lines is growing.[50] As Ruth Bader

Ginsburg wrote in her dissent on the *Gratz* opinion, "In the wake of a system of racial caste only recently ended, large disparities endure. Unemployment, poverty, and access to health care vary disproportionately by race. Neighborhoods and schools remain racially divided. . . . Irrational prejudice is still encountered in real estate markets and consumer transactions. Bias both conscious and unconscious, reflecting traditional and unexamined habits of thought, keeps up barriers that must come down if equal opportunity and nondiscrimination are even genuinely to become this country's law and practice."[51]

In the years since *Brown*, it has become now clear that institutionalized race, class, and gender privilege—and the benefits that accrue to certain groups as the result—are the problem, not just the harm done to victimized racial minorities. The more radical Black Power movement challenged the assumption in *Brown* that the problem of racism was in the pathology it created among black people. Instead, current analyses have learned from the more radical movement that the pathology lies, not in minority communities, but in the structure of systemic racism.[52]

The legal reasoning of *Brown* gives no recognition to the benefits that accrue to whites because of racial segregation; thus, those benefits were never challenged by *Brown*. Blacks were seen as benefiting from elimination of segregation only insofar as the framers of *Brown* believed that segregation caused harm. The brilliance and the dilemma of *Brown* is that it helps establish colorblindness as the law of the land, but we can now see that colorblind, gender-blind, and class-blind strategies are limited in their ability to reduce social inequality.

Brown established a moral framework for justice. But as the arena for establishing group rights has shifted from eliminating overt discrimination to overcoming the inequities in more systemic structures, we have an even more difficult challenge—that is, dismantling the systemic privileges that come from multiple and overlapping forms of oppression—those stemming from race *and* class *and* gender *and* age *and* sexual orientation, and so forth.[53] Furthermore, doing so happens where "context matters," as Sandra Day O'Connor wrote in the *Grutter* decision, echoing Cornel West's assertion that "race matters." That context now includes:

increased diversity in the U.S. population, brought in part through large-scale immigration of Latinos and Asian Americans and a globalizing economy;

fewer men and more women in the labor market in most racial and ethnic groups;

substantial growth of the black, Latino, and Asian American middle class;

growing class inequality—both across and within racial groups;

a movement toward the privatization of most major social institutions
   (education, health care, prisons, and others);
extensive resegregation of schools both in the South and all other regions;
increased college attendance among black Americans, although a marked
   decline in the presence of historically black colleges and universities;
fewer opportunities for upward mobility through employment in the
   manufacturing sector;
growth of a substantial and influential conservative movement.

Within this context, groups may purportedly have equality of opportunity,
but they do not live in a condition of equality. Moreover, the United States
seems to be losing its status as a symbol of democracy with the sympathy of
other nations. Huge differences in the economic, social, and political resources
of blacks, Latinos, Native Americans, Asian Americans, and whites; women and
men; working and middle classes and elites are making the promise of equality more a dream than a near reality. *Brown* may have forbidden "separate but
equal" but it surely did not dismantle white supremacy.

• • •

In conclusion, it is impossible to separate the impact of *Brown* from the social
movements and social context that surround it. Nonetheless, *Brown* laid a path
for raised expectations and new demands from multiple groups for a more just
society. In short, it helped establish a legal framework—limited as it is—for the
realization of many dreams.

There is significant debate among scholars about the legal utility and significance of the *Brown* decision[54]—a debate that will no doubt be augmented by the
fifty-year retrospective that the anniversary provides. Whatever one concludes
about the legal and social impact of the *Brown* decision, there is no doubt that
it is a touchstone for studying social change in the last half of the twentieth
century. As we recognize the anniversary of *Brown* we can remind ourselves
that "racism and discrimination are continuing and ongoing problems in this
society, but it is almost impossible to argue that our present problems of racism
would be less severe if legal segregation still existed. . . . The elimination of legal
segregation was a necessary step on the road toward racial equality. That the
road is a long and difficult one should not blind us to the necessity and value
of that very important step."[55]

Just as *Brown* was marked by optimism, faith in federal government, mass
mobilization, and legitimate use of social science, now it is fair to say that
the current climate is one of deep cynicism and pessimism, declining faith in
dominant institutions, and the absence of a mass movement for change. The

counterreaction from a deeply conservative movement that dominates the public discourse about race, gender, and class has frozen progressive change. Equal opportunity is in place in the law, but not in practice. The roots of institutional racism were never weeded out by the framework of *Brown*.

We can be reminded of the words of the man to whom we owe a great debt on this day of recognition. Thurgood Marshall said, "We can always stick together when we are losing, but tend to find means of breaking up when we're winning."[56] Since we seem to be losing, surely we should stick together.

Notes

The author thanks Benigno Aguirre, Maxine Baca Zinn, Valerie Hans, Elizabeth Higginbotham, and Richard Rosenfeld for their comments on an earlier draft of this paper.

1. See Alice Kessler-Harris, *Out to Work: A History of Wage-Earning Women in the United States* (New York: Oxford University Press, 1982).

2. Teresa Amott and Julie Matthaei, *Race, Gender, and Work: A Multi-Cultural Economic History of Women in the United States,* rev. ed. (Boston: South End Press, 1996).

3. U.S. Census Bureau, *Statistical Abstract of the United States 1956* (Washington, D.C.: U.S. Government Printing Office, 1956); U.S. Department of Labor, *Employment and Earnings* (Washington, D.C.: U.S. Government Printing Office, 2002).

4. U.S. Census Bureau, *Statistical Abstract 1956*, 209; note that the census did not enumerate white, black, or other groups at the time, using instead the designators "white" and "nonwhite."

5. Carmen de Navas-Walt and Robert Cleveland, *Money Income in the United States 2002* (Washington, D.C.: U.S. Census Bureau, 2002); U.S. Census Bureau, *Statistical Abstract 1956*.

6. U.S. Census Bureau, *Statistical Abstract 1956*.

7. U.S. Census Bureau, *Statistical Abstract of the United States 2002* (Washington, D.C.: U.S. Government Printing Office, 2002), 139.

8. National Center for Educational Statistics, *Digest of Educational Statistics* (Washington, D.C.: U.S. Department of Education, 2002).

9. See Darlington School, "History of Thornwood School for Girls," http://www .darlingtonschool.org/academics/library/archives/places/thornwood/thornwood-school.asp (accessed April 9, 2008).

10. Michelle Brattain, *The Politics of Whiteness* (Princeton: Princeton University Press, 2001).

11. Julie Ray, "Reflections on the 'Trouble in Little Rock,' Part II," *Gallup Poll*, March 4, 2003, http://www.gallup.com/poll/7900/Reflections-Trouble-Little-Rock -Part.aspx (accessed December 14, 2008).

12. Lewis M. Killian, *The Impossible Revolution* (New York: Random House, 1968), 35.

13. See Aldon Morris, *The Origins of the Civil Rights Movement: Black Communities Organizing for Change* (New York: Free Press, 1984); Richard Kluger, *Simple Justice: The History of Brown v. Board of Education and Black America's Struggle for Equality* (New York: Knopf, 1975); Juan Williams, *Thurgood Marshall: American Revolutionary* (New York: Times Books, 1998).

14. Killian, *The Impossible Revolution*, 43.

15. Lerone Bennett, *The Negro Mood* (New York: Ballantine, 1964), 40.

16. Aldon Morris, "The Genius of the Civil Rights Movement: Can It Happen Again?" in *Understanding Society,* ed. Margaret L. Andersen, Kim Logio, and Howard F. Taylor (Belmont, Calif.: Wadsworth, 2001), 503–8.

17. Killian, *The Impossible Revolution*, 35–44. Note: The title of this section, "God Has Spoken from Washington, D.C.," is from a black woman in Montgomery following the U.S. Supreme Court decision that made segregated seating on buses unconstitutional; quoted in Louis Lomax, *The Negro Revolt* (New York: Harper and Row, 1962), 94.

18. Robert Franklin Williams, *Negroes with Guns* (New York: Marzani Munsall, 1962); cited in *Eyes on the Prize: America's Civil Rights Year, A Reader and Guide,* ed. Clayborne Carson, David J. Garrow, Vincent Harding, and Darlene Clark (New York: Penguin, 1987), 29.

19. Ronald Takaki, *Strangers from a Different Shore: A History of Asian Americans* (Boston: Little Brown, 1989); *Ozawa v. United States* 260 U.S. 178 (1922); 43 S. Ct. 65 (1922).

20. *Brown v. Board of Education,* 347 U.S. 483 (1954).

21. Gunnar Myrdal, *An American Dilemma: The Negro Problem and American Democracy* (New York: Harper, 1944).

22. Ray, "Reflections on the 'Trouble in Little Rock' Part II."

23. James B. Mckee, *Sociology and the Race Problem: The Failure of a Perspective* (Urbana: University of Illinois Press, 1993), 311.

24. Josephine Mazzuca, "U.S. Race Relations by Region: The East," *Gallup Poll,* November 5, 2005, http://www.gallup.com/poll/7144/US-Race-Relations-Region-East.aspx; "The West," November 12, 2005, http://www.gallup.com/poll/7213/US-Race-Relations -Region-West.aspx; "The South," November 19, 2002, http://www.gallup.com/ poll/7234/US-Race-Relations-Region-South.aspx (all accessed December 14, 2008).

25. Morris, "The Genius of the Civil Rights Movement," 25.

26. Vilma S. Martinez, "Chicanos and Equal Educational Opportunity," in *The Continuing Challenge: The Past and the Future of Brown v. Board of Education: A Symposium,* ed. Howard Glickstein (Evanston, Ill.: Integrated Education Associates, 1975), 59–64.

27. *Hernandez v. Texas,* 347 U.S. 475 (1954).

28. Martinez, "Chicanos and Equal Educational Opportunity," n.28.

29. Robert J. Cottrol, Raymond T. Diamond, and Leland B. Ware, *Brown v. Board of Education: Caste, Culture, and the Constitution* (Lawrence: University Press of Kansas, 2003); Michael Klarman, "Brown, Racial Change and the Civil Rights Movement," *Virginia Law Review* 80 (1994): 80; Gerald Rosenberg, *The Hollow Hope: Can Courts Bring About Social Change?* (Chicago: University of Chicago Press, 1991); *Race, Law, and Culture: Reflections on Brown v. Board of Education*, ed. Austin Sarat (New York: Oxford University Press, 1997).

30. Peggy Cooper Davis, "Performing Interpretation: A Legacy of Civil Rights Lawyering in *Brown v. Board of Education*," in Sarat, *Race, Law, and Culture*, 23–48; David Garrow, "From *Brown* to *Casey:* The U.S. Supreme Court and the Burdens of History" in Sarat, *Race, Law, and Culture*, 74–88; Paul Gewirtz, "The Triumph and Transformation of Anti-Discrimination Law," in Sarat, *Race, Law, and Culture*, 110–34.

31. Gewirtz, "Triumph and Transformation," 111.

32. Morris, "The Genius of the Civil Rights Movement."

33. Gewirtz, "Triumph and Transformation."

34. Douglas McAdam, *Freedom Summer* (New York: Oxford University Press, 1990); Sara Evans, *Personal Politics: the Roots of Women's Liberation in the Civil Rights Movement and the New Left* (New York: Vintage, 1980).

35. Gewirtz, "Triumph and Transformation," 116.

36. Lawrence D. Bobo, "The Color Line, the Dilemma, and the Dream: Race Relations in America at the Close of the Twentieth Century," *Civil Rights and Social Wrongs: Black-White Relations since World War II*, ed. John Higham (University Park: Pennsylvania State University Press, 1999), 31–55.

37. Ibid., 38.

38. Ibid.

39. Heather Mason Kiefer, "Equal-Opportunity Education: Is It Out There?" *Gallup Poll*, July 1, 2003, http://www.gallup.com/poll/8731/EqualOpportunity -Education-There.aspx (accessed December 15, 2008).

40. Bobo, "The Color Line, the Dilemma, and the Dream"; Eduardo Bonilla-Silva, *Racism without Racists: Color-Blind Racism and the Persistence of Racial Inequality in the United States* (Lanham, Md.: Rowman and Littlefield, 2003); Michael Brown, Martin Carnoy, Elliott Currie, Troy Duster, David B. Oppenheimer, Marjorie M. Schultz, and David Wellman, *Whitewashing Race: The Myth of a Color-Blind Society* (Berkeley: University of California Press, 2003); Joe Feagin, *Racist America: Roots, Current Realities, And Future Reparations* (New York: Routledge, 2000); Charles A. Gallagher, "Color-Blind Privilege: The Social and Political Functions of Erasing the Color Line in Post Race America," *Race, Gender, and Class* 10 (2003): 23–37.

41. Williams, *Negroes with Guns*.

42. Joseph N. Cappella and Kathleen Hall Jamieson, "News Frames, Political Cynicism, and Media Cynicism," *Annals of the American Academy of Political and*

Social Science 546 (July 1996): 71, 84; Thomas J. Espenshade and Katherine Hempstead, "Contemporary American Attitudes toward U.S. Immigration," *International Migration* 30 (Summer 1996): 535, 570; Robert Hariman, "Prophecy, Phenomenology, and Democratic Politics: A Review of Hart's *Seducing America*," *Critical Studies in Mass Communication* 13 (June 1996): 180, 186.

43. Cedric Herring, James S. House, and Richard P. Mero, "Racially Based Changes in Political Alienation in America," *Social Science Quarterly* 72 (March 1991): 123, 134; Franklin D. Gilliam Jr. and Karen M. Kaufman, "Is There an Empowerment Life Cycle? Long-Term Black Empowerment and Its Influence on Voter Participation," *Urban Affairs Review* 33 (July 1998): 741, 766.

44. Frank Newport, "Military, Police Top Gallup's Annual Confidence in Institutions Poll," http://www.gallup.com/poll/8668/Military-Police-Top-Gallups-Annual -Confidence-Institutions-Poll.aspx (accessed December 15, 2008).

45. Sarat, *Race, Law, and Culture*, 4.

46. *Grutter v. Bollinger*, 539 U.S. 306 (2003).

47. *Metro Broadcasting Inc. v. FCC*, 497 U.S. 547 (1990).

48. Bonilla-Silva, *Racism without Racists*, 3.

49. Margaret L. Andersen, "Restructuring for Whom? Race, Class, Gender and the Ideology of Invisibility," *Social Forum* 16 (June 2001): 181, 201.

50. Ibid.

51. *Grutter v. Bollinger*, 539 U.S. 306 (2003).

52. Feagin, *Racist America*.

53. See Margaret L. Andersen and Patricia Hill Collins, eds. *Race, Class, and Gender: An Anthology*, 5th ed. (Belmont, Calif.: Wadsworth, 2004).

54. Jack M. Balkin, *What Brown Should Have Said: The Nation's Top Legal Experts Rewrite America's Landmark Civil Rights Decision* (New York: New York University Press, 2002); Cottrol et al., *Brown v. Board of Education*.

55. John P. Jackson Jr., *Social Scientists for Social Justice: Making the Case against Segregation* (New York: New York University Press, 2001), 225.

56. Cited in Gilbert Ware and William Hastie, *Grace under Pressure* (Oxford University Press, 1984).

4

Beyond School Desegregation

The Impact of *Brown*

Laughlin McDonald

The Supreme Court handed down the *Brown v. Board of Education* decision in May of 1954,[1] but it was not until the 1970s that a significant level of desegregation of public schools in the South was achieved. The causes for the delayed implementation of *Brown* were numerous and included the Court's directive the following year in *Brown* II that desegregation should be accomplished "with all deliberate speed,"[2] which was widely interpreted by whites in southern states as meaning that desegregation could be delayed indefinitely. Equally important, the South in the mid-1950s was completely and rigidly segregated. The public schools were an integral part of an extraordinary edifice of racial segregation, and dismantling it proved to be an onerous, time-consuming task.

As this chapter will discuss, the white leadership of the South was bitterly opposed to the *Brown* decision and did everything in its power to block its enforcement and maintain the Jim Crow system. *Brown* ultimately succeeded, however, not simply in invalidating the formal, legal structure of segregation in the public schools, but segregation in places of public accommodation, such as buses, restaurants and lunch counters, city parks, hospitals, courthouses, and prisons and jails. It was also used to strike down discrimination in the voting process, in the maintenance of public records, by labor unions, and against civil rights organizations and attorneys, interracial couples, illegitimate children, undocumented school-age children, and gays and lesbians. *Brown* was instrumental in transforming American society and significantly expanding the concept and reality of equal treatment under the law.

Underscoring the pervasive significance of race, Georgia state law at the time of the *Brown* decision defined "persons of color" as being "[a]ll Negroes, mulattoes, mestizos, and their descendants, having any ascertainable trace of either Negro or African, West Indian, or Asiatic Indian blood in their veins." To be admitted into the privileged circle of "white persons," one had to be free not only of all "colored" blood, but of Mongolian, Japanese, and Chinese blood as well. To maintain the purity of the white blood line, it was a felony "for a white person to marry any save a white person."[3] To ensure that this edict was strictly enforced, state law required all residents to register with the state board of health and to designate their race. Applications for marriage licenses were then cross-checked with the registration data to ferret out any would-be offenders. The board of health was obligated to report the birth of any mixed-race child to the state attorney general, whose duty it was to institute criminal proceedings against the parents of such a child.

State law required segregation of the races not only in public schools but in nearly every area of public life, including hospitals, prisons and jails, book-mobiles, training schools, public transportation (an exception was made for "colored nurses or servants" attending their employers),[4] courthouses, public housing, and tax records. Segregation in public accommodations was the pre-vailing norm—in theaters, restaurants, hotels, clubs, billiard rooms, civic and community organizations, the American Legion, golf courses, swimming pools, and libraries.

White preoccupation with race extended even to segregating the streets. In 1956 Georgia's Sumter County Board of Education tried to halt construction of a new black elementary school, not because segregation had been declared unconstitutional by the Supreme Court two years earlier, but because local white citizens complained that the school would be "too close" to an existing white school and that as a result "the children, both colored and white, would have to travel the same streets and roads in order to reach their respective schools." The school board was unable to get the state to halt construction of the new school because of the expense involved, but assured the white parents of the county that it "would do everything in its power to minimize simultaneous traffic between white and colored students in route to and from school."[5]

Jobs were regularly advertised and sought in the private and public sectors on a racial basis. The LaRue Company advertised in the *Harris County Journal* that "WE WANT WHITE LABOR!" in a Pine Mountain canning plant.[6] The McDuffie County Board of Commissioners wrote to the American Brake Shoe Company in February 1957 urging it to locate a plant in the county as a way of increasing "white male employment."[7]

Membership in the state bar association, which traditionally supplied much of the political leadership of the state, was reserved for whites only. Blacks had a separate organization, the Gate City Bar, but since none of the state's public or private law schools would admit blacks, it had fewer than two dozen members. The judiciary itself was a reflection and extension of the segregated, virtually all-white bar. According to Donald Hollowell, one of the state's few black at-torneys: "All the judges were white. Without exception, all the district attorneys were white, and virtually all the assistant district attorneys and prosecutors were white. All the clerks of court were white. All the bailiffs were white, and most of the juries who heard serious cases were white. You might find a black janitor, but there were no black citizens in any position of responsibility or authority."[8]

The police were also segregated, and those few blacks on the force typically had no authority to arrest a white person. Billy McKinney, one of the first blacks hired as a police officer in Atlanta in 1948, recalled that "we served in a segregated unit and patrolled only at night. We were called the '6 p.m. watch' and were told that we couldn't arrest a white person." After being on the force for four years, McKinney arrested a white man and was promptly suspended.[9] The only instrumentality of justice in the state that was not segregated was the electric chair. As of 2000 a total of 441 people had been electrocuted in Georgia, 80 percent of whom were black.[10]

J. B. Fuqua, a senator from Augusta and president of the state Democratic Party, summed up the reality of segregation in the state when he said that back in the 1950s he was one of "only three white people who would shake hands with a black man on Broad Street in Augusta, Georgia." The other two were Carl Sanders, who later became governor, and a man whose name Fuqua could no longer remember.[11]

Given the depth of Georgia's commitment to segregation, it is not surprising that *Brown* ignited an extraordinary white backlash. Immediately after the Supreme Court's decision, the state legislature passed a series of laws and resolutions designed to maintain segregation and defeat the federal assault on what white southerners reverentially called "The Southern Way of Life." In 1955 it provided that no money could be appropriated or spent for public schools unless they were racially segregated. The Georgia legislature formally asked the U.S. Congress to adopt an amendment to the Constitution giving the several states exclusive authority over schools so that they could be operated in perpetuity on a segregated basis. It also asked Congress to amend the Constitution to provide that no person could be required to serve in the armed forces with members of another race.[12]

At the invitation of Governor Marvin Griffin, a States' Rights Council of Georgia was organized in Atlanta in September 1955. The organizational meeting, according to press accounts, "was attended by 200 of the State's most prominent government officials and political, business and civic leaders representing all political factions in the state." At the meeting, the council dedicated itself to "preservation of the traditional establishment of segregation in both public and private areas."[13] States' rights councils were also soon established in other parts of the state.

Herman Talmadge, the state's governor and later a U.S. senator, lent his support to the states' rights movement by confidently announcing that no less an authority than "God advocates segregation." Drawing on the popular, and discredited, race mythology of the late nineteenth century, Talmadge claimed that God created "five different races: white, black, yellow, brown and red. . . . He did not intend them to be mixed or He would not have segregated them."[14]

In 1956 the legislature made appropriations to public schools on a racially segregated basis, authorized the governor to close schools rather than desegregate them, provided for tuition grants to enable white students to attend private schools, and gave local school boards the authority to lease public school property to private schools. It authorized the sale or leasing of parks, playgrounds, golf courses, swimming pools, and other public property to private citizens or associations rather than operate them on a desegregated basis, and it made it a crime to trespass on public property that had been closed to the public.[15]

With only one dissenting vote, the legislature adopted an "Interposition Resolution" in 1956 declaring that the *Brown* decision was "null, void and of no force or effect." The Supreme Court had acted beyond its powers, the legislature said, and it pledged "to take all appropriate measures honorably and constitutionally available to the State, to avoid this illegal encroachment upon the rights of her people."[16]

Expressing its disdain for federal school desegregation decisions, the legislature adopted a new state flag incorporating the stars and bars of the Confederate battle flag. Denmark Groover, the administration's floor leader, said the adoption of the new flag will "leave no doubt in anyone's mind that Georgia will not forget the teachings of Lee and Stonewall Jackson," and "will show that we in Georgia intend to uphold what we stood for, will stand for and will fight for."[17]

The attorney general of Georgia, Eugene Cook, compiled the state's constitutional and statutory provisions requiring segregation of the races and proudly announced that "A perusal of the many segregation laws included herein, affecting as they do almost every phase of human endeavor to which authority of government traditionally extends, convincingly demonstrates the predominant influence that racial segregation has exerted in the sociological development of the two races in this state." The compilation of state laws demonstrated, he said, the fundamental error of the *Brown* decision and the necessity of maintaining the existing racial "status." He expressed the hope that "a Supreme Court of tomorrow, dedicated to a different theory of sociology, may well find the 14th Amendment itself to be no longer tenable."[18]

A year later, the legislature adopted a resolution calling for the impeachment of Chief Justice Earl Warren and several other justices of the Supreme Court on the grounds that they had committed high crimes and misdemeanors by rendering decisions such as *Brown,* which gave aid and comfort to "Godless communism" and was part of a "procommunist racial integration policy."[19] In another resolution, the legislature by unanimous vote in both houses called for repeal of the Fourteenth and Fifteenth Amendments because they "were malignant acts of arbitrary power" and "are null and void and of no effect."[20]

Georgia, of course, was far from being the only southern state to condemn *Brown* and pledge to resist its threat to the racially segregated Southern Way of Life. In March 1956, nineteen senators and eighty-one members of Congress from the South signed the Southern Manifesto, which commended "those States which have declared the intention to resist forced integration by any lawful means," and pledged "to use all lawful means to bring about a reversal of this dangerous [*Brown*] decision which is contrary to the Constitution and to prevent the use of force in its implementation."[21]

But the months and years after *Brown* saw a steady parade of lawsuits in which the school desegregation principle was extended to all areas of public, and many areas of private, life. In applying the concept of equal treatment, *Brown* and the courts transformed the Southern Way of Life in a way unlikely ever to be undone.

A week after it decided *Brown,* the Supreme Court indicated that its ruling was not limited to education when it vacated and remanded a case involving segregated city parks in Louisville, Kentucky, for further consideration in light of "the Segregation Cases."[22] Despite this decision, state officials continued to argue—and some southern judges to agree—that *Brown* applied only to public schools. In South Carolina, for example, Judge George Bell Timmerman dismissed a suit challenging segregated buses in the state's capital city on the ground that "segregation in the field of public transportation is a valid exercise of State police power." In a remarkably obtuse opinion, the court noted that *Brown* relied upon "such intangibles as opportunities to engage in discussions and to exchange views with students of a different race, and the supposed sociological effect which segregation might have on a negro child's motivation to learn." But, the court reasoned, "no such effect can be legitimately claimed in the field of bus transportation. One's education and personality is not developed on a city bus."[23] Other courts agreed with Timmerman that *Brown* applied only to public education.

In Maryland, approximately two months after the *Brown* decision was announced, a federal district court, at the behest of the state's attorney general, dismissed a challenge brought by blacks to segregated public beaches, bathhouses, and swimming pools in Baltimore and the state of Maryland, concluding that the invalidation of "separate but equal" facilities in *Brown* was "limited to the field of education."[24] A court in Atlanta, in a case involving segregated public golf courses, reached a similar conclusion in deciding that *Brown* rejected the doctrine of separate but equal "only as it applied to public education."[25]

The appellate courts eventually reversed these decisions limiting *Brown* to the field of education. In the case from Maryland, the court of appeals concluded that the effect of *Brown* was to destroy the basis of the lower court's decision that separation of the races in recreational facilities was "normal treatment in

Maryland" and was justified as an effort "to avoid any conflict which might arise from racial antipathies."[26] The Supreme Court summarily affirmed.[27] In the public transportation case from South Carolina, the court of appeals similarly ruled that "the separate but equal doctrine . . . can no longer be regarded as a correct statement of the law." Segregation of the races in common carriers was "governed by the same principles as segregation in the public schools."[28] And in the case involving golf courses in Atlanta, the Supreme Court ordered the lower court to enter a judgment for the plaintiffs in conformity with the case from Maryland.[29]

Despite the decisions in the cases from Baltimore, Columbia, and Atlanta, the city of Montgomery, Alabama, continued to operate its buses on a racially segregated basis. Rosa Parks was one of those who challenged this segregation by refusing to yield her seat at the front of a bus to a white passenger, and in doing so she galvanized public attention and helped usher in the modern civil rights movement. When local blacks took the city to court, lawyers for Montgomery argued that the city's segregation laws were constitutional and valid. The federal court disagreed and concluded that, in light of *Brown*, "there is now no rational basis upon which the separate but equal doctrine can be validly applied to public carrier transportation."[30]

New Orleans also refused to desegregate its city parks. Borrowing the discredited arguments made by Judge Timmerman of South Carolina, it claimed that none of the "psychological considerations" that had informed *Brown* were applicable to the operation of segregated parks. The court dismissed the contention out of hand. There were too many decisions striking down segregation in public facilities, it said, "for us to take seriously a contention that such decisions are erroneous and should be reversed."[31]

Blacks in Memphis brought suit in 1960 to desegregate the city's public parks and other recreational facilities. The city admitted that the facilities were segregated but, invoking the doctrine of deliberate speed from *Brown* II, argued that desegregation should be phased in to prevent "interracial disturbances, violence, riots, and community confusion and turmoil." The Supreme Court rejected the argument noting that deliberate speed had no application to the desegregation of parks and recreational facilities, and that in any event "constitutional rights may not be denied simply because of hostility to their assertion or exercise."[32]

Although the equal protection clause of the Fourteenth Amendment reaches only state action, the Supreme Court, prior to passage of the Civil Rights Act of 1964,[33] relied on *Brown* to invalidate racial segregation by a privately owned restaurant located in a parking building owned by the city of Wilmington, Delaware. The fact, among others, that the restaurant was operated as "an integral part of a public building" was enough to bring it within the ambit of the Fourteenth Amendment's condemnation of state sanctioned discrimination.[34] In a similar case from Memphis, the Supreme Court rejected the arguments of the opera-tors of a racially segregated restaurant in the municipal airport that they had a right under state law "to exclude persons 'for any reason whatever.'" Relying on *Brown* and the Wilmington case, the Court ruled that the minority plaintiffs were entitled to injunctive relief against the discrimination they had challenged.[35]

In another variant on the state action theme, and again before passage of the Civil Rights Act of 1964, the Court held in a case from Greenville, South Carolina, that the segregation of a lunch counter in a privately owned building on privately owned property violated the Fourteenth Amendment when the segregation was pursuant to state law. The city had an ordinance prohibiting restaurants and lunch counters from providing meals "to white persons and colored persons" in the same facility. Demonstrating just how finely tuned Jim Crow could be in a southern city, the ordinance contained an exception allowing whites and blacks to be served in the same place, but only if completely sepa-rate facilities were furnished, including "[s]eparate eating utensils and separate dishes for the serving of food, all of which shall be distinctly marked by some appropriate color scheme or otherwise." And to further protect whites from presumed contamination from unsegregated dishwater, separate dishwashing facilities were mandated, that is, "[a] separate facility shall be maintained and used for the cleaning of eating utensils and dishes furnished the two races."[36] In the summer of 1960, twenty black young people entered the S. H. Kress store in Greenville, sat at the lunch counter, and waited to be served. The store manager turned off the lights and called the police, who came and arrested the young people and took them off to jail. They were subsequently convicted of trespass-ing, and their convictions were affirmed by the state supreme court, which concluded that the owner of a store "may lawfully forbid any and all persons, regardless of reason, race or religion, to enter or remain upon any part of his premises."[37] The Supreme Court of the United States disagreed and reversed the ruling. Citing the case from Wilmington, the Court set aside the convictions and held that a violation of the Fourteenth Amendment occurs where a state agency "passes a law compelling persons to discriminate against other persons because of race," and uses its law enforcement to enforce the discrimination.[38]

Two private hospitals in Greensboro, North Carolina, the Moses H. Cone Memorial Hospital and the Wesley Long Community Hospital, were sued in the wake of *Brown* for denying admission to black patients and staff privileges to black doctors and dentists. The court of appeals, relying on the Wilmington case, held the discrimination was unlawful state action in view of the financial support both hospitals received from the Hill-Burton program, which allocated federal and state aid to hospitals throughout the state.[39]

Brown was also used to desegregate courthouses in the South, which were literally the citadels of white supremacy and racial suppression. Herman Lodge, who was one of the first blacks elected to the county commission in Burke County, Georgia, after passage of the Voting Rights Act of 1965, explained that "the courthouse was a stigma. People were reluctant to go there. Everything about it was segregated—courtroom seating, juries, employment, drinking fountains. They even had two outhouses for blacks."[40] A middle-aged black woman from Sumter County, Georgia, noted the trauma she experienced when she went to the courthouse in 1963 to register to vote for the first time. "I went down to register and my knees were shaking and I could hardly sign my name," she said. "But it was all right, and maybe now I can get up the nerve to vote."[41]

Ford T. Johnson Jr., a black man attending traffic court in Richmond, Virginia, took a seat in the courtroom in the left-hand section that was reserved for whites. He was directed by the bailiff to move to the right, or black, section but refused to do so. He was then ordered to move by the presiding judge, and when he again refused was convicted of contempt of court. In reversing the conviction, the Supreme Court in a terse opinion relying upon *Brown* held that "segregation in a court of justice is a manifest violation of the State's duty to deny no one the equal protection of its laws."[42]

Blacks attending court in the South had to suffer indignities other than segregated seating, such as being referred to only by their first names. Mary Hamilton was a witness on her own behalf in a case being tried in Etowah County, Alabama. During examination by the prosecutor she refused to answer questions when she was addressed only by her first name, rather than as "Miss" and her last name. As the following exchange shows, and it tells us volumes about what it was like to be black in a courtroom in Alabama in the 1960s, Hamilton was convicted of contempt:

> Q: What is your name, please?
> A: Miss Mary Hamilton.
> Q: Mary, I believe—you were arrested—who were you arrested by?
> A: My name is Miss Hamilton. Please address me correctly.
> Q: Who were you arrested by, Mary?
> A: I will not answer a question--
> By ATTORNEY AMAKER: The witness's name is Miss Hamilton.
> A:—your question until I am addressed correctly.
> THE COURT: Answer the question.
> THE WITNESS: I will not answer them unless I am addressed correctly.
> THE COURT: You are in contempt of this court, and you are sentenced to five
>   days in jail and a fifty dollar fine.[43]

Following the service of her jail sentence, the state supreme court affirmed Hamilton's conviction, noting that "[t]he record conclusively shows that petitioner's name is Mary Hamilton, not Miss Mary Hamilton," and that the contempt citation was within "the sound discretion of the trial court."[44] The

Supreme Court disagreed and, citing the segregated courtroom seating case from Richmond, summarily reversed.[45]

Perhaps the last of the public accommodations to fall under the mandate of *Brown* were prisons and jails, which in most southern states were required to be segregated on the basis of race. In a case from Alabama, the district court struck down Alabama laws requiring segregation in all penal facilities, and cited *Brown* for the proposition that "racial discrimination by governmental authorities in the use of public facilities cannot be tolerated."[46] The state acknowledged that *Brown* was the law, but said it didn't apply in this instance. Inmates, it argued, were not schoolchildren but criminals; segregation was appropriate as a matter of routine prison security and discipline. The Court rejected this argument, but did add a proviso that race could be taken into account under limited circumstances to deal with discipline problems. On appeal the Supreme Court affirmed, finding the opinion of the lower court to be "unexceptionable."[47]

It was inevitable that southern states would go after civil rights organizations and lawyers in an effort to stem the tide of desegregation and other civil rights litigation. The state of Virginia enacted legislation in 1956 directly in response to *Brown,* expanding the definition of prohibited "fomenting and soliciting legal business," which the state courts held applied to the activities of the NAACP and their lawyers in assisting its members and others in seeking to vindicate their constitutional rights. Those found guilty of solicitation could be fined and/or imprisoned and in the case of lawyers disbarred. Other southern states—Arkansas, Florida, Georgia, Mississippi, South Carolina, and Tennessee—followed suit, bringing within the reach of their solicitation laws attorneys paid by organizations such as the NAACP and who represented litigants without charge. In invalidating Virginia's solicitation law, the Supreme Court held the activities of the NAACP were "modes of expression and association protected by the First and Fourteenth Amendments" that the state could not prohibit under the guise of regulating the legal profession. The Court also held that "a statute broadly curtailing group activity leading to litigation may easily become a weapon of oppression . . . [and] could well freeze out of existence all such activity on behalf of the civil rights of Negro citizens."[48]

The Supreme Court, prior to passage of the Voting Rights Act of 1965,[49] also applied the school desegregation cases to remedy discrimination in voting. Citing a school desegregation case from Knoxville, Tennessee, the Court invalidated a Louisiana law requiring candidates for public office to designate their race on nominating petitions and on the ballot. In rejecting as "superficial" the state's argument (which was a variant of the separate but equal concept) that the labeling was constitutional because it applied "equally to Negro and white" candidates, the Court said the vice of the labeling was "in the placing of the power of the state behind a racial classification that induces racial prejudice at the polls."[50] The same year, in *Reynolds v. Sims,* the Court cited and applied the invidious discrimination concept of *Brown* in holding that both houses of a bicameral state legislature must be apportioned on the basis of population. "Diluting the weight of votes because of place of residence," the Court said, "impairs basic constitutional rights under the Fourteenth Amendment just as much as invidious discrimination based upon factors such as race."[51]

In another application of *Brown,* the courts invalidated Virginia laws requiring the segregation by race of the names of persons on records for voting, property tax assessments, and divorce. The trial court, while acknowledging that the compilation of racial statistics may serve a useful purpose, concluded that the infirmity of the challenged laws lay in their mandate of separation of names by race. As the court held, "[t]he 'separate but equal' racial doctrine was condemned a decade ago in *Brown.*"[52] The Supreme Court summarily affirmed without further comment.[53]

In 1960, in response to the equal rights movement ignited by *Brown,* the state of Louisiana amended its constitution to require new applicants for voter registration to "be able to understand" as well as "give a reasonable interpretation" of any section of the state or federal constitution. The new measure was openly touted as a way of preventing blacks from voting and thus preserving segregation and white supremacy.[54] The local registrars had absolute discretion in administering the tests and did so in a way that disproportionately denied blacks access to the registration rolls. In twenty-one parishes in the state, 25,361 blacks were registered prior to the use of the interpretation tests. After the tests went into effect, and as of December 31, 1962, black registration in those twenty-one parishes dropped to 10,351, only 8.6 percent of the black voting age population. White registration remained essentially unaffected. The Supreme Court found the new registration test to be unconstitutional, describing it as "part of a successful plan to deprive Negroes of their right to vote."[55]

Each of the ex-Confederate states, in an effort to disfranchise black voters, adopted laws during the aftermath of Reconstruction requiring proof of payment of a poll, or head, tax as a condition for voting. As Carter Glass, the sponsor of a suffrage plan that included a poll tax, explained to the delegates of the Virginia Constitutional Convention of 1902: "Discrimination! Why that is precisely what we propose; that, exactly, is what this Convention was elected for—to discriminate to the very extremity of permissible action under the limitations of the Federal Constitution, with a view to the elimination of every negro voter who can be gotten rid of, legally, without materially impairing the numerical strength of the white electorate."[56]

Despite a similar history surrounding its adoption, in 1937 the Supreme Court upheld the Georgia poll tax as "a familiar and reasonable regulation."[57] But following *Brown,* and after passage of the Twenty-Fourth Amendment in 1964 banning the poll tax in federal elections, the Supreme Court considered again the constitutionality of the poll tax in a case from Virginia and held its use in state elections was in fact unconstitutional. Noting that *Brown* had overruled the separate but equal doctrine previously approved in *Plessy v. Ferguson*,[58] the Court held that "[n]otions of what constitutes equal protection for purposes of the Equal Protection Clause do change," and that "a State violates the Equal Protection Clause of the Fourteenth Amendment whenever it makes the affluence of the voter or payment of any fee an electoral standard."[59] The Court, building upon the expanded concept of equal protection articulated in the Virginia poll tax case that "[w]ealth, like race, creed, or color, is not germane to one's ability to participate intelligently in the electoral process," subsequently struck down state laws that limited voting in bond elections to taxpaying property owners.[60]

Another voting practice invalidated under the post-*Brown* equal protection doctrine was Alabama's disfranchisement of persons convicted of misdemeanor offenses involving moral turpitude. The scheme had been adopted at the state constitutional convention of 1901 as part of a package of measures designed to disfranchise blacks. John B. Knox, the president of the convention, asked rhetorically in his opening address: "And what is it that we want to do? Why it is within the limits imposed by the Federal Constitution, to establish white supremacy in this State."[61] The offenses that would disqualify a person from being eligible to vote included vagrancy, living in adultery, and wife beating, and were chosen because they were thought to be more commonly committed by blacks. The chief drafter of the statute, John F. Burns, a Black Belt planter, was reported as saying that the "crime of wife beating alone would disqualify sixty percent of the Negroes."[62] In invalidating the scheme under the equal protection clause of the Fourteenth Amendment, the Court concluded that it "was motivated by a desire to discriminate against blacks on account of race and . . . continues to this day to have that effect."[63]

One of the biggest phobias of southern whites was the so-called "amalgamation" or "mongrelization" of the white race that they believed would result from desegregation. Many whites feared that with the demise of separate but equal would come social equality and intermarriage, and inevitably the corruption and downfall of American civilization.

Herman Talmadge wrote in 1955 that "history shows that nations composed of a mongrel race lose their strength and become weak, lazy and indifferent. They become easy preys to outside nations." According to Talmadge, "[t]he decline and fall of the Roman Empire came after years of intermarriage with other races. Spain was toppled as a world power as a result of the amalgamation of the races."[64] Newell Edenfield, the president of the Georgia Bar Association in 1960, said that to mix the "superior" white race with the "inferior" black race would be a catastrophic form of "adulteration."[65]

When it was revealed that Charlayne Hunter, the first black to graduate from the University of Georgia, had been married to a white man in 1963 and was pregnant, there was a chorus of angry condemnation from prominent white officials. The president of the University of Georgia, O. C. Aderhold, issued a statement that neither Hunter nor her husband would ever be allowed to reenter the university. Governor Carl Sanders described the marriage as "a disgrace" and "a shame." Attorney General Eugene Cook said the marriage was "illegal" and that he was investigating the matter for a possible violation of the state's criminal laws.[66]

Indeed, as late as the mid-1960s, sixteen states, most of them in the South—Alabama, Arkansas, Delaware, Florida, Georgia, Kentucky, Louisiana, Maryland, Mississippi, Missouri, North Carolina, Oklahoma, South Carolina, Tennessee, Virginia, and West Virginia—prohibited miscegenation and made it a criminal offense.[67] The Supreme Court of Appeals of Virginia, in a decision upholding that state's antimiscegenation laws, said they were designed "to preserve the racial integrity of its citizens," and to prevent "a mongrel breed of citizens," "the obliteration of racial pride," and "the corruption of blood even though it weaken or destroy the quality of its citizenship."[68]

Despite the pervasive race phobias and race mythology that permeated the South, the courts used the *Brown* decision to strike down state laws regulating the private conduct of adults along racial lines. One of those cases decided by the Supreme Court involved an interracial couple in Florida who were convicted of violating a state law that made it a crime for an unmarried interracial couple simply to live in and occupy the same room at night. There was no comparable offense making it a crime for an unmarried white or black couple to live in and occupy the same room at night. The state supreme court affirmed, brushing aside the defendants' argument that their conviction violated the Fourteenth Amendment as "the new-found concept of 'Social Justice.'"[69] In reversing, the Supreme Court held the racial classification in the challenged statute was "an invidious discrimination forbidden by the Equal Protection Clause."[70]

Three years later, the Court struck down the state of Virginia's law making interracial marriage a crime. Mildred Jeter, who was black, and her husband, Richard Loving, who was white, pleaded guilty to violating the state's antimiscegenation law and were sentenced to a year in jail, suspended upon their leaving the state for twenty-five years. The trial judge, echoing the words of Herman Talmadge from a decade earlier, said: "Almighty God created the races, white, black, yellow, malay and red, and he placed them on separate continents. And but for the interference with his arrangement there would be no cause for such marriages. The fact that he separated the races shows that he did not intend for the races to mix." In reversing, and once again relying upon the precedent of *Brown,* the Supreme Court invalidated the Virginia law and held "[t]here is patently no legitimate overriding purpose independent of invidious racial discrimination which justifies this classification." "There can be no doubt," the Court continued, "that restricting the freedom to marry solely because of racial classifications violates the central meaning of the Equal Protection Clause." And even assuming the state's purpose was to protect the "integrity" of the races, the law was "repugnant to the Fourteenth Amendment."[71]

Brown was extended further to invalidate a Louisiana law prohibiting illegitimate children from suing for the wrongful death of their mother. The state courts had upheld the law as "based on morals and general welfare because it discourages bringing children into the world out of wedlock." Citing *Brown*, however, the Supreme Court said "we . . . have not hesitated to strike down an invidious classification even though it had history and tradition on its side." In the present case, it was "invidious to discriminate against [illegitimate children] when no action, conduct, or demeanor of theirs is possibly relevant to the harm that was done the mother."[72]

Brown's concept of equal treatment was later applied to undocumented school age children, whom the state of Texas excluded from its public schools. The Supreme Court was unable "to reconcile the cost or the principle of a state-based denial of basic education with the framework of equality embodied in the Equal Protection Clause" as articulated in *Brown*.[73]

Another institution that fell in the aftermath of *Brown* was segregated labor unions. In invalidating the maintenance of separate white and black longshoremen's unions in Texas because they resulted in employment discrimination against blacks, the court concluded: "It is ludicrous to say in the seventh decade of the twentieth century, 20 years after Brown v. Board of Education gave us our forceful education in race relations, as our society and courts have struggled with the great task of cleansing the various inequities which have beset our black citizens, that segregated unionism is to receive the statutory or constitutional blessing of our Congress or this Court. . . . Unions are not entitled to any separate enclave in our legal and sociological stratification."[74]

More recently, the Supreme Court struck down under the equal protection clause of the Fourteenth Amendment a Colorado constitutional provision that prohibited all legislative, executive, or judicial action designed to protect homosexuals from discrimination. In doing so, the Court began its discussion with a quote from the dissenting opinion of Justice Harlan in *Plessy v. Ferguson* that the constitution "neither knows nor tolerates classes among citizens."[75] Thus, the concept of equal treatment of the races embodied in Justice Harlan's dissent and subsequently adopted in *Brown* was applied to prohibit a state from denying the protection of its laws to gays and lesbians.

Much has been written about the failure of *Brown* to desegregate fully public education in America. That failure is the result in large measure of the continuing and divisive importance of race in this country. The entire history of opposition to equal rights—from slavery, to the overthrow of the Reconstruction experiment, to the rise of Jim Crow, to the massive resistance campaign against *Brown,* to the opposition to modern civil rights laws—starkly demonstrates that there is no quick and easy solution to the racial problems that continue to divide the country, in education and other areas of life.

Notably, when it enacted the Voting Rights Act in 1965, Congress subjected certain states (most of them in the South where discrimination against blacks in voting had been most pronounced) to the special preclearance provisions of section 5,[76] but only for a limited period of five years. Congress thought, in retrospect unrealistically, that a five-year "cooling-off" period during which proposed voting changes would be subject to scrutiny by federal officials would be sufficient "to permit dissipation of the long established political atmosphere and tradition of discrimination in voting because of color" in the covered jurisdictions.[77] But based on congressional findings of ongoing, widespread discrimination in voting, Congress extended section 5 in 1970, 1975, 1982, and again in 2006.

One of those who testified in support of the 1982 extension was C. Vann Woodward, the dean of southern historians. Noting the continuing dynamic effect of race, he warned that the failure to extend section 5 "will open the door to a rush of measures to abridge, diminish, and dilute if not emasculate the power of the black vote in southern states."[78] Congress heeded Woodward's warning and extended Section 5 for an additional twenty-five years.

In July 2006 Congress again extended section 5 for twenty-five years, and in doing so said the evidence before it "reveals that 40 years has not been a sufficient amount of time to eliminate the vestiges of discrimination following nearly 100 years of disregard for the dictates of the 15th amendment."[79] The continuing racial problems in voting, however, were cause, not for disparaging the act and its principle of equal voting rights, but for strengthening and extending it. By the same token, while the full implementation of *Brown* remains elusive, that is not a reason to retreat from its enforcement or disparage the principle of equal treatment that it embodies.

Following *Brown,* a broad array of groups has demanded the same equal treatment accorded to blacks by the school desegregation cases. The list of publications in the ACLU's *Rights* series provides a vivid illustration of the extent of the modern rights revolution. Aside from *The Rights of Racial Minorities,* there are now some thirty-five titles in the series, including the rights of aliens and refugees; authors and artists; candidates and voters; crime victims; the critically ill; doctors and nurses; employees and union members; ex-offenders; families; government employees; Indians and tribes; lawyers and clients; lesbians and gay men; military personnel; older persons; parents; patients; people who are

HIV-positive; people with mental disabilities; police officers; the poor; prisoners; public employees; reporters; single people; students; suspects; teachers; veterans; women; and young people. The list will surely grow as the legacy of *Brown* continues to unfold in the coming years.

Brown helped define America as a free, egalitarian society and in fundamental ways led the country out of the darkest regions of its past. It set the stage for passage of the modern civil rights acts, including the Civil Rights Act of 1964 and the Voting Rights Act of 1965. It has been applied to remedy discrimination in a multitude of contexts—restaurants, public parks, courtrooms, prisons and jails, the legal profession, civil rights organizations, voting, marriage, illegitimacy, labor unions—and to protect groups not defined by race, including the poor, illegitimate children, ex-offenders, lesbians and gays, non-taxpayers, and undocumented aliens. *Brown* fueled a rights movement that continues to transform American society consistent with the decision's vision of equality embodied in the Fourteenth Amendment.

Notes

1. *Brown v. Board of Education,* 347 U.S. 483 (1954).

2. *Brown v. Board of Education,* 349 U.S. 294, 301 (1955) (*Brown* II).

3. Ga. Laws 1927, pp. 272, 277–78.

4. Ga. Code of 1933, §§ 18-206 and 209.

5. Minutes of the Sumter County Board of Education, September 24, 1956, October 5, 1956, Americus, Ga.

6. *Harris County Journal,* November 8, 1945.

7. *Bowdry v. Hawes,* Civ. No. 176-128 (S.D.Ga., 1976), Pl. Ex. 56.

8. *Georgia v. Thornburg,* Civ. No. 90-2065 (D.D.C., 1990), Declaration of Donald L. Hollowell.

9. Billy McKinney, interview by author, September 8, 2001.

10. Georgia Department of Corrections, *A History of the Death Penalty in Georgia: Executions by Year, 1924–2004* (January 2005).

11. *Brooks v. Miller,* No. I:90–CV-1001–RCF (N.D.Ga., 1990), trial transcript, May 15, 1966, p. 407.

12. Ga. Laws 1955, pp. 4, 9, 174, 185.

13. *Stewart-Webster Journal,* January 12, 1956.

14. Herman E. Talmadge, *You and Segregation* (Birmingham, Ala.: Vulcan Press, 1955), 44.

15. Ga. Laws 1956, pp. 6, 9, 10, 11, 22, 753, 756.

16. Ga. Laws 1956, pp. 642, 647; *Georgia House Journal,* February 8, 1956, 782–83; *Georgia Senate Journal,* February 13, 1956, 629.

17. Ga. Laws 1956, p. 38; *Atlanta Journal,* February 10, 1956.

18. State Law Department, *Compilation of Georgia Laws and Opinions of the Attorney General Relating to Segregation of the Races* (April 1956), 2–3.

19. Ga. Laws 1957, pp. 553, 561–62.

20. Ga. Laws 1957, p. 348; *Georgia Senate Journal,* February 8, 1957, 257; *Georgia House Journal,* February 13, 1957, 661.

21. Southern Manifesto, 84th Cong., 2nd sess., *Congressional Record* 102, part 4 (March 12, 1956): 4515–16.

22. *Muir v. Louisville Park Theatrical Association,* 347 U.S. 971 (1954).

23. *Flemming v. South Carolina Electric & Gas Company,* 128 F. Supp. 469, 470 (E.D.S.C. 1955).

24. *Lonesome v. Maxwell,* 123 F. Supp. 193, 205 (D.C.Md. 1954).

25. *Holmes v. City of Atlanta,* 124 F. Supp. 290, 293 (N.D.Ga. 1954).

26. *Dawson v. Mayor and City Council of Baltimore,* 220 F.2d 386, 387 (4th Cir. 1955).

27. *Mayor and City Council of Baltimore v. Dawson,* 350 U.S. 877 (1955).

28. *Flemming v. South Carolina Electric & Gas Company,* 224 F.2d 752 (4th Cir. 1955).

29. *Holmes v. City of Atlanta,* 350 U.S. 879 (1955).

30. *Gayle v. Browder,* 142 F. Supp. 707, 717 (M.D.Ala. 1956).

31. *New Orleans City Park Imp. Ass'n v. Detiege,* 252 F.2d 122, 123 (5th Cir. 1958).

32. *Watson v. Memphis,* 373 U.S. 526, 535 (1963).

33. Title II of the *Civil Rights Act, U.S. Code* 42 (1964), §§ 2000a et seq., was the nation's first modern public accommodations law, and prohibits discrimination on the basis of race, color, religion, or national origin in virtually all private establishments that serve the public.

34. *Burton v. Wilmington Parking Authority,* 365 U.S. 715, 724 (1961).

35. *Turner v. Memphis,* 369 U.S. 350, 354 (1962).

36. *Peterson v. Greenville, S.C.,* 373 U.S. 244, 247–48 (1963).

37. *City of Greenville v. Peterson,* 239 S.C. 298, 122 S.E.2d 826, 828 (S.C. 1961).

38. *Peterson v. Greenville, S.C.,* 373 U.S. at 247–48.

39. *Simkins v. Moses H. Cone Memorial Hospital,* 323 F.2d 959, 967 (4th Cir. 1963).

40. Herman Lodge, interview by author, 1978.

41. Quoted in Pat Waters and Reese Cleghorn, *Climbing Jacob's Ladder* (New York: Harcourt, Brace and World, 1967), 146.

42. *Johnson v. Virginia,* 373 U.S. 61, 62 (1963).

43. Ex parte Hamilton, 275 Ala. 574, 156 So.2d 926 (1963).

44. Ibid. at 927.

45. *Hamilton v. Alabama,* 376 U.S. 650 (1964).

46. *Washington v. Lee,* 263 F. Supp. 327, 331 (M.D.Ala. 1966).

47. *Lee v. Washington,* 390 U.S. 333, 334 (1968).

48. *NAACP v. Button,* 371 U.S. 415, 429, 435, 445 (1963) (Douglas, J., concurring).

49. *Voting Rights Act, U.S. Code* 42 (1965), §§ 1973 et seq.

50. *Anderson v. Martin,* 375 U.S. 399, 402, 404 (1964).

51. *Reynolds v. Sims,* 377 U.S. 533, 566 (1964).

52. *Hamm v. Virginia State Bd. of Elections,* 230 F. Supp. 156, 157 (E.D.Va. 1964).

53. *Tancil v. Wools,* 379 U.S. 19 (1964).

54. *United States v. State of Louisiana,* 225 F. Supp. 353, 378 (E.D.La. 1963).

55. *Louisiana v. United States,* 380 U.S. 145, 151 (1965).

56. *Harman v. Forssenius,* 380 U.S. 528, 543 (1965).

57. *Breedlove v. Suttles,* 302 U.S. 277, 283 (1937).

58. *Plessy v. Ferguson,* 163 U.S. 537 (1896).

59. *Harper v. Virginia State Board of Elections,* 383 U.S. 663, 666 (1966).

60. *Cipriano v. City of Houma,* 395 U.S. 701 (1969). See also *Kramer v. Union Free School District,* 395 U.S. 621 (1969), and *Hill v. Stone,* 421 U.S. 289 (1975).

61. *Hunter v. Underwood,* 471 U.S. 220, 229 (1985).

62. *Underwood v. Hunter,* 730 F.2d 614, 620 (5th Cir. 1984).

63. *Hunter v. Underwood,* 471 U.S. at 233.

64. Talmadge, *You and Segregation,* 44–45.

65. Newell Edenfield, Address of the President, *Report of the 77th Annual Session of the Georgia Bar Association* (1960), 204.

66. *Atlanta Journal,* September 3, 1963; *Atlanta Constitution,* September 6, 1963.

67. *Loving v. Virginia,* 388 U.S. 1, 6 n.5 (1967).

68. *Naim v. Naim,* 197 Va. 80, 90, 87 S.E.2d 749, 756 (1955).

69. *McLaughlin v. State,* 153 So.2d 1, 2–3 (1963).

70. *McLaughlin v. Florida,* 379 U.S. 184, 193 (1964).

71. *Loving v. Virginia,* 388 U.S. at 3, 11, 12, 12 n.11.

72. *Levy v. Louisiana,* 391 U.S. 68, 70–72 (1968).

73. *Plyler v. Doe,* 457 U.S. 202, 222 (1982).

74. *EEOC v. International Longshoremen's Ass'n,* 511 F.2d 273, 279 (5th Cir. 1975).

75. *Romer v. Evans,* 517 U.S. 620, 623 (1996).

76. *U.S. Code* 42 § 1973c.

77. 89th Cong., 1st Sess. 15 (1965), H. Rept. 439, reprinted in *United States Code Congressional and Administrative News,* 1965, 1:2446.

78. House Committee on the Judiciary, *Extension of the Voting Rights Act: Hearings before the Subcommittee on Civil and Constitutional Rights,* 97th Cong., 1st sess., June 24, 1981, 2001.

79. *Fannie Lou Hamer, Rosa Parks, and Coretta Scott King Voting Rights Act Reauthorization and Amendments Act of 2006,* Public Law 109–246, *U.S. Statutes at Large* 120 (2006): 577, Sec. 2(b)(7).

5

"A Mind Is a Terrible Thing to Waste"

The Advertising Council, the United Negro College Fund, and Educational Access for African Americans

Jason Chambers

On a quiet day in early 1943 Dr. Frederick Patterson of Tuskegee Institute in Alabama sat down at his desk to compose a letter. Foremost on his mind that day was the financial future of his institution and others like it. Tuskegee, like other historically black institutions, had little assistance from state or federal funds and depended on contributions from private donors. Given its history and the legacy of its well-known founder, Booker T. Washington, Tuskegee fared better financially than many other black schools. But, "better" was a relative assessment. For while Tuskegee did not have the same difficulty generating funds as other schools, it was far from being a wealthy institution. So as Patterson sat down that day he had his own institution's future in mind as well as that of other black schools.[1]

Dr. Patterson had a desire to help in educating all black students, no matter what school they attended. As a student at Iowa State University, Patterson knew the difficulty black students had in paying for higher education. To support his own education Patterson worked at various times as a cook, janitor, waiter, and cotton picker. Hence, he had a vested desire in easing the financial burden for other black students and in seeing black educational institutions succeed. So, with a clear picture in mind of the financial picture of black schools he crafted a unique fund-raising proposal. On that day Patterson outlined the basic structure for what became the United Negro College Fund (UNCF). He believed that instead of black schools individually soliciting funds, a central fund that spoke for a body of institutions would be more effective. After completing the letter Patterson sent it to the presidents of other black colleges, and he published a portion of it in the *Pittsburgh Courier*. The initial response from college presidents to the idea was one of support. Little more than a year later his vision became reality with the founding of the UNCF.[2]

The UNCF was created ten years before the *Brown v. Board of Education* decision and would, at first glance, appear unconnected to the decision. In fact, in the wake of the ruling many people believed that the desegregation order meant that black schools would soon close. Some began to question the role of segregated institutions in a country where educational segregation was (at least theoretically) outlawed. Yet, rather than launching plans to close their doors, black institutions were among the first to ensure that their charters and admissions policies adhered to the *Brown* ruling. The leadership of the UNCF and of member institutions not only realized the importance of their institutions to higher education, but also the hypocrisy inherent in arguments as to their imminent demise. For while their closure was assumed to be a natural outgrowth of the *Brown* decision, the same assumptions were not made about historically white institutions that had openly and aggressively pursued segregationist policies. Instead of closing their doors, the *Brown* ruling meant that black colleges and universities could now attract students of all races. The decision meant that Americans were now free to choose the institution that best suited their needs and interests rather than being restricted because of race. Therefore, the *Brown* ruling meant that, rather than closing, black schools now had the genuine opportunity to become first rank institutions.[3]

The spirit of the *Brown* decision was about the equality of opportunity. Yet this equality meant little without access. In other words, while it was important to offer black children the chance to receive an education, *Brown* offered them little tangible support to reach that goal. The UNCF has been part of the "access" phase of the *Brown* decision because it has offered African American children the means to achieve the educational opportunities the *Brown* decision guaranteed. Consequently, any examination of the impact of the *Brown* decision necessarily involves the presence and impact of the UNCF. In 2003, as part of the University of Illinois's commemoration of the *Brown* decision, my research examined the history of the advertising campaign that supported the UNCF. Through a retrospective of the print, television, and radio advertisements from the campaign, viewers were exposed to the myriad appeals the campaign has used over the years. This exhibit also highlighted the role of advertising beyond that of goods and services. The advertising campaign for the UNCF not only brought more positive images of blacks to the nation's advertising landscape, it also helped initiate a national conversation about race and opportunity. The campaign has presented black people as agents in their own advancement and as a group worthy of investment and support rather than pity.

When Dr. Patterson penned his early outline of the UNCF he had been president of Tuskegee for nearly ten years. During his tenure he had many opportunities to participate in the traditional fund-raising practices of black college presidents. Because there was a small pool of major donors to black institutions, presidents often competed with one another for funds. It was not uncommon for the president of one institution to leave the office of a donor only to run into the leader of another school waiting in the foyer. While the process did garner results, Patterson believed that they could be increased. The catalyst for his thinking was the successful March of Dimes campaign. Instead of looking for major contributions, the March of Dimes asked people to contribute a small sum (i.e., dimes), and campaign organizers had received tremendous contributions. Consequently, Patterson believed that a similar process would work for black institutions. He felt that if more people were asked for their contributions and were given a cause to believe in and support, they would respond with donations. After all, pennies, nickels, and dimes eventually added up to dollars, and those dollars could make the UNCF a strong resource for black colleges and students.[4]

The first public campaign for the UNCF was in 1944. To the consternation of some member presidents, Patterson set the initial goal for the campaign high, at $500,000. Several members of the group felt that the goal could not be reached and that the failure to do so would damage the public image of the fledgling organization. Conversely, Patterson believed that if the group did not have a substantial goal they would receive a minimal response. "I learned early in the game that many people give according to the size of your goal; if you're asking for peanuts, you get peanuts."[5] With an initial investment of $100,000 contributed by the twenty-seven member institutions, the campaign raised over $700,000. This was an enormous improvement in fund-raising for black schools. The year before joining the UNCF Tuskegee had spent over $20,000 alone on fund-raising and had produced only $40,000. Now, with a much smaller investment the school had received a substantial return. With each successive campaign the contributions to the UNCF increased. Clearly Patterson had hit upon a successful fund-raising formula.[6]

Over the decades following its creation the UNCF used the services of several volunteer advertising agencies. From year to year the agency servicing the account changed, and there was no strong unifying theme to the advertisements. Although the UNCF continued to receive substantial contributions, it lacked an immediately visible national stature. Instead the group was simply one of any number of charitable organizations, educational and otherwise, seeking donations. In 1970, in search of that national presence, the leadership of the UNCF sought the help of the Advertising Council, the nation's leading public service advertising organization.

The Advertising Council first entered the public service arena during the Second World War. Initially known as the War Advertising Council, the group was responsible for coordinating messages of support for the American war effort. At the end of the war, members agreed the group should remain in operation, and they shifted focus from wartime concerns to a host of social issues. Over the years these have included seat belt use, drunk driving, forest fires, environmental pollution, and drug abuse. The council is supported by a variety of media organizations, trade groups, advertising agencies, and various media outlets. Advertising created by the council is done largely for free by volunteer advertising agencies, and the ads are placed in space donated by media organizations. Clients, like the UNCF, are responsible for paying only for the production and distribution of campaign materials. This massive donation of time and talent far exceeds the advertising budgets of the majority of council clients. If the Advertising Council's time and labor were measured in billings, it would be one of the largest agencies in the nation.[7]

When UNCF executives turned to the council for support, it found an organization with a lengthy résumé of successfully generating public support for causes, issues, and groups. Yet when the Advertising Council took over the campaign it was within a nation mired in crisis. The economy was beginning a slide into recession, the war in Vietnam continued without foreseeable end, and African Americans continued to struggle to secure full equality. So UNCF and council leaders realized that, if improperly handled, the advertising campaign for the UNCF might present blacks as charity cases, or be viewed as patronizing to the black community. Therefore, the creators of the campaign chose to focus on the potential inherent in the African American community, potential denied because of discrimination and prejudice.

The task for creating the UNCF campaign fell to executives at Young & Rubicam (Y&R), who immediately saw an array of challenges. The primary one was how to ask the public to give money for institutions that appeared to be segregated when years of public discourse had argued that segregation and "separate but equal" was wrong. Beyond simply generating income the campaign had to change the public perception that these institutions were relics from a bygone past that was best forgotten. After consulting with UNCF leaders, Forrest Long, a copywriter at Y&R, suggested a theme-line for the campaign: "A mind is a *hell* [*italics mine*] of a thing to waste." The goal of the campaign Long and others envisioned was to pointedly place a human face on the impact of educational discrimination: "We wanted to make supporting the UNCF a human issue and not a race issue." But despite the need for the directness so well encapsulated by Long's initial slogan, executives at both the Advertising Council and the UNCF felt it was too profane. The slogan might insult some potential donors, and, more seriously, keep media organizations from donating space for its running. After more thought Long came back to the two groups with the now famous tagline: A mind is a terrible thing to waste.[8]

In changing a single word Long had succeeded exquisitely in making support of the UNCF a human issue. With just eight words he encapsulated the importance of educational access for all Americans. In conjunction with the tagline the images created for the advertising campaign encouraged a personal connection between the viewer and prospective student. Blacks were not presented as objects of pity. Instead, emotional connections emphasized the impact of lost human potential. Further, true to Patterson's vision, the advertisements stressed that any size donation was welcomed and that each one made a difference. Also, the slogan and campaign tapped what may be commonly described as American values—hard work, achieving dreams and aspirations, contributing to the societal good—all of which are possible with an education. The ads helped lead Americans to confront the individual and societal impact of educational discrimination and prejudice that limits the human and economic resources of a large segment of the population.

The Advertising Council Takes Over

With the development of the slogan in place, advertising for the UNCF became significantly more focused. Rather than the campaign theme changing from year to year, examination reveals six major themes have been developed and incorporated into UNCF advertisements: Unrealized Dreams and Lost Potential, Achievers from Historically Black Colleges and Universities, Family Support and Sacrifice for Education, History of Educational Discrimination, Investing in Helping People Help Themselves, and Celebrity Support of UNCF Goals. These themes have addressed different audiences as well as UNCF organizational goals for the year in question. Each theme and representative ads are discussed below.

The most powerful and consistent theme incorporated into the advertisements was that of *Unrealized Dreams and Lost Potential.* Importantly, these children were not just presented as students but as deserving students who were capable of real achievement. These were kids who had the talent and drive to succeed but simply lacked the money to achieve their potential. One advertisement within this theme was entitled "All dressed up and no place to go" (see figure 5.1). Sitting on the steps of his high school it was clear that the student had graduated, but his future was now in question. Without contributions to the UNCF, it was certain that he would not attend college. Consequently, both the individual and the larger society lost when talented students were tragically denied an education. After all, as another advertisement declared, "You can't cure cancer with a monkey wrench."

Other advertisements encouraged people to consider the various social and physical ills that blacks might be able to cure if only they had access to an

FIGURE 5.I.

All Dressed Up and No Place to Go, University of Illinois Archives, Record Series 13/3/218, courtesy of the University Archives of the University of Illinois, Champaign.

All dressed up and no place to go.

A student who not only meets but exceeds the demands of high school deserves to go on to college. But if he can't afford such an education, he won't be going anywhere.

Please help us keep tuitions down for these deserving students by sending your check to the United Negro College Fund, 500 East 62nd Street, New York, NY 10021.

United Negro College Fund.
A Mind Is A Terrible Thing To Waste.

education. In one print ad a black man walked down an alley on his way to an evidently blue-collar job. The headline over the advertisement made its implications clear: "He could've been searching for a cure to the common cold." A radio spot further developed the point: "There are people born every day who could cure disease, make peace, create art, abolish injustice, create jobs, end hunger. There are people everywhere who could do a lot to make his world a much better place. But if they're not encouraged . . . if they don't get an education, they may never get a chance to do anything worthwhile."[9] Therefore, rather than allowing the waste to continue, listeners were told that contributing to the UNCF was one active step to help put an end to the waste. For, as another advertisement asked, "Who ever said the man who discovered a cure for cancer is going to be white, or even a man?"

Funds from the UNCF have not only supported individual students but also provided operating capital for member institutions. Thus it has been important for viewers to see the outstanding record and contributions of alumni from these schools. This second theme, *Achievers from Historically Black Colleges and Universities,* has incorporated actors, politicians, artists and societal leaders. Persons like actor Samuel L. Jackson, Atlanta mayor Maynard Jackson, singer Leontyne Price, and Martin Luther King Jr. were the focal point of campaigns. These men and women were prominently pictured with their accomplishments described (see figure 5.2). Although not all students would go on to the achievements of Dr. King or other famous alumni, without the existence of black colleges and universities many would never get the opportunity to try. This theme has been used to balance the assumption that because many students at black colleges need financial support, the schools were by relation inferior.

The third theme, *Family Support and Sacrifice for Education,* encouraged individuals to sacrifice and make a donation just as black families sacrificed and worked to send their children to school. The headline for one ad read:

FIGURE 5.2.
Your Gift Could Produce a King, University of Illinois Archives, Record Series 12/2/219, courtesy of the University Archives of the University of Illinois, Champaign.

"My brothers and sisters wear other folks' clothes so I can become an engineer." Beneath the line was a picture of a young boy and girl dressed in threadbare clothes and looking forlornly at the camera. Other advertisements did not use the theme of lack but emphasized the important lessons black parents had communicated to their children. "My father gave me ambition, courage and dignity," read one advertisement. A black father and son were presented standing next to each other, with the father wearing a work shirt and jeans with the son in a shirt and tie. The implication of the advertisement was the father had given the son everything he needed to succeed—except money. Additionally, the attire suggested that the son now had the opportunity to advance farther professionally than did the father. Viewers were reminded of American notions of an expected return for hard work and that sometimes the dreams of parents and grandparents were realized through their children (see figure 5.3). Advertisements strongly implied there should be some reward for diligence and effort

Once this man dreamed of going to college. Today he finally made it.

For more than fifty years, The College Fund has helped thousands of young men and women achieve goals their grandparents could only dream of. We are proud to have made a critical difference in the lives of so many. But our job is not done. With your help, we will continue to bring many more dreams within reach.

SUPPORT THE COLLEGE FUND/UNCF.
A MIND IS A TERRIBLE THING TO WASTE.

Ad Council

1-800-332-UNCF

FIGURE 5.3.

A Dream Realized. University of Illinois Archives, Record Series 12/2/219, courtesy of the University Archives of the University of Illinois, Champaign.

on the part of both students and their families. Lost dreams were presented as being intergenerational, with children striving for the educational dreams their parents had been unable to reach. Like the theme of *Unrealized Dreams,* this emphasis on family support and sacrifice presented the viewer with a personal and emotional connection to students in a manner that emphasized the human impact of being denied an education.

The theme of the *History and Impact of Education Discrimination* was often used in the early years of Advertising Council support for the UNCF. The ads were designed to remind the viewer that, as one advertising executive noted, "The injustices that exist today were born yesterday."[10] Thus, given the length of time blacks had struggled to receive an education, there was an immediate need for donations and an improvement in their educational opportunities. Advertisements described the centuries-long struggle of African Americans to get an education and the actions of others who had supported their efforts. Viewers were reminded that "There was a time when supporting black education could have cost you your freedom. Today it just costs money." Or, "Once you had to put your life or liberty on the line to support black education. Today we just need your signature." Advertisements featured images of blacks clandestinely meeting in the woods and teaching one another to read. Other advertisements featured pictures and descriptions of white Americans who had been hanged for educating blacks. Thus, the current struggle of blacks to go to college was part of a much longer and complex historical legacy.

The business community has been a key source of contributions for the UNCF. Nearly one-third of all funds contributed to the organization come from corporations. So when reaching out to business executives, the theme of *Investing in Helping People Help Themselves* was often utilized and featured in business periodicals. From the beginning, however, this theme also underlay the UNCF campaign insofar as it emphasized that blacks were not to be pitied or scorned (see figure 5.4). Radio advertisements within this theme told listeners, "We're not asking for a handout. Just a hand." Just as African Americans struggled to help themselves, companies and individuals could provide much needed assistance. As one advertisement noted, "No one can do it alone." Investing in African American higher education also provided corporations with the added benefit of a larger pool of educated employees to draw from. In another advertisement viewers were introduced to a young man working as a landscaper to help pay for his education. The headline read: "A part-time job only pays for part of his education." The implication was that one day the young man would graduate and become an important contributor to the nation's economic system as a small business owner or a corporate leader. Additionally, viewers were reminded that educational achievement was difficult under the best circumstances, let alone when one was struggling financially.

FIGURE 5.4.

A Check to the UNCF, University of Illinois Archives, Record Series 12/2/219, courtesy of the University Archives of the University of Illinois, Champaign.

Over the years a variety of entertainment celebrities have lent their faces and talents in support of the UNCF and its goals. The final theme, *Celebrity Support of UNCF Goals,* utilized the support of well-known African Americans from a variety of occupations. Actors such as Ossie Davis and Laurence Fishburne have provided the voiceovers to commercials. Musical artists including Ray Charles, the Temptations, Dionne Warwick, and Leontyne Price have lent their talents to radio and television commercials. Sports stars such as Arthur Ashe, Michael Jordan, and Henry Aaron, as well as political figures like Colin Powell have also voiced their support. Some of these celebrities are graduates of UNCF institutions or other historically black institutions, but many are not. Regardless of their connection to black institutions, celebrity support has long been important in generating contributions to the UNCF. In fact the long-running telethon the *Lou Rawls Parade of Stars* has been essential to UNCF coffers, and its success was based upon celebrity support.

The Legacy of Frederick Patterson

Shortly before his death in 1988 Frederick Patterson was awarded the Presidential Medal of Freedom, the highest civilian honor presented in the United States. It was a measure of the nation's appreciation for the impact his creation had on hundreds of thousands of individual lives and the nation as a whole. The campaign for the UNCF has been an unprecedented success, raising a total in excess of $2 billion over the life of the fund. Today the UNCF supports students at over nine hundred universities throughout the country. UNCF scholarships are also available to nonblack students who attend one of the thirty-nine current UNCF member schools.[11]

Although the advertising campaign is not the only part of UNCF fund-raising efforts, it is the most well known. The tagline for the campaign has become a part of the American lexicon. A survey conducted in the early 1990s revealed that over 75 percent of the public recognized the slogan and could identify its benefactor. Moreover, the advertisements for the UNCF have been at the forefront of changing public perceptions of African American educational desires and achievements. Long before the *Brown* decision was handed down, blacks sought opportunities for higher education. Since its issuance blacks have only intensified that struggle as part of their fight for equality in America. The campaign for the UNCF has placed blacks at the center of that struggle as agents in their own individual and group uplift.[12]

The UNCF campaign has also helped lead Americans to understand, or at least grudgingly recognize, the role of black colleges and universities within the educational structure. The campaign has evolved from one underlining the historic struggle for educational equality to one that currently acknowledges the many strides that have been made without allowing viewers to believe the job is complete. Far from being institutions destined to be closed, black colleges are now the chosen destination for high-achieving students of all racial backgrounds.

The idea that a mind is a terrible thing to waste has been more than words or a slogan to be butchered by former vice presidents.[13] Rather it has been a call to action on the importance of individuals having the opportunity to go as far in life as their abilities will allow. Therefore, while the *Brown* decision opened the door to educational opportunity, it was the UNCF that was part of the action mechanism that allowed blacks to step through and to broaden educational access within America. Additionally, the campaign has helped America to continue to confront the importance of wiping out educational discrimination and prejudice.

Notes

UNCF name, slogan, and advertisements used by permision of UNCF.

1. Frederick D. Patterson and Martia Graham Goodson ed., *Chronicles of Faith: The Autobiography of Frederick D. Patterson* (Tuscaloosa: University of Alabama Press, 1991).

2. Ibid.

3. Mark Lowery, "United Negro College Fund: 50 Years and Going Strong," *Black Enterprise* (September 1994): 132–38.

4. Patterson and Goodson, *Chronicles of Faith,* 137.

5. Ibid., 132.

6. Ibid., 140.

7. See Daniel L. Lykins, *From Total War to Total Diplomacy: The Advertising Council and the Construction of the Cold War Consensus* (Westport, Conn.: Praeger, 2003).

8. Mariko Fujinaka, "United Negro College Fund," in *Encyclopedia of Major Marketing Campaigns,* ed. Thomas Riggs (Detroit: Gale Group, 2000), 1826.

9. Ibid., 1827.

10. "Market Analysis Underlies Negro College Fund Push," *Advertising Age,* June 5, 1967, 16.

11. Ronald Roach, "UNCF Gray's Way," *Black Issues in Higher Education,* September 30, 1999, 18.

12. Fujinaka, "United Negro College Fund," 1827.

13. The most notable misquoting of the slogan came from former vice president Dan Quayle who intoned: "What a waste it is to lose one's mind. Or not to have a mind is being very wasteful. How true that is." See Reference.com, *United Negro College Fund* (Los Angeles: Lexico Publishing Group, 2006), http://www.reference .com/browse/wiki/United_Negro_College_Fund (accessed April 9, 2008).

6

Success *and* Failure

How Systemic Racism Trumped the
Brown v. Board of Education Decision

*Joe R. Feagin and
Bernice McNair Barnett*

U.S. schoolchildren have long pledged allegiance to a "nation . . . with liberty and justice for all," yet from the beginning this has been hypocritical rhetoric. When it comes to schools, African American children and many other children of color historically have rarely gotten justice. Never in U.S. history has there been a year when even half the country's black children attended schools where a majority of children were white.[1] Today, even officially "desegregated" schools—which are decreasing in number—are intentionally divided internally into ability tracks that reflect racial, class, and gender stratification. Typically, a desegregated school facility is internally segregated with different educational experiences for most white and black children—a kind of "second-generation segregation." Despite supporting the ideal of a desegregated society in surveys, white leaders and citizens have been unwilling to implement the thoroughgoing desegregation of any major institution.[2]

Today, in many larger cities there are relatively few white children left in public schools. Various factors, such as the rise of private academies, the increase in populations of color in cities, the flight of middle-class whites to predominately white school districts, the movement of middle-class blacks into predominately white neighborhoods, and the acceptance of resegregation in neighborhood schools by federal courts, have greatly limited the possibilities for present and future school desegregation. As a result, the separation of white children from children of color is increasing. Indeed, recent government data indicate that segregation of black from white children in urban schools is high and has increased a little over the last decade.[3] Increased school segregation is particularly significant because residential segregation has decreased slightly during this same period.[4]

In this essay we discuss numerous reasons why desegregated schooling is important for all children, including the provision of improved social and learning environments for all. Indeed, school desegregation is important for segregated children of color because, as is often said, "green follows white"—that is, schools with white student majorities typically get better educational resources from those (usually white) officials who have the power to provide such socioeconomic resources.

In the next section we briefly examine the development of the racist foundation of the United States and define the concept of *systemic racism*. We argue here that racial segregation in schools has long been a central part of systemic racism in the United States and that attempts at serious desegregation of schools were limited mostly to the decades from the 1950s to the 1970s. These efforts at significant school desegregation were soon followed by backtracking by most white authorities on earlier commitments to desegregation such as those announced in the celebrated 1954 *Brown I* decision. The next two sections review the successful strategies of the NAACP in persuading U.S. courts to knock down the wall of legal segregation, including a discussion of the *Brown I* decision and its mixed impact on U.S. schools and society. We then examine the slow implementation of *Brown I* until the mid-1960s and the backing off on significant implementation that began by the mid-1970s. We also briefly assess the recent reassertion by the federal courts of the previously discredited *Plessy* doctrine that school segregation is natural and cannot be eradicated successfully by government intervention. Next we examine some of the successes of school desegregation, including the greater access of children of color to the educational, networking, and job access resources and opportunities generally available to white students. We also discuss the importance of school desegregation for all students, including white children, and for the future of a country that will, in coming decades, contain a majority of people whose origins lie in areas of the world other than Europe. In the following section we evaluate the impact of early desegregation on the child pioneers and the continuing segregation that exists within ostensibly desegregated schools, largely because of discrimination within schools by white students, faculty, and administrators. We also delineate the continuing institutionalized discrimination in school curricula, tracking, and testing programs and the linkages of racial stratification to class stratification. Next we examine the role of leading white policymakers and politicians in failing to provide the support, resources, and services needed to enable teachers and students of all racial, gender, and class backgrounds to achieve society's often expressed goal of educational excellence. In the conclusion we summarize the successes and failures of school desegregation and accent the strengths of black children, parents, and communities in working for racial desegregation against great odds and in successfully pressing the United States closer to its long expressed ideas of "liberty and justice for all."

The Racist Foundation of U.S. Society

This great and growing segregation of schoolchildren along racial lines is unsurprising for those familiar with U.S. history. Over centuries of colonial and U.S. development, whites created a system of systemic racism—initially in the enslavement of African Americans and genocidal land-taking that targeted Native Americans. The fifty-five white men who drafted the U.S. Constitution, and then implemented it, built into the country's foundation certain mechanisms designed to maintain the enslavement of African Americans for the purpose of unjustly enriching many white Americans. These enslavement mechanisms were not removed until eight decades later, and racial segregation was soon put in place. Legal segregation was a system of near-slavery for most African Americans; it was enshrined in state statutes and federal and state court decisions for nine decades. Whites have enforced various types of racial separation since the mid-seventeenth century, when the status of African Americans became that of enslavement for life.[5] Today, school segregation is but part of a centuries-old system of racism.

Systemic racism involves the racialized exploitation and subordination of Americans of color by white Americans. It encompasses the racial stereotyping, prejudices, and emotions of whites, as well as the discriminatory practices and racialized institutions engineered to produce the long-term domination of African Americans and other people of color. At the heart of systemic racism are discriminatory practices that generally deny Americans of color the dignity, opportunities, and privileges available to whites individually and collectively.

Some recognition of racism's systemic character is occasionally seen at the highest levels of national leadership. For example, Justice John Marshall Harlan, dissenting in the 1883 *Civil Rights Cases,* explained why oppression of blacks persisted after slavery: "That there are burdens and disabilities [that] constitute badges of slavery and servitude, and that the power to enforce by appropriate legislation the Thirteenth Amendment may be exerted by legislation of a direct and primary character, for the eradication, not simply of the institution, but of its badges and incidents, are propositions which ought to be deemed indisputable."[6]

In his minority view, the government had the right to eradicate racial badges, burdens, and the disability of slavery in the form of persisting discrimination.[7] More recently, in the 1968 case of *Jones v. Alfred H. Mayer Co.,* the Supreme Court condemned housing discrimination, ruling that "[w]hen racial discrimination herds men into ghettos and makes their ability to buy property turn on the color of their skin, then it too is a relic of slavery."[8] In his concurring opinion, Justice William O. Douglas added: "Some badges of slavery remain today. While the institution has been outlawed, it has remained in the minds and hearts of many white men. Cases which have come to this Court depict a spectacle of slavery unwilling to die. . . . Negroes have been excluded over and again from juries. . . . They have been made to attend segregated and inferior schools. . . . They have been forced to live in segregated residential districts."[9] Moreover, since the end of legal segregation, many whites have continued imposing the burdens of a "slavery unwilling to die" in a wide range of discriminatory practices.

The imposed segregation of racial groups and the larger reality of systemic racism are the normal condition of U.S. society. School segregation separates, on the basis of race, those defined by whites as different, and segregation is buttressed by an ideology that asserts that whites are superior. As one commentator has noted: "Black school children are not injured as much by a school board's placement of them in a school different from that in which it has placed white school children, so much as by the reality that the school exists within a larger system that defines it as the inferior school and its pupils as inferior persons."[10]

Attempts at desegregation in the 1950s to 1970s were part of a brief period of progressive impulse. Such efforts need constant renewal, for arrangements established for centuries have a strong social inertia. Systemic racism stays in place so long as there is no counter pressure forcing change. Briefly, the civil rights movement—together with increased black political participation and international competition with the former Soviet Union for the allegiance of non-European peoples[11]—pressed some white leaders to take notice of racial discrimination and move toward increased justice.

During the 1950s and 1960s, under pressure from black leaders, churches, and civil rights organizations, white liberals pressed for desegregation, especially in the South. By the 1970s, however, most white liberals were backtracking on commitments to substantial desegregation. Backtracking has been widespread since the 1980s due to the rise of presidential administrations and courts controlled by conservatives. White conservatives have been joined by a few conservatives of color, such as Supreme Court justice Clarence Thomas and former University of California regent Ward Connerly, in blocking further progress in societal desegregation. The failure of school desegregation lies primarily in the hands of those with the greatest political, economic, and civic power, who have long been mostly white. White elites—including school board members, leaders of civic and business organizations, state and local legislators, and judges in state and federal courts—have made decisions that have reversed progress toward substantial school desegregation since the 1970s. A recent example is the June 28, 2007, ruling of the U.S. Supreme Court, which outlawed the voluntary use of race-conscious admissions procedures by local school districts to desegregate racially isolated schools in Seattle, Washington (*Parents Involved in Community Schools v. Seattle School District No 1*), and Louisville, Kentucky (*Meredith v. Jefferson County Public Schools*).

Before *Brown*: Successful Strategies of the NAACP

In the early 1950s, on the eve of *Brown,* the United States, and especially the South, had in place extremely oppressive conditions for African Americans and many other people of color. U.S. apartheid was extensive, and the civil rights movement was accelerating. One gets some feeling for the continuing burdens of "slavery unwilling to die" in this comment from a black teacher who long lived under legal segregation:

> In those days, black people in their community had all the things that they had, because they were set aside from the white community, and we had all the things we needed to sustain us. . . . We had no affiliation with the whites [in school] whatsoever. Everything was separate and unequal. . . . We had aspirations but we were limited since we were in the black world, that's where we lived. . . . You thought . . . that everything was alright, and we were not looking out onto the white world because if you ventured out, you were stopped before you could even get started. And in those days there was just a definite dividing line of black or white. White over here; black over here. . . . It was a black and white world. No coming together on anything.[12]

In most U.S. areas, African Americans were forced by law or by informal discrimination to live in very segregated conditions, attend very segregated schools, suffer discrimination in public facilities, take less desirable jobs, face higher unemployment, and live on family incomes less than half those of whites.[13] In the South, African Americans faced an extreme racial etiquette requiring constant deference to whites of all ages. Resistance often brought severe punishment—loss of jobs, burned houses, home evictions, mortgage foreclosures, loss of credit, beatings, and lynchings.

In the face of real or threatened violence, it took great courage for African Americans, including NAACP members and lawyers, to mount large-scale legal efforts to bring down the walls of segregation, first in colleges and universities in the period from 1930 to 1950, and then in public schools.[14] This effort eventually culminated in the pathbreaking *Brown v. Board of Education,* which broke dramatically with legally coerced segregation.[15] Mounting legal attacks in several states, courageous NAACP lawyers sought school desegregation as a strategy to secure equal educational opportunity.[16] The intent was to dethrone the *Plessy v. Ferguson* doctrine of "separate but equal" as the defining law.[17] Robert Carter, an

NAACP lawyer and later a federal judge, concluded these efforts were necessary to move to broader goals: "It was not until *Brown I* was decided that blacks were able to understand that the fundamental vice was not legally enforced *racial segregation* itself; that this was a mere by-product, a symptom of the greater and more pernicious disease—white supremacy."[18]

The *Brown* Decision: Constitutional, Moral, and Political Successes

Successful efforts by African Americans to end legal segregation showed how pervasive racism was in American society. The organized efforts of African Americans and their nonblack allies motivated elite whites to end apartheid, and thus enter the modern sociopolitical world. The *Brown* decision did not transpire because of the goodness of white hearts, but rather as the culmination of a long struggle by black children, men, and women.[19] Without this enormous effort, the United States today might still be a backwater among the world's industrialized countries, indeed as a country trying to come to terms with apartheid institutions.

Finally, in 1954, nine white men were pressed by these efforts to see how unjust racial segregation was. At the heart of *Brown* was this broadly framed declaration:

> We conclude that in the field of public education the doctrine of "separate but equal" has no place. Separate educational facilities are inherently unequal. Therefore, we hold that the plaintiffs and others similarly situated for whom the actions have been brought are, by reason of the segregation complained of, deprived of the equal protection of the laws guaranteed by the Fourteenth Amendment.[20]

With this statement, and with the rejection of previous court decisions upholding segregation, the Supreme Court rejected legal school segregation in the numerous states that still required or allowed it. With this broad framing, the Court asserted that the federal government has an obligation to extend full rights to African Americans, who were finally recognized by the Court as first-class citizens—a category to which they had been denied membership for centuries: "Segregation in the public schools is condemned for producing second-class citizenship for African Americans both because it imposed a stigma on them (as persons not fit to go to school with whites) and because it did not adequately prepare them to be effective citizens."[21]

Brown had an important psychological impact on black Americans and others committed to desegregating U.S. society, for it indicated that desegregation struggles were sanctioned by whites on the country's highest court. *Brown* provided moral encouragement for those active in accelerating the civil rights movement. As one commentator has noted, "Civil rights leaders repeatedly invoked *Brown* in their political and moral arguments against segregation."[22] They also cited the decision as moral authority for demonstrations. At the beginning of the 1955 Montgomery bus boycott, Dr. Martin Luther King Jr. alluded to *Brown* in a speech: "If we are wrong, the Constitution of the United States is wrong."[23] The success of that boycott was in turn facilitated by lawyers who filed suits against bus segregation.

Brown provided the moral and legal authority for ending segregation. The decision was interpreted by numerous judges as a mandate to dismantle state-created segregation. New discrimination cases came to courts in such areas as public accommodations and voting, and an end to discrimination was mandated in most cases, including interracial marriages. Official segregation in public facilities began to end, first in border states, then in most southern areas.[24] *Brown* remains a beacon of liberty for many people in the United States and globally, including those seeking voting rights, gender equity in sports, freedom from harassment based on gender and sexual orientation, multicultural education, bilingual education, special education, and international human rights.[25] As one commentator has noted: "Many people take the Constitution to express the nation's deepest moral commitments. When the Supreme Court said that segregation could not be reconciled with the Constitution, it told the nation that segregation was wrong. . . . Even today *Brown* stands as the Court's deepest statement on the central issue in American history—how Americans of all races should treat one another."[26]

Problems and Failures Since *Brown*: The Timidity of Federal Courts

We now turn to the reasons why the *Brown* decision has not brought the extent or quality of school desegregation originally envisioned by the NAACP and other groups that sought major changes in U.S. racism. *Brown* and its implementation signaled that ending racial apartheid would come only at the pace that whites in the governing elite would allow. In this sense, the modest character of the decision reflected many elements of systemic racism, for few white leaders, including federal judges, envisioned fully dismantling that racism. Neither the 1954 *Brown* decision (*Brown* I) nor the 1955 implementation decision (*Brown* II)[27] clearly spelled out what constituted "desegregation," nor what the steps were to end segregation described and mandated. One reason for the failure of *Brown* I to significantly desegregate the schools in the first decade after 1954 was the weakness of the 1955 *Brown* II decision, which articulated the "with all deliberate speed" formula for implementing desegregation.[28] This failure was amplified by the unwillingness of President Dwight Eisenhower to back the Court's decrees with full federal authority in the face of intense opposition by millions of white parents, school officials, civic leaders, legislators, and governors, as well as by local supremacist groups. Given the racist views of most white leaders, including a president who revealed his racist stereotypes to Chief Justice Warren,[29] the vacillating action against racial discrimination was unsurprising. Systemic racism was too fundamental for them to accede to a head-on attack on its many oppressive realities. For that reason, school desegregation would come only slowly in the South and would never be fully realized in most northern and western cities.

Not until the late 1960s and early 1970s did the Supreme Court and other federal courts begin to force meaningful school desegregation on the South. A series of important cases finally expanded the requirements for desegregation. In a 1968 case, *Green v. County School Board of New Kent County,* the Court held that "freedom of choice" plans were insufficient, and belatedly put pressure on segregated school systems to make greater progress by requiring that segregation be eliminated "root and branch"—that students, teachers, staff, transportation, and extracurricular facilities be desegregated.[30] In *Swann v. Charlotte-Mecklenberg Board of Education,* in 1971, the Court ruled that desegregation plans grounded in residential patterns for student assignments were inadequate, and aggressive action had to be taken to desegregate, including busing if necessary.[31] Gradually, as evidenced by the "root and branch" language, justices of the Supreme Court began to realize the extent of the systemic racism underlying school segregation.

Then, by the mid-1970s, new conservative appointments to the Court presaged a long-term movement—lasting to the present day—away from eradicating the burdens of "slavery still unwilling to die" in public schools, as well as other institutions.[32] For example, in *Milliken v. Bradley,* a conservative Supreme Court blocked local officials' attempts at a metropolitan-wide school desegregation plan combining the city of Detroit and its suburbs.[33] Dissenting in this case, Justice Marshall (joined by three other justices) noted that after decades of steps toward desegregation, the Court was seriously backtracking: "Notwithstanding a record showing widespread and pervasive racial segregation in the educational system provided by the State of Michigan for children in Detroit, this Court holds that the District Court was powerless to require the State to remedy its constitutional violation. . . . Our precedents . . . firmly establish that where, as here, state-imposed segregation has been demonstrated, it becomes the duty of the State to eliminate root and branch all vestiges of racial discrimination and to achieve the greatest possible degree of actual desegregation."[34]

Since this decision, the Supreme Court and courts of appeals decisions have generally retreated on the commitment to desegregate. In a 1986 case, *Riddick v. Norfolk,* the Fourth Circuit was the first to allow a southern school district that declared itself "unitary"—that is, not officially segregated—to abandon its desegregation plan and escape federal supervision.[35] By the 1990s, courts allowed many school systems to abandon desegregation. The *Board of Education of Oklahoma v. Dowell* and *Freeman v. Pitts* decisions indicated that the Supreme Court would permit large-scale resegregation of schools.[36] The *Freeman* decision gave lower court judges much discretion to abandon supervision of desegregation before a school district was in full compliance.[37] Today, as Orfield and Eaton note, "[d]esegregation remedies can even be removed when achievement gaps between the races have widened, or even if a district has never fully implemented an effective desegregation plan."[38] The current Supreme Court view, which was recently reflected in the 2007 rulings in *Parents Involved in Community Schools v. Seattle School District No 1* and *Meredith v. Jefferson County Public Schools* prohibiting the use of race conscious admissions plans to achieve desegregation, seems similar to assumptions discredited by *Brown* that segregation in schools is "natural," cannot be eradicated by government, and that authorities can be trusted to act in a nondiscriminatory way in decisions about educating black children.[39] For the current Court, "separate but equal" is constitutional if racial segregation is not openly directed by government officials.

Advantages to Desegregation: Access to Resources and Opportunities

When and where government officials have implemented substantial school desegregation with commitment, resources, and significant public support, it has generally worked to the benefit of all. Even where officials have only partially desegregated schools, we see substantial gains. In numerous ways, school desegregation has been successful, despite its limitations.

Providing Greater Access to Educational Resources

From the beginning, black parents and community leaders sought desegregation primarily to secure greater access to educational and related socioeconomic resources. They did *not* seek desegregation because they felt that black children needed to sit with whites to be educated. The assumption has always been that better school resources come in racially desegregated schools, and this in turn usually means better learning environments and greater achievements for children of color.

In general, these assumptions have been correct. Research shows that attending desegregated schools usually facilitates achievement for black students. One major study found that "black third-graders in predominantly white schools read better than initially similar blacks who have attended predominantly black schools."[40] Another extensive review found that most research studies of desegregation showed some positive effects on academic performance: "African American and Hispanic students learn somewhat more in schools that are majority White as compared to their academic performance in schools that are predominantly non-White."[41] In addition, research on more than 1,800 students in Charlotte-Mecklenburg schools found that black *and* white children did better in substantially desegregated schools than in segregated schools. Mickelson, the study's author, concludes from extensive data that "the more time both black and white students spend in desegregated elementary schools, the higher their standardized test scores in middle and high school, and the higher their track placements in secondary school."[42] One major reason that desegregation in schools facilitates achievement for black students is that the most segregated schools (with children of color as the majority) get less in the way of socioeconomic and human resources.

Providing Greater Access to Networking Resources

School desegregation has brought African American, Latino, Native American, Asian American, and other students of color improved access to important job networks, most of which are controlled by white employers. Often greater in desegregated schools, networking resources help students later on in securing good jobs and advanced education. Black students from desegregated, substantially white schools typically are more successful in entering into the high-paying job and college networks than those students from traditionally segregated schools. Going to a substantially desegregated high school significantly increases the chance that a black or Latino student will attend college.[43] Black students in desegregated schools are more likely to attend historically white colleges, work and live in desegregated environments, and have friends from other racial groups. Going to desegregated schools increases the "pool of contacts and informants from whom African Americans can obtain information about available jobs," thereby increasing opportunities.[44] For children of color without much previous contact with whites, school desegregation may also help them develop coping strategies for dealing with racist whites in other settings.[45]

Desegregation has often forced white officials to deal with insufficient resources in historically black schools.[46] When schools are substantially desegregated, white officials typically spend *more money* on schools. When school systems resegregate with court approval, as many are now doing, per-student expenditure differentials again increase sharply. This is the lesson of big cities such as Milwaukee, where a recent report shows that the "separate but equal" notion increasingly accepted by courts fails. Per capita school expenditures for Milwaukee's children, mostly children of color, are now far lower than per capita expenditures for suburban children, who are mostly white. The differential is considerably more than one thousand dollars per child.[47] As the report notes: "Half a century after the U.S. Supreme Court outlawed separate and unequal schools based on race, the Milwaukee area has firmly returned to both separate and unequal education . . . [A]s the percentage of African-American students and students of color has risen in the Milwaukee Public Schools (MPS), funding per pupil has plummeted compared to funding in overwhelmingly white suburban districts."[48] The report also notes the role of state government: "The state of Wisconsin is constitutionally responsible for providing public education. Yet the state not only tolerates the funding gulf between Milwaukee and its suburban counterparts, it has instituted policies that allow the gap to widen."[49] This increasing gap is one consequence of state-sanctioned resegregation now spreading across the United States. Such resegregation will, doubtlessly, result in sharply reduced access for many students of color to those critical college and job networks that desegregation provides.

While the school desegregation process stemming from the _Brown_ decisions brought new opportunities and better access to resources for many children of color and their parents, at no point has a desegregated system equalized the array of educational resources. White officials and citizens are still unwilling to spend the money necessary to eradicate the long-term impact of racism in education. Interestingly, several studies of desegregation, including the famous Coleman report, downplayed school resources in explaining racial differentials. The 1966 Coleman report, for example, concluded that resources, such as per-pupil expenditures, were not greatly different between predominantly black and predominantly white schools and had no significant correlations with achievement; the important correlations of achievement were with socioeconomic status and family characteristics.[50] Many analysts have interpreted those studies as meaning that significant differentials in school resources no longer exist—or that what differences remain are not critical for achievement. However, even the Coleman report acknowledged that, while the differences in resources available to predominately white schools as compared to predominantly black schools are relatively small, those differences can _accumulate_ to a major difference in quality: "[T]he child experiences his environment as a whole, while the statistical measures necessarily fragment it. . . . [T]he statistical examination of difference in school environments for minority and majority children will give an impression of lesser differences than actually exist . . . so that the subsequent sections will probably tend to understate the actual disadvantage in school environment experienced by the average minority child compared to that experienced by the average majority child."[51]

To assess whether critical resources are different in predominantly white and predominantly black schools, one must consider the accumulation of small differences and an array of resources often neglected in comparative assessments of schools. Even the best desegregation plans are unable to equalize historically black and historically white schools in fundamental ways. Researchers examining desegregated Charlotte-Mecklenburg schools have found many differences in the level of resources available to predominantly black schools as compared to predominantly white schools. Schools with more white children are more likely to have adequate media centers, computers, and other technology, as well as newer buildings and more classes for advanced students. On the average, such schools have more teachers (regardless of race) with substantial teaching experience.[52] Research indicates that other critical resources, such as the availability of small classes and college placement courses, are not equitably distributed.[53] Today, de facto segregated schools are segregated not only by racial group, but also by income. Most black and Latino children remain in schools where low-income children are the majority, yet most white children attend schools where the majority of students are middle class. Schools where the children's parents have higher incomes usually have an array of resource advantages, while those in low-income communities are likely to have fewer teachers, less adequate libraries, and fewer advanced courses.[54] Again, the problem of racial segregation is inextricably linked to class stratification in U.S. society.

Providing Greater Opportunities to Experience Diversity

School desegregation has generated not only increased opportunities for black, Latino, and other children of color and their parents, but also new experiences for white children, parents, and teachers. Although since *Brown* many whites, in all regions, have chosen private schools and moved into higher-income communities where most children of color do not reside, the challenges of cooperatively living, learning, working, and participating democratically in a multiracial society and within a global economy are greater than ever before for all Americans.

Racial segregation exacts costs for whites in terms of fear, ignorance, conflict, and inhumanity.[55] Population trends indicate that by 2050 the United States will likely have a population in which people of color will compose a majority. Moral and practical reasons dictate building a country that expands socioeconomic and political participation in a multiracial-democracy framework.[56] School desegregation provides opportunities for all, including whites, to dismantle historical barriers, because students in truly desegregated schools gain opportunities to learn about and associate with those with whom they might not otherwise interact. For example, in a study of young children in a multiracial preschool, researchers Debra Van Ausdale and Joe Feagin found that white children learn racial differences and how to discriminate at an early age, and that it is by experience, interaction, and education with children of color that they are able to reduce stereotypes and gain opportunities to establish friendships and understanding of others.[57]

Negative Impacts: Children in Desegregated Schools

The Severe Impact on Pioneering Black Children

In the first era of school desegregation, which took place in the late 1950s and early 1960s, Supreme Court justices, congressional leaders, and presidents failed dismally to provide strong supervision of court-ordered school desegregation. This lack of supervision signaled weak commitment to change and, as was quite foreseeable, encouraged white resistance. Federal officials left much actual desegregation up to courageous black children, parents, and community leaders. Children were lonely pioneers thrown into extremely hostile, formerly all-white environments. Desegregation's costs were very heavy for these child pioneers—costs that few whites, including white policymakers, have yet to acknowledge.

The social scientists testifying in the *Brown* I case presented data that segregation had a harmful impact on children by damaging self-esteem.[58] Ironically, because of feeble enforcement, desegregation also had a damaging psychological, and often physical, impact on numerous children of color. While there have been a few autobiographies, such as that written by Melba Pattillo Beals vividly recounting the traumatic experiences of nine Little Rock Central High students,[59] few studies have systematically examined the impact of desegregation on child pioneers. One attempt to examine such impact was a study conducted by sociologist Leslie Inniss in the 1990s of twenty-five black adults who had desegregated high schools in the South decades earlier. On the positive side, several reported making white friends, and most felt they received a better education under desegregation.[60]

Even though newly desegregated schools had some positive effects on black children, they limited other opportunities. For example, in predominantly black schools, a black child could try out for the cheerleading squad or run for class president, but this was not possible in newly desegregated schools. In addition, all these pioneers paid a high psychological and emotional price. Two were so hurt by the process that they had nervous breakdowns.[61] Interviewed as adults, numerous respondents were still in pain as they recalled negative desegregation experiences. Most reported being tormented constantly by white students, and sometimes even by teachers. One reported that "after a while all hell broke loose and they really started harassing us," while another noted that "we had a little group [of whites] that would meet us every morning, I mean they would say little ditties to us, it was sort of like entertainment."[62]

Inniss herself was a black student pioneer at a formerly white high school in the 1960s. She later recounted her emotionally battering experience: "During the first year, parents spit on me, called me a monkey, and used other intimidating behaviors while lining up on both sides of my morning pathway to the school, forming what I called a 'tunnel of terror.' The students defaced my locker, stole my books, and tore my clothing." She continued with an account of what happened the next year when President John F. Kennedy was shot: "Through my tears and sobs I heard one white student shout that was good for him because he was 'only for niggers anyway.' The third year brought more threats and indignities, ranging from warnings not to participate in certain extracurricular activities to a white boycott of a traditional school slumber party."[63]

As a result of extreme harassment, most students had a sense of decreased self-esteem or self-confidence. One former student noted that "desegregation left me with feelings of alienation and incompetence." Another explained: "We had to learn their way of doing things—acting, talking, dressing their way of being, but nobody was interested in our way. We wanted so badly to be accepted, we tried to do and be all they wanted and we were still rejected. Even today, I have a really big problem with rejection of any kind." Yet another described the severe physical effects: "To this day . . . I never eat breakfast. . . . I know it's because for those four years my stomach was so much in knots I couldn't eat before I went to school and then I couldn't eat lunch. I wouldn't sit in the lunchroom because of the things they would do. . . . [D]eep down you know that it's stuff that still affects you."[64]

How did they manage to survive the trauma perpetrated or allowed by white judges, politicians, teachers, principals, superintendents, school boards, parents, and bus drivers? Those who survived the experience reported on the importance of staying focused.[65] One child pioneer, now a successful lawyer, explained: "You just maintain and say, look my goal is to get out of here and make my grades and to get out of here and you just stay focused on that and you know it's a transition."[66] Recalling her own experiences, Inniss explained how she focused "on the belief that my endurance would make things better for my own children and others who would follow me."[67] Another pioneer noted that "forced integration was the worst thing that happened to our race," and added: "[W]e were forced to play their game by their rules but now my goal is to extract all their knowledge and use it to beat them at their own game. My job is not to help white folks but to educate my son so that he is prepared and he is able to compete with those people at a very early age and that's what I'm trying to teach him."[68]

What is most striking is that not one of these pioneers would do it over if they faced the situation again, and several shared the opinion that "they would never even consider sending [their] children to an integrated school."[69] In one of our recent interviews, another pioneer in southern school desegregation, now a successful administrator in higher education, recounted with great pain: "They beat me. They beat me every day that I went into that white school . . . I can't forget . . . I can't love them now."[70]

Reflecting on survival and resistance strategies that she used during the voluntary school choice period of desegregation in her southern town, Bernice Mc-

Nair Barnett has explained that she protected herself from the everyday "grind of racially motivated negative incidents" by withdrawing inwardly and using "tactics similar to those of POWs who successfully survive systematic personal attack and isolation. . . . I swore never to let 'them' see me cry. I was silent and found inner strength in the knowledge that I had done nothing to engender such race-based animosity." The costs were high, as Barnett describes:

> The years of spatial and social distancing, ostracizing, name-calling, pushing, shoving, jeering, and threatening were all a part of my daily . . . battles that gradually promoted my aloofness and silence. I was isolated and cut off from the world of my former Black peers (who saw my school desegregation choice as "trying to be White") as well as my new White peers (who were both hate filled bullies and otherwise good hearted but silent bystanders). Mine was a battle that was fought not in the newspapers or in front of the television cameras, but alone and with the everyday survival-resistance strategies I used in a small southern school. Thus, divorced from and unaccepted in both worlds, I lost my "voice."[71]

Significantly, in her analysis Inniss ponders another question: "I wonder what, if anything, did my experiences accomplish? The cumulative, multigenerational experience of entrenched racism has never been adequately presented, examined, or analyzed from a black point of view."[72] A key problem throughout the societal desegregation process, including that of schools, is that relatively few whites have ever cared about black experiences—what Lisa Delpit categorizes as the experiences of "other people's children."[73]

Continuing Discrimination in Schools: Teachers and Students

Since the days of child pioneers in desegregated schools, many white students, teachers, counselors, administrators, and parents have moderated their behavior, yet much racial hostility and discrimination remain in ostensibly desegregated schools. In the literature, we have not seen a study indicating that *any* historically white school has eliminated "root and branch" all major "burdens and disabilities" of racism. Most school desegregation has done little more than change the demographic mix of students and, less often, of faculty and administrators. Often the senior administrative staff at schools has remained overwhelmingly, if not entirely, white. In most desegregated schools, teachers are disproportionately, if not predominantly, white, and many other features of school settings remain white-normed. Given the realities of institutionalized racism, black children in desegregated schools with white majorities have continued to face racial harassment and other discrimination.[74]

Significantly, hostile racial climates in desegregated schools seldom have been researched systematically. Reviewing the literature, we have found relatively little discussion of racial attitudes of, or discrimination by, white teachers, principals, staff, and students.[75] We see little analysis of how discrimination affects everyday school performance. Some analysts even argue that significant racial bias on the part of white (and other) teachers exhibited in learning settings is unlikely or unimportant. Thus, Jere Brophy has argued that "[f]ew teachers can sustain grossly inaccurate expectations for many of their students in the face of daily feedback that contradicts those expectations."[76] Emil Haller has argued that, while there are likely prejudiced teachers, "the problem [of student achievement] does not seem to be of that nature. Conceiving it so is to confuse the issue, to do a serious injustice to the vast majority of teachers."[77] Whites tend to downplay the importance of the racial thinking or discrimination exhibited by whites in desegregated schools. One study of a desegregated New England middle school found that most teachers said they tried to ignore racial issues; they "denied that they noticed children's race not only when the researchers were present but also among themselves."[78]

We have found no specific surveys of white teachers and students in desegregated schools, yet it seems probable that many of these whites hold views similar to the majority of whites questioned in recent national surveys. In these studies, a majority admit to holding negative stereotypes of African Americans.[79] Given the likelihood that many white teachers, principals, parents, and students hold similar stereotypes, future research studies of children of color will probably find in school settings substantial discrimination that is linked to stereotypes. Researchers have found that racial bias in white (and other) teachers' expectations affects student performance; as Ronald Ferguson shows, this discrimination takes the form of teachers not expecting the same performance from black and white children, or from black and white children with comparable test scores. Four experimental studies show that teachers are less supportive of black students than white students in situations where they are matched for ability or randomly assigned. In one study, black students got less feedback after mistakes and fewer hints than comparable whites. Similarly, observation studies in desegregated classrooms have found that teachers are more likely to encourage white students than black students to participate actively in class. This discriminatory behavior on the part of teachers likely affects student achievement. Reviewing the literature, Ferguson concludes that "teachers' perceptions, expectations, and behaviors probably do help to sustain, and perhaps even to expand, the black-white test score gap."[80]

One famous study of white children showed that those who feel stereotyped often do not perform as well as they would without the stereotyping. Teacher Jane Elliott divided her all-white third-grade class into privileged and unprivileged children based on eye color. Those with the favored color got better treatment from the teacher. The experiment showed the strong impact of negative and positive teacher expectations on students.[81] Whatever their socioeconomic backgrounds, black children carry the burden of regularly confronting white negativity—a symbolic reality that affects everyday interactions and achievements. Research by Claude Steele and Joshua Aronson indicates that academically successful black students are often concerned that scoring low on a test will feed stereotypes that blacks are less intelligent. In research where racial characteristics of successful black students are highlighted for them prior to an academic test, such as by having them indicate on a form their "race," they do not do as well as when nothing is said about racial characteristics. Accenting the "stereotype threat" can have negative effects on how well black students, regardless of class backgrounds, do on tests and other performance situations.[82]

Still, even these important studies do not examine the array of other discriminatory actions targeting children of color in desegregated schools. White teachers, principals, counselors, and students—as well as office, cafeteria, janitorial, transportation, and security personnel—act in ways that undermine the self-confidence of students of color and make learning difficult. In a biographical account, white professor Sharon Rush, who is raising a biracial adopted daughter, gives numerous examples of how whites regularly sabotage the educational growth of her talented daughter. White teachers have discriminated against her daughter over many years in public and private schools. This discrimination involves differential expectations and discrimination in class assignments, curriculum, placement of desks, and sports.[83] In their study of a multiracial daycare center, Van Ausdale and Feagin found that white children also caused substantial psychological harm to children of color. They also found that white students often do discriminatory things that interfere with school performance of children of color.[84]

Continuing Racial Bias in the School Curriculum

In almost all desegregated school systems, the curriculum has stayed mostly the same as it was before desegregation—with, for the most part, token gestures to the history of formerly excluded students. The orientation of many white teachers and administrators in desegregated schools seems to be one-way acculturation of children of color into a white worldview. In a 1978 study of desegregated classrooms, Ray Rist found a widespread orientation among teachers to having black students acculturate to white ways.[85] Since the 1970s, multicultural education has been added to school curricula—and accented in teacher education—yet most schools have not successfully integrated people of color, and their histories and experiences, throughout the kindergarten through twelfth-grade curriculum and over the school year.

Textbooks provide one example of the whitewashed curriculum, as they often communicate much inaccurate or elliptical historical information, especially in regard to racial discrimination, stereotyping, and conflict. Assessing high school history books, James Loewen found that the books ignored or downplayed the harsh realities of racial oppression, past and present.[86] For example, New York City's Wall Street is celebrated in textbooks for its economic role, yet none note that it began as a large colonial market where whites bought enslaved African Americans in a bloody business.[87] Not one major textbook made significant use of African American sources in regard to racial issues, and not one "lets African Americans speak for themselves."[88]

Another curriculum bias lies in the uncritical use of literary "classics" that are often part of required reading. Analyzing schools' use of Mark Twain's *Huckleberry Finn*, Sharon Rush shows how widespread the requirement of reading this racist novel is in schools and what the consequences are for children. Not only does the novel bombard readers, including black children, with more than two hundred "nigger" epithets, but it is also riddled with racist stereotypes of African Americans, such as the explicit portrayal of heroic action by the enslaved protagonist "Jim" as indicative of his soul really being "white." While many teachers may use the novel to problematize slavery, typically the novel is not taught as a book that is pervaded with racist assumptions and stereotyping by its prominent author.[89]

More Second-Generation Segregation: Ability Tracking

One sees systemic discrimination in ostensibly desegregated schools in the widespread use by authorities of ability tracking that creates "second-generation" segregation. In desegregated schools, most children of color learn in segregated classroom tracks with fewer resources and less rigorous teaching than tracks for allegedly "more talented" students, most of whom are white because of bias in the selection process.[90] Derrick Bell underscored this problem over two decades ago: "Extra money for special programs with better, higher-paid teachers follows white students into special, upper-track classes even within integrated schools, where most blacks are trapped in lower-track, generally ineffective and less expensive course offerings."[91]

Tracking is well-remembered by students. In our interviews with people who attended desegregated schools, one white college student recounted his experience:

> I found out that even though we were always in mixed classes in elementary school, they were tracking us, like they had us divided into groups and were kind of watching us as we developed. . . . If you look at the racial mix of the classes, [the] honors track seemed to be predominately white and the lower,

like regular classes, would be predominately African American. . . . They'd be placed in the lower track so early on, that it was just impossible to break out of even if they had the ability level.[92]

Much research now shows that tracking assigns students of color "unjustifiably and disproportionately to lower tracks and almost excludes them from the accelerated tracks; it offers them inferior opportunities to learn and is responsible, in part, for their lower achievement."[93] Recalling this pattern, a middle-aged white teacher in our interview study recently commented:

I remember in the fourth grade when the first time I actually had a black classmate. I specifically remember [him] reading along in class, and I think it was the word Nazi that came up. And I didn't know what the word was, but he knew; and I was kind of impressed by that. By the time I got to high school, or even junior high, when I started getting separated from other students . . . the number of minorities dropped precipitously. So by the time I was in high school, in honors classes, there were perhaps you know some Arab or Indian students in those classes with me. . . . African Americans and Latinos weren't in those classes.[94]

Significantly, African American students often get placed in tracks lower than their measured abilities indicate, even as measured by the racially biased conventional tests. Students in higher tracks typically get more attention and better resources, often including more experienced teachers and more rigorous instruction. Students in privileged tracks in early grades tend to perform better in later schooling, and thus over time "racially stratified tracks create a discriminatory cycle of restricted educational opportunities for minorities who are disproportionately assigned to lower tracks irrespective of their academic abilities."[95]

Several early studies showed that desegregated school systems that eliminated or significantly reduced ability tracking had better achievement results than those that maintained or increased tracking.[96] More recently, Roslyn Mickelson has summarized much school research: "[W]hen schools consistently employ practices to enhance equality of opportunity (including the elimination of tracking and ability grouping), desegregation brings clear, though modest academic benefits to black students and does no harm to whites."[97]

Interestingly, in her own Charlotte-Mecklenburg study, Mickelson found that breaking down tracking benefits whites, as well.[98] Thus, tracking has negative effects on all children, for they are much less likely to learn effective ways of interacting with people of different backgrounds. Homogeneous socializing limits the breakdown of racial-ethnic stereotyping.[99] Significant amounts of literature now indicate that the more diverse the learning milieu, the more likely people are to progress beyond rigid and stereotyped ways of thinking.[100]

Problems of Testing: Racial and Class Bias

Substantial racial and class biases exist in testing procedures used for placing children in educational programs. Most standardized tests, including so-called intelligence tests, measure learned skills, not some broad "intelligence."[101] Skills learned depend on resources in home and school environments, which often disadvantage the learning process of lower-income children.[102] Black and Latino children often do less well than whites on paper-and-pencil tests standardized on whites and created by educators who are overwhelmingly white. Such tests are typically skewed toward the knowledge—including subtle understandings—of the white middle-class minds that generate test items from within a limited racial-class experience. Traditional tests measure only certain skills and acquired knowledge—skills and knowledge not equally available to all racial groups because of centuries of discrimination. Successful achievement-test taking is a skill that white middle-class children are more likely to possess than working-class children, including most children of color. Aptitude tests, research indicates, have "on the whole favored prosperous youths and penalized poor ones."[103] Such testing clearly reflects the racial-class system. In addition, the testing situation can create the problem of test anxiety noted previously. At best, a small portion of human abilities are revealed on any achievement test.[104]

"Acting White": A Secondary Factor

Some researchers, such as John Ogbu, view achievement differences between black and white children as more likely the result of negative black school cultures than of problems with institutionalized racism in schools. That is, academically successful black students are put down so much by their black peers that they cannot achieve as well as whites. Ogbu gathered ethnographic data supposedly showing the severe effects of being put down for "acting white," as well as showing that black students and their parents do not put as much emphasis on education as whites.[105] We will examine later the fallacious notion that African Americans do not value education as much as whites, but we should note here that much research contradicts the notion that pressure from other students has severe and lasting effects on achievement of talented students. For example, Cook and Ludwig summarize that research as follows: "Black high school students are not particularly alienated from school. They are as likely as whites to expect to enter and complete college, and their actual rate of high school completion is as high as that among whites from the same socioeconomic background. Also, black and white students report that they spend about the same amount of time on homework and have similar rates of absenteeism."[106]

Despite the widespread belief that typical black students do not work as hard in school as white students, no research evidence exists for this stereotyped notion. Black and white high school students who do well in school are no more likely to be socially unpopular than other students. While successful students—black, white, Latino, Asian, Indian, and others—do periodically get taunts from less successful students, such comments usually "do not inflict especially grievous social damage."[107]

Children's Continuing Burdens:
Great Expectations, Little Support

Over the history of school desegregation, educators and politicians have often forgotten about the everyday lives and well-being of children. Repeatedly, children are sent to fight with bravery to implement and achieve society's desegregation goals, regardless of casualties. The enormity of the children's burden is seen in the unforgettable images of six-year-old Ruby Bridges bravely walking up steps escorted by federal marshals to a previously segregated school in New Orleans; of Elizabeth Eckfort walking resolutely with her head held high while flanked by whites yelling venomous epithets in Little Rock; of Vivian Malone and James Hood attempting to enter the University of Alabama as Governor George Wallace stands in the door; of James Meredith trying to enter "Ole Miss" as Governor Ross Barnett fuels rioters by declaring "segregation today, segregation forever"; or of Charlayne Hunter and Hamilton Holmes escorted by police at the University of Georgia after rioting whites burned crosses and Governor Ernest Vandiver vowed to let "not one, no, not one" black student enter. Such searing images emphasize the significance of black children's burden in achieving what adults had not achieved over centuries of oppression.

In a 2003 Supreme Court opinion regarding a University of Michigan affirmative action program, Justice Sandra Day O'Connor expressed the view that in twenty-five years the United States may not need to consider racial characteristics to achieve educational diversity.[108] Reflection on the 170–year history of racism in education casts doubt on that expectation. Over the last four presidential administrations, national school reform plans for enhancing the achievement of "all children" prompt both hope and caution for the next twenty-five years. It will likely take much more time for children of color to achieve parity with white children.

The four most widely publicized educational plans over the past twenty years have been controversial. *A Nation at Risk, America 2000: An Educational Strategy, Goals 2000: Educate America Act,* and *No Child Left Behind* are problematic in terms of expectations and results for children.[109] Some have fundamental flaws in design that are insensitive to the realities of many working-class children, a disproportionately large number of whom are African American, Latino, or Native American.

A Nation at Risk, a 1983 report of President Ronald Reagan's National Commission on Excellence in Education, had well-publicized expectations and strategies. It evaluated public schoolchildren unsympathetically: "Our nation is at risk, . . . [The] educational foundations of our society are presently being eroded by a rising tide of mediocrity that threatens our very future as a Nation and a people. . . . If an unfriendly foreign power had attempted to impose on America the mediocre educational performance that exists today, we might well have viewed it as an act of war."[110]

A Nation at Risk advocated education to support U.S. economic competition for "international standing and markets."[111] Excellence meant accountability for scores on standardized tests in English, mathematics, science, social studies, and computer science. Recommending a market-oriented educational system, higher standards and expectations, more learning time, school choice, teacher training, school-business alliances, and more citizen support, the report's goals were supposed to bring "all children" to a level of excellence.[112] *A Nation at Risk,* however, ignored the structural inequality in education demonstrated above—inequalities in resources from racism and classism—and placed an unfair burden on working-class children and parents from all backgrounds to meet its goals.

In the early 1990s, President George H. W. Bush proclaimed *America 2000: An Educational Strategy* as his plan for attaining excellence in public schools. *America 2000* again emphasized excellence in English, math, science, history, and geography, as well as common values, technical training, and business participation in a market-type system with school choice and vouchers.[113] Like *A Nation at Risk,* it did not achieve its goals, in large part because it failed to deal honestly with extreme inequalities generated by racism and classism in schools.

President Bill Clinton accented similar themes in his *Goals 2000: Educate America Act.* The Clinton plan called for "all children" to achieve excellence by 2000. Incorporating *America 2000* goals, it heralded great expectations: all children will enter school with a readiness to learn; the country will achieve a 90 percent high school graduation rate; children will demonstrate competency in challenging subjects; the United States will become first in the world in science and mathematics achievement; teachers will have new resources; schools will increase parental participation; all adults will be literate; schools will be free of drugs.[114] Again, *Goals 2000* did not adequately address the racial and class inequalities governing many children's lives. Indeed, while poor children are at much greater risk of academic failure than economically advantaged children, their families were attacked by the era's so-called welfare reforms,[115] which reduced the resources available for poor families to achieve educational goals.

More recently, President George W. Bush decreed his *No Child Left Behind* plan. Building on previous plans and emphasizing the pieties that "no child should be left behind" and that "every child should be educated to his or her full potential," Bush proposed closing the achievement gap through increased accountability in the form of extensive testing of children, annual assessments, and school transfers for students who "fail to make progress."[116] Such national testing strategies, however, have been tried before and have not achieved the expectations for "all children," particularly working-class children of color.

During school desegregation efforts following *Brown,* and under the afore-mentioned national reform plans, children (especially children of color) have borne the actual burden of school change and policy regression. National plans, like earlier court orders, have generated programs to improve educational per-formance, such as magnet schools. Yet the majority of children in public schools have been unable to achieve the plans' grand goals. In formulating national education plans, adults have not sufficiently considered the heavy burden placed on children and have neglected the great expenses in monetary and human capital necessary for children to reach parity in an educational footrace with a legacy of ball-and-chain impediments placed around the feet of children of color and/or working-class children.

Conclusion: Strengths of Black Children, Parents, and Communities

We see significant successes and major failures following in the wake of *Brown.* Racial desegregation is a major break with apartheid, and desegregation works best when resources—economic, educational, legal, and political—are put into it wisely. The racial world of the United States is much different now than it was in the decade before *Brown.*

We have documented important successes in desegregating educational in-stitutions as well as in the larger society. Research shows that desegregated schooling has a positive impact on academic achievement for most students, typically with substantial gains for students of color. Research demonstrates, too, that black students attending desegregated schools tend to do better in job and educational attainments later in life. Those students who have attended desegregated schools are more likely to attend college, work in desegregated environments, and have diverse friends. Researchers have shown that many stu-dents in desegregated schools become less stereotypical in their thinking about other groups—which equips them better for life in this increasingly multiracial society. Clearly, *Brown's* impact is not limited to education, for, as Judge Robert Carter has underscored, *Brown* brought about "a radical social transformation in this country and whatever its limited impact on the educational community, its indirect consequences of altering the style, spirit, and stance of race relations will maintain its prominence for many years to come."[117] *Brown,* together with other contemporaneous desegregation efforts, dismantled much of the legal architecture of antiblack oppression in the United States.

In spite of the substantial hostility African American students and other students of color face in desegregated schools, they have managed to achieve much. While historically and predominantly white school settings are social comfort zones for most whites, most black students integrated into these settings find themselves in difficult environments well outside their social comfort zones.[118] When black children face racism routinely, it is extraordinary that most do as well as they do in desegregated settings. The energy loss alone that results from dealing with hostility and discrimination may be enough to account for the remaining differences in school performance of white and black children. The extraordinary strength shown by black children in getting through a racialized day, as well as the academic achievements under these conditions, gets little discussion in most analyses of desegregation.[119] These strengths deserve extensive research, as they are likely based in the collective values and knowledge that African Americans have accumulated over centuries of struggles against racism.[120]

Indeed, we see evidence of the impact of successes in the civil rights struggle against racism and in the educational achievements of African Americans. Over the course of the 1950s and 1960s black students made dramatic educational gains. By the mid-1960s large numbers of black students were graduating from high school. The percentage graduating in the South increased from 35 percent in 1960 to 71 percent less than two decades later.[121] Historically black colleges saw dramatic increases in black college graduates, as did formerly segregated white colleges.

Nonetheless, research documents the continuing significance of discrimination in majority white colleges,[122] as well as the increasing disparity in the gender ratio among black students, especially because black men are more likely to drop out of college.[123] Thus, current problems in education reveal the interrelatedness of racial, gender, and class factors in the pipeline to achievement—with some parents and educators of black children now supporting the idea of Afrocentric (often all-male) academies.[124]

Today, African Americans, including students, place great emphasis on the importance of education in the larger society, despite historical relations of racial privilege that structure experiences of black students inside and outside of school classrooms. In one recent analysis, Judith Blau found that black students "have high educational aspirations, and they are more likely than whites to continue with their schooling at given test score levels." Black Americans with jobs are more likely to pursue education into adulthood than comparable whites. In surveys, African Americans show as much, or more, desire for education as whites, yet they are more likely than whites to understand the structural barriers African Americans face in attaining more education. Whites are more likely than blacks to view low socioeconomic status and lesser performance in school as indicators of personal failure, while blacks are more likely than whites to accent structural factors as barriers.[125]

We should situate the great difficulties in desegregating schools in the context of structural barriers created in this racist and classist society. In our interviews, a middle-aged white teacher recently commented: "I think what needs to be done nobody wants to do it. Like they talk about building one big giant school around here and everybody would go to it. . . . You can't have [names affluent school]—that's where all the money is at. . . . [B]ut [names poor school], they don't have a chance, and that's 80 percent, probably, minorities there."[126]

We cannot bring profound change in one area of this racist society by dismantling discrimination in schooling alone, no matter how well done. Racism is systemic and reflected in all major U.S. institutions. Those Americans who are not white are generally at a huge disadvantage relative to whites. Because the privileged are resistant to significant change, successful progress against racial discrimination constantly faces the threat of backtracking. In American society constant organization for change is necessary.

The Declaration of Independence articulated the great American ideal that "all men are created equal," a doctrine the founders meant to apply to white men with property. However, once this grand doctrine was articulated, subsequent generations have pressed for its application to ever-expanding groups of Americans. Thus, the Fourteenth Amendment was enacted to make newly freed African Americans into the full U.S. citizens they had not been before the Civil War: "All persons born or naturalized in the United States . . . are citizens of the United States and of the State wherein they reside. No State shall make or enforce any law which shall abridge the privileges or immunities of citizens of the United States; nor shall any State deprive any person of life, liberty, or property, without due process of law; nor deny to any person within its jurisdiction the equal protection of the laws."[127]

All government actions that overtly or covertly create or sustain racial segregation in any area of society operate to subordinate and stigmatize African Americans and thereby blatantly violate the Fourteenth Amendment's promise of full citizenship "privileges and immunities" and the "equal protection" of the laws for African Americans. The authors of the *Brown* decision glimpsed the great promise of equality for all that is embedded in the Declaration of Independence and in the Fourteenth Amendment, yet neither they nor their official governmental descendants have been willing to turn this rhetorical promise into a social and political reality. *That* is now *our* task.

Notes

We are indebted to Roslyn Mickelson for comments on an earlier draft, and to Danielle Dirks, Molly Recar, and Dana Schulte for comments and research assistance. This article was originally published in the *University of Illinois Law Review* 5 (2004): 1099–1130. Copyright to the *University of Illinois Law Review* is held by The Board of Trustees of the University of Illinois.

1. Peter Irons, *Jim Crow's Children: The Broken Promise of the Brown Decision* (New York: Viking, 2002), 338.

2. See Lawrence Bobo, James R. Kluegel, and Ryan A. Smith, "Laissez-Faire Racism: The Crystallization of a Kinder, Gentler, Anti-black Ideology," in *Racial Attitude in the 1990s: Continuity and Change,* ed. Steven A. Tuch and Jack K. Martin, 15–44 (Greenwood, Conn.: Praeger, 1997).

3. Irons, *Jim Crow's Children,* 289, 291–92.

4. John R. Logan, "Choosing Segregation: Racial Imbalance in American Public Schools 1999–2000" (unpublished research report, on file with authors, March 29, 2002).

5. Joe Feagin, *Racist America: Roots, Current Realities, and Future Reparations* (New York: Routledge, 2000), 9–10, 21–25.

6. *The Civil Rights Cases,* 109 U.S. 3, 35 (1883) (Harlan, J., dissenting).

7. Ibid. at 35–36 (Harlan, J., dissenting).

8. *Jones v. Alfred H. Mayer Co.,* 392 U.S. 409, 442–43 (1968).

9. Ibid., at 445 (Douglas, J., concurring) (internal citations omitted).

10. Charles Lawrence, "'One More River to Cross'—Recognizing the Real Injury in *Brown*: A Prerequisite to Shaping New Remedies," in *Shades of Brown: New Perspectives on School Desegregation,* ed. Derrick Bell (New York: Teachers College, Columbia University, 1980), 49, 53.

11. See Philp A. Klinkner and Rogers M. Smith, *The Unsteady March: The Rise and Decline of Racial Equality in America* (Chicago: University of Chicago Press, 1999), 3–4.

12. Wilhelmina Johnson, interview by Joel L. Buchanan, Samuel Proctor Oral History Program, University of Florida, Gainesville, Fla., May 27, 1981.

13. Feagin, *Racist America,* 57–66.

14. For colleges and universities, see, e.g., *Sipuel v. Board of Regents of the University of Oklahoma,* 332 U.S. 631 (1948); and *Sweatt v. Painter,* 339 U.S. 629 (1950). Public school cases include *Webb v. School District No. 90,* Johnson County, 206 P.2d 1066, 1073 (Kan. 1949) (stating that if a school district wants to maintain two buildings in its district, the allocation of students must be made "upon a reasonable basis without any regard at all as to color or race of the pupils within any particular territory"); *Mendez v. Westminster School District,* 64 F. Supp. 544, 549 (S.D. Cal. 1946) (concluding that segregation practices "clearly and unmistakably disregard rights secured by the supreme law of the land").

15. *Brown v. Board of Education,* 347 U.S. 483 (1954).

16. Robert L. Carter, "A Reassessment of *Brown v. Board,*" in Bell, *Shades of Brown,* 20, 21, 27.

17. *Plessy v. Ferguson,* 163 U.S. 537 (1896).

18. Carter, "A Reassessment of *Brown v. Board,*" 23.

19. Bernice McNair Barnett, "Invisible Southern Black Women Leaders in the Civil Rights Movement: The Triple Constraints of Gender, Race, and Class," *Gender and Society* 7 (1993): 162, 168–69; and Bernice McNair Barnett, "Unsung Women of *Brown v. Board of Education*" (unpublished study, on file with author, August 1, 2002).

20. *Brown v. Board of Education,* 347 U.S. at 495.

21. T. Alexander Aleinikoff, *Semblances of Sovereignty* (Cambridge, Mass.: Harvard University Press, 2002), 40.

22. Mark V. Tushnet, *Brown v. Board of Education: The Battle for Integration* (New York: Franklin Watts, 1995), 130.

23. Ibid., 131.

24. Richard Kluger, *Simple Justice: The History of Brown v. Board of Education and Black America's Struggle for Equality* (New York: Knopf, 1976), 750–51.

25. See, e.g., A. Reynaldo Contreras and Leonard A. Valverde, "The Impact of *Brown* on the Education of Latinos," *Journal of Negro Education* 63 (1994): 470, 478.

26. Tushnet, *Brown v. Board of Education,* 132, 136.

27. *Brown v. Board of Education,* 349 U.S. 294 (1955).

28. Ibid., at 301.

29. Feagin, *Racist America,* 113.

30. *Green v. County School Board of New Kent County,* 391 U.S. 430, 437–38 (1968).

31. *Swann v. Charlotte-Mecklenberg Board of Education,* 402 U.S. 1, 22–31 (1971).

32. Justices Blackman, Powell, and Rehnquist were all appointed by President Nixon between 1970 and 1971. See Ronald D. Rotunda, *Modern Constitutional Law,* 6th ed. (St. Paul, Minn.: West Group, 2000), lix.

33. *Milliken v. Bradley,* 418 U.S. 717, 745 (1974).

34. Ibid., at 782 (Marshall, J., dissenting).

35. *Riddick v. School Board of Norfolk,* 784 F.2d 521, 535–36 (4th Cir. 1986).

36. *Board of Education of Oklahoma v. Dowell,* 498 U.S. 237 (1991); *Freeman v. Pitts,* 503 U.S. 467 (1992).

37. *Freeman v. Pitts,* 503 U.S. at 492–99.

38. Gray Orfield and Susan E. Eaton, *Dismantling Desegregation: The Quiet Reversal of Brown v. Board of Education* (New York: New Press, 1996), 4.

39. See ibid., 26–27.

40. Christopher Jencks and Meredith Phillips, introduction to *The Black-White Test Score Gap,* ed. Christopher Jencks and Meredith Phillips (Washington: Brook-

ings Institution Press, 1998), 31. There was less effect on reading at higher grade levels and no consistent effect on math scores.

41. Jomills Henry Braddock and Tamela McNulty Eitle, "The Effects of School Desegregation," 5 (unpublished research paper, on file with authors).

42. Roslyn Arlin Mickelson, "The Academic Consequences of Desegregation and Segregation: Evidence from the Charlotte-Mecklenburg Schools," *North Carolina Law Review* 81 (2003): 1546 ("[T]he more time both black and white students spend in desegregated elementary schools, the higher their standardized test scores in middle and high school, and the higher their track placements in secondary school.").

43. Orfield and Eaton, *Dismantling Desegregation,* 53–54.

44. Braddock and Eitle, "The Effects of School Desegregation," 8–9.

45. Debra Van Ausdale and Joe R. Feagin, *The First R: How Children Learn Race and Racism* (Lanham, Md.: Rowman and Littlefield, 2001), 191–92.

46. Orfield and Eaton, *Dismantling Desegregation,* 64–71.

47. The Editors of Rethinking Schools, "The Return to Separate and Unequal: Metropolitan Milwaukee School Funding through a Racial Lens," *Rethinking Schools* 15, no. 3 (2001): i–ii.

48. Ibid., i.

49. Ibid.

50. James S. Coleman et al., *Equality of Educational Opportunity* (Washington: U.S. Department of Health, Education and Welfare, Office of Education, 1966), 3–34.

51. Ibid., 37.

52. Mickelson, "The Academic Consequences of Desegregation and Segregation," 1547.

53. Jencks and Phillips, introduction to *The Black-White Test Score Gap,* 12.

54. Orfield and Eaton, *Dismantling Desegregation,* 53, 69.

55. Feagin, *Racist America,* 197–202.

56. Ibid., 237–38.

57. Van Ausdale and Feagin, *The First R,* 126–27.

58. *Brown v. Board of Education,* 347 U.S. at 494.

59. Melba Pattillo Beals, *Warriors Don't Cry: A Searing Memoir of the Battle to Integrate Little Rock's Central High* (New York: Pocket Books, 1994).

60. Leslie Baham Inniss, "Historical Footprints: The Legacy of the School Desegregation Process," in *The Bubbling Cauldron: Race, Ethnicity, and the Urban Crisis,* ed. Michael P. Smith and Joe R. Feagin (Minneapolis: University of Minnesota Press, 1995), 142, 155.

61. Ibid., 151–53, 148, 149–50.

62. Leslie Baham Inniss, "Desegregation Pioneers: Casualties of a Peaceful Process," *International Journal of Contemporary Sociology* 31 (1994): 253, 259.

63. Leslie Baham Inniss, "School Desegregation: Too High a Price?" *Social Policy* 6 (1993): 6, 7.

64. Inniss, "Historical Footprints," 157, 154–55.

65. Ibid., 148.

66. Inniss, "Desegregation Pioneers," 259.

67. Inniss, "School Desegregation," 7.

68. Inniss, "Historical Footprints," 152.

69. Inniss, "Desegregation Pioneers," 268.

70. Bernice McNair Barnett and Joe Feagin, "Schooling Experiences: Voices of Many Colors" (unpublished research paper, on file with authors, November 1, 2003).

71. Bernice McNair Barnett, "Race, Gender, & Class in the Personal-Political Struggles of African Americans: Reclaiming Voice," in *Race, Gender, and Class in Sociology: Toward an Inclusive Curriculum*, ed. Jean Belkhir and Bernice McNair Barnett (Washington, D.C.: American Sociological Association, 1999), 34, 35–36.

72. Inniss, "School Desegregation," 7.

73. See Lisa Delpit, *Other People's Children: Cultural Conflict in the Classroom* (New York: New Press, 1995), xiii–xv.

74. Desegregation has also had a negative impact on black teachers, principals, and communities. In our research, we have accounts from black teachers that they have been forced out of classrooms, been demoted, or treated as assistants to white teachers. We also have accounts of desegregation's negative impact on the role of the black community's schools as community centers.

75. For some discussion, see Amanda Lewis, *Race in the School Yard: Negotiating The Color Line In Classrooms And Communities* (New Brunswick: Rutgers University Press, 2003), 12; Pamela Perry, *Shades of White: White Kids and Racial Identities in High School* (Durham: Duke University Press, 2002), 5–8, 199–202.

76. Jere E. Brophy, "Teacher-Student Interaction," in *Teacher Expectancies,* ed. Jerome Dusek (Hillsdale, N.J.: L. Erlbaum, 1985), 304.

77. Emil J. Haller, "Pupil Race and Elementary School Ability Grouping: Are Teachers Biased against Black Children?" *American Educational Research Journal* 22 (1985): 465, 481. We draw here on the summary in Ronald F. Ferguson, "Teachers' Perceptions and Expectations and the Black-White Test Score Gap," in Jencks and Phillips, *The Black-White Test Score Gap,* 273, 275–94.

78. Janet Ward Schofield, *Black and White in School: Trust, Tension, or Tolerance* (New York: Praeger, 1982), 51.

79. Lawrence Bobo, "Inequalities That Endure? Racial Ideology, American Politics, and the Peculiar Role of the Social Sciences" (unpublished research paper, on file with authors, October 26, 2001); see also Feagin, *Racist America,* 108–15.

80. Ferguson, "Teachers' Perceptions and Expectations," 294–95, 300, 313.

81. William Peters, *A Class Divided: Then and Now* (New Haven: Yale University Press, 1987), 163–70.

82. Claude M. Steele and Joshua Aronson, "Stereotype Threat and the Test Per-

formance of Academically Successful African Americans," in Jencks and Phillips, *The Black-White Test Score Gap,* 401–27, esp. 401, 422–26.

83. Sharon E. Rush, *Loving across the Color Line* (Lanham, Md.: Rowman and Littlefield, 2000), 1–8, 36–42, 51–71.

84. Van Ausdale and Feagin, *The First R,* 175–96.

85. Ray C. Rist, *The Invisible Children: School Integration in American Society* (Cambridge, Mass.: Harvard University Press, 1978).

86. James W. Loewen, *Lies My Teacher Told Me: Everything Your American History Textbook Got Wrong* (New York: New Press, 1995), 137–99.

87. See ibid., 142. Loewen notes: "In 1720, of New York City's population of seven thousand, 1,600 were African Americans, most of them slaves. Wall Street was the marketplace where owners could hire out their slaves by the day or week."

88. Ibid., 168.

89. Sharon E. Rush, "Emotional Segregation: Huckleberry Finn in the Modern Classroom," *University of Michigan Journal of Law Reform* 36 (2003): 305, 306, 308.

90. See generally Kenneth J. Meier, Joseph Stewart, Jr., and Robert E. England, *Race, Class, and Education: The Politics of Second Generation Discrimination* (Madison: University of Wisconsin Press, 1989).

91. Derrick Bell, "A Model Alternative Desegregation Plan," in Bell, *Shades of Brown,* 124, 136.

92. Barnett and Feagin, "Schooling Experiences."

93. Mickelson, "The Academic Consequences of Desegregation and Segregation," 1513, 1529–33.

94. Barnett and Feagin, "Schooling Experiences."

95. Mickelson, "The Academic Consequences of Desegregation and Segregation," 1532.

96. Thomas F. Pettigrew, "A Sociological View of the Post-*Milliken* Era," in *Milliken vs. Bradley: The Implications of Metropolitan Desegregation* (Washington, D.C.: U.S. Commission on Civil Rights, 1974), 53, 58.

97. Mickelson, "The Academic Consequences of Desegregation and Segregation," 1528–29.

98. Ibid.; telephone interview with Roslyn A. Mickelson, Professor of Sociology, University of North Carolina at Charlotte, January 19, 2004.

99. Mickelson, "The Academic Consequences of Desegregation and Segregation," 1533, 1532.

100. Patricia Gurin, Eric L. Dey, Sylvia Hurtado, and Gerald Gurin, "Diversity in Higher Education: Theory and Impact on Educational Outcomes," *Harvard Educational Review* 72 (2002): 330, 330–66.

101. N.J. Block and Gerald Dworkin, "IQ, Heritability, and Inequality," in *The IQ Controversy,* ed. N. J. Block and Gerald Dworkin (New York: Pantheon, 1976), 410, 411.

102. Joe R. Feagin and Clairece Y. Feagin, *Racial and Ethnic Relations,* 7th edition (Upper Saddle River, N.J.: Prentice Hall, 2003), 164–65.

103. Nicholas Lemann, *The Big Test: The Secret History of the American Meritocracy* (New York: Farrar, Straus and Giroux, 2000), 271.

104. Block and Dworkin, "IQ, Heritability, and Inequality," 411.

105. John U. Ogbu, *Black American Students in an Affluent Suburb: A Study of Academic Disengagement* (Mahwah, N.J.: L. Erlbaum Associates, 2003), 198–203, 219–21.

106. Philip J. Cook and Jens Ludwig, "The Burden of 'Acting White': Do Black Adolescents Disparage Academic Achievement?" in Jencks and Phillips, *The Black-White Test Score Gap,* 375, 390.

107. Ibid., 391.

108. *Grutter v. Bollinger,* 539 U.S. 306, 343 (2003). O'Connor wrote, "We expect that 25 years from now, the use of racial preferences will no longer be necessary to further the interest approved today."

109. *A Nation at Risk: The Imperative for Educational Reform* (Washington, D.C.: National Commission on Excellence in Education, 1983); U.S. Department of Education, *America 2000: An Educational Strategy* (Washington, D.C.: U.S. Department of Education, 1991); *Goals 2000: Educate America Act,* Public Law 103–227, 108 Stat. 125 (1994); *No Child Left Behind Act of 2001,* Public Law 107–110, 115 Stat. 1425 (2002).

110. *A Nation at Risk,* 5–6.

111. Ibid., 6.

112. William A. Firestone et al., *The Progress of Reform: An Appraisal of State Education Initiatives* (New Brunswick, N.J.: Center for Policy Research in Education, 1989), 8–9.

113. U.S. Department of Education, *America 2000.*

114. *Goals 2000: Educate America Act,* 108.

115. *Personal Responsibility and Work Opportunity Reconciliation Act of 1996,* Public Law 104–193, 110 Stat. 2105 (1996).

116. *No Child Left Behind Act of 2001,* 115.

117. Carter, "A Reassessment of *Brown v. Board,*" 21.

118. Joe R. Feagin, Hernan Vera, and Nikitah Imani, *The Agony of Education: Black Students at White Colleges and Universities* (New York: Routledge, 1996), 7–9.

119. See generally Jencks and Phillips, *The Black-White Test Score Gap.*

120. See, e.g., Yanick St. Jean and Joe R. Feagin, *Double Burden: Black Women and Everyday Racism* (Armonk, N.Y.: M. E. Sharpe, 1998), 192–208, which discusses history and its effects on African American women.

121. Gavin Wright, "The Economics of Civil Rights," 12 (unpublished paper prepared for the Citadel Conference on the Civil Rights Movement in South Carolina, on file with authors, March 5–8, 2003).

122. Joe R. Feagin, *The Continuing Significance of Racism: U.S. Colleges and Uni-*

versities (Washington, D.C.: American Council on Education, Office of Minorities in Higher Education, 2002).

123. Karen W. Arenson, "Colleges Struggle to Help Black Men Stay Enrolled," *New York Times,* December 30, 2003, A1.

124. Ronnie Hopkins, *Educating Black Males: Critical Lessons in Schooling, Community, and Power* (Albany: State University of New York Press, 1997), 94.

125. Judith R. Blau, *Race in the Schools: Perpetuating White Dominance?* (Boulder, Colo.: Lynne Rienner Publishers 2003), 209, 208.

126. Barnett and Feagin, "Schooling Experiences."

127. U.S. Constitution, amend. 14, sec. 1.

7

From Racial Liberalism to Racial Literacy

Brown v. Board of Education and the Interest-Divergence Dilemma

Lani Guinier

On its fiftieth anniversary, *Brown v. Board of Education* no longer enjoys the unbridled admiration it once earned from academic commentators. Early on, the conventional wisdom was that the courageous social engineers from the National Association for the Advancement of Colored People Legal Defense and Educational Fund (NAACP LDEF), whose inventive lawyering brought the case to fruition, had caused a social revolution. Legal academics and lawyers still widely acclaim the *Brown* decision as one of the most important Supreme Court cases in the twentieth century, if not since the founding of our constitutional republic. *Brown*'s exalted status in the constitutional canon is unimpeachable, yet over time its legacy has become complicated and ambiguous.[1]

The fact is that fifty years later, many of the social, political, and economic problems that the legally trained social engineers thought the Court had addressed through *Brown* are still deeply embedded in our society. Blacks lag behind whites in multiple measures of educational achievement, and within the black community, boys are falling further behind than girls. In addition, the will to support public education from kindergarten through twelfth grade appears to be eroding despite growing awareness of education's importance in a knowledge-based society. In the Boston metropolitan area in 2003, for example, poor people of color were at least three times more likely than poor whites to live in severely distressed, racially stratified urban neighborhoods. Whereas poor, working-class, and middle-income whites often lived together in economically stable suburban communities, black families with incomes above $50,000 were twice as likely as white households earning less than $20,000 to live in neighborhoods with high rates of crime and concentrations of poverty. Even in the so-called liberal North, race still segregates more than class. Gerald N. Rosenberg, emphasizing the limited roles courts can generally play, bluntly summed up his view of *Brown*'s legacy: "The Court ordered an end to segregation and segregation was not ended." If *Brown* was a decision about integration rather than constitutional principle, Mark Tushnet observed in 1994, it was a failure.[2]

Even as constitutional principle, the Court's analysis and the formal equality rule it yielded became more troubling in the intervening years. Presented with psychological evidence that separating black children from whites "solely because of their race generates a feeling of inferiority as to their status in the community that may affect their hearts and minds in a way unlikely ever to be undone," Chief Justice Earl Warren led the Court to declare segregation unconstitutional. *Brown*'s holding became the gold standard for defining the terms of formal equality: treating individuals differently based on the color of their skin was constitutionally wrong. However, once the Court's membership changed in the 1970s, advocates of color blindness used *Brown*'s formal equality principle to equate race-conscious government decisions that seek to develop an integrated society with the evils of de jure segregation. The new social engineers on the right adapted the Warren Court's rhetoric to create a late twentieth-century constitutional principle that forbids government actors from remediating societal discrimination. They changed *Brown* from a clarion call to an excuse not to act.[3]

The academy has produced a host of explanations for the discontinuity between *Brown*'s early promise and its present reality. Some scholars have challenged the Warren court's motives; others have criticized its reasoning; still others have found fault with its method of implementation. For example, focusing on motivation, Derrick A. Bell Jr. questioned the case's power to promote social justice because it was shaped, not by the intentional coalescing of a transforming social movement that reached across boundaries of race and economic class, but by the calculated convergence of interests between northern liberals, southern moderates, and blacks. The resulting alliance was temporary, lacked deep populist roots, and built on a tradition of treating black rights as expendable. For throughout United States history, Bell contended, the rights of blacks have regularly been sacrificed to preserve the greater interests of the whole society.[4]

In an influential article published in 1980 in the *Harvard Law Review*, Professor Bell concluded that the *Brown* decision represented the interest *convergence* between blacks and middle- and upper-class whites:

> [The] principle of "interest convergence" provides: The interest of blacks in achieving racial equality will be accommodated only when it converges with the interests of whites. However, the fourteenth amendment, standing alone, will not authorize a judicial remedy providing effective racial equality for blacks where the remedy sought threatens the superior societal status of middle and upper-class whites. . . . Racial remedies may instead be the outward manifestations of unspoken and perhaps subconscious judicial conclusions

that the remedies, if granted, will secure, advance, or at least not harm societal interests deemed important by middle and upper-class whites.[5]

In the post–World War II period the alignment of interests of a biracial elite shifted to accommodate legal challenges to Jim Crow, Bell argued. The Court gave its imprimatur to the desegregation of public schools to add legitimacy to the U.S. struggle against Communism; to reassure blacks that precepts of equality heralded in World War II would be applied at home (and thus to quiet the resentment and anger of black veterans who returned from the war only to be denied equality); and to eliminate an important barrier to the industrialization of the South and the transition from a plantation to a modern economy. Consistent with Bell's interest-convergence thesis, Philip Elman, special assistant to the attorney general, filed a brief on behalf of the United States in which he framed the problem of racial discrimination "in the context of the present world struggle between freedom and tyranny."[6]

The ideals of racial liberalism helped fashion the legal strategy of the biracial elite. Racial liberalism emphasized the corrosive effect of individual prejudice and the importance of interracial contact in promoting tolerance. Racial liberals stressed the damaging effects of segregation on black personality development to secure legal victory as well as white middle-class sympathy. The attorneys in *Brown* and their liberal allies invited the justices to consider the effects of racial discrimination without fear of disrupting society as a whole. The Court responded by seeking to mollify southern whites even as it declared the end to the de jure separate but equal system. Yet, to the extent that *Brown* reflected the alliance of some blacks and some upper-class whites unthreatened by desegregation, it left out crucial constituencies for change, including southern black educators and poor rural blacks.[7]

Reservations also abound about the Court's reasoning, which was influenced by the litigation tactics of *Brown*'s advocates and allies. The lawyers wanted to dismantle segregation so that all black children would have access to resources presumptively enjoyed by all white children. The lawyers chose to achieve their goal by encouraging the Court to assume the role of protecting black children from the intangible effects of stigma and self-hate. This intangible damage thesis seemed to offer the best possible means of directly dismantling Jim Crow (de jure, formal inequality) and *indirectly* dismantling its effects. Unfortunately, in this court-centered universe, the tactic of desegregation became the ultimate goal, rather than the means to secure educational equity. The upshot of the inversion of means and ends was to redefine equality, not as a fair and just distribution of resources, but as the absence of formal, legal barriers that separated the races.

Advocates for the NAACP made a conscious choice to abandon cases that demanded that states equalize the facilities, staff, and budgets of separate white and black schools to focus the Court's attention on segregation itself. As part of their litigation strategy, they appended studies by social scientists to their brief in *Brown*. The plaintiffs' attorneys successfully mobilized social scientists to support the fight against segregation, presenting racism as pathological because of the "toll it took on the black psyche." In a magisterial study, Daryl Michael Scott faulted the Court's dependence on psychological damage imagery to demonstrate the intangible costs of segregation. Segregation's evils had social and economic, not just psychological, ramifications. Even more, as others have pointed out, the psychology of segregation did not affect blacks alone; it convinced working-class whites that their interests lay in white solidarity rather than collective cross-racial mobilization around economic interests. Writing in 1935, W. E. B. Du Bois described the "public and psychological wage" paid to white workers, who came to depend on their status and privileges as whites to compensate for low pay and harsh working conditions.[8]

The Court's reasoning suffered once it considered the caste system of Jim Crow narrowly, as a function of individual prejudice. The Court's minimalist analysis had legal, sociological, and psychological consequences. In legal terms, the focus on prejudice alone cast a long doctrinal shadow, allowing subsequent courts to limit constitutional relief to remedying acts of *intentional* discrimination by local entities or individuals. Absent evidence that local officials or state actors intentionally manipulated school boundaries because of racial animus, *Brown*'s principled conclusion ultimately excused inaction in the face of a gradual return to racially segregated schools that are unquestionably separate *and* unequal. The sociological ramifications—that de facto separation became invisible—were predictable, given the Court's lopsided psychological framing. The Court's measure of segregation's psychological costs counted its apparent effect on black children without grappling with the way segregation also shaped the personality development of whites. This analytic asymmetry influenced the reaction of blue-collar whites and arguably re-stigmatized blacks. The decision modified but did not eliminate "the property interest in whiteness" that Du Bois earlier observed and that came to define the Court's equal protection jurisprudence. As Cheryl I. Harris has written, "*Brown I*'s dialectical contradiction was that it dismantled an old form of whiteness as property while simultaneously permitting its reemergence in a more subtle form" by failing to redress "inequalities in resources, power, and, ultimately, educational opportunity."[9]

Other scholars deplore the Court's remedial approach as overly deferential to southern whites; some also criticize integration efforts as benefiting very few poor blacks. What blacks won was not freedom, but tokenism. A cadre of middle-class blacks has enjoyed the privileges of upward mobility, but for the mass of blacks (and poor and working-class whites), educational opportunities remain beyond reach.[10]

A few scholars have sought to demonstrate that a bench-based, lawyer-crafted social justice initiative was ill equipped to address complex social problems. *Brown* actually had little effect on educational opportunity, Michael J. Klarman has argued, serving instead to reenergize white racial consciousness, while providing little in the way of integrated or improved educational facilities. Without executive and legislative branch leadership, the courts could not bring about the dynamic social change envisioned by the *Brown* lawyers. The federal judge John Minor Wisdom, renowned for his landmark decisions ordering desegregation in the wake of the Supreme Court's ruling in *Brown,* was candid about the lack of judicially inspired progress in the face of fierce white backlash. Like Wisdom, Rosenberg concluded that "the courts acting alone have failed." It was not until nonviolent and courageous civil rights activists were violently brutalized on national television that blacks won their "freedom" from state-sanctioned oppression. But they won through legislative action, which was after all the more democratic and sustaining force for change.[11]

Beyond the academic debates, many black activists struggle to reconcile their early optimism and contemporary hopelessness. A sense of lost opportunity has sparked increasing cynicism among some. There is an eerie nostalgia for the feeling of community that was destroyed post-*Brown.* As Adam Fairclough has noted, school integration has long divided the black community. For a surprising number of blacks, the question is not whether we mistook integration for the promised land. Confusion, even skepticism, reigns in some quarters over whether the promised land can exist in a United States that has yet to come to terms with the way slavery and the racialized compromises it produced shaped our original understanding of the nation as a republic.[12]

Racism—meaning the maintenance of, and acquiescence in, racialized hierarchies governing resource distribution—has not functioned simply through evil or irrational prejudice; it has been an artifact of geographic, political, and economic interests. In the United States racism was foundational, indeed constitutional. Mainstream historians are now busy tracing the constitutional legacy of the three-fifths clause that gave southern states, and most often southern plantation owners, disproportionate electoral clout at the national level. For roughly fifty of our country's first seventy-two years, the presidency was won by southern slave owners. Indeed, before and after the Civil War the social alliances between northern and southern elites encouraged both to suppress the ideological dissonance of a country "of free men" that "worshipped liberty while profiting from slavery" and "left the public arena to men of propertied independence." Such histories remind us that the northern "lords of the loom" and the southern "lords of the lash" were complicit in the maintenance of slavery and its aftermath. As David Brion Davis has explained, the South may have lost the Civil War battles, but it won the ideological civil war, propagating white acceptance nationwide of both "Negro inferiority" and white supremacy for most of the nineteenth and twentieth centuries.[13]

Under those circumstances, it is an open question whether any legal analysis, even one grounded in more rigorous social science research or employing a more balanced assessment of segregation's causes and effects, could have accomplished the goals of the *Brown* attorneys or could now accomplish the massive tasks that still await us: to extirpate a complex system of relationships that have tortured this country from its earliest beginnings and then to refashion a new social and economic order in its place. Formal legal equality granted through the courts could never guarantee economic, political, and social opportunity for the mass of blacks, for whom civil rights alone were not the measure of success. Their struggle was for "jobs and freedom" and encompassed many of the principles of self-government and property ownership that animated the early American revolutionaries.[14]

While Bell focused on interest *convergences* to explain the limited reach of the Court's initiative in *Brown,* geographic, racial, and class-based interest *divergences* were also at work ordering social, regional, and class conflict between northern and southern elites; between white elites and poor whites, north and south; between poor blacks and poor whites, whose concern was not unequal treatment but the maldistribution of resources and opportunity; and between poor and middle-class blacks, who arguably benefited most. When *Brown* is read in light of these divisions, it is clear that the task confronting those who took on Jim Crow would prevent even the most ambitious policy-minded experts from challenging white supremacy as it reemerged in new garb. The social engineers in *Brown* identified state-sponsored segregation as the visible manifestation of American racism. This understandable preoccupation with de jure segregation disabled the plaintiffs' attorneys and their liberal allies from comprehending Jim Crow as the visible manifestation of a larger, constantly mutating racialized hierarchy. That hierarchy was racialized both by elites to consolidate their power and privilege and by poor whites to palliate their own debased circumstances.

Brown's legacy is clouded at least in part because post–World War II racial liberalism influenced the legal engineers to treat the symptoms of racism, not the disease. Their strategy was to eliminate desegregation, which they assumed would strike a fatal blow to racialized hierarchies. The lawyers' assumption and its corollary remedial emphasis were limited by the nature of their allies, who wanted to do good without sacrificing any of their own privileges, believing integration was possible without significant resource redistribution. The legal engineers failed to anticipate the downsides of a singular preoccupation with desegregation, because their analysis essentialized all white children without identifying the regulatory role race and class played within the white community. The lawyers and their allies went to court to enforce a right without consciously considering the remedy, which ended up re-stigmatizing blacks, reinforcing white working-class fear of economic downward mobility, and reserving for a privileged few the resources they needed to learn. Finally, while dismantling Jim Crow was a noble imperative, the lawyers did not realize that the disease Jim Crow betokened could and did easily reappear in a new guise. Racism was not ended by the defeat of Jim Crow, even in school systems that achieved unitary status. As Judge Robert Carter, one of the NAACP LDEF lawyers in *Brown,* has since written, "Both northern and southern white liberals and blacks looked upon racial segregation by law as *the primary* race relations evil in this country. It was not until *Brown I* was decided that blacks were able to understand that the fundamental vice was not legally enforced *racial segregation* itself; that this was a mere by-product, a symptom of the greater and more pernicious disease— white supremacy."[15]

Even when race is no longer explicitly coded by appearance or ancestry, the allocation of seats in a classroom, the use of buses to transport schoolchildren, or the hue of the dolls with which those children play, race is, and was, about the distribution of power. Race in the United States is a by-product of economic conflict that has been converted into a tool of division and distraction. It is not just an outgrowth of hatred or ill will. Racism has had psychological, sociological, and economic consequences that created the separate spheres inhabited by blacks and whites in 1954 but extended well beyond them.

To address the full range of racialized inequities in this country, racial-justice advocates need to move beyond the early tenets of racial liberalism to treat the disease and not just its symptoms. A first step would be to make legible racism's ever-shifting yet ever-present structure. The oppressive conditions that most blacks still confront must not be ignored, but the continuing puzzle is how to address the complex ways race adapts its syntax to mask class and code geography. Racism is a structural phenomenon that fabricates interdependent yet paradoxical relationships between race, class, and geography—what I am calling the interest-divergence dilemma. It is the interest-divergence dilemma that requires a new racial literacy, meaning the capacity to decipher the durable racial grammar that structures racialized hierarchies and frames the narrative of our republic. To understand why *Brown v. Board of Education* has not lived up to its promise, I propose a paradigm shift from racial liberalism to racial literacy.

Racial Liberalism and the Interest-Divergence Dilemma

Post–World War II racial liberalism rejected scientific racism and discredited its postulate of inherent black inferiority. At the same time, racial liberalism positioned the peculiarly American race "problem" as a psychological and interpersonal challenge rather than a structural problem rooted in our economic and political system. Segregation was a "symptom of some psychological mal-adjustment" among those who imposed it; it was also a source of psychological maladjustment among those who were subjected to it. Reeling from the horrors of fascism abroad, fearing the specter of totalitarian domination, and facing continued pressure to fight racial inequities at home, proponents of greater tolerance suggested that racism was irrational and would surrender to logic and interpersonal contact. Equality before the law, through the persistent pursuit of civil rights, was the goal. That goal would be realized through racial integration. And that goal, in its singular and universalistic truth, would provide the ultimate reconciliation. The defining elements of postwar racial liberalism were its pragmatic devotion to a single strategy, its individualized and static view of American racism, and its focus on top-down social reform.[16]

The coalition promoting racial liberalism took hold only after northern elites began to align their interests with black emancipation rather than with the interests of their putative southern counterparts who used legal segregation to preserve upper-class power. In the shadow of the cold war, international pressure and elite-dominated racial liberalism gave the civil rights quest moral and strategic heft; but it also reconfigured civil rights advocacy. According to some scholars, the alliance between middle-class blacks and white moderates filled the void as labor influence eroded in the late 1940s due to anticommunist assaults, the slow pace of reform through administrative changes, and union leaders' unresponsiveness to the specific needs of black union members. The result was a more conservative civil rights movement. Martha Biondi has argued that anticommunism propelled desegregation efforts while displacing grass-roots movements that had focused on building economic coalitions across lines of race.[17]

In the struggle between a grassroots insurgency emphasizing both political and economic issues and top-down elite control of a social agenda based on a single principle, the elites prevailed. Relying on psychological evidence of the intangible damage segregation does to black personality development, the strategic shift to challenge Jim Crow enabled many white allies to maintain their social and economic advantages without giving up the moral high ground. While anticommunist fervor helped fuel the willingness of national elites to take on segregation, it also channeled dissent from the status quo into status-based legal challenges that focused on formal equality through the elimination of de jure segregation.[18]

Scholars such as Biondi have suggested that biracial activism around common economic interests existed prior to, and was displaced by, *Brown*, while others find minimal evidence of such coalitions. The real surprise, the latter have argued, has been the antipathy to the civil rights movement that northern working- and lower-middle-class whites displayed. Guided by the assumption that closer contact with whites would ensure dignity and citizenship rights for blacks, the "new integrationist orthodoxy" failed to connect its version of the psychology of blacks with an equally probing analysis of the psychology of whites. The bargain struck by northern elites—that desegregation would restore credibility to the United States during the cold war and provide social stability as it eased the dissonance experienced by black veterans returning from World War II—disregarded the substantial investment poor whites had in their superior social status vis-à-vis blacks.[19]

In the North and South many working-class and poor whites had acquired an investment in white racial privilege even before the decision in *Brown*. Not surprisingly, remedies involving desegregation evoked virulent hostility among such whites, who were the people initially targeted by those remedies. After the Supreme Court's decision in *Milliken v. Bradley*, which held that only districts found to have intentionally discriminated could be subject to a school desegregation plan, they became the group of whites most affected by desegregation in both North and South, as wealthier whites fled inner cities for surrounding suburbs. Even the most committed proponents of racial integration of the schools acknowledge that it is poor rather than rich whites who have experienced dislocation in the transition to integrated schools. As Bell has recognized, poor whites and blacks have much in common, yet poor whites "feared a loss of control over their public schools," a loss "intensified by the sense that they had been betrayed."[20]

Racial liberalism identified a thin slice of the problem, while the multiple interest divergences that defined the country in 1954 continued to incubate. The conflicts were transformed but not overcome. Indeed, in the petri dish of racial liberalism, those conflicts were allowed to fester. Ironically, the change the racial liberals wrought was not always the change they sought. A preliminary, and mostly tentative, review of the historical literature suggests that the *Brown* court's doctrine that "separate but equal is inherently unequal" had unanticipated consequences. It intensified divergences between northern elites and southern whites, solidified the false interest-convergence between southern white elites and southern poor whites, ignored the interest divergences between poor and middle-class blacks, and exacerbated the interest divergences between poor and working-class whites and blacks.

Interest Divergence: Racialized Geography and the Psychology of White Solidarity

Unlike the Jim Crow system it challenged, *Brown*'s asymmetric focus on the psychological damage segregation did to blacks gave the psychological benefits segregation conferred on whites short shrift. In the ideology of racial liberalism, the class and geographic interests of rural and poor southern whites—and of working-class northern whites—also receded from view. That inattention had two consequences. First, many poor and working-class whites saw themselves as victims. Second, they saw desegregation as downward economic mobility. To poor whites, compulsory association with blacks brought no added value and endangered the sense of autonomy and community they did have. *Brown's* racial liberalism did not offer poor whites even an elementary framework for understanding what they might gain as a result of integration. Neither the opinion nor the subsequent legal strategy to implement *Brown* made clear that segregation had offered elites an important means of exercising social control over poor and working-class whites as well as a means of dominating or disadvantaging blacks.[21]

Little attention was paid to the disparities between the educational resources of poor and working-class whites and those of more affluent whites, who had access to better education through private schools or geographic mobility. Although whites in the aggregate enjoyed educational resources that far exceeded those available to blacks, poor whites, especially in rural communities in the South, were often educational orphans. Levels of schooling declined with falling income more precipitously in the South than in other parts of the country. In 1940 nearly three-quarters of the wealthiest seventeen-year-olds in the South, but less than one-sixth of the poorest, had completed at least eleven years of schooling. There were also rural-urban disparities. According to the 1950 census, among southerners in their late twenties, the state-by-state percentages of functional illiterates (defined as people with fewer than five years of schooling) for whites on farms overlapped with those for blacks in cities. In most southern states, more than half of urban whites in their late twenties had completed high school, but less than a quarter of whites of the same age living on farms had done so. The majority of southern whites, considering older and younger people and farm, village, and city dwellers, were semiliterates (defined as those with fewer than twelve years of schooling) who shared disadvantages with blacks, while an affluent white minority completed elementary and high school, standing far apart from the rest of the whites and from virtually all blacks.[22]

Ideologically committed to an integrationist orthodoxy, racial liberalism initially failed to contemplate a mechanism for acknowledging the psychological paradox of poor whites or their need for greater material resources and other tangible benefits. As a result, poor whites experienced desegregation, in Bell's terminology, as a net "loss." That sense of loss was exploited by demagogic politicians, who have successfully used racial rhetoric to code American politics to this day and who continue to solidify the original bargain between poor and wealthy southern whites. Regional differences remain pronounced, as evidenced in the "red" and "blue" states that defined media maps of the 2000 presidential election. And yet regional differences are less evident when race and class are disaggregated.[23]

In the South, for example, integration was successfully portrayed as downward mobility through compulsory association with blacks. The dramatic events accompanying the integration of Central High School in Little Rock, Arkansas, illustrate the dynamic. In 1957 there were three high schools serving Little Rock: the new all-white Hall High School, the all-black Horace Mann High School, and Central. Central had been the only white high school in Little Rock, but in summer 1957, Hall opened in the western and more affluent portion of the city. Middle- and upper-middle-class white students transferred to the new high school just before the school year began. This meant that once the senior class at Central graduated in 1958, Central would lose its "citywide character." The school board had approved a plan to integrate Central in 1955. It was scheduled to take effect in fall 1957, at the very time when affluent whites were exiting to attend the new school. Horace Mann would remain all black; Hall would be all white. Only Central would experience integration, albeit with nine carefully chosen black students. Despite the academic credentials and middle-class appearance of the black trailblazers, those white students who remained at Central perceived a twisted symmetry: poor blacks and rich whites would remain in the isolated, racially homogeneous environments of Horace Mann and Hall high schools, while working-class whites became the guinea pigs in the integration experiment at Central. In their minds, the "symmetry" was not coincidental; school superintendent Virgil Blossom had "sold" his desegregation plan to the leadership in Little Rock by reassuring them that their children could attend the new Hall High School, "a high school segregated by both class and race." As Elizabeth Huckaby, who was then assistant principal of Central High School, recalled, "Except for a hundred of our seniors who had elected to stay at Central for their final year, we would have no more boys and girls from [the northwest] section of Little Rock where the finest houses were being built, where the families of the most successful businessmen were moving, where the country clubs are."[24]

The exodus of white elites from Central High School threatened working-class dreams of upward mobility and put working-class students' virtual membership in the "dominant class" at risk. The sociologist Beth Roy subsequently interviewed some white students who were then at Central. Even thirty years later, her interviewees criticized the disruption desegregation brought into their lives: "I became very disenchanted with the whole thing. I just kept thinking, This is my senior year, and this is not what I was looking forward to. This is just unfair." Another, searching for a way to explain her hatred for one of the black students who entered Central in 1957, exclaimed, "She walked the halls as if she belonged there." To working-class whites, integration, timed to coincide with the flight of the city's elite, was a stigmatizing force that interfered with their ability to pursue the American dream. Thus they resisted it.[25]

Goaded on by the racial demagoguery of local politicians, such whites came to view the potential economic consequences of desegregation in psychological terms. Politicians preyed on their sense of betrayal and unfair sacrifice, deliberately organizing the conversation about desegregation around a white racial consciousness. Although working-class whites initially saw this "experiment in interracial education" in class terms, a racially polarized contest was easily manufactured using antebellum conceptions of race and class that had crystallized under segregation. Lacking a vocabulary of either class or structure, Roy's working-class white informants were still fluent in the language of racial scapegoating some thirty years later. Disappointed with their own economic and social status, they blamed blacks. Cause and effect were reduced to race.[26]

Although poor and working-class whites were among the most visible protesters, they acted with the tacit approval of the more affluent whites in their communities. According to some accounts, southern elites, with the exception of a few moderates, remained defiant post-*Brown,* often encouraging massive resistance in the South. For example, during the 1940s white elites in Birmingham, Alabama, had played the race card to defuse opposition to the poll tax, which disenfranchised poor whites as well as blacks. Poor whites, more than half of whom did not vote, acquiesced in the downplaying of their economic and political interests in favor of a vigorous defense of white supremacy. Post-*Brown* the Birmingham elites ensured their continued dominance by undermining any class identity among poor and working-class whites. Aided by the same fear of communism that may have led the Court to rule unanimously in *Brown,* ambitious southern politicians quickly perceived the benefits to be derived from racial demagoguery. It had long been in the interests of the white upper class, whether planters or industrialists, to "make all whites think in racial or sectional ways—indeed, in any terms *except* class." As "the only class fully conscious of its power and purpose," the Birmingham "industrialists, and the lawyers and politicians who served them," continued, after *Brown* as before, to deploy a white racial consciousness as an instrument of social control.[27] Upper-class whites in the South, however, were not monolithic; some scholars have argued that the *Brown* decision radically altered elite treatment of race issues as the focus of white moderates shifted from labor reforms to eliminating de jure segregation.

Resistance within the South was more muted in those metropolitan areas where local leadership had fewer incentives to mine a white racial consciousness in order to maintain political power. Michael J. Klarman, for example, argues that affluent city residents who were cocooned within racially and economically segregated housing patterns were less likely to lead resistance. Wealthier whites "retained the option of exiting the public school system altogether either by educating their children privately or by fleeing to the (generally white) suburbs."[28]

Politicization of the experience of desegregation as loss existed in the North, not just the South, and affected blue-collar workers, not just poor whites. In a study of white neighborhood associations in Detroit in the 1950s, Thomas J. Sugrue found that government programs that subsidized white home ownership or defined political boundaries to determine access to education were taken for granted and remained largely invisible. Government programs designed to give blacks a hand up were highly visible and resented. Blue-collar whites in Detroit measured their success by their ability to control their distance from blacks as a group. Failure meant being forced to share community, schools, or economic status with blacks.[29]

Arnold Hirsch's study of public housing in Chicago and Sugrue's account of homeowner associations in Detroit suggest that maintaining racially homogeneous neighborhood enclaves was central to white working-class identity in the North. Aspirations to upward mobility, bonds of family and community, and the "white racial identity premised on American individualism" depended on maintaining residential distance from blacks. Although it was often the more affluent and educated blacks who sought to move into white neighborhoods, all their prospective white neighbors could see was a deluge of poor black people crowded together in crime-ridden neighborhoods. Working-class whites interpreted the poverty they associated with blacks in two ways. First, the "wretched conditions" in predominantly black communities "were the fault of irresponsible blacks." Second, those neighborhoods served as a "grim prophesy" of what theirs would become if they welcomed upwardly mobile black pioneers. They equated racial integration with crime and violence.[30]

Many white working-class people perceived the American dream as assuring them a right to a racially homogeneous community. While it appeared that race trumped class, it was equally true that class was defined by race and urban-suburban geography. Sugrue's study demonstrates the post–New Deal political realignment of blue-collar workers in Detroit with their corporate bosses living in Grosse Pointe, an exclusive suburb. No longer did they direct their rage at the economic or social conditions that kept them off balance. Politicians and real estate brokers were able to reorient populist rage to target civil rights organizations and their upper-class white allies. It was those groups who threatened to destroy racial homogeneity within the blue-collar homeowners' community and thus to undermine a precondition for achieving the American dream, especially in uncertain economic times.[31]

The stories told by Hirsch about housing desegregation in Chicago and by Sugrue about working-class white resistance, abetted by government policies and private real estate brokers, to social or residential intermingling with blacks in Detroit suggest the key role played by politicians and self-interested business people who resorted to a racially coded rhetoric to manipulate or divert attention from economic conditions. On the one hand, the approaches to desegregation instituted by political and judicial actors represented burden shifting. Although a few middle- and upper-class whites exercised constraint and exhorted moderation, many took advantage of their power to shift the burden from themselves artificially. The method used in Little Rock was also employed in other cities: the establishment in upper-class neighborhoods of new schools that would remain segregated. The formation of new towns and cities based on racial geography had the same effect. Because *Brown* did not change the funding structure of public education and did not reduce geographic segregation by class (and consequently race), it left the costs of integration to already underfunded schools in poor white areas. Those schools were often geographically closest to the poor black areas, and their students often experienced great anxiety about their own educational abilities and future opportunities. In addition, because small and medium-sized cities and therefore school districts were often dominated by a single racial group, preexisting race-based borders hindered *Brown's* capacity to provide meaningful integration.[32]

On the other hand, some costs of integration under the *Brown* framework fell "naturally" on poor and working-class whites. Explicit burden shifting was often unnecessary. Class geography, untouched by *Brown,* would have sheltered upper-class whites from the "burden" of integration even without subsequent selfish or racist manipulations, as Richard Thompson Ford, for example, has argued.[33]

Whether the geographic boundaries were natural or political, poor whites felt stigmatized by black demands for first-class citizenship. Watching the dismantling of their psychological position of relative privilege, they were left without an alternative understanding of their actual condition relative to more affluent members of the society. According to Sugrue, racial liberalism succumbed to "simmering white discontent," constrained by "the politics of race and neighborhood." For many white workers from Little Rock to Detroit, the explanation has been simple. With the aid of the federal government, blacks absconded with the American dream.[34]

Witness Beth Roy's working-class white informants in Little Rock, who collectively assigned their own failures to blacks. Whites who succeeded believed they did so because of individual merit; they earned their success. By contrast, in the stories reported to Roy, if they failed, it was because black people "stole" the American dream. Working-class whites did not get into the colleges of their choice, did not get the jobs they needed, or were the victims of crime because blacks benefited from affirmative action, lived on welfare, or chose to hustle rather than perform honorable work. The stories of Little Rock, Detroit, and Chicago suggest that it was middleclass and often suburban whites who were subsidized in large measure by government programs for homeownership and highways and who tended to monopolize access to the best educational resources, the good jobs, and the safe streets. Yet poor and working-class whites accepted the terms of racial solidarity rather than confront the fundamental need to organize collectively and across racial lines to obtain similar benefits.[35]

Their fears inflamed by economic insecurity as constructed by the individualism of the American dream, many whites turned to race as an explanation and an identity. According to Jennifer L. Hochschild, the American dream is an inclusive, optimistic, and high-minded myth that "evokes" "unsullied newness, infinite possibility, [and] limitless resources." The dream has universal elements of sharing opportunity broadly: everybody should have the chance to succeed as measured by income, a good job, and economic security. The opportunity for everyone to succeed is an inclusive fantasy, but that opportunity is presumptively obtained through one's individual effort. Those who succeed are those who exert strenuous effort so that their talents prevail; they work hard, take risks, and imagine a better future for themselves and their children. Virtue leads to success; success is evidence of virtue. Therefore, those who fail to climb up the ladder of success must be without talent or without discipline. The losers are not only miserable failures; they also lack character unless they assume personal responsibility for their flaws.[36]

While it is easy to see success as a sign of merit rather than luck, few people willingly accept an equally self-referential explanation of failure. Race arguably fills the gap, providing a believable account of all that went wrong. Race functions as a pragmatic explanation for the fact that few working-class and poor whites achieve their version of the American dream. The choice of race as the explanatory covariant is neither irrational nor aberrant, given the otherwise highly individualized structure of this metanarrative. In the words of Du Bois, the psychological wage of whiteness put "an indelible black face to failure." Once blackness becomes the face of failure, race then influences and constrains social, economic, and political opportunities among and between blacks and whites and among and between blacks and other people of color.[37]

In a somewhat incongruous fashion, race is the variable explaining failure for both whites and blacks. Blacks think racial discrimination inhibits their chances to participate in the American dream; whites think reverse discrimination is the culpable party. For many blacks, success and failure are both understood in more collective terms. Indeed, contemporary sociological and psychological research suggests that an understanding of failure as a product of systemic rather than personal deficiencies is a healthy psychological response, at least insofar as it may lead to collective action to change one's circumstances.[38]

Interest Divergence: Stigmatizing Race

Brown helped change the quality of life for many blacks. It educated the country about the changing meaning of the United States Constitution and allowed blacks to claim the Constitution as theirs despite the tragic role race had played in its earliest formulation. It overruled *Plessy v. Ferguson,* the constitutional straitjacket in which the Court had put itself in 1896. It represented the triumph of racial liberalism over scientific racism and other theories of inherent black inferiority. It also served for most of the second half of the twentieth century as the "principal ideological inspiration" to those who sought racial justice through the courts, according to Jack Greenberg, Thurgood Marshall's successor as head of the NAACP LDEF and one of the lawyers who argued a companion case to *Brown.*[39]

Yet as Marshall's colleague Robert Carter concluded, *Brown* promised more than it could give. *Brown*'s analysis was limited by its singular focus on the harm segregation caused the personality development of black children. Predicated on experiments purportedly showcasing blacks' lack of self-esteem, the opinion reinforced the stigma long associated with blacks, even as it attributed the stigma to segregation rather than biology. Subsequent cases added insult to injury as the Court began to label the legal claim as arising from differential treatment rather than demeaning treatment within a racialized hierarchy.[40]

Significantly, the Court's analysis was framed as requiring racial desegregation to end damage to black psyches. The district court judge and later the Supreme Court adopted almost verbatim testimony by the psychologist Louisa Holt in the Kansas case that segregation, especially when sanctioned by law, had a detrimental effect on the personality development of the Negro child." One of the lawyers in *Brown* found in her testimony, which he attributed to a "God-given eloquence," "the seeds of ultimate victory." Linking responsibility for educational disadvantage to black self-loathing and connecting that to a psychological abstraction did little, however, to disrupt the powerfully negative views of blacks in the popular imagination. As Charles R. Lawrence III has written, many whites do not believe that racial discrimination is the principal cause of black inequality. The explanation lies instead in some version of black inferiority. "Few will express this belief openly. It is no longer consistent with American ideology to speak in terms of inherent racial traits. But the myth of racial inferiority remains embedded in the fabric of our culture."[41]

Basing its opinion on the psychological research of the time, the Court misunderstood the source of self-esteem for many blacks and unwittingly contributed to the divergence of interests along class and geographic lines within and without the black community. These outcomes can be traced, in part, to the flawed studies on which plaintiffs relied to prove that physically equal but segregated facilities had a negative psychological impact on all black children. The most famous of the psychological studies cited by the Court was the doll experiment of Kenneth Clark and Mamie Clark. The Clark study aggregated findings of northern and southern black children, light-skinned and dark-skinned black children, and middle-class and poor black children to conclude that segregation caused feelings of inferiority among all blacks. Black children in the more integrated North had more frequently preferred the white dolls than black children in the South. Many northern black children also verbalized unease when prompted to consider their physical similarity to the brown dolls, yet Kenneth Clark concluded that northern black children were actually psychologically healthier. A historian has summarized Clark's argument: The reaction of the northern children showed their "discomfort with the complicated and harsh reality of racial mores rather than resignation," whereas racial segregation and isolation had caused southern black children to accept their inferior social status as normal. "Such an acceptance," Clark reported, "is not symptomatic of a healthy personality." Clark argued that the racial identification of the southern children, almost 80 percent of whom identified themselves in some way with the brown dolls, was tainted because of the terms they used to verbalize their choices. The southern black children described the black dolls as "pretty," "nice," or "good" but accompanied their choices with statements such as, "This one. It's a nigger. I'm a nigger."[42]

Clark's message was that group self-hatred among blacks begins at an early age, involves the rejection of brown skin color by black children, and becomes embedded in the personality of blacks as a result of the "damage inherent in racial segregation." These conclusions may have had some merit, but none was entirely consistent with his research. According to Daryl Scott, Clark's conclusions (unlike his data) also contradicted other contemporary studies that suggested that black children with greater contact with whites experienced the most psychological distress. While many blacks hailed the Court decision, especially for its vast symbolic value, the opinion's emphasis on the psychological damage segregation does to blacks camouflaged the ways *de*segregation "hurt" some blacks, while segregation motivated others to excel, a possibility Holt had conceded. For some black children, segregated schools provided a sanctuary from psychological conflict. More recently, psychological literature has also suggested that those blacks who are the most invested in achieving academically within the larger society are often more vulnerable to what Claude Steele and others term stereotype threat, the situational threat of being negatively stereotyped. Unlike Clark's "self-fulfilling prophecy" that black students internalize and then fulfill negative stereotypes and low expectations for achievement, stereotype threat is context-dependent rather than intrinsic. Moreover, social psychologists have found that in some circumstances the ability to maintain a sense of self-worth in a hostile environment may actually enhance self-esteem. The key point is that data on self-esteem differences between black kids and white kids were not well developed then; even today "there's not much evidence of chronic psychological damage done to blacks' self-esteem as a result of segregation" per se.[43]

A desegregation solution based on concerns about psychological stigma did not necessarily have the desired effect of providing meaningful educational and economic opportunity even for those middle-class blacks whom compulsory segregation had denied a first-class education. For example, desegregation meant that some black teachers, the backbone of the black middle class at the time, lost their jobs. And the mentoring provided to high-achieving middle-class black students at some all-black elite public high schools, such as Dunbar High School in Washington, D.C., was neither replaced nor reproduced in more integrated environments. Within integrated schools, the interaction with white students was often limited literally and figuratively by tracking, skepticism about blacks' intellectual ability by their teachers and white classmates, and the loss not only of black mentors but also of a sense of community in which the adults were invested in the students' achievement.[44]

In addition, the prejudice-centered approach set in motion forces that have cemented the connection between public education and damaged goods in a way that disadvantaged poor blacks in particular. Much of Derrick Bell's scholarship and that of others presents evidence that poor blacks were abandoned by middle-class blacks who now had the opportunity to choose educational situations consistent with their class interests. Similarly, Carter, an NAACP LDEF lawyer in *Brown*, later concluded that "to focus on integration alone is a luxury only the black middle-class can afford. They have the means to desert the public schools if dissatisfied." Poor blacks suffered as urban public schools became the primary locus of integration; the change fomented an unhealthy battleground of racial tensions. Race became synonymous with poor blacks, and public education itself became stigmatized as it became more and more closely associated with racialized poverty.[45]

The focus on educational quality soon abated, as administrators, teachers, and students became political figures or political pawns rather than learners; educational funds were diverted to conflict avoidance and resolution and education budgets manipulated to promote political goals about race policy. Although *Brown* heralded the crucial role that public education plays in a democracy and gave eloquent voice to the importance of an educated citizenry to society as a whole, its legal analysis forestalled political interest convergences to the detriment of poor people of all colors: black, brown, and white, urban and rural. The Court's analysis became the basis for a doctrinal distinction between race and class that lifted unequal resource distribution out of the constitutional canon.[46] What appeared to be "eloquence from God" in the testimony of a witness at the trial court in Kansas that compulsory segregation damages children's ability to learn soon became manifest in a different prophecy: that black children simply cannot or do not wish to learn. Legally compelled segregation became socially acceptable separation; separation became stigma; stigma became association with blacks who still occupied and defined separate, albeit public, education. Integration was reduced to diversity, a benefit to be enjoyed by a critical mass, but not by the masses.

Sadly, it was the appellees in Brown whose prognostications came closest to describing current realities. In his oral argument before the Supreme Court in the companion case of *Davis v. County School Board,* Attorney General Lindsay Almond of Virginia argued that integration would "destroy the public school system as we know it today" because the "people would not vote bond issues through their resentment to it." Colgate Darden, then president of the University of Virginia and a former governor of Virginia, testified that desegregation would "impair the opportunities for both races" because goodwill toward the public school system would be "badly impaired," which would lead to a "sizable falling off of the funds required for public education." Indeed, urban and rural public schools became stigmatized as the dumping ground for those with nowhere else to go.[47]

The ambiguity of *Brown*'s legacy is as much a consequence of interest divergence as of the temporary alliance between northern elites and civil rights advocates to promote social reform through biracial top-down cooperation grounded in the values of racial liberalism. The Court relied on incomplete data regarding the damage segregation did to the self-esteem of blacks while it underestimated the potentially negative impact of *de*segregation on the self-esteem of some blacks and perhaps inadvertently reinforced the identification of blackness with inferiority and stigma in the minds of whites. There was also a divergence of interests inside the black community between poor and middle-class blacks arising from the practical consequences of *Brown* (including the loss of community and the exodus of middle-class blacks from urban public schools).

That the divergences were relegated to the background was partly a result of the prejudice-centered orthodoxy of racial liberalism. That the divergences remain mostly intact may also have been a function of the elevated and preeminent role of legal analysis in fashioning a social change strategy. The Court, acting alone, was not in a position to explore the triangulation of interests along race, class, and geographic lines.

Racial Literacy and the Interest-Divergence Dilemma

The apparent interest convergence between northern liberals and southern blacks ultimately perpetuated a more durable divergence of interests within and between the black and white communities. The ideals of racial liberalism produced a legal icon but did little to disrupt the historic pattern in which race was used to manufacture dissensus, complicating relationships inside and outside communities of color. That dissensus was not produced by race, but by social and economic conflict that was simultaneously revealed and concealed by race. Post-*Brown*, the ability to use race to code and cloak diverging interests sustained racial hierarchies—a phenomenon that tainted our founding arrangements and remains at our ideological core.

Through the creation and maintenance of racialized hierarchies, the plight of poor blacks and poor whites was mostly ignored; similarly, under the shibboleth of equal opportunity, urban and rural communities were abandoned as the maldistribution of material resources persisted undisturbed. Just as significant, the psychological bribe that segregation offered working-class and poor whites was not examined or countered even as white racial solidarity assumed crucial importance in the decision's aftermath. Indeed, the focus on race as a source of one-way psychological stigma had deleterious consequences for the public school system. Public education became a battlefield rather than a constructive gravitational force within many communities. Race was used to pathologize blacks rather than to reveal how economic and social privilege hid behind racial fault lines. Ultimately, the class interests of those who could afford to invest personally in their children's education triumphed.

The first step in understanding these diverging interests is to make them legible. A racially literate analysis seeks to do just that by deciphering the dynamic interplay among race, class, and geography. In contrast to racial liberalism, racial literacy reads race as epiphenomenal. Those most advantaged by the status quo have historically manipulated race to order social, economic, and political relations to their benefit. Then and now, race is used to manufacture both convergences and divergences of interest that track class and geographic divisions. The racialized hierarchies that result reinforce divergences of interest among and between groups with varying social status and privilege, which the ideology of white supremacy converts into rationales for the status quo. Racism normalizes these racialized hierarchies; it diverts attention from the unequal distribution of resources and power they perpetuate. Using race as a decoy offers short-term psychological advantages to poor and working-class whites, but it also masks how much poor whites have in common with poor blacks and other people of color.[48]

Racial liberalism triumphed in *Brown* by presenting racism as a departure from the fundamentally sound liberal project of American individualism, equality of opportunity, and upward mobility. But racial liberalism's individualistic and prejudice-centered view of formal equality failed to anticipate multiple interest divergences, helped fuel a white backlash, and doomed both integration and the redistribution of resources. Racial literacy, in contrast, requires us to rethink race as an instrument of social, geographic, and economic control of both whites and blacks. Racial literacy offers a more dynamic framework for understanding American racism.

There are many differences between what I call racial literacy and racial liberalism, but for the purposes of this essay three stand out. First, racial literacy is contextual rather than universal. It does not assume that either the problem or the solution is one-size-fits-all. Nor does it assume that the answer is made evident by thoughtful consideration or expert judgment alone. Racial literacy depends upon the engagement between action and thought, between experimentation and feedback, between bottom-up and top-down initiatives. It is about learning rather than knowing. Racial literacy is an interactive process in which race functions as a tool of diagnosis, feedback, and assessment. Second, racial literacy emphasizes the relationship between race and power. Racial literacy reads race in its psychological, interpersonal, and structural dimensions. It acknowledges the importance of individual agency but refuses to lose sight of institutional and environmental forces that both shape and reflect that agency. It sees little to celebrate when formal equality is claimed within a racialized hierarchy. Although legally enforced separation was identified as a dignitary harm and the issue being litigated ridiculed as a matter of "racial prestige" by John W. Davis, attorney for South Carolina in the *Brown* case, it soon became distorted into an issue of mere separation rather than subjugation. Indeed, it is precisely as a legal abstraction that we are now being asked to honor equality. But things seldom are equal, as W. E. B. Du Bois pointed out in 1935 as he weighed the benefits of segregated and integrated education for blacks. He concluded that blacks needed education for their minds, not just integration of their bodies: "Other things being equal, the mixed school is the broader, more natural basis for the education of all youth. It gives wider contacts; it inspires greater self-confidence; and suppresses the inferiority complex. But other things seldom are equal, and in that case, Sympathy, Knowledge, and the Truth, outweigh all that the mixed school can offer."[49]

Third, while racial literacy never loses sight of race, it does not focus exclusively on race. It constantly interrogates the dynamic relationship among race, class, geography, gender, and other explanatory variables. It sees the danger of basing a strategy for monumental social change on assumptions about individual prejudice and individual victims. It considers the way psychological interests can mask political and economic interests for poor and working-class whites. It analyzes the psychological economy of white racial solidarity for poor and working-class whites and blacks, independent of manipulations by "the industrialists and the lawyers and politicians who served them." Racial literacy suggests that racialized hierarchies mirror the distribution of power and resources in the society more generally. In other words, problems that converge around blacks are often visible signs of broader societal dysfunction. Real interest convergences among poor and working-class blacks and whites are possible, but only when complex issues are analyzed and acted upon with their structural, not just their legal or their asymmetric psychological, underpinnings in mind. This means moving beyond a simple justice paradigm that is based on formal equality, while contemplating what it will take to create a moral consensus about the role of government and the place of the public itself.[50]

One of the original architects of the *Brown* strategy apparently understood the importance of further interrogating the interest divergences that promote a purely formal, legal equality within a system where social and economic inequalities persist. Charles Hamilton Houston, the former vice-dean at Howard Law School, director-counsel of the NAACP LDEF, and the consummate social engineer, declared six years before the case was decided:

> There come times when it is possible to forecast the results of a contest, of a battle, of a lawsuit all before the final event has taken place. So far as our struggle for civil rights is concerned, the struggle for civil rights is won. What I am more concerned about is that the Negro shall not be content simply with demanding an equal share in the existing system. It seems to me that his historical challenge is to make sure that the system which shall survive in the United States of America shall be a system which guarantees justice and freedom for everyone.[51]

• • •

Race is a powerful explanatory variable in the story of our country that has been used to explain failure in part by associating failure with black people. Racial literacy suggests that legal equality granted through the courts will not extirpate the distinctive, racialized asymmetries from the DNA of the American dream. The courts can be and often have been a critically important ally, but neither the judiciary nor lawyers acting alone possess the surgical skill required to alter the genetic material of our organizing narrative. Nor is the attainment of civil rights by itself an adequate measure of success, in part because the problem is not just race but race as conjugated by class, geography, and the organizing narrative of upward mobility.

Through its invocation of the language of prejudice, the Court in *Brown* converted the structural phenomenon of racism into a problem of individual psychological dysfunction that whites and blacks are equally capable of exhibiting. In the 1950s prejudice was understood as an aberration in individuals who disregard relevant information, rely on stereotypes, and act thoughtlessly. Prejudice was a function of ignorance. Educated people, it was assumed, are not prejudiced. Yet many who acquiesce in racialized hierarchy derive tangible benefits from such a hierarchy. They are acting rationally, not irrationally, when they ignore the ways hierarchy systematically disadvantages groups of individuals and privileges others consistent with socially and culturally constructed definitions of race that predictably order and rank.

In legal terms, *Brown*'s rule of "equality by proclamation" linked segregation to prejudice and reinforced the individuating of both the cause of action and the remedy. By defining racism as prejudice and prejudice as creating individual psychological damage, the Court's opinion paved the way for others to reinterpret *Brown* as a case mandating formal equality and nothing more. Subsequent courts have tended to limit the equal protection clause of the Fourteenth Amendment by a symmetrical, perpetrator-oriented focus on color blindness. If the problem is that separate is inherently unequal, then equality is simply presumed when the separation is eliminated. Any remaining inequality is the fault of black people themselves.[52]

In the end, *Brown*'s racial liberalism had little to offer poor and working-class whites to counter the psychological benefits of white racial solidarity. Jim Crow was a caste system that oppressed all blacks, regardless of class and geographic lines, but the psychology of Jim Crow allowed white elites to limit the educational and economic opportunities of poor and working-class whites. Working-class whites were also complicit, as they perceived their own advancement as dependent on their ability to separate and distinguish themselves from blacks as a group. It is the conflation of psychological benefits with economic and political self-interest that crafts the popularly accepted fiction that failure is not only measured by race but also *explained* by it.

Brown's effect on public education, for example, showed why it is critical to link race and class without losing sight of race, and in ways that invite the people most directly affected to speak for themselves. *Brown* relied on the lawyers' and the justices' understanding of the key role played by public education in a democracy. Yet it unwittingly nationalized the southern white racial consciousness, which downplayed the collective interest in a vigorous public in favor of the social interest of one class in private, individual choice. Nevertheless, it is important to remember that, although the trisection of interests along race, class, and regional lines haunted *Brown* from the beginning, the stark lines of divergence emerge more clearly in retrospect, viewed from the perspective of significant social progress that was inconceivable in 1954.

To be sure, the NAACP lawyers were audacious social engineers. Their ingenious litigation strategy bolstered insurgent efforts to dismantle de jure segregation. But for all their brilliance, the lawyers in *Brown* were unable to kindle a populist revolution in which the people, not just the lawyers, come to understand the crippling effects of race and racism on our entire social, economic, and political order. Race matters not just for blacks, in other words, but for every citizen of the United States. Because of its foundational role in the making of this country's history and myths, race, in conjunction with class and geography, invariably shapes educational, economic, and political opportunities for all of us.

My proposed paradigm shift to racial literacy is more a thought experiment than a judicial brief. We need to learn to use the courts as a tool rather than a panacea to overcome the structured dissension race has cemented in our popular consciousness as well as in our lived experience. If we can become more literate about the role racism continues to play in structuring and narrating economic and political opportunity, we may be better able to combine legal and legislative advocacy that enlists support among people of all colors, whites as well as blacks. It may be that the time has come for "a new policy compass," as Derrick Bell recently wrote, "to assert petitions for racial justice in forms that whites will realize serve their interests as well as those of blacks." But however petitions for racial justice are framed, they need to avoid confusing tactics with goals, forever freezing a formalistic theory of racial equality into the Constitution, which can then be used to undermine opportunities for progressive innovation in the future.[53]

If there is only one lesson to be learned from *Brown*, it is that all Americans need to go back to school. The courts acting alone cannot move us to overcome, and the federal government has not assumed leadership in this arena since the 1960s. At the beginning of the twenty-first century, a racially literate mobilization of people within and across lines of race, class, and geography might finally be what it takes to redeem the optimistic assessment of those early academic commentators. Of course, a racially literate analysis, meaning the ability to read race in conjunction with both contemporary institutional and democratic hierarchies and their historical antecedents, may not resolve the interest-divergence dilemma. Nor should it. But at least it may help us understand why *Brown* feels less satisfying fifty years later.

Notes

This article was originally published under the same title in *Journal of American History* 90, no. 1 (2004): 92–118, and is reprinted with permission from the Organization of American Historians.

1. On the importance of the *Brown* decision, see Jack Greenberg, *Crusaders in the Courts: How a Dedicated Band of Lawyers Fought for the Civil Rights Revolution* (New York: BasicBooks, 1994), 197; James T. Patterson, *Brown v. Board of Education: A Civil Rights Milestone and Its Troubled Legacy* (New York: Oxford University Press, 2001), xxvii–xxviii; Jordan Steiker, "American Icon: Does It Matter What the Court Said in *Brown*?" *Texas Law Review* 81 (November 2002): 305; Martin Guggenheim, "Symposium: Translating Insights into Policy: Maximizing Strategies for Pressuring Adults to Do Right by Children," *Arizona Law Review* 45 (Fall 2000): 779; David

A. Strauss, "Interdisciplinary Approach: Afterword: The Role of a Bill of Rights," *University of Chicago Law Review* 59 (Winter 1992): 547; and Jack M. Balkin, ed., *What Brown v. Board of Education Should Have Said: The Nation's Top Legal Experts Rewrite America's Landmark Civil Rights Decision* (New York: New York University Press, 2001), 3. See also Ronald S. Sullivan Jr., "Multiple Ironies: *Brown* at 50," *Howard Law Journal* 47 (Fall 2003): 29.

2. Nancy McArdle, "Beyond Poverty: Race and Concentrated-Poverty Neighborhoods in Metro Boston," December 2003, *The Civil Rights Project,* Harvard University, http://www.civilrightsproject.ucla.edu/research/metro/McArdleBostonPoverty.pdf (accessed January 2, 2009). For figures on declining levels of school-age children enrolled in Boston public schools by race and as total percentages of the population, see "Lessons for the Boston Schools," *Boston Globe,* March 14, 2004. After ten years of court-ordered desegregation, barely 1 percent of black children in the eleven southern states attended school with whites, according to Gerald N. Rosenberg, *The Hollow Hope: Can Courts Bring About Social Change?* (Chicago: University of Chicago, 1991), 52. See also Adam Fairclough, *Better Day Coming: Blacks and Equality, 1890–2000* (New York: Viking, 2001), 329; Patterson, *Brown v. Board of Education,* 202–4, 211–12, 229, 231; and Lani Guinier, "Admissions Rituals as Political Acts: Guardians at the Gates of Our Democratic Ideals," *Harvard Law Review* 117 (November 2003): 113, 118–19 nn.24–27. Mark Tushnet, "The Significance of *Brown v. Board of Education,*" *Virginia Law Review* 80 (February 1994): 175.

3. *Brown v. Board of Education,* 347 U.S. 483, 494 (1954). Decisions that rejected race-conscious governmental policies and/or required a showing of prior intentional discrimination to justify a limited racial classification as a remedy include *Regents of the University of California v. Bakke,* 438 U.S. 265 (1978); *City of Mobile v. Bolden,* 446 U.S. 55 (1980); *Wygant v. Jackson Board of Education,* 476 U.S. 267, 274 (1986) (plurality opinion); and *Richmond v. J. A. Croson Co.,* 488 U.S. 469, 496 (1989). The Court held that a school desegregation plan must be limited to districts with an actual history of racial discrimination in *Milliken v. Bradley,* 418 U.S. 717, 744–45 (1974).

4. Derrick A. Bell Jr., "*Brown v. Board of Education* and the Interest-Convergence Dilemma," *Harvard Law Review* 93 (January 1980): 518–33.

5. Ibid., 523.

6. For the interest-convergence principle framed broadly, see Derrick A. Bell, *Race, Racism, and American Law* (Boston: Little, Brown, 1980). On desegregation and the cold war, see Greenberg, *Crusaders in the Courts,* 164–65; Mary L. Dudziak, "Desegregation as a Cold War Imperative," *Stanford Law Review* 41 (November 1988): 61–120; and Mary L. Dudziak, *Cold War Civil Rights: Race and the Image of American Democracy* (Princeton: Princeton University Press, 2000). On the arousal of civil rights consciousness among blacks during World War II, see, for example, Earl Lewis, *In Their Own Interests: Race, Class, and Power in Twentieth-Century Norfolk, Virginia* (Berkeley: University of California Press, 1991), 173–76; Martin

Sosna, *In Search of the Silent South: Southern Liberals and the Race Issue* (New York: Columbia University Press, 1977); and Michael J. Klarman, "*Brown,* Racial Change, and the Civil Rights Movement," *Virginia Law Review* 80 (February 1994): 17–18. On desegregation and southern industrialization, see ibid., 56. The brief on behalf of the United States is quoted in Yale Kamisar, "The School Desegregation Cases in Retrospect: Some Reflections on Causes and Effects," in *Argument: The Oral Argument before the Supreme Court in Brown v. Board of Education of Topeka, 1952–55,* ed. Leon Friedman (New York: Chelsea House Publishers, 1969), xiv. On Special Assistant to the Attorney General Philip Elman, see Robert J. Cottrol, Raymond T. Diamond, and Leland B. Ware, *Brown v. Board of Education: Caste, Culture, and the Constitution* (Lawrence: University Press of Kansas, 2003), 161–62. On the embarrassment to foreign visitors who were mistaken for American blacks, see Brief for the United States as Amicus Curiae at 4–5, *Brown v. Board of Education,* 347 U.S. 483 (1954) (No. 1).

7. The Court itself refocused on segregation per se: "Here, unlike *Sweatt v. Painter,* there are findings below that the Negro and white schools involved have been equalized, or are being equalized, with respect to buildings, curricula, qualifications and salaries of teachers, and other 'tangible' factors. Our decision, therefore, cannot turn on merely a comparison of these tangible factors in the Negro and white schools involved in each of the cases. We must look instead to the effect of segregation itself on public education" (*Brown v. Board of Education,* 347 U.S. at 492). On racial liberalism, see Daryl Michael Scott, *Contempt and Pity: Social Policy and the Image of the Damaged Black Psyche, 1880–1996* (Chapel Hill: University of North Carolina Press, 1997), xiii. On constituencies *Brown* ignored, see David S. Cecelski, *Along Freedom Road: Hyde County, North Carolina, and the Fate of Black Schools in the South* (Chapel Hill: University of North Carolina Press, 1994), 8, 12. According to the National Association for the Advancement of Colored People lawyer Constance Baker Motley, many black teachers became major foes of school desegregation after *Brown.* See Adam Fairclough, *Teaching Equality: Black Schools in the Age of Jim Crow* (Athens: University of Georgia Press, 2001), 62–65, esp. n.46. See also Martha Biondi, *To Stand and Fight: The Struggle for Civil Rights in Postwar New York City* (Cambridge, Mass.: Harvard University Press, 2003), 164–65, 170–71, 180–85.

8. The social scientist survey on the psychological effects of segregation submitted to the Supreme Court as an appendix in *Brown* is cited in Kenneth B. Clark, *Prejudice and Your Child* (Boston: Beacon Press, 1955), 39–41. Scott, *Contempt and Pity,* xii–xiv, 125–26, 138; W. E. B. Du Bois, *Black Reconstruction in America, 1860–1880* (New York: Russell and Russell, 1935), 700.

9. For an example of the judiciary's perception of racism as a matter of prejudice, see Justice Anthony M. Kennedy's concurrence in *Board of Trustees of the University of Alabama v. Garrett,* 531 U.S. 356, 374–75 (2001). On the development of a specific intent theory of equal protection, see John Charles Boger, "Willful Colorblindness: The New Racial Piety and the Resegregation of Public Schools," *North Carolina Law*

Review 78 (September 2000): 1794. *Washington v. Davis*, 426 U.S. 229 (1976); *Mobile v. Bolden*, 446 U.S. 55 (1980). On the cost of segregation to black schoolchildren and ultimately their communities, one source noted "the contrasts in support of white and Negro schools are appalling . . . the median expenditure per standard classroom unit in schools for white children is $1,160 as compared with $476 for Negro children." See Brief of the American Federation of Teachers as Amicus Curiae at 9, *Brown v. Board of Education*, 347 U.S. 483 (1954) (No. 1). Derrick A. Bell, "Bell, J., Dissenting," in Balkin, *What Brown v. Board of Education Should Have Said*, 185–200. Stephen E. Gottleib, "*Brown v. Board of Education* and the Application of American Tradition to Racial Division," *Suffolk University Law Review* 34 (2001): 282–83. See also George Lipsitz, *The Possessive Investment in Whiteness: How White People Profit from Identity Politics* (Philadelphia: Temple University Press, 1998), 34. But contrast Fairclough, *Teaching Equality*, 66. Cheryl I. Harris, "Whiteness as Property," *Harvard Law Review* 106 (June 1993): 1714.

10. On the Court's deference to southern whites, see Harris, "Whiteness as Property," 1753 n.9. For criticism of integration efforts, see Derrick A. Bell Jr., "Serving Two Masters: Integration Ideals and Client Interests in School Desegregation Litigation," *Yale Law Journal* 85 (March 1976): 470–516. For a critique of Bell's view that it was middle-class blacks who sought integration, see Tomiko Brown-Nagin, "Race as Identity Caricature: A Local Legal History Lesson in the Salience of Intraracial Conflict," *University of Pennsylvania Law Review* 151 (June 2003): 1913–76. On tokenism, consider that as recently as 2002, in a flagship state school that was the subject of a precedent on which *Brown* relied, nearly 90 percent of the undergraduate classes "with five to twenty-four students had no or only one African American to contribute their experiences or perspectives to a class discussion" (Office of Admissions, University of Texas at Austin, "Diversity Levels of Undergraduate Classes at the University of Texas at Austin, 1996–2002," November 20, 2003 http://www.utexas.edu/student/admissions/research/ClassroomDiversity96-03.pdf (accessed January 2, 2009). Cf. *Sweatt v. Painter*, 339 U.S. 629 (1950).

11. Michael J. Klarman, "How *Brown* Changed Race Relations: The Backlash Thesis," *Journal of American History* 81 (June 1994): 81–118; Klarman, "*Brown*, Racial Change, and the Civil Rights Movement," 7–150. Some commentators have suggested Klarman may have exaggerated the possibilities of northern and southern biracial cooperation or treated the role of litigation without sufficient nuance. See, for example, David Garrow, "Hopelessly Hollow History: Revisionist Devaluing of *Brown v. Board of Education*," *Virginia Law Review* 80 (February 1994): 151. Robert Korstad and Nelson Lichtenstein, "Opportunities Found and Lost: Labor, Radicals, and the Early Civil Rights Movement," *Journal of American History* 75 (December 1988): 787. On the role of courts in implementing desegregation, see *U.S. v. Jefferson County Board of Education*, 372 F. 2d 836, 847 (1966); Rosenberg, *Hollow Hope*, 52.

12. Cecelski, *Along Freedom Road*, 8, 10, 12, 15, 34, 36. Cf. Fairclough, *Better Day Coming*, 148, 219, 221–23; and Fairclough, *Teaching Equality*, 62–65. Patterson,

Brown v. Board of Education, xxvi–xxix, 201–5. See also Bell, "Serving Two Masters," 470–516.

13. For a definition of racism, see Lani Guinier and Gerald Torres, *The Miner's Canary: Enlisting Race, Resisting Power, Transforming Democracy* (Cambridge, Mass.: Harvard University Press, 2002), 302. On the role of racial hierarchy in American history, see, for example, David Brion Davis, "Free at Last: The Enduring Legacy of the South's Civil War Victory," *New York Times,* August 26, 2001; Garry Wills, "The Negro President," *New York Review of Books,* November 6, 2003, 45, 48–49; Gordon S. Wood, "Slaves in the Family," *New York Times,* December 14, 2003; and Lipsitz, *Possessive Investment in Whiteness,* 18. Eric Foner, *The Story of American Freedom* (New York: W. W. Norton, 1998), 31–32; Henry Wiencek, "Yale and the Price of Slavery," *New York Times,* August 18, 2001; Davis, "Free at Last," 1.

14. Biondi, *To Stand and Fight,* 183; Foner, *Story of American Freedom,* 21.

15. On racism as the "dominant interpretative framework" for understanding and securing social stability in the United States, see Bell, "Bell, J., Dissenting," 185, 187–90. See also Lipsitz, *Possessive Investment in Whiteness,* 2, 19. On the difficult relationship between the legal rights in *Brown* and potential remedies, see Jack M. Balkin, "*Brown v. Board of Education*—A Critical Introduction," in Balkin, *What Brown v. Board of Education Should Have Said,* ed. Balkin, 64–71. Robert Carter, "A Reassessment of *Brown v. Board,*" in *Shades of* Brown: *New Perspectives on School Desegregation,* ed. Derrick A. Bell (New York: Teachers College Press, 1980), 23. See also Kenneth B. Clark, "The Social Scientists, the *Brown* Decision, and Contemporary Confusion," in Friedman, *Argument,* xl. Lewis, *In Their Own Interests,* 199–200.

16. While color blindness was also a goal, most racial liberals were willing to endorse a temporary period of race consciousness. On racial liberalism, see Scott, *Contempt and Pity,* xiii.

17. On the creation of a more conservative civil rights movement, compare Biondi, *To Stand and Fight,* 171, 182–83; Lewis, *In Their Own Interests,* 144–46, 165; and Korstad and Lichtenstein, "Opportunities Found and Lost," 800–801, 804–5.

18. Biondi, *To Stand and Fight,* 171; Scott, *Contempt and Pity,* 184; Lewis, *In Their Own Interests,* 148, 165, 199–202.

19. On the new integrationist orthodoxy, see Biondi, *To Stand and Fight,* 182–83. On the extent of biracial activism and the antipathy of northern working-class whites toward coalition building, compare Klarman, "*Brown,* Racial Change, and the Civil Rights Movement," 102–3; Thomas J. Sugrue, "Crabgrass-Roots Politics: Race, Rights, and the Reaction against Liberalism in the Urban North, 1940–1964," *Journal of American History* 82 (September 1995): 551–78; and Arnold R. Hirsch, "Massive Resistance in the Urban North: Trumbull Park, Chicago, 1953–1966," *Journal of American History* 82 (September 1995): 522–50. On social scientists' underestimates of the effect of racism on blacks and whites in North and South, see Clark, "Social Scientists, the *Brown* Decision, and Contemporary Confusion," xl–xlv, xlix.

20. On desegregation and white flight, see Paul Gewirtz, "Remedies and Resis-

tance," *Yale Law Journal* 92 (March 1983): 628–65; Jeffrey A. Raffel, *The Politics of School Desegregation: The Metropolitan Remedy in Delaware* (Philadelphia: Temple University Press, 1980), 177; and Finis Welch and Audrey Light, *New Evidence on School Desegregation* (Washington, D.C.: U.S. Commission on Civil Rights, 1987), 74. For the debate on whether white flight was a response to school desegregation, see Gary Orfield, *Must We Bus? Segregated Schools and National Policy* (Washington, D.C.: Brookings Institution, 1978); Gary Orfield and David Thronson, "Dismantling Desegregation: Uncertain Gains, Unexpected Costs," *Emory Law Journal* 42 (Summer 1993): 759–90; and Charles T. Clotfelter, "Are Whites Still Fleeing? Racial Patterns and Enrollment Shifts in Urban Public Schools, 1987–1996," *Journal of Policy Analysis and Management* 20 (Spring 2001): 199–221. See also James S. Coleman, Sara D. Kelly, and John A. Moore, *Trends in School Segregation, 1968–73* (Washington, D.C.: Urban Institute, 1975), 53–80; and David J. Armor, *Forced Justice: School Desegregation and the Law* (New York: Oxford University Press, 1995), 174–93. On poor whites weathering the transition to integrated schools, see Gary Orfield, "Metropolitan School Desegregation: Impacts on Metropolitan Society," *Minnesota Law Review* 80 (April 1996): 831. Bell, "*Brown v. Board of Education* and the Interest-Convergence Dilemma," 525. See also Linda Hamilton Kreiger, "The Content of Our Categories: A Cognitive Bias Approach to Discrimination and Equal Employment Opportunity," *Stanford Law Review* 47 (July 1995): 1240.

21. Beth Roy, *Bitters in the Honey: Tales of Hope and Disappointment across Divides of Race and Time* (Fayetteville: University of Arkansas Press, 1999), 318; Pete Daniel, *Lost Revolutions: The South in the 1950s* (Chapel Hill: University of North Carolina Press, 2000), 270. Many whites believed that if race relations changed, they could only lose social status and power. See Robert J. Norrell, *Reaping the Whirlwind: The Civil Rights Movement in Tuskegee* (New York: Knopf, 1985), 107.

22. C. Arnold Anderson, "Social Class Differentials in the Schooling of Youth within the Regions and Community-Size Groups of the United States," *Social Forces* 25 (May 1947): 440, 436; C. Arnold Anderson, "Inequalities in Schooling in the South," *American Journal of Sociology* 60 (May 1955): 553, 549, 557. See also Allison Davis, "Socio-Economic Influences upon Children's Learning," in *Proceedings of the Midcentury White House Conference on Children and Youth,* ed. Edward A. Richards (Raleigh, N.C.: Health Publications Institute, 1951), 7; Robert L. Marion, *Rural Education in the Southern United States* (Austin, Tex.: National Educational Laboratory Publishers, 1979); and Rashi Fein, "Educational Patterns in Southern Migration," *Southern Economic Journal* 32, no. 1, pt. 2 (1965): 106–24.

23. Bell, "*Brown v. Board of Education* and the Interest-Convergence Dilemma," 525; Armor, *Forced Justice,* 174–93, 206–7. See also Charles E. Kimble, "Factors Affecting Adults' Attitudes toward School Desegregation," *Journal of Social Psychology* 110 (April 1980): 216. On regional differences based on race, see, for example, Thomas Byrne Edsall with Mary D. Edsall, *Chain Reaction: The Impact of Race, Rights, and Taxes on American Politics* (New York: Norton, 1991). On maps that

color code the electorate, with red for Republican states and blue for Democratic states, see Robert David Sullivan, "Beyond Red and Blue," *Commonwealth Magazine*, 2007, http://www.massinc.org/index.php?id=110&pub_id=1616 (accessed January 2, 2009); and Tom Zeller, "One State, Two State, Red State, Blue State," *New York Times*, February 8, 2004.

24. Daniel, *Lost Revolutions*, 251; Elizabeth Huckaby, *Crisis at Central High: Little Rock, 1957–58* (Baton Rouge: Louisiana State University Press, 1980), 1–13. The Central High School integration plan had originally called for the desegregation of grades ten through twelve with three hundred black students. Over time, the number was scaled back to twenty-five. See Greenberg, *Crusaders in the Courts*, 228–29. On the twisted symmetry of the integration process, see Daniel, *Lost Revolutions*, 254–55; and David R. Goldfield, *Black, White, and Southern: Race Relations and Southern Culture, 1940 to the Present* (Baton Rouge: Louisiana State University Press, 1990), esp. 108. Huckaby, *Crisis at Central High*, 2. In 1960 the per capita income in the geographic region associated with Central High was $3,826; in the region associated with Hall High it was $8,012. See Donald Bogue, "Census Tract Data, 1960: Elizabeth Mullen Bogue File" (University of Chicago, Community and Family Study Center, 1975), computer file, Inter-University Consortium of Political and Social Research (ICPSR) version, http://www.icpsr.umich.edu/cocoon/ICPSR/STUDY/02932.xml (accessed January 2, 2009).

25. Daniel, *Lost Revolutions*, 257; Roy, *Bitters in the Honey*, 179, 206, 338, 343–44.

26. On the role of Gov. Orval Faubus and others in manufacturing the conflagration and violence that attended the desegregation of Central High in Little Rock, see Greenberg, *Crusaders in the Courts*, 228–43. Goldfield, *Black, White, and Southern*, 108.

27. Robert J. Norrell, "Labor at the Ballot Box: Alabama Politics from the New Deal to the Dixiecrat Movement," *Journal of Southern History* 57 (May 1991): 201, 234, 227, 233. On antebellum conceptions of race and class and political use of white supremacy, see W. J. Cash, *The Mind of the South* (1941; New York: Vintage Books, 1991), 38–39, 109–10. See also Norrell, *Reaping the Whirlwind*, 92–102.

28. Norrell, "Labor at the Ballot Box," 227. Some scholars argue that in several southern states, the postwar political elite was dominated by progressives who campaigned successfully for the interests of poor blacks and whites. After *Brown*, southern elites who were not threatened economically seemed to acquiesce in racial progress, as in Little Rock. See Goldfield, *Black, White, and Southern*, 48, 108; and Klarman, "*Brown*, Racial Change, and the Civil Rights Movement," 85–90, 102–3. On urbanization in the South, the way an influx of northern whites affected southern racial reform efforts, and the gradual weakening of Jim Crow's hold on the region, see ibid., 52–65, 67–71; and Daniel, *Lost Revolutions*, 282. Klarman, "*Brown*, Racial Change, and the Civil Rights Movement," 64–65.

29. On how northern white working-class residents came to expect racially segregated neighborhoods, largely because of New Deal policies, and how the stage

was set for the "backlash" long before the racial liberalism of the 1950s and 1960s, see Thomas J. Sugrue, *The Origins of the Urban Crisis: Race and Inequality in Postwar Detroit* (Princeton: Princeton University Press, 1996); and Hirsch, "Massive Resistance in the Urban North," 522–50. See also Charles R. Lawrence III, "The Id, the Ego, and Equal Protection: Reckoning with Unconscious Racism," *Stanford Law Review* 39 (January 1987): 342. Lipsitz, *Possessive Investment in Whiteness*, 18.

30. Hirsch, "Massive Resistance in the Urban North"; Sugrue, "Crabgrass-Roots Politics," esp. 561, 560.

31. On the alignment of working-class and upper-class whites to resist civil rights, see Roy, *Bitters in the Honey*, 46–48, 132–33, 148–66, 179–84; and Sugrue, "Crabgrass-Roots Politics." See also Hirsch, "Massive Resistance in the Urban North."

32. Hirsch, "Massive Resistance in the Urban North"; Sugrue, "Crabgrass-Roots Politics." A comparison of the desegregation methods in Wilmington, Delaware, and the more evasive ones used in Dallas, Texas, illustrates how upper-class whites used political and social power to tailor the implementation of desegregation to limit their burden. Compare Raffel, *Politics of School Desegregation*, 13, 20, 110–11, 210; and Glenn M. Linden, *Desegregating Schools in Dallas: Four Decades in the Federal Courts* (Dallas: Three Forks Press, 1995), 24. On racial segregation in the formation of new towns, see Nancy Burns, *The Formation of American Local Governments: Private Values in Public Institutions* (New York: Oxford University Press, 1994), 35–36.

33. Burns, *Formation of American Local Governments*, 112; Richard Thompson Ford, "The Boundaries of Race: Political Geography in Legal Analysis," *Harvard Law Review* 107 (June 1994): 1847–57.

34. Sugrue, "Crabgrass-Roots Politics," 570, 578; Roy, *Bitters in the Honey*, 326, 338.

35. On working-class whites' racializing of failure, see Roy, *Bitters in the Honey*, 324–25, 338–44; Sugrue, "Crabgrass-Roots Politics," 551–78; and Sugrue, *Origins of the Urban Crisis*, 213–14.

36. Jennifer L. Hochschild, *Facing Up to the American Dream: Race, Class, and the Soul of the Nation* (Princeton: Princeton University Press, 1995), 15.

37. See Guinier and Torres, *Miner's Canary*, 102–4, 224–29. David Levering Lewis, "'The Souls of Black Folk,' a Century Hence," *Crisis* (March–April 2003): 18.

38. See Guinier and Torres, *Miner's Canary*, 74–86.

39. *Plessy v. Ferguson*, 163 U.S. 537 (1896). Jack Greenberg made the statement in a 1974 speech delivered to the New York City Bar Association. See Gerald N. Rosenberg, "*Brown* Is Dead! Long Live *Brown*!: The Endless Attempt to Canonize a Case," *Virginia Law Review* 80 (February 1994): 171 n.32.

40. Robert Carter quoted in Kamisar, "School Desegregation Cases in Retrospect," xxv. In recent cases challenging affirmative action, the Court's analysis often sees race merely as phenotypic difference, fails to recognize the asymmetrical ways in which race functions in American society, and allows whites to claim reverse discrimination. See Guinier and Torres, *Miner's Canary*, 32–66.

41. Greenberg, *Crusaders in the Courts*, 130–32. Cf. Brief for the United States as Amicus Curiae at 3, *Brown v. Board of Education*, 347 U.S. (No. 1). Lawrence, "Id, the Ego, and Equal Protection," 322, 374–75, esp. 375. Scott, *Contempt and Pity*, 71–91; Charles R. Lawrence III, "If He Hollers Let Him Go: Regulating Racist Speech on Campus," *Duke Law Journal* (June 1990): 439–40, 466.

42. Initially hailed for bringing a measure of reality into the legal proceedings, the evidence cited in *Brown*'s famous footnote 11 was primarily (though not exclusively) from one social science—psychology. In the years after *Brown*, it was the doll studies that gained cultural salience. The Court also cited a sociologist and an economist: E. Franklin Frazier, *The Negro in the United States* (New York: Macmillan Co., 1949); Gunnar Myrdal, *An American Dilemma: The Negro Problem and Modern Democracy*, 2 vols. (New York: Harper and Brothers, 1944). The other citations in footnote 11 of *Brown*, which described the psychological effects of segregation, included Max Deutscher and Isidor Chein, "The Psychological Effects of Enforced Segregation: A Survey of Social Science Opinion," *Journal of Psychology* 26 (1948): 259–87; and Isidor Chein, "What Are the Psychological Effects of Segregation under Conditions of Equal Facilities?" *International Journal of Opinion and Attitude Research* 3 (Summer 1949): 229–34. For the doll studies, see, for example, Midcentury White House Conference on Children and Youth, "The Effects of Prejudice and Discrimination," in *Personality in the Making: The Fact-Finding Report of the Midcentury White House Conference on Children and Youth*, ed. Helen Lelan Witmer and Ruth Kotinsky (Palo Alto, Calif.: Science and Behavior Books, 1952), 135–58, esp. 142; and Clark, *Prejudice and Your Child*, 19–20, 22–24. On the methodological problems of these studies, see Scott, *Contempt and Pity*, 93–136. On the children examined in the doll studies and Kenneth Clark's conclusions about them, see a historian's account: Ben Keppel, "Kenneth B. Clark in the Patterns of American Culture," *American Psychologist* 57 (January 2002): 29–37, esp. 32.

43. Clark, *Prejudice and Your Child*, 50. Scott, *Contempt and Pity*, 124. On contemporary testing situations that trigger vulnerability to negative stereotypes, see Claude M. Steele, "Thin Ice: 'Stereotype Threat' and Black College Students," *Atlantic Monthly* 284 (August 1999): part 2 http://www.theatlantic.com/doc/199908/student -stereotype/2 (accessed January 2, 2009). On how stigmatization may strengthen self-esteem, see Jennifer Crocker and Brenda Major, "Social Stigma and Self-Esteem: The Self-Protective Properties of Stigma," *Psychological Review* 96 (October 1989): 608–30. On the lack of evidence that segregation by itself damaged self-esteem, see Geoffrey Cohen to Lani Guinier, e-mail, Dec. 4, 2003 (in Lani Guinier's possession). See also David Glenn, "Minority Students with Complex Beliefs about Ethnic Identity Are Found to Do Better in School," *Chronicle of Higher Education* [online version], June 2, 2003, http://sitemaker.umich.edu/daphna.oyserman/files/ chronicle_of_ higher_education.htm (accessed January 2, 2009); and D. Oyserman, M. Kemmelmeier, S. Fryberg, H. Brosh, and T. Hart-Johnson, "Racial-Ethnic Self-Schemas," *Social Psychology Quarterly* 66 (December 2003): 333–47.

44. On black teachers' losing their jobs due to integration, see Cecelski, *Along Freedom Road,* 8. On the loss of outstanding black high schools, see Derrick Bell, *Silent Covenants: Brown v. Board of Education and the Unfulfilled Hopes for Racial Reform* (New York: Oxford University Press, 2004), 124–25.

45. Bell, "Serving Two Masters," 470–516; Brown-Nagin, "Race as Identity Caricature," 1913–76. See also Coleman, Kelly, and Moore, *Trends in School Segregation,* 53–80; Armor, *Forced Justice,* 174–93; Lewis, *In Their Own Interests,* 199–202; and Sugrue, *Origins of the Urban Crisis,* 268. On efforts by middle-class blacks to separate themselves from poorer blacks, see Grace Carroll, *Environmental Stress and African Americans: The Other Side of the Moon* (Westport, Conn.: Praeger, 1998), 9; Orfield and Thronson, "Dismantling Desegregation," 774; Lisa W. Foderaro, "A Suburb That's Segregated by Money More than Race," *New York Times,* November 24, 2003. Class differences within the black community also influenced who led in challenging segregation. See Goldfield, *Black, White, and Southern,* 90–91. But cf. Klarman, "*Brown,* Racial Change, and the Civil Rights Movement," 56–62. On "racial outsiders" who have sought the privileges of whiteness, see Lipsitz, *Possessive Investment in Whiteness,* 3. See also Patterson, *Brown v. Board of Education,* 42–44, 200–201; and Cecelski, *Along Freedom Road,* 34. Carter, "Reassessment of *Brown v. Board,*" 28.

46. The Court rejected the possibility that the Fourteenth Amendment implicated distributional considerations, striking down a judicial attempt to mandate equalization of resources, stating that "at least where wealth is involved, the equal protection clause of the Fourteenth Amendment does not require absolute equality or precisely equal advantages." See *San Antonio Independent School District v. Rodriguez,* 411 U.S. 1, 24 (1973). Dissenting, Justice Thurgood Marshall lamented the Court's refusal to consider how much governmental action itself had caused the wealth classifications (ibid., 123–24).

47. *Davis v. County School Board,* 103 F. Supp. 337 (E.D. Va. 1952). For Lindsay Almond's statements, see "Oral Argument," in *Removing a Badge of Slavery: The Record of Brown v. Board of Education,* ed. Mark Whitman (Princeton, N.J.: Markus Wiener Pub., 1993), 157. For Colgate Darden's testimony, see "Colgate Darden," in Whitman, *Removing a Badge of Slavery,* 83, 84.

48. I define racial literacy at greater length in Guinier, "Admissions Rituals as Political Acts," 201–12. See also Guinier and Torres, *Miner's Canary,* 29–31.

49. John W. Davis quoted in "1953 Argument," in Friedman, *Argument,* 216. W. E. B.Du Bois, "Does the Negro Need Separate Schools?," *Journal of Negro Education* 4 (July 1935): 335.

50. Norrell, *Reaping the Whirlwind,* esp. 57.

51. Charles Hamilton Houston (1949) quoted in *The Road to Brown,* dir. Mykola Kulish (San Francisco: California Newsreel, 1990).

52. Emphasis on formal equality gave birth to the Warren E. Burger and William H. Rehnquist Courts' legal doctrine interpreting the Constitution narrowly, limiting

relief to proven acts of intentional discrimination. See, for example, *Washington v. Davis*, 426 U.S. 229 (1976); and *City of Mobile v. Bolden*, 446 U.S. 55 (1980). Even when the Court finds diversity to be a compelling governmental interest, it diverts concern and resources away from the real barriers to educational opportunity, according to Derrick Bell, "Diversity's Distractions," *Columbia Law Review* 103 (October 2003): 1622–33.

53. Derrick A. Bell, "Comments from the Contributors," in Balkin, *What Brown v. Board of Education Should Have Said*, 206. Bell, *Silent Covenants*, 119–20; W. E. B. Du Bois, *Dusk of Dawn: An Essay toward an Autobiography of a Race Concept* (New York: Harcourt, Brace and Co., 1940), 303.

Section II

Brown and Lived Experience

Joseph A. De Laine Jr. and Ophelia De Laine Gona, the children of the leader of the desegregation movement in Clarendon County, South Carolina, begin these personal accounts. De Laine's "*Briggs*: South Carolina's Bold Step that Led to *Brown*" and Gona's "About Integration: In Memory of the Reverend J. A. De Laine" describe firsthand the conditions in the rural South Carolina county and the courage and dignity of Reverend De Laine in the face of virulent white supremacy. The pioneering historian John Hope Franklin recalls his experiences working with the legendary civil rights attorney Thurgood Marshall on the *Brown* case. Constance Curry follows with her essay, "The Intolerable Burden," which tells the story of the Carters in rural Mississippi. Despite repercussions from recalcitrant white southerners, this family sent its African American children to a previously all-white school. Curry brings their tribulations and triumphs to life.

In the years following *Brown,* the spirit of the decision spread to other aspects of life across the nation. African Americans and their allies began to test desegregation laws in other venues than public schools. The Freedom Riders, which the Congress of Racial Equality organized in 1961, drew on the ideas of the Fourteenth Amendment's application in public accommodations for travelers. James C. Onderdonk's "The Freedom Riders: Two Personal Perspectives" explores two of the Riders' experiences. Onderdonk uses their speeches and interviews to write this personal perspective from inside the buses as they traveled in the South. Following Onderdonk, Freedom Rider Ed Blankenheim provides his account of the journey in "Looking Back at the Freedom Riders." Kal Alston closes this section with her experiences growing up in the only African American family in a Pennsylvania suburb after the decision in *Brown*. "The Middle Generation after *Brown*" speaks directly to a young audience Alston charges with bringing further change through their everyday interactions.

Together, these essays recount strength in the face of adversity and African Americans' continuing push for equality before, during, and after the *Brown* decision. These firsthand accounts and personal tales offer readers moving testimony of the bravery of participants in the civil rights movement.

8

Briggs

South Carolina's Bold Step
That Led to *Brown*

Joseph A. De Laine Jr.

The *Brown v. Board of Education* U.S. Supreme Court decision of 1954 represented a significant milestone in the history of the United States. Since the rendering of this decision, historians, legal scholars, and, consequently, the general public have tended to infer that the case from which the decision took its name, *Brown et al. v. Board of Education of Topeka et al.,* was the primary challenge that precipitated the decision. In fact, there were a total of five cases involved. Although the cases were argued separately, the Supreme Court heard them consecutively over a period of three days. The first four (from the states of South Carolina, Kansas, Virginia, and Delaware) alleged that public school segregation violated rights guaranteed by the Fourteenth Amendment; the fifth case (from the District of Columbia) alleged violation of the Fifth Amendment. Because all five addressed a common legal question, the Supreme Court delivered a consolidated opinion for the first four cases and based the opinion for the fifth on that previously delivered consolidated opinion. These cases, and the Court's opinions, have come to collectively be known as *"Brown v. Board."*

By focusing on the case from Kansas, we lose sight of the far more compelling arguments presented in the South Carolina and Virginia cases. Additionally, the failure to give proper emphasis to the South Carolina case (*Briggs et al. v. Elliott et al.*) has led to an erroneous belief that the NAACP had decided to challenge the "Separate but Equal" doctrine prior to accepting a case from South Carolina. When the *Briggs* case is remembered and discussed, history is often distorted by one or more recurring errors.

In this essay, it is my intent to correct the record by relating the true context in which the *Briggs v. Elliott* case developed. This will include an examination of *Briggs* as a grassroots effort, its leadership by the Reverend Joseph Armstrong De Laine (my father),[1] and the hardships encountered by those who so fervently supported the effort.

My comments and views on the history of *Briggs* are based on personal knowledge and on accounts given by individuals who also had direct knowledge of the events. From very early childhood, my father, the Reverend Joseph A. De Laine, took me with him as he went about his business—whether it was personal, civic, school, or church related. Thus, I was present at many of the relevant discussions and events. When the chain of events that led to *Briggs* began, I was fourteen years old and extremely interested in what people I knew did and said. It is safe to say that not much escaped my attention in those days.

I have been motivated to develop an expertise on the *Briggs* case because of my deep concern over the discordance between what is often promulgated and what I remember as fact. Fortunately, I have had access to my father's personal papers, a rather complete set of documents (letters, newspaper clippings, etc.) about some of the events surrounding *Briggs*. Most of these are housed at the University of South Carolina;[2] others remain in the possession of family members. In addition, I have interviewed and talked with many of the people who were involved in some way with *Briggs*, examined federally archived data on the petitions and arguments in the five *Brown* cases, referred to Richard Kluger's masterful work *Simple Justice*, and served as a member of the Fiftieth Anniversary Brown v. Board Presidential Commission. By virtue of this latter capacity, I was privileged to be involved in numerous discussions and symposia and to listen to scholars from various fields interpret the history of *Briggs* and *Brown*.

• • •

On December 22, 1950, *Briggs et al. v. Elliott et al.* was filed in United States Federal District Court as a lawsuit that asked for an injunction to abolish legal segregation in public schools on the grounds that segregation infringed on rights guaranteed by the Fourteenth Amendment to the Constitution. It was the second time that plaintiffs from Clarendon County, South Carolina, had filed a lawsuit with the very same name. The case was heard in May 1951. A three-judge panel issued a non-unanimous, two-part decision the following month, on June 23. The first part denied an injunction to abolish segregation, while the second directed the Clarendon County School District to equalize educational facilities and opportunities and report to the court within six months. Judge J. Waties Waring registered his dissenting opinion in a masterful twenty-page document.

The plaintiffs immediately appealed the 1951 decision of the three-judge panel on the *Briggs* desegregation case to the U.S. Supreme Court. To the dismay of the litigants, the case was remanded to the lower court for a review of progress by the county. By this time Judge J. Waties Waring had retired from the courts and was replaced on the district court panel by another judge. The 1952 ruling by the district court was unanimous, admitting that there were inequities in the dual system of South Carolina, but also stating that there was no evidence to support the eradication of the dual school system. By the time *Briggs* returned to the Supreme Court, the case from Kansas had also arrived. The two were scheduled to be heard in October, but when the Court learned that other similar cases were in the pipeline, it ordered them held until all had arrived. Although argued separately in December 1952, and again in December 1953, decisions were not announced until May 17, 1954. The question of relief was argued in April 1955.

• • •

In the years before 1950, Clarendon County, with a population majority of about 70 percent people of color, was rigidly controlled in all respects by a relatively small group of whites. This power structure was highly effective in maintaining separation of the races and the subservience of the majority. The inability of many people of color to read, write, or perform simple math calculations was alarmingly high. Encouragement by the power structure to continue these conditions was the prime method of control. Opportunities for nonwhites were limited to labor-intensive careers to maintain food on the table and clothes on their backs, with the lowest of wages.

It was common practice for many minority individuals to sign their names using the mark "X," attesting to statements they rarely understood and having to rely on what they were told. Yet, these individuals recognized their plight and were convinced that change, particularly for their children, would only occur through personal zeal, perseverance, persistence, and effective leadership by demanding an equitable share in the American Dream. I might add that similar tactics, but tactics more sophisticated in nature, exist today in an effort to retain some modicum of control.

It was after the conclusion of World War II that several issues affecting South Carolinians began to reinforce the thoughts and hopes of these plighted people to the possibility of potential redress for their situation. The first issue dealt with Negro[3] veterans returning from World War II, now being again subjected to conditions they so valiantly fought to eradicate. Then there were two federal court decisions, one dealing with the right to register and vote and the other focused on the right to equal pay for Negro and white teachers. Federal District Court Judge J. Waties Waring issued the decision in both of these cases. There was a developing confidence among African Americans that court decisions, particularly in the federal courts, might provide some objectivity and fairness in rulings that affected minorities, particularly in Judge Waring's court.

A number of the published conclusions specifically related to the genesis of the *Briggs* case erroneously imply that the Reverend Joseph A. De Laine was a plaintiff, that the core of the support was among his parishioners, that the NAACP solicited this community to initiate litigation, and that the core of the community's activities centered on one church's congregation.

The leadership role of this movement is most credited to my father. Having relocated to his boyhood home in Clarendon County, in 1934, he immediately began to establish himself not only as a clergyman, but also as a spokesman and advisor for the poor and the underprivileged. By the end of World War II, he had gained the respect and confidence of most African Americans in the county, not only for his religious teachings, but also for his efforts in the educational process and the facilitation of personal services (health, legal, civic, personal, and family problems, among other issues).

My father's formal training included degrees in the liberal arts and theology, a certificate in agriculture, and apprenticeships in carpentry and masonry. Prior to completing his formal education, he had worked as a laborer, operated a home-repair business in the state of Michigan and attempted several entrepreneurial businesses in South Carolina. I believe his varied professional skills, along with his charisma and willingness to become personally involved in social or civic issues, gave impetus to confidence bestowed upon him as a leader. His continued self-study as an adult seemed to focus on the areas of history, literature, social science, and religion. These subjects seemed to have offered him knowledge of pathways through which he would effectively bring this community together and lead its members toward a challenge for change. The African American church had the potential to and did effectively serve as a critical role in the progress of African Americans. This was especially true in Clarendon County, where Reverend De Laine, along with local colleagues with a vested interest in the community, were most successful in their leadership roles: as clergymen, as individuals with a personal desire to help others, and in their ability to address issues of concern. Most notable among these ministers were the Reverends Edward E. Richburg and James W. Seals.

Having a background with these characteristics was formidable for any individual or group of individuals, and it allowed them to encourage a large segment of minority citizens to openly question or demand improvement in their respective lots. Not only were these people almost totally dependent on the power structure for their meager economic livelihood, but minorities also feared for their physical safety from these same authorities. However, through their religious convictions and quest for a better life, they courageously followed their leadership with tenacity and a conviction that this was an optimal strategy for their chance to achieve some degree of equality.

Their first attempt in this movement dealt with a challenge in federal courts demanding bus transportation for Negro children in Clarendon County. The case filed by Mr. Levi Pearson under the aegis of the NAACP State Conference was the result of efforts by seventeen parents from the Davis Station area of the county. Its cost was to be underwritten by the Palmetto State Teachers Association (the state Negro teachers association). Due to a technicality regarding the school district in which Mr. Levi Pearson (the plaintiff) paid his property taxes in 1948, the case was withdrawn for the courts.

• • •

Reverend De Laine then made requests through Attorney Harold Boulware, legal counsel for the South Carolina State NAACP, for a meeting with attorney Thurgood Marshall to seek further help from the National NAACP for a case against Clarendon County demanding equity in the dual school systems. This meeting was held in Columbia, South Carolina, in March 1949, and agreement was reached that the NAACP would entertain a case demanding "The Equalization of Educational Opportunity for Negro Children." The November 1949 case, known as *Briggs v. Elliott,* which had 107 plaintiff signatures (both adults and children), narrowed the scope of potential coverage from a countywide effort to a focus on one school district located around the town of Summerton. The petition was first presented to local officials for action. Upon their failure to act, the case was filed in Federal District Court in May 1950. During a formal hearing, Judge Waring strongly urged the NAACP lawyers to refocus the case from the reliance on relief for the plaintiffs within the *Plessy v. Ferguson* precedent to a challenge to the constitutionality of segregation itself without regard for the quality of facilities.[4]

The new case, also known as *Briggs v. Elliott,* challenged the constitutional legality of the separate but equal practices of public schools in South Carolina. The number of plaintiffs then narrowed to twenty parents (one per family). This became the *Briggs* case that was ultimately joined with the four other cases that collectively became known as *Brown v. Board.*

Retributions, from the vicious to the ridiculous, were swift as a consequence of such bold moves taken by African Americans in the county and the state. The state legislature had already enacted a law making it illegal for a teacher to be a member of the NAACP. A resolution passed by the legislature called for one-way tickets out of the state to be issued to Judge Waring and his wife and the provision of grave markers to be installed in a cattle stall at Clemson University upon their deaths. Plaintiffs, suspected sympathizers, and individuals believed to have relatives supporting the cause were fired from their positions of employment. Sharecroppers and tenant farmers were abruptly evicted with no compensation for the fruits of their labor or consideration for a place where they might live. One individual, Mr. James McKnight, a member of Reverend De Laine's church, was brutally murdered as his family watched helplessly. It was widely rumored that he was suspected of being one of the plaintiffs. Willie

Stukes accidentally lost his life within two months after becoming a plaintiff due to unsafe conditions working at home after being fired and in an effort to earn money to support his family. A cow owned by another plaintiff was even arrested and taken to the local jail for trespassing in the white cemetery.

As for Reverend De Laine, his home in Summerton was totally destroyed by arson in 1951. After the Supreme Court's 1955 "with all deliberate speed" decision was announced, a series of acts of vandalism were committed at his Lake City residence (a parsonage) over a three-month period. On October 1, 1955, Reverend De Laine received a letter giving him ten days to leave town or die. On the seventh day, his church, St. James AME Church, was destroyed by arson. On October 10, 1955, gunfire erupted at the church parsonage. To protect himself, Reverend De Laine finally returned the gunfire. It is alleged that several of the attackers were injured. The culprits fled the scene. Within an hour after the attack, Reverend De Laine fled Lake City in fear of his life. He remained a fugitive from his home state for the remainder of his life. The warrant for his arrest, charging him with "assault and battery with the intent to kill," was finally rescinded by the state of South Carolina in 2000, twenty-six years after his death.

Forty-nine years later, a gentleman approached my brother in a distant city and related an incident that happened after the shooting. He stated that his uncle had been the sole Negro police officer on the Lake City police force at that time. He said that his uncle "was instructed to lure De Laine to the police station for talks." The police officer came to the parsonage and informed my father of his instructions and said he suspected that they intended to kill him at the police station. He urged my father to flee and told him he would report that no one was found at the house. A neighbor next door was already sheltering my mother.[5] Within thirty-six hours of the incident, my father was seeking safe haven in New York City.

During the years between 1949 and 1965 many African Americans in Clarendon County relocated to other areas of the country as a direct result of the harsh pressures placed upon them because of this civil rights struggle. These pressures included a myriad of tactics, such as efforts by the local power structure to starve the Negroes into submission through not only economic pressures, but also the actual denial of food and other necessities of life through retail outlets.

Today, the efforts of these Clarendon County people, who were responsible for the seeds of a movement that has changed the entire American social structure with regard to the rights guaranteed to all citizens under the Fourteenth Amendment to the U.S. Constitution, have experienced little benefit. The public schools in Summerton remain primarily all black, with a quality of education that barely meets state minimum standards. Whites generally attend private academies or are sent to other school districts. Student performance appears on average to be at or below state standards. School funding, although comparable to similar rural poor districts, continues to reflect a crisis situation in the district's ability to provide bare necessities. The races generally do not mix on a social basis or for the common good of the community. The few whites that tend to speak out or seek understanding between the two groups often find themselves in uncomfortable or untenable situations among individuals thought to have been lifelong friends. The African Americans generally tend to avoid confrontation and exhibit suspicious attitudes towards their white counterparts. Yet, there are a few exceptions from both races who espouse an open dialog and the spirit of cooperation.

An arduous uphill journey must be undertaken before citizens of this county can achieve even a modicum of equity in the economic and educational fruits enjoyed by so many Americans as a consequence of the *Brown* ruling. It is also lamentable that those in South Carolina who so boldly planted the seeds of this court challenge have been relegated to minor national recognition for their community's role in this effort. In four of these cases, action was initiated by groups of plaintiffs who in some manner suffered greatly because of their bold demands. Yet, our press and other publications have tended to highlight only the first name appearing on the petitions as the only person with recognized credit for this effort. In reality, however, other petitioners may have been far more influential in the success of the effort or may have endured greater hardships, but have been forgotten only because their name did not appear first.

It is true that my father played a vital leadership role in organizing the efforts that led to the formation of the *Briggs* case. I am also quite grateful that many are now recognizing his contribution to the cause. However, I am often embarrassed when, in the presence of individuals who are descended from one of the plaintiffs in the cases grouped together under *Brown*, their parents' achievements are ignored as accolades are given to that name that heads the list, with no acknowledgment of others.

Regardless of how history has portrayed them, the facts are somewhat inconsequential. The mission of our fore-parents has not been completed. We as Americans continue to have a formidable task that must be addressed in our future. That task still includes the eradication of racial bias in our economic, educational, and social structures.

Notes

1. Richard Kluger, *Simple Justice: The History of Brown v. Board of Education and Black America's Struggle for Equality* (New York: Vintage Books, 1977). Richard Kluger incorrectly reported Rev. De Laine's middle name as being Albert, and many authors continue to perpetuate this error.

2. De Laine Papers, Caroliniana Library, University of South Carolina, Columbia.

3. As they were referred to at the time.

4. Leon Friedman, *Arguments: The Oral Arguments before the Supreme Court in Brown v. Board of Education of Topeka, Kansas, 1952–55* (New York: Chelsea House Publishers, 1969), xxxii.

5. Years later, I discovered that this neighbor was the aunt of actor Ossie Davis.

9

About Integration

In Memory of the
Reverend J. A. De Laine

Ophelia De Laine Gona

Our '48 Ford was passing a large bush laden with cascades of lavender flowers. My daddy (the man known to everyone else as the Reverend J. A. De Laine) looked to his right and remarked, "That's integration."

In the segregated world of 1950 South Carolina, integration was neither a common word nor a common sight. My younger brother and I, sitting in the back seat, immediately looked out of the window. We were happy to have learned what integration was.

Our journey continued, and the two of us kept looking ahead for another example. We saw unpainted barns, women hanging out wash, groves of pine trees, men in fields, another one of those lavender flower bushes. We spied our example and shouted, "There's more integration."

"Where?" Daddy asked.

"There! There!"

Daddy missed it and we continued our journey. Fortunately, another example was just ahead. We knew he couldn't possibly miss this one.

He looked. Understanding dawned and he gave his special little "harrumph" laugh. Then patiently, as he always did when teaching, he told us what he had called "integration" was some black and white children playing together by the road.

"But, Daddy," we chorused. "What about those lavender bushes?"

"Oh!" he said, "They're called wisteria."

• • •

On May 16, 1950, *Briggs et al. v. Elliott et al.,* a public school desegregation law-suit that arose in South Carolina's Clarendon County, was filed in federal court. In a previous incarnation, *Briggs v. Elliott* had been filed as a lawsuit seeking equal educational facilities. But, because of events during pretrial proceedings in the chambers of Federal District Court Judge J. Waties Waring, the case had been withdrawn. Under the leadership of NAACP lawyer Thurgood Marshall, *Briggs* was completely changed and submitted in a new form, retaining the same name, as a public school desegregation lawsuit. As a result of *Briggs,* the word "integration" would soon be in common use throughout the nation.

Acknowledged by the people of Clarendon County as the leader of the *Briggs* plaintiffs, my father had indeed provided the impetus that led to the filing of the case. For a while, he even came to be referred to, by some in South Carolina, as "the nigra who started that integration mess." To others, he would be rightfully acknowledged as the catalyst that caused legal and mandatory racial segregation in the public schools of the United States to come to an end. Some more insightful people would recognize his key role in making the civil rights era possible. Indeed, in the future, following in Daddy's footsteps would be movements for women's rights, handicapped rights, immigrant rights, etc.

An elementary school principal and a rural church pastor, Daddy didn't start out thinking about integration. He regarded himself as a simple shepherd—a shepherd whose flock included everyone he encountered, not just worshipers who attended his churches. He believed his mandate was to lead the flock to the green pastures of both earth and heaven. He made it his duty to help prepare his followers to reap the bounty that could be found in these pastures. The green pastures of his mind included an earthly place where all Americans enjoyed the rights "guaranteed" by the U.S. Constitution and its Amendments.

By 1947 it was apparent to Daddy that he had to help the flock get to a place where skin color didn't determine whether children walked or rode buses to school. By 1949 he knew that place had to be one where educational facilities were equal for all children. In the green pastures he had to help the flock find, 75 percent of the education budget would never be allocated, on the basis of race, to one-fourth of the children.

So, as a good shepherd, he led all from the community who would follow. Undaunted when obstacles blocked the way in their quest for school bus transportation, he helped the flock search for a path leading to equal educational facilities. When Judge Waring pointed out the pitfalls of that way to lawyer Marshall, Daddy convinced the flock to take the new, unmarked trail. Because of Daddy's tenacity and grassroots leadership, *Briggs* became the first petition of its kind—arguing that segregation in public schools violated the Fourteenth Amendment to the U.S. Constitution—to reach the federal court system. *Briggs* set the stage, and in less than two years became one of the five cases heard by the Supreme Court as *Brown v. Board of Education.*

Without *Briggs,* there could never have been *Brown.*

And without *Brown,* segregation might still be a fact of life the United States.

For his leadership role, by 1951 Daddy had been fired from his principalship, sued for slander, and threatened with death. Our home was burned down. Some people were afraid to be seen talking with him. Yet, standing tall and erect, honest and resolute, determined and down-to-earth, he remained unbowed and unafraid.

A great admirer of Mahatma Gandhi and his philosophy of nonviolence, Daddy had led the little Clarendon County flock in their peaceful quest for equality. They all had suffered as a consequence of their efforts, but the reward was that bus transportation was now provided for both black and white children. The small shacks that had served as schools for black children had become things of the past. And yet, there were newer schoolbooks and classrooms had more resources. South Carolina was fighting hard to maintain segregation as the status quo.

The schools for black children were still not equal to those for whites. There could never be equality as long as South Carolina law held that "no white child shall ever attend school with a black child." As Judge Waring so aptly wrote in his June 1951 dissenting opinion for the Federal District Court ruling on *Briggs,* "Segregation is per se inequality." In order for the little boys and girls for whom he cared so deeply to have a chance at their share of the American Dream, Daddy knew the public schools of South Carolina had to be integrated.

Daddy was a practical idealist—like Gandhi—and a very sensible man. He had long since taken precautions to ensure his own safety—precautions like carrying a firearm in the car. An excellent marksman himself, he also made sure we children and Mother could handle the shotguns he hung inside over doors and windows of our house.

In May 1954 the Supreme Court ruled in favor of *Briggs* and the other cases that constituted *Brown.* The Court implied that integration was to be the new order of the day.

The South dug in, saying there would be no new order.

In May 1955 the Supreme Court declared that public schools must be integrated "with all deliberate speed."

By the latter half of 1955, reactionary White Citizens' Councils were common throughout the South. For the councils' members—both Ku Klux Klan adherents and misguided but otherwise reasonable community members—the words "desegregation" and "integration" fanned the flames of fear, meanness, and hatred. In early October, the church that Daddy pastored was destroyed by arson, our residence (the church parsonage) was vandalized, and a cross was burned across the street.

If he was afraid, no one knew it, not even Mother. He went about his daily business relaxed and confident, radiating good cheer. He even stopped to talk with rude young white men, their necks red from ill-fitting shirts and too much sun, their venomous speech punctuated by the spitting of tobacco juice.

But even Daddy, however law-abiding and God-fearing, had limits to his patience. One night, in response to gunfire that had rung out in the night—and under advisement of the police chief, he finally took action, protecting his family and home by answering gunshots with gunshots. During the next forty-five minutes, while waiting in vain for town police to appear, he took stock of his situation. Finally, he did something he never thought he would do. In the dead of the night of October 10, 1955, Daddy fled from South Carolina, becoming a fugitive from justice and thus—in all likelihood—saving his life from the South's peculiar brand of justice reserved for people of color.

• • •

Integration did become the order of the day. And the South, often ranting and resisting, ultimately obeyed. As the integration drama unfolded in the South and throughout the nation, Daddy had to be content watching from the sidelines in New York State.

In 1971, retired and with a warrant still out for his arrest in South Carolina, Daddy and Mother returned to the South—to Charlotte, North Carolina. It was just about as close as he could get to his beloved home state without endangering his freedom.

• • •

The Supreme Court had just upheld a lower court ruling that the Charlotte-Mecklenburg School District must use a busing plan to achieve true integration of schools. Daddy was elated to be able to witness firsthand the implementation of one outcome of his efforts.

Almost every day he went to a particular elementary school. Although he was seventy-five years old and hadn't been a principal for twenty years, he was still keenly interested in the education of children. The school community, with a racially mixed faculty and a 70 percent white student body, quickly began to look forward to his visits.

He read to the students, helped them with their math, and listened when they talked. Clad in suit, white shirt, and tie, he had no compunctions about sitting on the floor to play with a child. I think he must have been every child's idea of a wonderful grandfather, a grownup who treated them as equals and with respect.

Captivated by his personableness and ready laugh, impressed by his strong grasp of history and current affairs, the teachers learned from him as easily and painlessly as the children did.

Daddy didn't talk much about his visits to the integrated school. The principal, however, occasionally expressed admiration of him to my brother, whose son attended the school. Once she told my brother of a fight my father had stopped. Addressing the small combatants as "young men," the old man—fired from his principalship more than twenty years before because he wanted equal educational opportunities for all children—calmly separated the children. Sitting on the steps of the school, the three of them—Daddy cool in his three-piece suit, the boys panting and disheveled—quietly talked. The school administrators stared in almost open-mouthed amazement when the boys amicably walked away.

One day in 1973—about a year before Daddy died—my brother happened to stop by that school. Some children—black and white—played together on the playground, apparently oblivious of race. Daddy was watching the children, a satisfied little smile occupying the corner of his mouth.

For a while my brother also watched. Then he jokingly asked, "Is this integration?"

Solemnly, the little smile gone, Daddy glanced at his thirty-six-year-old son, perhaps remembering the day when the now-man had first learned the word. Then he looked thoughtfully around the playground. It was not the right time of year to see cascades of wisteria blossoms.

His eyes came back to the children, dozens of distinctly human little beings—talking, pushing and shoving, holding hands, doing things that are done by children all over the world. In a few minutes they would be sitting in the same classroom, listening to the same teacher, learning from the same books. From where my father and brother stood, only patches of skin and tufts of hair showed the children's differences.

A long minute passed before Daddy slowly nodded. He had always understood that integration was not just a matter of black and white children playing together. It meant the chance for children, unhampered by barriers of race, sex, or creed, to have equal access to educational opportunities. It meant the absence of legal and enforced segregation. As Judge Waring had written: "Segregation is per se inequality."

Ever so quietly, with a flicker of a smile, the good shepherd—seeing with his eyes as well as in his mind the green pastures he had sought—replied, "Yep. This is integration."

10

My Life and Times with Thurgood Marshall

John Hope Franklin

During the summer of 1948 I settled into a routine of teaching for diversion at a place other than my regular tenured position at Howard University, which I had taken up the previous year. I went back to my old job at North Carolina College for Negroes, later called North Carolina College at Durham, and even more recently given the modern, integrated title of North Carolina Central University. It was a most pleasant interlude before what was to become an extraordinarily busy year, made even busier for it being the year that I met Thurgood Marshall. He seemed informally attached to the Howard University Law School, although by that time he had joined the legal staff of the National Association for the Advancement of Colored People, already universally known as the NAACP. He was in and out of Washington, where he, James Nabrit (Secretary of Howard University), and other members of the law faculty held mock court and discharged other responsibilities in preparing Howard Law School students for their postgraduate years.

Marshall was already in the midst of preparing for one of the early legal battles in the long fight to desegregate the nation's public educational institutions. I was deeply flattered and honored when he asked me to join him on one of the cases, *Lyman T. Johnson v. the University of Kentucky.* Johnson, a graduate of the Kentucky State College for Negroes and a history teacher in the Louisville Public Schools, applied for admission to the University of Kentucky to pursue graduate studies in history. He had been summarily denied admission because he was African American and advised to apply to the Kentucky College for Negroes at Frankfort. Having graduated from the Frankfort college and having taken all or most of the courses in history that the institution offered, Johnson declined to apply. Instead, he sought help from the legal arm of the NAACP, and Marshall took his case. Marshall thought that it would be easy to prove that the college at Frankfort was not a match for the large and prestigious all-white university at Lexington. He asked me to assist him by studying the library resources, history curriculum, and department personnel at Lexington and Frankfort and preparing testimony that the two programs were not even competitive. I took delight in the assignment, went to Frankfort and Lexington, where my friends at the University of Kentucky were happy to assist me in gathering information so that Marshall could make his case against the university. At the end of my visit I was able to report to Marshall that the two institutions could not be compared by any reasonable means. The institution for blacks was so thoroughly inferior that the only way to discuss them at the same time was to *contrast* them.

Several weeks later, when the case was to be argued in Frankfort before Judge H. Church Ford of the United States District Court, I had the great pleasure of returning to Frankfort in the company of James Nabrit, who was assisting Marshall and who treated me as though I was a lawyer on the case. From the time that I went with my father to court and listened to him examine and cross-examine witnesses in his role as an attorney, I looked forward to testifying in court and making a few powerful, even decisive points that would impress the lawyers *and* the judge. Imagine my surprise, bordering on chagrin, when at the end of the defendant's poor showing, Marshall rose and made the observation to Judge Ford that since the defendant had not made and could not make a case, he respectfully suggested that Ford should order Johnson admitted to the University of Kentucky. How could he do that without my testimony? I asked in silence. And when Judge Ford told Marshall that he would indeed order the admission of Johnson *forthwith,* I was almost as disappointed as the officials from the University of Kentucky. It took a few minutes for me to appreciate the sweeping victory that Marshall had achieved, and that we all had reason to celebrate. I hope that no one had seen my immediate disappointment and, instead, saw how delighted I was to realize, moments later, that we all had won a complete and historic victory!

I had no immediate subsequent contact with Thurgood Marshall except to encounter him in Washington from time to time. On such occasions we would reminisce about Kentucky and rejoice in *our* victory! Meanwhile, I proceeded with my career, teaching at Howard University during the regular academic year and assisting major universities salve their consciences by accepting their invitations for brief visiting professorships. Thus, I taught at Harvard University in the summer of 1951, at the University of Wisconsin in Madison for the spring semester in 1953, and Cornell University in the summer of 1953. Toward the end of my summer school stint at Cornell University, I received a telephone call from Thurgood Marshall inquiring about my plans for the autumn of 1953. I responded that I would be returning to the only regular job that I had, the one at Howard University. He told me that I would also be working for him, and if I did not agree to do so, he would regret the fate that the gods would dispense on me. I replied that under the circumstances there was nothing I could do but bow to his command. After describing my duties and my schedule he wished me well for the remainder of the summer and bade me farewell.

The legal suit to desegregate the public schools in Kansas, the District of Columbia, Delaware, Virginia, and South Carolina had been argued before the Supreme Court in the term just ended. The justices, dissatisfied with the arguments set forth by both sides, declined to reach a decision in the case. Instead, they ordered the case to be reargued in the next term and requested that the attorneys for both sides answer several critical questions, including what evidence was there to show that the state legislatures and conventions that voted to ratify the Fourteenth Amendment had in mind that the amendment would abolish segregation in the public schools? The Court ordered that counsel on both sides be prepared to answer such questions during its autumn term, 1953. There were other questions that the justices raised, and all of them were serious questions in constitutional history. Thurgood and his colleagues turned to historians to assist them in finding the answers.

Upon my return from Ithaca to Washington in August, Thurgood and I agreed on a regular work schedule for me for the late summer and early fall. If I could arrange my teaching schedule, I would go to New York and work in the offices of the NAACP Legal Defense Fund offices from Thursday afternoon until Saturday afternoon, at which time I could return to Washington for the weekend and presumably prepare for the three days of classes at the university and any assignments I brought with me from the Legal Defense Fund offices. I followed that schedule from mid-August to the end of November 1953. My chairman, Rayford Legan, was more than pleased to adjust my teaching schedule. I would take an early afternoon train from Washington, check in at the Algonquin Hotel, and then report for duty at the Legal Defense Fund offices, just around the corner. Thurgood was *always* there, working at his desk, somewhat disheveled in appearance, shirt open at the neck, necktie loose, a lit cigarette in an ashtray or dangling from his lips. He would greet me cordially, tell me what they were doing, and tell me what he wished me to do. He would ask me if I had any news, as if during the week I had found all the answers to the questions raised by the Court. He would seem a bit dejected upon learning that I had not found all the answers to those intimidating questions. I would then tell him what my most recent study of the legislative history of the Fourteenth Amendment had revealed and report how far along I had gotten on any writing assignment he had given me or I had given myself. I would then work until about midnight, when Thurgood would say, "Why don't we take a fifteen minute break?" Whereupon I would return to the hotel for my night's rest.

I do not know how long Thurgood worked, but when I greeted him the following morning, he would appear to have worked through the night. Indeed, it would not be an exaggeration to say that Thurgood Marshall worked harder than anyone I ever knew. He was obsessed with his work, especially appreciating the historic significance of the case pending before the Court and knowing what the outcome would mean for public education in the United States. Although he worked without pause, it seemed, it was clear that he relied heavily on his staff as well as the attorneys associated with him. He certainly depended on the lawyers on his staff, such as Constance Baker Motley, who traveled to the communities where the cases originated, and Bob Carter and Jack Greenberg, who were in the office around the clock, it seemed. In and out of the office were attorneys from the communities where the cases originated: Louis Redding from Wilmington, Delaware; James Nabrit and George E. C. Hayes of Washington, D.C.; and Spottswood Robinson and Oliver Hill of Richmond, Virginia, among others. Among the nonlegal scholars in and out of the office, who participated in seminars, wrote papers, and the like, were Alfred Kelly of Wayne State University, C. Vann Woodward of Yale, Rayford Logan of Howard University, and Herbert Gutman of the University of Rochester. These and others were on call and would do much of their work from home. This was an exciting experience for the nonlegal scholars, as they saw how eager the legal luminaries were to hear what they had to say on anything dealing with the questions advanced by the Court at the end of the previous term.

At Thurgood's request, I wrote a paper on the history of segregation in the public schools. I read it to him and his colleagues at one of our sessions. It was called "Jim Crow Goes to School: The Genesis of Legal Segregation in Southern Schools" and was later published in the *South Atlantic Quarterly*. The piece elicited many comments from the historians and the lawyers, who said that they could use some of my findings in the brief that they were preparing. The historians added to my findings by citing from their own research, while the lawyers seemed to be in awe of what we were able to dig up. In the discussions that followed the reading of my paper and in other discussions, one of them would say, "Let's hear what Vann [Woodward, the preeminent historian of the South] has to say," while another would ask "Al" Kelly, the great constitutional historian, what he thought of my findings. It was obvious that they would take whatever morsels we had to offer and be grateful for them. As for me—and I suspect the same was true for the other scholars—it was exhilarating.

Regardless of how pointed our questions were or how significant our discoveries might be, the one thing that Thurgood would not tolerate was speculation about possible opinions of the Court. If one of the nonlegal researchers declared that the Court simply *had* to rule in our favor, because of our findings or the power of our arguments, Thurgood would come as close to a reprimand as I ever heard him. Our task, he would say, was not to speculate, but to make a case so persuasive that the Court would be compelled to rule in our favor. We should, therefore, work on the case and not on the Court's opinion, which we would not be writing anyway! On the other hand, all of us who were nonlegal participants in the discussions in Thurgood's offices were immensely gratified and impressed with the way in which our work was appreciated by the lawyers. They spoke with precision about what transpired in the House of Representatives in the sessions of 1867 and 1868. They could quote what Thaddeus Stevens said about the racial segregation of the schools or any portion of society. They were remarkably familiar with what transpired in both houses of the Congress from day to day and seemed to have no difficulty in placing the events that transpired in the Congress in the proper context. They even seemed to understand the relationship of events that transpired in, say, 1868, with those that were occurring on the contemporary scene. The lawyers seemed to have no difficulty in juxtaposing the past with the present, because they had become legal historians. I could not have asked for a greater transformation.

It was in early November that the draft of the Legal Defense Fund's brief began to take shape. We were all invited to comment on it, to offer suggestions, corrections, criticisms, or whatever observations came to mind. It was at this point that the tables were turned. While a few weeks earlier we historians had regarded ourselves as authorities on Reconstruction and the legislative history of the Fourteenth Amendment, we were now awed by the very appearance of the brief: its formality, its legalistic wording, and its deference to the Court. It was not altogether new to me, for I had seen some of the briefs that my father had presented in cases before the Oklahoma Supreme Court. Even so, I was enormously impressed with what Thurgood Marshall and his colleagues had done with the material we had provided and the vast amount of information they had generated on their own. In a sense the tables had indeed been turned. The previous summer, we had every reason to feel that we were in a superior position, because at that stage the lawyers appeared to be pitifully dependent on the historians. By November, thanks to the crash course we had provided the lawyers and the diligence and speed with which they became legal historians, I was quite confident that they would have no difficulty in presenting their arguments, even the historical arguments, to the United States Supreme Court.

I knew early on that Thurgood's nonlegal staff would not be able to hear the arguments before the Court, because of the demand for tickets by persons much higher on the eligibility list than we were. It really did not matter to me. I had observed the transformation of our lawyers, including Thurgood Marshall, from insecure novices in the history of Reconstruction to confident professionals who could argue with the best Reconstruction historians about what transpired during those troubled years and why. I was confident that they would "hold up the side" and that we would all be proud of them. Thurgood had thanked me for what I had done. It was nothing when compared to what he had done, and I told him so.

On May 17, 1954, I was in my office at Howard University, giving little thought to the possibility that this would be a historic day in the life of the nation. My wife, Aurelia, called me from her office at Spingarn High School, where she was the librarian. Had I heard the news, she inquired. What news? I replied. She told me that the decision in *Brown* had just been handed down and that it was unanimous in favor of Brown. I called Thurgood Marshall to congratulate him but was unable to reach him. Aurelia and I celebrated quietly. While the Brown decision was historic, even revolutionary, it did not mean that black and white children would be going to school together in the fall of 1954. Indeed, resistance already began to build on the afternoon of May 17, and it continued to build over the succeeding days and months. Indeed, the resistance began to build so rapidly in the Congress and among the general public that the Court sought to rein in the opposition in a subsequent ruling, called *Brown II,* in which the Court ruled that the desegregation of the public schools should go forward "with all deliberate speed," whatever that meant. The imagination and creativity of those resisting any kind of change would be revealed in the succeeding generations, thus giving the warriors of 1954 reason to wonder if the time would ever come when peaceful desegregation of the nation's public schools would enjoy anything resembling widespread support.

I saw very little of Thurgood following the decision in *Brown.* In due course he would leave the Legal Defense Fund and become a judge on the second circuit of the United States Court of Appeals. Later, President Lyndon Johnson sent him to the Department of Justice to become solicitor general of the United States. I do not know how much credence to put to the claim, ascribed to President Johnson, that since he intended to appoint Marshall to the Supreme Court, he wanted to be certain that he had adequate experience in the federal judicial system. True or not, President Johnson appeared to derive much pleasure from making the spectacular and historic appointment of Thurgood Marshall to the position of Associate Justice of the United States Supreme Court in 1967. This would be the first time that an African American had been appointed to such an exalted position. Marshall would sit on the Court until 1991.

Although we would speak by telephone from time to time, I never saw Thurgood after he went to the high court. Whenever we visited over the telephone, I made myself available to share my opinion or assistance about any matter he desired; and I provided him with whatever historical information he sought. On one occasion, he called to request some citations for something on which he was working. I had learned not to inquire about the context of the citation he was seeking or, indeed, what case he was working on. When I provided him with the citation, he thanked me and was about to end the conversation without an exchange of the usual pleasantries that had been a part of our relationship in the past. When I asked him why he was so glum, he replied in a straightforward way that, if I knew what he knew, I would be glum too. When the decision came down in the case of *Regents of the University of California v. Bakke*, I wondered if it was the debate in the Court's chambers that made Marshall so down. The Court held that in considering applicants for admission to the University of California at Davis, the university could take a variety of factors into consideration that, indeed, could outweigh the matter of race, thus not guaranteeing the admission of any African American to the university.

He could have been unhappy about yet another development. Thurgood and his colleagues, including Charles Houston and the legal generation immediately preceding Thurgood, had risked their lives repeatedly by urging African Americans to vote, by urging aggrieved African Americans to use the courts and other legal instruments to protect their rights as citizens. Yet, since the Montgomery bus boycott, the Selma Voting Rights March, and the March on Washington, few gave any attention to the risks and sacrifices that the Houstons and the Marshalls had made in the earlier years. It was as though the pioneers had been forgotten and the focus was permanently on the later, more "glamorous" generation. Perhaps Thurgood paid little attention to what was occurring in the streets and on the hustings. It was just as well if he did not. By the time he had settled in as an associate justice of the United States Supreme Court, the civil rights battle had entered an entirely new stage.

Two years before *Bakke,* Thurgood Marshall sent me a draft of the speech he had been invited to deliver before the American Bar Association meeting in Hawaii and asked for my comments. It was "vintage Marshall." In it he called the United States Constitution a "flawed document." I congratulated him on the speech and encouraged him to deliver it as written. After delivering the speech he was criticized in some quarters for being a critic of the Constitution while sitting on the Supreme Court. In urging him to deliver the speech as written, I took the position that the Constitution was not sacrosanct and calling attention to its flaws was a sign of civic health.

In a televised press conference after Marshall announced his retirement from the Court, one reporter asked him why he was stepping down. In frank and characteristic fashion, he replied that he was old. He could have added that he could look back on a life of ceaseless service, courage, and sacrifice and was tired. He could also have added that he was still feisty.

11

The Intolerable Burden

Constance Curry

For the past ten years, I have been savoring the second gift of my life—writing about some of the people that I met during the civil rights movement of the 1960s. The first gift was to actually be part of that movement. I was associated with the Student Nonviolent Coordinating Committee from 1960 until 1964, when I joined the staff of the American Friends Service Committee (AFSC). As their Southern Field representative, I spent the next eleven years wandering around the South, following the wonderful tenet of the Quakers—"Proceed as way opens."

Some background is in order.

After the passage of the 1964 Civil Rights Act—of which Title VI mandated a plan for school desegregation—many southern schools, particularly in rural areas, submitted a "freedom of choice" plan to Washington. This scheme theoretically allowed all parents to send their children to the schools of their choice. The white power structure knew full well that black parents, in most southern states trapped in the economic peonage of the sharecropping system, would not dare choose a white school for their children.

However, in every Southern state there were black families who faced the challenge, and it was my pleasure and honor to meet and try to assist several of these "ordinary" people—people willing to make the choice and face the consequences. From 1965 until 1975, I worked closely with the Carter family of Sunflower County, Mississippi. Matthew and Mae Bertha Carter had thirteen children and sharecropped on a cotton plantation not far from Drew, Mississippi, in the heart of the Delta. Drew is a few miles from Parchman Penitentiary, a few miles from Ruleville, home of Fannie Lou Hamer, and not far from Senator James Eastland's 5,800–acre cotton plantation in Doddsville. Right outside Drew, the remnants of a barn mark the site where Emmett Till was lynched in 1955 for allegedly whistling at a white woman.

The first five Carter children graduated from the ill-equipped "colored" school and left home immediately to join the military or to find jobs outside of the state. Mae Bertha and Matthew were determined to get a better education for the rest of their children, filled out the "freedom of choice" forms, and in the fall of 1965 sent their seven school-age children to the previously all-white schools in Drew. For five years, the Carter children were the only blacks attending these schools and were subjected to insults, harassment, and humiliation until the courts ordered full desegregation in 1970. The suit that prompted that order, filed by Marian Wright Edelman and others with the NAACP Legal Defense and Educational Fund in Jackson, asked for injunctive relief against the operation of a racially segregated system that placed a "cruel and intolerable burden" on black pupils and parents.

In the meantime, shots were fired into the Carter house, their crops were plowed under, their credit was cut off, they were evicted from the plantation, and they could not find jobs for some time. Finally, with the help of the AFSC and other groups they were able to find a house in Drew, jobs with Head Start, and better treatment in general when the powers in Drew realized that the Carter family had support from the outside world. I lost track of the Carters in 1975 when I left the AFSC and went to work for Atlanta city government, but I ran into Mae Bertha at the King Center in 1988, when she attended a conference on women in the civil rights movement.

We hugged each other, and in answer to my question about the family she told me that Matthew had died earlier that year; the children, including Carl (the baby in 1965) had graduated from the Drew High School, all eight had gone on to college, and seven of them had graduated from Ole Miss. I realized then that I wanted to tell their story, and *Silver Rights* was published in 1996. Aaron Henry, another and better-known civil rights leader in Mississippi, read *Silver Rights* and asked me to help tell his story, and *The Fire Ever Burning* was published in 2000. *Deep in Our Hearts: Nine White Women in the Freedom Movement* was also published that year, and I wrote a chapter and was facilitator for this book. At the thirtieth anniversary celebration of 1964 Freedom Summer in Mississippi in 1994, Bob Moses had encouraged us all to tell our own stories, so that history might be more accurate. In 2002, my collaboration with Mrs. Winson Hudson of Leake County, Mississippi, *Mississippi Harmony: Memoirs of a Freedom Fighter,* was published.

After *Silver Rights* was published, several people asked Mae Bertha to tell her story on video and film, and what an experience it was to see! All of her humor, vitality, and courage came shining through, and with the help of Chea Prince, an associate in Atlanta, we finished a documentary called *The Intolerable Burden* in the spring of 2003. Initially, we had planned to tell the Carter story and show the successes the Carter children had made of their lives in spite of the trauma of earlier years. We interviewed all eight of them, and I was amazed at some of the stories they told—stories that they had not told me in the interviews for *Silver Rights*. Beverly, who desegregated A. W. James Elementary school as the lone black third grader, cries in the film as she tells of never having anyone to play with—standing alone against the school wall during play period, watching the little white girls jump rope and wishing that she could also jump, because she was good. One day they approached her, but she found that they would only allow her to throw the rope.

We interviewed white people from Drew, some of whom had attended school with the Carters and were sorry for their ignorance of what was taking place or sorry for their silence if they did know. Other whites remain adamant today in their belief that the civil rights movement ruined "the Southern way of life." The head mistress of the all-white private North Sunflower Academy told us the history of its establishment, and the assistant school superintendent spoke of the high dropout, expulsion, and suspension rates in the now mostly black Drew High School. Senator Willie Simmons, the first black state senator from the Delta since reconstruction, decried the enormous state allocations for prisons and corrections rather than education.

As we developed the documentary, we tried to look at it through the eyes of Mae Bertha Carter. She passed away in 1999, and as we worked it became clear to us that, as a fighter in the struggle for justice until she drew her last breath, she would have wanted us to tell the whole and continuing story of racism. Thus, the film is divided into three parts, segregation, desegregation and resegregation. There is a fourth part, however: incarceration.

The film ends with an epilogue, "Education vs. Incarceration," that points out the Sunflower County pattern of failing public education for blacks and minorities, and poor people in general, and the fast track to prison is being replicated throughout the United States. It is sobering indeed to see that one of Mae Bertha's grandchildren, Lorenzo, son of one of the older Carter men but raised by his maternal grandmother in Drew, is serving a long term in Parchman Penitentiary for dealing drugs. The film reflects the dismal conditions of these poor rural towns like Drew, with zero-tolerance policies in the schools, no jobs, no industry, and deserted streets. One young black man we interviewed says in the documentary, "Can't go to school, no jobs, no way to get to the next nearest town to work—nothing to do but get caught up in the street life."

The reactions to the documentary have been a revelation. We have shown it in venues from Ithaca, New York, to Cambridge, Massachusetts, from South Carolina to California, to AFSC groups, universities, historical associations and high schools, and a corporate diversity training group. I suppose one pervasive reaction of note is the general lack of knowledge of the civil rights movement and the conditions that precipitated the struggle of the 1960s. This was, after all, only forty years ago—we are not talking about ancient Roman history here. This comes mostly from younger people, but surprise at the treatment of the family and the lives of blacks in general are expressed often by adult audiences from outside the South.

The film is generally accepted with warmth and enthusiasm by black audiences, and I have noticed tears on the faces of people who have told me that it brought back their own experience as the first black child in a white school in Tallahassee, or in Florence, South Carolina, or Richmond and other places. In an audience that was mostly white, I was told that it was too depressing and why couldn't I just end with the Carters all graduating from Ole Miss?

In an all-black high school in Jackson, Mississippi, the students cheered when Mae Bertha Carter says that it's useless to be afraid to die—that you are already dead if you let people control your life. After viewing the film many black activists have said that just having children in integrated schools won't ever make any difference as long as the curriculum is geared to a white world and how success or achievement is measured in that world. Little by little people are recognizing the reverberations of "resegregation" in their own communities, where those (mostly white) who can afford it are sending their children to private academies. And they talk of "desegregated" schools, where more specious segregation occurs in honor programs or advanced-placement classes that are almost always majority white. We are continuing to create a "better-educated" white elite.

The year 2004 was the fiftieth anniversary of the *Brown* decision, when the Supreme Court declared that segregated schools were unconstitutional. I received many invitations to show *The Intolerable Burden* at related events, including a conference at the University of Illinois. When I was working in Mississippi in 1964, I remember thinking that this was ten years after the *Brown* decision, and there were still no black children in the public schools in the state, except for the few who had been placed by court order in the cities of Biloxi and Jackson and in Leake County. This was a general pattern in most of the southern states. The resistance to following the decision, which included the harassment and violence that the Carters and many other families faced, came up in all of the conferences and panels on the anniversary of *Brown*. I learned many things in these discussions of *Brown* and its aftermath. One historian pointed out that we had totally underestimated the massive resistance that implementation of the decision would face. The White Citizens' Councils were born in Mississippi and quickly spread the most-feared of all messages behind racism—that the mongrelization of the white race would result when black and white children went to school together. And of course, the ensuing message from the courts that the decision must be implemented "with all deliberate speed" played out with lots of deliberation and little speed. There was little to no planning on *how* to implement the decision in terms of human relationships, or thought given to what would happen to school personnel. Was the decision partially just political in the aftermath of the recognition of our world leadership following World War II—an attempt to live up to our reputation as a nation of freedom and justice? At one conference on the *Brown* decision, I heard a black man talk about the closing of his high school in North Carolina in 1969 and of his being transferred to a previously all-white school: "It was like our school and history had never existed—we had no past. None of our trophies or photos or black history books came with us. Our principal was sent to the desegregated schools to become the assistant to the assistant to the white principal."

Almost all audiences viewing the film have been surprised at the direct connection between the failure of public education and the fast track to prison for youth of color. They are quite willing to admit that the issue of education versus incarceration exists everywhere and to acknowledge how much money is being spent on building prisons and keeping them filled. They are stunned, however, to learn that with more than 2 million people in prison, the United States has the world's highest incarceration rate. If you add those on probation and parole, the figure is 6.5 million or one in every thirty-two adults. The majority of U.S. inmates are black men, but prison populations are increasingly inclusive of Hispanics, other minorities, and poor people in general. Racism and discrimination cover a broad spectrum ranging from police profiling to disproportionate death penalty convictions. In between are issues of prison privatization, mandatory sentencing, lack of indigent defense, prison sentences instead of drug treatment, abominable prison conditions, and lack of reentry or aftercare programs.

My own civil rights orientation makes me perhaps most outraged over statistics concerning felony disfranchisement. More than 4.6 million Americans—or 2 percent of the voting-age population—are barred from voting because of past criminal convictions (even if they have completely served their sentences and are not on probation or parole). Because more than 60 percent of the prison population is black or Latino, the voting power of these groups is disproportionately diluted.

On a nationwide basis, one in eight African American men is denied the right to vote. This translates to about 1.4 million black men. The number of Hispanic voters similarly disfranchised is approaching 15 percent.

Whose interest does this serve? Depriving convicted felons of the vote is done on a state-by-state basis and the procedures for reinstatement vary. There is movement in several states to do away with these laws. As Mae Bertha Carter used to say in an irate voice, "People died so black people could vote."

So here we are today, still bearing the burden of a majority that does not want to see minorities receive a quality education, if any. And added to that, we in the South are particularly reaping the whirlwind from criminal justice concepts and policies planted some thirty years ago. We have been surrounded by messages of "get tough on crime," "three strikes and you're out," mandatory sentencing, disparities in drug sentencing for crack and for cocaine, and media portrayal of "young black predators." Most of the southern states now spend more on incarceration than on education. George W. Bush's application of the underfunded *No Child Left Behind* program takes a great toll on children who don't test well, and feeds right into the school-to-prison pipeline. Also, under Bush and the Republicans, private prisons flourished, often in rural areas where people have been duped into believing that the prisons will improve their economy, and these politicians allowed a system where people are traded on Wall Street instead of off a slave block in Charleston, South Carolina.

These public-education and criminal-justice injustices, hidden and ignored, have spread from the South to infect present-day America. Remedying them must become the focus of the human rights movement in this country.

12

The Freedom Riders

Two Personal Perspectives

James C. Onderdonk

And other voices echoed the freedom words,
. . . Ride! And I rode the bus for freedom.
—Naomi Madgett,
"Alabama Centennial" in *The Black Poets,* 198.

On May 4, 1961, thirteen men—seven whites and six blacks—boarded buses in Washington, D.C., bound for New Orleans to test whether the principles of equal access affirmed in several Supreme Court cases would apply to public transportation across the South.[1] All believed firmly in the power of nonviolent protest and in personal resistance to injustice. These were the original Freedom Riders. The ordeals they endured, and the courage they demonstrated, are now justly honored within the history of the civil rights movement.

As part of a series of programs designed to commemorate the *Brown v. Board* fiftieth anniversary, the University of Illinois at Urbana-Champaign invited the four surviving original Freedom Riders to campus. One, John Lewis, was unable to attend. The others, Ben Cox, Hank Thomas, and Ed Blankenheim, made a series of public appearances, visited public schools, and spoke to university students in seminars. They offered a highly personal look at a momentous event in the history of American race relations. Ed Blankenheim's reminiscences are recorded in the next chapter of this volume; my essay is built up from the comments and presentations of the two other riders. Their memories of the ride offer a searing view of the racism of the time. Yet at the same time both men, inspired by the idealism of the early '60s, stressed the integrated nature of the Freedom Rides. While they are black, they wished to call attention to the equally heroic white activists alongside whom they fought for justice. An integrated society still remains for them a central goal of social change, and they envision their activism as something undertaken on behalf of all of humanity. Hank Thomas, for instance, held up the example of a Jew he met while demonstrating for equal rights for African Americans as a model of the humanity, inclusivity, and nobility of spirit that characterized the Freedom Rides:

I remember in the suburbs of Washington D.C., walking the picket line, and there was a . . . a survivor of Auschwitz, and he showed me his tattoo number on his arm. Later on I had the chance to ask him—I did not know a great deal about the Holocaust at that particular time—why he had only been in this country about eight or nine years. So here he was just fifteen, sixteen years removed from the Nazi concentration camps, and he is walking a picket line on behalf of my rights, and I will never forget what he had said. It was something to the effect that there was nobody in Germany to stand up for the Jews. He wanted to make certain that if he ever had the opportunity to stand up for what is right for truth and justice, that he did it. So, he said, "It is not just for you, it is for everyone, every minority who has been put upon."[2]

During their visits to the University of Illinois, Cox and Thomas spoke to high school students in Urbana-Champaign, telling of the original Freedom Ride and inspiring them with the idealistic spirit of their vision of social change.

• • •

In 1961 Hank Thomas was a nineteen-year-old student at Howard University. At the last minute he replaced a rider who had to drop out due to illness. Thomas would go on after the rides to become a successful businessman in the Atlanta area. The Reverend Ben Elton Cox was born in Whiteville, Tennessee, the seventh of sixteen children. When he was five years old, his family moved to Kankakee, Illinois, where they lived in the "colored" section of town. Ben dropped out of school and worked to help his family pay the bills, but he eventually earned his high school equivalency and attended Livingstone College, a historically black college in Salisbury, North Carolina. He graduated in 1951 with a bachelor's degree in sociology and a minor in history. He then attended Hood Seminary, affiliated with Livingstone College, and Howard University, a historically black institution in Washington, D.C. He received a master of divinity degree from the School of Religion at Howard in June of 1957. When he joined the Freedom Ride in 1961, he was serving as a field secretary for CORE, the Committee of Racial Equality (later Congress of Racial Equality), a civil rights organization founded in Chicago in 1942.

After the Freedom Rides, Reverend Cox continued his work for civil rights. He remained with CORE until 1966 and traveled to various universities teaching students, both black and white, how to use nonviolent protest techniques to achieve social change. In December 1961, some months after the Freedom Ride, he led a demonstration of Southern University students in Baton Rouge, Louisiana. After participants recited the Pledge of Allegiance and sang several hymns, including "God Bless America," Ben suggested to the group that they have lunch at one of the many segregated lunch counters in stores downtown. He was arrested the next day and charged with disturbing the peace. In January of 1965 the United States Supreme Court reversed his conviction on the grounds that it violated his right of free speech. The Court held that free speech "may indeed best serve its high purpose when it produces a condition of unrest, creates dissatisfaction with conditions as they are, or even stirs people to anger."[3] *Cox v. Louisiana* is widely considered to be a landmark decision in support of the rights of free speech and free assembly.

To understand the full significance of Cox's and Thomas's memories it is helpful to recall some of the details of the first Freedom Ride. The riders carefully selected their expected date of arrival and destination with eyes directed toward the history of race relations in the United States. They planned to arrive on May 17, the seventh anniversary of the *Brown v. Board of Education* decision. They chose New Orleans because it was the site of *Plessy v. Ferguson,* a decision handed down by the Supreme Court in 1896 that upheld the constitutionality of racial segregation on public conveyances. Although justices did not use the phrase "separate but equal" in the Court's decision, *Plessy v. Ferguson* is widely acknowledged as the legal foundation used throughout the South to enforce segregation of the races. Thus, the riders wanted to juxtapose the racial integration proposed by the *Brown* decision with the racial segregation enforced by laws and practices in the spirit of *Plessy.*

The riders were sponsored by CORE, which had already attempted to test segregation laws, and these actions were themselves inspired by the deeds of a few heroic individuals. In July of 1944 a young black woman, Irene Morgan, a defense worker and mother, had refused to give up her seat to a white passenger on a Greyhound bus traveling from Norfolk, Virginia, to Baltimore, Maryland. Forcibly removed from the bus in Saluda, Virginia, Morgan was convicted of resisting arrest and of violating Virginia's 1930 statute against mixed-race seating on public conveyances. Although she pled guilty to the charge of resisting arrest (she apparently offered a spirited resistance to the officers who removed her from the bus) and paid the hundred-dollar fine, she refused to pay the ten-dollar fine for violating the segregation laws and fought her conviction. She appealed through the Virginia courts and eventually to the United States Supreme Court. The National Association for the Advancement of Colored People (NAACP) helped overturn Morgan's conviction, and in *Morgan v. Virginia* (1946), the Court narrowly defined the rights of interstate passengers for equal treatment when traveling.

To test the effect of *Morgan,* in April of 1947 CORE organized the Journey of Reconciliation—a bus trip by eight blacks and eight whites through Virginia, North Carolina, Tennessee, and Kentucky. At bus terminals along the way, the riders were met with hostility and arrest, and some of the riders served time on a chain gang in Roxboro, North Carolina, for violation of segregation laws. In one trial, the riders witnessed the most insidious racism—the courtroom had two Bibles, one labeled "white," the other "black." When black witnesses testified, the bailiff instructed them to hold the Bible in their left hand and raise their right to swear. When a white witness testified, the clerk held up the "white" Bible while the witness raised his or her right hand to swear. It was obvious to the riders that the white clerk would not touch the "black" Bible.[4]

In 1958, in another test of the constitutionality of segregation laws in interstate commerce, police arrested a black law student, Bruce Boynton, after he ordered a sandwich and tea in a whites-only section of a restaurant in the Trailways bus station in Richmond, Virginia. Like Morgan, Boynton appealed his case to the Supreme Court, and in December of 1960 the Court ruled in *Boynton v. Virginia* that the maintenance of separate facilities, such as restaurants, waiting rooms, and restrooms, for interstate passengers was unconstitutional.

The Freedom Ride of 1961 drew on the *Morgan* and *Boynton* precedents and constituted a further test of Supreme Court decisions. Because the riders were, according to federal law, acting within their rights, perhaps their deeds should not be understood as civil disobedience. These rights, however, were not enforced in the South, where the simplest act, such as eating together at a bus station lunch counter, was labeled criminal.

After three days of preparation, including training in nonviolent techniques, the riders met in a restaurant the night before they were to leave Washington, D.C. One of the riders likened the gathering to the Last Supper. At that meal, James Farmer, the leader of the riders, told them that no one was obligated to go on the trip and that should they choose to withdraw, they would face no recriminations. At breakfast the next morning, he was gratified to find all the riders ready and determined to begin.[5]

Once en route, the strategy of the Freedom Riders was simple. As Cox explains: "We rode on the two main bus lines in America, Trailways and Greyhound, and we would go and seat ourselves opposite of where our race was expected to be seated. The blacks were to sit up front and the whites were to go to the back."[6] Cox continues:

> Of course our seating arrangements scared a lot of [other] riders and so many of them would get up and leave rather than sit beside us. Some of the drivers resented us in that seating pattern, but they had to continue. When we got to a bus station, the whites would go into the old "colored" waiting room and we blacks went into the white. We would try to drink out of the white drinking fountain. We would try to sit down at the lunch counter and we went into the white restrooms. We did this knowing that we would not get served at the lunch counter but we would try to order anyhow.[7]

While the Freedom Riders were challenging the separation of the races in nearly all public accommodations in the South at that time, the specific choice of challenging segregation on buses was strategic. Segregated buses had become a synecdoche for the entire system of racial oppression. For example, the African American social satirist Dick Gregory titled his first book, published in 1962, *From the Back of the Bus* and often used the image in his humor. ("Do you realize how many people are still in jail from those Freedom Rides? I mean, if you buy a bus ticket to Alabama and it says GOOD FOR ONE YEAR—you better believe it!")[8]

Initially, the riders' trip through Virginia and North Carolina was uneventful, and the riders thought that perhaps they had overestimated the racial animosity in the South. That feeling changed in Rock Hill, South Carolina, where a group of white toughs at the bus station attacked three of them. Although badly beaten, the riders did not resist and passed the first test of their commitment to the principle of nonviolent resistance. They faced many such tests.

Black riders of course faced great danger in challenging segregation in the white-dominated South, but both Cox and Thomas, perhaps reflecting the idealism, generosity, and respect for others that characterized the civil rights movement, wished to stress the heroism of their white colleagues. Cox noted the special violence meted out on whites: "The whites would go into the black side of the bus stations and there was quite an uproar. There, naturally, some blacks didn't know what was happening and they resented the whites coming in, you know, and doing that. So at some bus stations a mob greeted us, pushing and shoving and beating, and the odd thing about it was that the whites always got the worst beating."[9] Indeed, the white riders suffered some of the worst injuries. For instance, James Peck's wounds received at the Birmingham, Alabama, bus station required fifty-three stitches.[10]

In his talks to students, Thomas, too, stressed the integrated nature of the Freedom Ride and the special heroism of the non–African American riders: "our fight for integration, our fight for freedom was an integrated one. Of the thirteen freedom riders, seven were white, three were Jews. So I always like to stand, whether it is before an audience like this or an integrated audience, to pay homage and tribute to those whites who stood with us and some who suffered tremendously and especially to the Jews."[11]

The violence meted out on the white riders has a number of explanations. Cox perceptively attributes it to the racist attitudes of white supremacists who felt that African Americans were too stupid or cowardly to lead themselves: "the segregationists said that if they [the whites] were not leading us, then we . . . would not follow. So that is why the whites were called communists and all the other nasty names."[12] Exacerbating hatred further was the idea among whites who assaulted the riders that the white riders were race traitors who violated the unspoken mores of white supremacy that had oppressed African Americans for centuries. Perhaps, too, southern white racists perceived the riders' measured, nonviolent response as a challenge to their own sense of masculinity. Finally, at the height of the cold war, in the midst of competition between the United States and the Soviet Union for the fealty of nonaligned nations, and immediately on the heels of the failed American-backed invasion of Cuba, the Freedom Riders exposed the gulf of hypocrisy between the American creed and the American deed. Whites who did nothing to prevent the abuse used the propaganda that the riders were Soviet ploys as their excuse. The *Birmingham News* alluded to this in their front page article on May 15, 1961, describing the violence at the bus terminal by condemning the riders—"these people were moving through the South to create racial trouble to make headlines not only here but in every city in the United States and in quite a few foreign capitals."[13]

In the end the violence succeeded in bringing the first Freedom Ride to an early and tragic end. Cox takes up the story after Atlanta, when the riders split up into two groups, each on a separate bus:

> One went north to Birmingham, and then the other went to a southern route to Birmingham. The Greyhound bus took the southern route and went through a little town called Anniston, Alabama, and a mob greeted them. A lot of pushing and shoving took place, and the police kept them from killing the Freedom Riders. What they did was they slashed the tires of the Greyhound, knowing that that bus eventually would slow down and stop, and then they followed that Greyhound bus down the road until it stopped and then they began beating on the bus door but the driver would not let them in. The last resort was they threw a fire bomb into the back window of the Greyhound bus and then they came around again and tried to open up the side door or the front door. While they were doing that the fire exploded one of the gas tanks and of course everybody ran or tried to hide from them. So the smoke inside the Greyhound bus was choking the passengers, including the Freedom Riders, but it just so happened that Happy [Albert] Bigelow was an old Navy man. We had the passengers get down on the floor and breathe their air from the floor. By this time the mob was still throwing fire bombs at the buses and finally they decided that we either had to get off or be incinerated. So as they came off the bus, the mob of course took charge with chains, nightsticks, and baseball bats. A state trooper, after he thought he had seen enough, pulled his gun and shot in the air twice. "Get back; there will be no killing here today."[14]

The bus on the northern route fared no better:

> Now, the Trailways bus was on its way to Birmingham and when they got there they attacked them and whipped them. The burning bus flashed around the country and around the world. Reverend Fred Shuttlesworth, who was a Baptist minister in Birmingham, sent a dispatch of cars to the burning Greyhound bus, and . . . his people put the Freedom Riders in the cars and took them to the hospital, but the administrator refused to let his staff wait on them and

to tend to their bruises, because he thought the mob would burn the hospital down. So Reverend Shuttlesworth had his people bring the Freedom Riders to his church along with the same ones from the Trailways bus.[15]

Despite the brutality of the white racists that ended the ride, both Cox and Thomas single out for praise the courage of a young white girl, twelve-year-old Janie Miller. Of all the whites at the scene of the firebombing, she was the only one to help the injured Freedom Riders. Cox recalls,

> Yes, the bus was burning. The Freedom Riders are now on the ground and choking from the heat and the smoke. In this crowd of people that came from this Church of God, a little girl broke away from her mother's hand. She ran to her house which was nearby and pumped a pail of water and brought it over to the Freedom Riders. When the whites in town later on found out that she did that, they ran her mother and father out of town. Later on, one of the Freedom Riders named Henry "Hank" Thomas found that girl out West somewhere, and years later he brought her to a rally to thank her for helping us, probably saving us![16]

Thomas describes Janie Miller as follows:

> Remember, I said to you that there were many white people of good will in the South, but they could not or were afraid to speak up. What happened to this little girl is an example of it. She was twelve years old, and after we had gotten off the bus, finally escaping from the burning bus, all of us had a great deal of smoke in our lungs and so obviously you want water or you want just something to ease your suffering. This little girl, who was there because the bus stopped in front of her house, broke away from her mother to run into the house to get a pitcher of water and some cups. She came out and she started giving us water, each one of us. But we then found out later on that the people of the town, some of the people of the town, turned on her family. They set fire to the family's house. The family came to move. Twelve years old. This girl was twelve years old. They had to send her out of town because of the death threats by adults against a twelve-year-old girl. That was just an example of the ugliness that existed.[17]

In addition to recounting their experiences in 1961, both Freedom Riders told audiences that much work remained undone in the struggle to achieve civil rights in the United States for all. Cox told students: "America to me is the greatest country on earth, but we have some dark spots, one of them being racism. . . . If *you* don't work to bring about equality, it will never come about."[18] Thomas spoke of movement toward the realization of the American dream and the promises of the Constitution and also returned to the theme of personal action. Improvement came about "because of not just the work that the civil rights blacks have done, but because people of 'good will,' Americans of good will, whether you lived in the South or you lived in the North you said, 'Enough, we have got to make this country what it is supposed to be.' And once again as I said, I was happy to have a small part of it."[19]

Despite the importance of the '60s in their lives neither man would wish to return to them. Cox notes: "We have traveled a great distance and most of it has been progressive. I would not want to go back and live before the '60s, and I would not want to relive the '60s because we have come so far. You see there was a time when a black could not get his name in the newspaper and was never addressed as 'mister.' In the pages where people got married they would never let a black picture come right up and touch the white pictures. They would always have a line through there. Many newspapers had a section called 'Colored News.'"[20]

For both Cox and Thomas, personal experience of racism led them directly to activism. Cox remembers that, even as a kindergartner, the last line of the Pledge of Allegiance, which promises "liberty and justice for all," had moved him. At the age of five, however, he knew that only six blocks away from his school in downtown Kankakee, he had to move off the sidewalk if white people approached, that he should never look white people directly in the eye, and that he had always to use the "colored" water fountain and restroom. The injustice and hypocrisy that forced him to do these things in a northern state, the so-called "Land of Lincoln" was not lost on him.[21] De facto segregation was widespread in the North, and was especially galling in the home state of the president who had issued the Emancipation Proclamation and whose most memorable public address on a Civil War battlefield reiterated the promise of an American truth that all people are created equal.

Thomas's motivation for participating in the ride, like that described in Blankenheim's essay in this volume, came of racism in the United States and service with the armed forces: "the cruel irony of what happened to me is that while I could not enjoy certain rights and privileges as an American in the state of Alabama and throughout the South, our government thought that it would be a nice idea if I would come and go to Vietnam and help the Vietnamese enjoy some of the same things that I could not enjoy here. The old biblical saying goes that God doesn't put any more on you than you can possibly bear, so I guess that was part of my burden as well."[22]

• • •

By 1961 three Court decisions, *Morgan* in 1946, *Brown* in 1954, and *Boynton* in 1960, had all guaranteed equal access for all Americans to simple justice and dignity in interstate travel. As the riders convincingly demonstrated, however, these decisions were unenforceable in most of the South, where state governments vigorously upheld segregation laws and ordinances while the rest of the country turned a blind eye and left de facto segregation in place. The enforcement of laws depends on more than the laws themselves, but also on a political will. It was the courageous actions of a few individuals in 1961 that helped to create that will. When images of the bloodied and beaten riders and of their bombed out bus were flashed around the country and world, the political will to enforce law began to coalesce. Although gains in civil rights have been significant since 1961, progress has been uneven and slower than many of the riders would have wished. Nevertheless, the contributions of the riders to the struggle for social justice have been enormous. Through direct, nonviolent personal action the Freedom Riders provided the impetus for issues of social justice and moral reform to inform political will. They succeeded in placing civil rights squarely in a national context and moved it onto the national agenda where in large measure it remains today. By speaking to youth on the anniversary of *Brown v. Board,* these Freedom Riders continued their legacy of activism, a lesson brought from nearly fifty years ago that personal commitment in the face of monstrous injustice can effect positive social change.

Notes

1. For a complete history of the Freedom Rides see Raymond Arsenault, *Freedom Riders: 1961 and the Struggle for Racial Justice* (Oxford: Oxford University Press, 2006).

2. Address by Henry Thomas (transcript in possession of the author, May 12, 2004).

3. *Cox v. Louisiana,* 379 U.S. 536 (1965).

4. Arsenault, *Freedom Riders,* 49.

5. Ibid., 108–9.

6. Reverend Ben Cox, interview by author, January 19, 2006, tape in the possession of the author.

7. Ibid.

8. Dick Gregory, *From the Back of the Bus* (New York: Avon Books, 1962), 67.

9. Interview with Cox.

10. Kenneth O'Reilly, "The FBI and the Civil Rights Movement During the Kennedy Years–from the Freedom Rides to Albany," *Journal of Southern History* 54, no. 2 (1988): 207.

11. Address by Thomas. Thomas is referring to three civil rights workers, Michael Schwerner, James Chaney, and Andrew Goodman, who were murdered while they worked on voter registration in Mississippi; Schwerner and Goodman were Jewish. On June 21, 1964, they disappeared in Neshoba County, Mississippi, after having been arrested on a trumped up charge of speeding by the local sheriff. Their bodies were discovered nearly seven weeks later in an earthen dam. A number of white Klansmen and police officials were charged with the federal crime of depriving the men of their civil rights. Seven of the defendants, including the deputy sheriff, were

convicted (although none of either manslaughter or murder) and eight were acquitted, and in three cases the jury failed to reach a verdict. Trial records make it clear that the police and the Ku Klux Klan collaborated in the murders. It was not until June of 2005, forty-one years after the murders, that a white Mississippian would be convicted of manslaughter in the case. For a detailed description of the murders and trial see Douglas Linder, *The Mississippi Burning Trial,* http://www.law.umkc .edu/faculty/projects/ftrials/price&bowers/Account.html; and Ben Chaney, *Schwerner, Chaney and Goodman: The Struggle for Justice,* available at the American Bar Association's Web site, http://www.abanet.org/irr/hr/spring00humanrights/chaney .html (both accessed April 9, 2008).

12. Cox interview.

13. "Where Were the Police?" *Birmingham News,* May 15, 1961.

14. Cox interview.

15. Ibid.

16. Ibid.

17. Address by Thomas.

18. Cox interview.

19. Address by Thomas.

20. Cox interview.

21. Ibid.

22. Address by Henry Thomas.

13

Looking Back at the Freedom Riders

Ed Blankenheim

I joined the Marine Corps when I was sixteen. As a high school dropout with no plans and even less ambition, I somehow found myself in South Carolina, in the Marines. Here I found plenty to do and a host of new friends. There was one in particular, Richard, whom I met on my first day in boot camp. Richard and I were both from Chicago and we shared the same birthday (he was also underage). We had both left home without our parents' knowledge.

There the similarities ended.

Richard was black and his parents were college professors. The family lived in Hyde Park, an integrated, liberal, and wealthy section that was centered around the University of Chicago. He had graduated from the University High School at age sixteen.

I, on the other hand, lived in a segregated working-class neighborhood where I had dropped out of school at fifteen only to bum around and get into trouble till I joined the Marines.

We were a pretty unlikely pair, but we got on famously. I had never known any black people, but my parents' Catholic influence held that all men are created equal and that was good enough for me.

So we embarked on the three months of boot camp and, to be quite honest, I was a little in awe of Richard. He taught me a great deal, especially about music. I helped him become more street smart, as he had lived a very sheltered life.

He did not have any friends anywhere near his age so I showed him the ropes.

We finished boot camp and were sent to Camp Lejeune, North Carolina. All this time we had never left the base or gone into town. When we finally got a weekend pass we decided to go into Jacksonville, a town twenty miles outside the base. We were pretty excited when the base bus came to our barracks and picked us up to take us to town. We settled into seats immediately behind the driver and were talking about our upcoming adventure when the bus cleared the main gate and the bus driver pulled into a turnaround area.

The driver got up, stood in the aisle, and said, "Now all you niggers get in the back of the bus."

I turned to Richard and asked him what in the hell this guy was talking about. Richard could not answer. He just sank further in his seat, if that were possible. He was embarrassed beyond the ability to speak to or look at me. Just then two military policemen, one black and one white, came on board the bus. The white one took a pink card from his shirt pocket and read: "The United States Marine Corps are guests of the Great State of North Carolina and as such will respect all of its laws and customs."

The black one explained that we had a choice. Go back to the base on a returning bus or ride into town with Richard riding on the back of the bus and me in the front. Richard could not get off that bus fast enough. Something in him died. Back in the barracks when I tried to talk to him he would just say, "Not now, Ed, not now."

I was so furious that I'm certain what came out of my mouth was unintelligible. It was like living in a dream, a nightmare. I couldn't believe that what was happening *was* happening. There had to be an explanation. This had to be a mistake. The United States Marine Corps with its proud traditions, its motto, Semper Fidelis, Always Faithful, could not let this indignity to one of its own go unchallenged.

The next morning I went to see my commanding officer because I knew that he would make sure that nothing like that would ever happen again. The first sergeant told me not to bother, but I insisted on seeing the CO. When I went into his office the CO held up his hand and said, "Look, kid, I've got a war to win and so do you. We can't be wasting our time feeling sorry for some nigger. Now go on back to your platoon, or better still, go see the fucking chaplain." Now, I can't say why, but I did go to see the "fucking chaplain."

The chaplain was much more soft spoken, but the message was still the same. He allowed as how the treatment of Richard was wrong but that we had to understand that the church was working to change that. But this change would take time. "God sees the truth, but waits." I just couldn't resist using that line. It's the title of a story by Dostoyevsky Richard had just given me.

I left the good chaplain with that and retired to barracks to sort things out. We (Richard and I) had been betrayed by the Marine Corps and the Holy Roman Catholic Church. There was nothing to sort out. There was nothing we could do. We were powerless!

So when an opportunity like the Freedom Ride came along some eleven years later, I had to take it. Finally there was a chance to redeem myself.

While none of us could have predicted exactly how the country would respond, we were certain that the black community, especially the black students already loosely organized, would not let the opportunity provided by the Freedom Ride die. After all, we were slapping Jim Crow in the face. Just as surely as if we had thrown down a gauntlet and challenged him to a duel. We felt that we were seeing the beginning of the end of blatant segregation in the southern United States. I think history backs up that claim.

Before the ride began we spent two weeks training for all the situations we might encounter. We all knew the dangers. On the night before we were to leave on the Freedom Ride, Jim Farmer (the organizer) took each aside and told us that if, after the training, we were not sure about the ride we probably should not go. No one would blame us. All thirteen of us showed up at the bus station the next morning.

Anniston, Alabama, was a horrid time and place for me. The violence, the beatings, the fear, and the hatred were beyond anything any of us had ever had or ever would again experience. I would for years try to silence the hatred that reared its ugly head whenever the subject of Anniston was mentioned.

In 2001, on the fortieth anniversary of the Freedom Ride, the Greyhound bus company carried a number of Freedom Riders as they retraced part of the route of the original ride. Anniston was part of that commemorative route. There we were greeted by about half of the townspeople, black and white. I was to give a speech but was so overcome with emotion that I had to ask fellow rider Hank Thomas to do it. Hank was brilliant. He had everyone in tears. It turned into a 1960s San Francisco–style love fest. I exorcised all of my demons that day.

The Freedom Rides succeeded because we were able to command the spotlight long enough that the media and the government could no longer ignore the United States of America's system of apartheid. The cat was out of the bag. The mobs chased us around Anniston and Birmingham and finally to the Birmingham airport. Now the airlines cater to a different clientele than do bus lines.

14

The Middle Generation
after *Brown*

Kal Alston

This essay is an introduction to a story that, on the one hand, probably seems as familiar as Black History Month and, on the other hand, chronicles events that happened more than fifty years ago. This story is addressed specifically to those of you born post-1960s from someone with a slightly different generational perspective. It is meant to be a bridging story, one story about what it meant to be too young to march but too old ever to believe in racism as simply an historical artifact.

I am going to address the aftermath of a famous legal case that reached the United States Supreme Court long before you were born. In fact, before I was born. I believe, for all its ultimate limitations as a piece of litigation, that *Brown v. Board of Education of Topeka, Kansas,* which banned racial segregation in public schools, changed the weave of the American social fabric during the second half of the twentieth century. Further, I propose to you that this case, its consequences, and its successors have reverberated directly and indirectly through the lives of everyone in this room.

Now, if you are anything like I was at your age, you are perhaps more interested in the present (or perhaps the near future) than you are in the past. Your interest in the Supreme Court may well be negligible. You may be more familiar with the judges on *American Idol* than with Justices Scalia and Ginsburg. You may know less about the lives of Linda Brown or Spotswood Thomas Bolling than about the lives and loves of Tiger Woods or Jennifer Lopez.

But I want to ask you to look at the story of *Brown* as a story about the hopes of many American families and the dreams of a nation. I want to ask you to listen to my story and to look for the ways that *Brown* touches you here and now.

I am going to tell you a little bit about my early life. I am even going to make the supreme sacrifice of revealing to all of you my age—because *where* and *when* matters in the making of a "who." I was born in the first half of 1959 in Greensboro, North Carolina. I mention this because, although I wasn't old enough to hear about *Brown* until much later, I did become aware at an early age that I was living in a time of change.

Our neighbor across the street, Miss Boulware, was one of the young people who "sat in" at the Woolworth's counter. Woolworth's, like every other business downtown, depended on its black customers but insisted on a segregated snack bar. Miss Boulware and her college friends withstood taunts and physical assaults to break down the barriers of segregation. My parents used to worry that Miss Boulware's yellow Volkswagen Bug would be blown up, but it wasn't. The threat of violence and the societal willingness to sacrifice black bodies was, however, a constant worry for my parents and others. One of the first news stories I remember being told (other than the assassination of President Kennedy) was a school bus accident involving black children. My mother was infuriated by the story of these children being turned away from the closest hospital and sent across town to the colored hospital, where I had been born. Being diverted to L. Richardson Hospital cost precious time for the injured and dying children. This incident took place almost a decade after the *Brown* decisions, but segregation was still the law and the custom of the land.

My parents grew up during the Great Depression and gave service to their country—my father in the U.S. Navy at the close of World War II and my mother in a government-sponsored program for teacher-training in Ethiopia and Japan. They both grew up believing in education as the motor for success, and they could look to their own lives for supporting evidence.

My father grew up in Norfolk, Virginia, attending segregated schools through college. In the early 1950s he pursued graduate education at Union Theological Seminary in New York City, where he met my mother. She was doing graduate work at Teachers College at Columbia University—across Broadway. My parents were being educated to what were then the most open professions for African Americans—teaching and the ministry. These were the same occupations my paternal grandparents held, but my parents were part of the first generations to receive their advanced training at *integrated* institutions of higher learning.

My father became part of the Southern Christian Leadership Conference in Georgia and then in North Carolina. He helped build church communities and marched for civil rights with colleagues and friends like Andrew Young and Ralph Abernathy. He marched in cities throughout the South before moving our young family to Pennsylvania in 1964 in order to join the national staff of the United Church of Christ in Philadelphia.

You might have been taught that racial segregation was a problem solely of the southern states, but that wasn't so. Restrictive covenants barring homeowners from selling to nonwhites continued to be a strategy for maintaining segregated communities and segregated schools well past 1954—in all parts of the country. But with three school-age children and armed with their belief that better education was the key to better lives, my parents were determined to move into the town with the best schools. They worked with the Fair Housing

League of Delaware County to move into the house they wanted *in the school district they wanted* for their children.

Of course, we kids were most excited about moving from a house with one bathroom to a house with three. I don't think we realized that we were moving from a world that was socially and legally all black to a world, a neighborhood, and schools that were virtually all white. We kids had no idea what that would mean, but my parents were aware that the world was changing after the *Brown* decision and that they had different options, opportunities, and obligations—both private and public—than they had had before.

The NAACP Legal Defense team had made the decision during the late 1940s to consolidate five cases from Kansas, Delaware, Virginia, South Carolina, and the District of Columbia into the case we know as *Brown*.[1] These schooling equity cases became a wedge to end the dominance of Jim Crow laws. But why did they choose schooling cases as their wedge? Streetcars, buses, hotels, and restaurants were important public accommodations, and they were segregated, too. In part the answer is that children, education, and the public space of schools were foundational ways that equality was *experienced* and *measured* by many American citizens.

The common schools movement of the early nineteenth century meant that schools were to be the free and open spaces for the development of *all children* into active and participating citizens. Of course the "all" in that sentence meant something different in 1840, 1880, and 1940, but black children were not in any of those times being—in general—educated to participate in that open citizenry. The *Brown* decision overturned more than a century of state and federal court cases from Massachusetts to Kansas that protected the status quo. *Brown* declared unequivocally that separating children by race *could not result* in equal education. Segregated schools *could not result* in equal social and political opportunities.

My parents—and many other parents as well—knew the direct connection of educational opportunity to life chances. They took seriously the legacy of Oliver Brown, Sarah Bulah, Ethel Belton, Lena Mae Carper, and the other parent plaintiffs of *Brown*,[2] who had demonstrated that parents had the moral obligation to do everything in their power to make those opportunities available to their children.

For my parents, this political and moral obligation meant allying with the Fair Housing League to exert counterpressure to the pressure the Singer family encountered when they agreed to sell their house to us, the first black family in Lawrence Park. Deciding to be first is not a decision that every couple would choose to make, either for themselves or for their family. I believe that the legal challenges of real estate acquisition were actually exciting for people of my parents' backgrounds and temperaments. They certainly displayed enthusiasm and commitment to the cause—in energy, money, and time.

Through that experience they were able to connect to colleagues from many ethnic backgrounds who became long-term political allies. Yet their decision to move to our school district—and schooling was the basis of the decision—changed the context of life for my parents, even though they were well educated, worldly, and cosmopolitan. They moved into a neighborhood in which the neighbors were initially suspicious, if not hostile. The folks behind us built a fence within weeks after we moved in to keep our balls—and us—out of their yard and to prevent the spoiling of the aesthetic pleasures of the suburban backyard barbecue.

My parents were both professional educators and were committed to living as examples of their beliefs. My mother was a gifted elementary school teacher who helped students, parents, and other teachers bridge differences, because she really did believe that we could all live together in harmony. I wish she were alive now so that I could ask her about the challenges of going from teaching in the segregated South to being in some years the only black teacher at Swarthmore Elementary School. What social negotiations were necessary to convince white parents that she was the perfect teacher for a new gifted program in Lower Merion School District—at a time when the very idea of a black professional must have been baffling to some folks?

My parents moved away from being very much a part of a community, of social networks that bridged from home to work to church. They knew their neighbors, and their neighbors knew them. They sacrificed that familiar social world to ensure that we would go to the best schools to which they could send us.

So we (unknowingly) became their little ambassadors, meeting other children on the common ground—the school grounds—and changing the fabric of our community, one friendship at a time. And we did form friendships, my sister, my brother, and I. My sister made friends in marching band and in plays during junior high and high school. My brother made friends in little league and Cub Scouts, and ultimately as captain of the high school football team.

We had friends who were Catholic and Jewish, Italian, Swedish, and Asian—but almost none who were black like us. Nevertheless, we were invited to birthday and slumber parties and bat mitzvahs and sweet sixteens, and we had friends with whom to go to the zoo, the circus, the art museum, the mall, and the prom. And, of course, we gained a world-opening education. The great social risk my parents had taken paid off just as they believed it would.

Having desegregated our suburban Pennsylvania neighborhood, my parents imbued us with a sense of moral triumphalism. They had made a political decision that had profound implications for the phenomenal experience of their children, since for us, blackness was experienced as totally intimate and familial or as totally public and performative. When Pearl Bailey or Sammy Davis Jr. or civil rights news came on the (pre-1968) television, my younger brother and

I would run screaming through the house, "There's a Negro on TV! There's a Negro on TV!"

This jubilant cry was part recognition, part celebration, and part reminder. I enjoyed the benefits of my parents' racial struggles without having to engage in very many battles on my own behalf. When my classmate and neighbor Patty told me I couldn't play in her yard because it upset her next-door neighbors, I turned the other cheek and invited her around the corner to my house (where the fences protected the delicate sensibilities of the neighbors). The occasional smashed pumpkin or graffiti on the sidewalk did not, in my family, provide an occasion for self-doubt, but of compassion for the "ignorant" one whose rage at the changing world could not be expressed in any words—or at least words that expressed more thought than feeling. Our very good friends and neighbors, the Falcones, who had sons about my age, were given "friendly" counsel to watch out for the adolescent sexual temptations that could lead to blood mixing and other pernicious consequences. (The parents remained firm in their friendship, and believe me, none of us kids were the least bit interested in mixing any bodily fluids!)

So this successful story of racial integration post-*Brown* did not come without stress and conflict. It is also not the only story that could be told, even about my own family. But it is nevertheless true that we were not encouraged to think of life as a tragic story about race and racism in America.

Instead, we were taught to see ourselves as the *beneficiaries* of an ongoing struggle, as *entitled* to be participants in the next phase of America's attempts to include all her sons and daughters, as *responsible* for pushing forth her democratic dreams.

We stayed busy with school and our friends, with our activities and accomplishments. We moved through a childhood world that continued to change. The time of the *Flip Wilson Show* paved the way for the time of *Roots* . . . and on to the *Bernie Mac Show*. We were observers as a time of sit-ins and marches became a time of riots and assassinations, which in turn became a time when venerable American institutions—like Ivy League colleges, professional schools, Congress and even the Supreme Court—opened to entrants across the lines of race, gender, religion, and class.

If you are interested in more about the social and educational effects of *Brown*, one book I will recommend to you is by Peter Irons, *Jim Crow's Children: The Broken Promise of the Brown Decision* (2002). That book gives testimony to the fact that the positive legacy of *Brown* (as is so often true of laws, legal decisions, and other social policy over the course of American history) is not without disappointment and unintended consequences. As the decision in 2003 in the Michigan Law School case, *Grutter v. Bollinger,* shows us, we are enmeshed in *ongoing debates* about the relationship of race, equality, and educational opportunity.

I should admit that, as a child, I never understood *Brown* or the other pieces of the civil rights movement as having direct effect on my life (even though from my current standpoint, that seems preposterous). In early adulthood, as I entered the world of work and later graduate school I circled back to those early lessons on race through gender politics. In my day-to-day childhood world the consequence of being the only black child was that race was not the everyday difference that marked struggle and competition. The relevant everyday difference was being a girl—a girl who couldn't wear pants until seventh grade, who couldn't be a school safety monitor, who had to take cooking instead of making a lamp. The effects of Title IX didn't kick in for me until high school, and even there, no one had anything to say about the fact that there were only three girls out of a possible eighteen in my pre-calculus class.

My father wanted me to be part of the next wave of social change and pushed me to go to do my generational bit and sexually desegregate an Ivy League college. The ways in which the decision to go to Dartmouth in the fourth class of women has had a major effect on my life, politics, and choices is the subject for another day. But it is absolutely true that as an undergraduate I was never attacked directly by verbal or physical aggression that was not sexually based (even if on some rare occasions race was mixed in). My own coming of age into racialized political understanding throughout my twenties was thoroughly interpolated with the experience of feminist awakening in late adolescence. It was my father who pointed out that quiet acceptance of "the way things have always been" is *not* the price of admission into previously closed hallways, boardrooms, and classrooms—in the context of telling me and some of my classmates that it was our job to get the words to the alma mater—"Men of Dartmouth"—changed to include us. For all the critiques offered by myself and others of the limitations of integrationist/traditional liberal politics, my father constantly reminded me that individuals can effect change through everyday acts of resistance and rebellion.

In my family, my parents did walk through a door opened by Thurgood Marshall and Chief Justice Earl Warren. They dreamed—and realized—a new (and more broadly drawn) American Dream implied by the *ideals* of *Brown*. Fifty years later, that same door and others are open for you today—whatever your racial, gender, religious, or cultural background—the doors opened by educators, courts, and alums whose names you may never know. Opened by your parents, teachers, grandparents, and mentors. Opened by those who helped you realize the value of your educational possibilities and enabled you through a good word, a good deed, or a good dollar to be here today.

You are the beneficiaries of an ongoing struggle; *you* are entitled to be participants in the next phase of America's attempts to include all her daughters and sons; *you* are responsible for pushing forth her democratic dreams.

As you choose your classes and your major, as you try out for an athletic team or a play, as you assume leadership in your house or run for student government—take up the legacy of *Brown*. Experience as fully as you can your fellow students and your faculty in all the forms of their diversity. Learn from their different backgrounds, experiences, and worldviews.

Brown's message was not simply that black kids should have better school buses. *Brown* stated as a matter of faith that American social life would be transformed—would *blossom*—if our children shared classrooms and teachers and educational experiences. Coming to a great American institution of higher learning, you have the opportunity to see things you haven't seen, to speak in new languages, to experience new worlds, and to figure out what you can give back to the world and contribute to the future.

My story was intended to situate my family and myself in a personal and political context that so marked and prepared me. You are part of a history of the present that will mark you and prepare you for making your own mark in the world.

Notes

The bulk of this essay was prepared for the fall 2003 convocation for new students at the University of Illinois at Urbana-Champaign, where I was the Director of Gender and Women's Studies and taught in GWS and Educational Policy Studies. As a campus, UIUC designated 2003–4 as a yearlong commemoration of the *Brown* decision, and I was honored to be the faculty speaker chosen to open the fantastic series of talks, art exhibits, films, and other celebrations—all of which I missed in order to take an ACE Fellowship at Smith College. In February, 2004, I adapted the remarks for Black History Month at Smith, and it is largely that version found here.

1. The cases were *Gebhardt v. Belton, Briggs v. Elliot, Davis v. County School Board of Prince Edward County,* and *Bolling v. Sharpe,* in addition to *Brown v. Board of Education.*

2. These are four of the parents who were plaintiffs in one or another of the combined cases. See Peter Irons, *Jim Crow's Children: The Broken Promise of the Brown Decision* (New York: Viking, 2002), and *Brown v. Board of Education*, Brown Foundation for Educational Equity, Excellence and Research, April 3, 2006, http://brownvsboard.org/ (accessed April 9, 2008).

Section III
The Arts and *Brown*

The arts can awaken us from our everyday habits and help us to imagine new possibilities. They can allow us to understand people with different cultural orientations while at the same time provide a way to understand our common humanity. The *Brown* commemoration at the University of Illinois at Urbana-Champaign recognized these special qualities of the arts and granted them an important place in its activities.

This section gathers together a variety of essays related to cultural events that took place during the academic year devoted to *Brown*. The poet Sekou Sundiata reflects on the special powers of the arts even as he criticizes the standard strategies for achieving diversity through them. The graphic designer John Jennings considers the lessons learned from a student poster competition sponsored by the UIUC to commemorate *Brown*. The choreographer and dancer Ralph Lemon writes about his experiences in the Deep South that helped to inspire his highly acclaimed *Come Home Charlie Patton*. David O'Brien discusses the works shown in an exhibition entitled *Social Studies: Eight Artists Address Brown v. the Board of Education,* and illustrates examples of work by the artists in the show: Dawoud Bey, Sanford Biggers, Brett Cook-Dizney, Virgil Marti, Gary Simmons, Pamela Vander Zwan, Carrie Mae Weems, and Jennifer Zackin. And, finally, O'Brien interviews Weems on the subject of integration and the art museum.

15

Why Colored Faces in High Places Just Won't Do

Sekou Sundiata

Like many Americans, I have been recalled to citizenship in the past few years. Not an unexamined citizenship of flag waving and fear, but a critical citizenship that demands radical new ways of imagining and acting in the world. If the fall of the Berlin Wall signaled the end of the cold war, then 9/11 and its aftermath brought us into a completely new reality. And at the advent of new realities, artists have always been called to respond to the shifting grounds of their life and times, to give weight and meaning to those times. Think the Surrealists and Word War I, the Be-bop musicians and Word War II, the Beat poets in the cold war era, and so on.

For those of us living and working in America in these times, it is impossible to ignore or deny the imperial power that America exerts in the world as well as the consequences of that power at home. I came across an article that does a good job of framing this new reality:

> what word but "empire" describes the awesome thing that America is becoming? It is the only nation that polices the world through five global military commands; maintains more than a million men and women under arms on four continents; deploys carrier battle groups on watch in every ocean; guarantees the survival of countries from Israel to South Korea; drives the wheels of global trade and commerce; and fills the hearts and minds of an entire planet with its dreams and desires.[1]

The subtitle of the article posed a question that gets to the heart of the matter: "With a military of unrivaled might, the United States rules a new kind of empire. Will this cost America its soul?"

Look at the power of that language: America "drives the wheels of global trade and commerce . . . fills the hearts and minds of an entire planet with its dreams and desire. . . . Will this cost America its soul?" With so much at stake, and after decades of discussing diversity, why do we find ourselves "revisiting" it? The studies have been done. The diversity committees have reported.

The target-of-opportunity positions have been filled. The puny engines of the diversity initiatives have been set in motion. And, most of all, the books have been written. But, here we are, at the same ol, same ol: colored people trying to break off something proper for themselves. Why are we here, again? What needs to change in our thinking?

I don't have any definitive answers, but I do have some ideas. The first has to do with language and how it can conceal even when it seems to reveal. "Diversity," for example, is a very neutral-sounding word for a complex issue. It has come to mean so many things that it actually means not much. In the Black Power days we fought for more black people in the media, on the police force, in the boardroom and so on. That got translated into some "black faces in high places." Just get some black faces and put them in there.

I am old enough to remember when certain "time-saving" products hit the market. Time-saving products were a big thing in the first half of the cold war. I can recall the first commercials and ads for food that came in boxes, and all you had to do was "add and stir" and presto! "Presto!" was also a big word back then. Presto! you had your meal. It was a sign of progress. That approach carried over into the social sphere. As if you could "add and stir" to achieve something called Diversity. Same thing with women. And Latinos. And Asians. Add + Stir = Diversity.

Somewhere along the line, the militant, radical principle that brought about the demands for change got lost in "strategic planning" and "measurable objectives." I am using the word "diversity," but what I really mean is "democracy." For the moment, I want to set aside the idea of democracy as it relates to matters of state. I am thinking of it instead as a humane social practice that elevates and promotes the best in individuals because it requires each of us to see and accept the Other as both different from us and the same as us at a fundamental level. It makes each democratic practitioner a better citizen and a better person because it brings together the inner need for the freedom to be who you are with the outer need for a social and political and economic ecology that can feed and care for the whole human being. And when I say "the freedom to be who you are," I am talking about the freedom to be whomever you have come to identify yourself as: Straight, Transgender, Master Carpenter, Professional Dissenter, African American, Latino, Pioneer, Explorer, Space Cadet, A Being Disrupted and Displaced during Interplanetary Travel, Cowboy Poet, and, yes, A Peeps of Color. You should be free to be all of that without facing punishment or brutalization or murder or subjugation because of it. Short of committing acts that violate basic human solidarity (rape, murder, political and corporate corruption, for example), you should be free to realize the Self that comes from the interior life of the mind and soul. And although it may come from this interior life, it is shaped in the context of history and social reality.

And the overarching purpose of the social order should be to bring that Self out of you, to honor it, and to use it as human capital to be spent in the interest of the human being. The world is full of ancient wisdom about the human desire for balance between the inner life and the outer life. A truly democratic society promotes and supports this balance.[2]

When you use democracy in this way, the discussion has to expand, it has to elevate, it has to point us toward the purpose of diversity, and the discussion has to be about more than "colored faces in high places." I think that we have to insist on linking diversity to democracy. Post-9/11 diversity conversations must have a different sense of time and place and urgency than those old, tired pre-9/11 conversations. Once again, just look at the language describing this gathering, how diversity is linked to the notion of artists and civic engagement.

"*Democracy* in the arts" brings us to a different place in our thinking than "*diversity* in the arts." "Democracy in the arts" fosters critical conversations about funding, programming, and audience development, and, *at the same time,* frames those practical matters as matters of national security. And that is precisely the way I've come to think about the arts in America: as a matter of national security. And if liberals and progressives don't understand that, then conservative and right-wing forces do, because when they attack works of art they don't bombard them with critiques about craft and form and the meaning of beauty. They attack on the basis of ideas. You and I may see Art, with a big A, but they see ideas. And they attack because they want to control the flow of ideas in society, because they know that whoever controls the ideas controls the society. In other words, they want to organize your thinking in the image of theirs. That is why their unrelenting efforts to silence, shut down, and disqualify any art that they find offensive are finally antidemocratic. This is why when I say "diversity" I am not talking about a diversity of colors but a diversity of ideas as expressed through different cultures. And that diversity of ideas is absolutely essential to democracy. This is why the arts are a matter of national security.

Think about the news about Michael Moore's film *Fahrenheit 9/11,* a film that is highly critical of George Bush and the Bush family's ties to wealthy Saudis. Disney, which financed the film, decided not to release it because it was so critical of the president. Michael Moore found another way to release it, but the strategy of Disney and the Right is apparent: silence dissent.

Think about the case of the Poet Laureate of New Jersey, Amiri Baraka. Baraka's poem "Somebody Blew Up America" implies that the Israeli government (and others) had prior knowledge about the 9/11 attacks.[3] He was then attacked as an anti-Semite, and asked to resign. He refused, and, according to the law, he couldn't be fired. He had to serve out his term. So the courageous and principled members of the New Jersey State Legislature abolished the position altogether. If it can't have the poet it wants then it will have no poets!

I want to be as clear as possible about the following point. Democracy in the arts or anywhere else, for that matter, is useless without what Professor Elaine Scarry calls "authorizations."[4] I take this term to mean the need for structures (voting laws, programming, staffing patterns, public policy) that realize and enforce the strategies and tactics of democracy. Without "authorizations," the practice of democracy depends on what she calls "generous imaginings." In other words, it is not enough to rely on a generous heart or mood to imagine others. Sentiments and moods come and go.

The key point in this: you cannot put into place "authorizations" that honor and protect the Self without "authorizations" honoring and protecting the Other. *Democracy: You can't have it unless you permit others to have it too.* And you cannot have it, let alone practice it, without a willing and robust imagination, because it is through the imagination that we can begin to "empty our cups" and see the world through eyes other than our own.

Scarry describes a useful way to approach "picturing others." She suggests that when we seek equality through generous imaginings, we start with our own weight, then attempt to acquire knowledge about the weight and complexity of others. The alternative strategy is to achieve equality between the Self and Other not by trying to make one's knowledge of others as weighty as one's self-knowledge, but by making one ignorant about oneself and, therefore, as weightless as all others.[5] In the absence of a willing and robust imagination, we find ourselves caught up in this ineffectual cycle of revisiting diversity after we visited it and revisited it before. To paraphrase Malcolm X, if you think those old ways will produce new results you've been had, you've been took, and you've been misled!

When we start talking about the imagination, artists enter the picture. The imagination is our field of operation. Just to be clear: when I say imagination, I am thinking of both the private realm of the individual and the public realm of social life: how one shapes the other and vice versa. I think of the imagination as a necessary and sacred space, a space in which "if not probable, all is possible." And although the imagination exists within material borders and is shaped, to a large degree, by the material world, it can transcend those borders and conjure infinite possibilities of being. Here is Albert Einstein on the subject: "I am enough of an artist to draw freely upon my imagination. Imagination is more important than knowledge. Knowledge is limited. Imagination encircles the world."[6]

I am not talking about imagination as some kind of benevolent place from which nothing but good will flow. We know that is not true. If the twentieth century has shown us nothing else, it has demonstrated the capacity of the human imagination to create nearly insurmountable horrors. Yet, at the same time, I believe it is only through the imagination that society can advance.

When I was in grade school, my class went on a field trip to the United Nations. I saw a plaque inscribed with a quote from the preamble to the Constitution for UNESCO. For reasons I never fully understood, the words stayed with me all these years: "since wars begin in the minds of men, it is in the minds of men that the defenses of peace must be constructed." At that age, I understood war to be like a schoolyard fight: it begins when someone strikes the first blow. So, I was troubled by this idea of war beginning in the mind. Years later, I started to understand how hurt and destruction directed toward another begins with the failure to fully imagine the Other as a human being. The violence that comes out of that failure can be widespread and far-reaching, but it comes from a narrow, restricted place in the mind. A writer once put it this way: "Fantasies are more than substitutes for unpleasant reality; they are also dress rehearsals, plans. All acts performed in the world begin in the imagination."[7]

We have all heard this next point before, but it bears repeating: the products of the artist's imagination add new value to culture and society. That value may be a commodity, entertainment, inspiration, insight, knowledge, or understanding. Each work of art, at its best, presents us with a new way of seeing and knowing. It adds to the great storehouse of knowledge or understanding about what it means to be human. It sheds light on the enduring, utterly mysterious human drama. So if we insist on diversity in the arts we are saying that people of color bring new value and new knowledge to the democratic enterprise *and* that what we bring is absolutely essential to national security in a democratic society *and* that openness to new values and new knowledge is essential to global peace, justice, and well-being.

So as we come around to another conversation about diversity in the arts, I am aware that the conversation is being repeated for many reasons, and that one of the main reasons is a failure of the imagination on the part of both People of Color as well as People of Whiteness. For People of Whiteness the problem is twofold: one, a failure to imagine anything other than themselves as the defining reality; and two, a willingness to see the Other in terms that erase the humanity of the Other.

Recently I was one of the featured poets at the Skagit River Poetry Festival in La Conner, Washington, located between Seattle and Vancouver. It is a very beautiful, mostly rural area: mountains, rivers, eagles, and so on. The festival is modeled on the Dodge Poetry Festival in that it involves hundreds of high school students from surrounding towns and counties, as well as the general public. The invited poets come from different parts of the country: one was a Chicano poet, three were black poets, and the rest were white poets. The headliner was former Poet Laureate of the United States and superstar Billy Collins.

It felt strange being the only black face in many of the events, in restaurants, and on the street. People were friendly. Some people even recognized me and knew my work. Others slowed down in their cars to get a good look as I walked down the street: *Stranger in town. Black stranger in town. Strange black poet in town.* While I never get used to this, I have come to view it as the American way. Which is to say, I ain't trippin'.

Then, one morning, I was having lunch with a woman poet who now lives and teaches in Alaska. She was telling me about her son, a musician who lives in New York and is also a recovering drug addict. She was talking about how he went about getting off drugs and she says, "if you don't mind me bringing up race, he had a black mentor that saved his life." As benign as that sounded, I wondered what in her mind was the significance of the mentor's race to the story. And, second to that, why would she think I would mind? After my reading at the closing ceremony a couple of days later, a woman came over to me, very excited and effusive, and said: "I'm just a white woman who loves what you're doing." Then another woman came over and said: "It must be hard to be around this many white people all this time."

This is how Whiteness gets People of Color to scratch their heads. What was going on? A black man could go nuts in America trying to figure out people's motives, but I think it was the disturbing presence of the black body in the white mind. I think all of these people meant well, but what they said amounted to the smiling erasure of my individuality, of what it is that makes me a singular, irreplaceable human being. It turned me into a racial figure, a type, and a representative. Now, I know how to represent when it's time to represent, but here I was representing without even trying. The effect and meaning of these kinds of well-meant speech is *unintended,* which means that they are difficult to address.

The other thing that struck me about the festival was the way in which the white poets introduced their poems or talks. Most of them quoted or made references to composers, writers, thinkers, musicians and others who shaped their thinking in one way or another. They made these references with great ease. Not one of them quoted a person of color. I heard Brahms and Philip Glass and Laurie Anderson and Bob Dylan, but not one Eddie Palmieri or Mario Bauza or Thelonius Monk or Cornel West, Julia Alvarez, Derek Walcott, or Arundhati Roy. When it comes to referencing powerful ideas that shape the intellectual and aesthetic lives of these poets, the issue was not the disturbing presence of the black (or colored, if you will) body, but the disturbing absence of the black (or colored) mind. While you could argue that it is not necessary for these poets to be informed by artists and thinkers of color, it is difficult to find an artist or thinker of color who is not informed by white influences. Artists and thinkers of color have to be informed by white influences because that is how we are trained, and because our survival depends on knowing what they have written and composed and painted and choreographed, because, in the end, they are the defining reality against which all others are judged. But what is the democratic imperative for these poets to know what artists and thinkers of color have written and composed and painted and choreographed? And if there is no such democratic imperative, where is the democracy? Or, what we have been calling "diversity"?

To appreciate all of this, it is important to understand what such a festival signifies. People who organize festivals like this believe they are bringing together some of America's best contemporary poets. Not only are the poets invited to read their work, but also they are asked to talk about such high-minded things as Craft, Identity, Grief, Violence, and Politics. The idea is that poets speak to our life and times, to the state and soul of the nation and the world in special ways. These are conceived and designed to reach the next generation through linkages with high schools, because they believe that literate, well-educated young people need poetry, that poetry tutors the heart and the mind, and that, in the words of William Carlos Williams:

> It is difficult
> to get the news from poems
>   yet men die miserably every day
>   for lack
> of what is found there[8]

Yet, in its own quiet and insidious way, the festival in La Conner, Washington was a failure of the imagination and perpetuated the status quo. And these are well-intentioned people!

What would it take to overcome this kind of failure of the imagination? As I said earlier, language is one starting point, beginning with the words "democracy" and "diversity" and "people of color." One of the signs of a society in trouble is the degradation and devaluation of language leading to a kind of cognitive dissonance that so many of us experience nowadays, wherein it becomes increasingly difficult to trust the language we encounter on a day-to-day basis. It's a pickpocket language. It doesn't say what it means. It claims, "the children come first because they are the future," but it's really trying to sell you something or get your vote. This is why artists who work with language are so important. They struggle for honest language that means what it says whether it is fashionable or not. And this leads to the next point about what it takes to overcome this failure of the imagination: it takes Art.

Consider the following: "The way we act towards 'Others' is shaped by the way we imagine others. . . . Both philosophic and literary descriptions of such imagining show the difficulty of picturing other people in their full weight and solidity. This is true even when the person is a friend or acquaintance; the problem is further magnified when the person is a stranger or 'foreigner.'

. . . It is therefore, important to come face to face with the limits of imagining other people."[9]

The key phrase here is "the difficulty of picturing other people in their full weight and solidity." This points to how hard it is for anyone to imagine other people as fully human as themselves. I think this is a particular challenge to Whiteness, with its long history of power and privilege. But this is the great advantage of Art in a democratic context. It can facilitate and compel the imagination in irresistible ways. We know that Imagination alone cannot solve real world problems, but real world problems cannot be solved without it.

It is worthwhile to think about how Art can do this great thing—how anything can make us look, but Art can make us see. Chinua Achebe, the great Nigerian writer, described the ways in which fiction uncovers something true about the human condition.[10] Although he is talking about fiction, what he has to say is really about all Art. In the essay, he introduces a term that he calls "imaginative identification" to describe the way fiction (Art) addresses imagining the Other. To paraphrase Chinua Achebe, things are not merely happening before us; they are happening, by the power and force of the imagination, to us. We not only see, we suffer alongside the hero. When the hero loses, we lose. When the hero triumphs, we triumph.

I said earlier that the constant "revisiting" of the issue of diversity frustrated People of Color and pointed to a failure of the imagination. Asking "People of Color" to say something useful about the fullness of our humanity, when what one really wants to hear about is our relationship to Whiteness, perpetuates this situation. It relates to the troubling, rarely mentioned failure to imagine each other. In her essay, Elaine Scarry points out that part of the difficulty of picturing others also has to do with the fact that most people have a low tolerance for features that are different from their own. People view the subjects of race, gender, and ethnicity as an occasion for self-reflection and affirmation, rather than an opportunity for reflection upon and affirmation of people different from oneself.

What is the consequence of this? One of the most notable consequences, to my mind, is an absence of collaborations between People of Color. I'm not talking about a few integrated companies or casts. I mean real collaborations in which peers deeply engaged in critical and creative conversations create new value and new knowledge. I have a feeling that the new form, vocabulary, syntax, and images that society needs so desperately are waiting to be uncovered in the mix and clash of those collaborations because they will come from people most likely to push for democracy, for freedom, for a rupture with the past. The passion and urgency of that push has the potential to create Art that is irresistible, to make diversity (democracy) irresistible. But where do we go to find such work—work that carries audiences (sometimes against their will) into the thing they may believe is so unlike them, only to discover more than they bargained for about themselves?

I often look at the state of American society and wonder if it is possible to pull back. Not to retreat to some fabled past romanticized by reactionaries, but to pull back from this unsustainable level of fear, violence, and distrust. I would be turning my back on the history of struggle and sacrifice if I did not believe that society could be redeemed. But it cannot pull back and cannot be redeemed without a fierce and radically imagined democracy.

Let me summarize my argument:

1. We find ourselves (as "People of Color") revisiting diversity because of "historical patterns of exclusion and invisibility." This is an old, tired story that requires new ways of thinking.
2. A possible new way of thinking begins with a critique of what People of Color represents, and with the idea that the aim of diversity is not more "colored faces in high places," but the humane practice of democracy.
3. A willing and robust imagination is absolutely essential to democracy because it depends on the capacity to imagine others in their full weight and solidity.
4. The cycle of never-ending diversity discussions is due, in large part, to a failure of the imagination. The failure of People of Whiteness to imagine People of Color, and the failure of People of Color to imagine one another.
5. Art works on our consciousness in special ways that compel us and enable us to imagine the Other.
6. When we talk about Art we are talking about Culture and Ideas. And the point is not to diversify the culture, but to change it.

I think it would be irresponsible of me to present a critique without suggesting some possible ways of addressing some of the issues I raised. Back in the day, in the movement, we were fond of telling the backseat drivers and weekend critics of our movement: *no participation, no right to observation.* Although speech is a form of participation, I can add some more concrete forms of addressing current problems:

1. Collaborations and critical conversations between People of Color: artists, presenters, and so forth. If I had to choose in order of importance, the critical conversations would come first. There is an advocacy and convening role here for organizations, institutions, and funders to create the time and space for artists, scholars, and others to discuss ideas without the pressure of an expected outcome.

2. Form real partnerships with universities. Universities are the largest
   funders of art in America. Yes, universities have resources to support
   the production and distribution of art, but their greatest value is the role
   they play in educating the next generation of citizens.
3. The purpose of artist residency activities needs to be reimagined.
   These are the activities that artists are usually obligated to conduct on
   campuses and in communities as they tour. They often have an "add
   and stir" quality, meaning they are often make-work kinds of things
   that allow the presenters to comply with the terms of various funding contracts. Or, they are directly linked to promoting the show to
   sell tickets. These activities can also be narrowly conceived teaching
   situations in which the visiting artist conducts master dance classes
   for dance students, composition workshops for music students, writing workshops for writing students, and so on. I am interested in the
   teaching and learning possibilities of interdisciplinary classes, or music
   classes for architecture students, or writing classes for dance students,
   dance classes for physics students. This is not just a warmed up idea
   about "art-across-the-curriculum." It has more to do with finding in-
   novative ways to make and learn new knowledge with the imagination
   engaged with the body engaged with the intellect. The idea is to connect
   feeling and thinking to imagination, creativity, learning, and, hopefully,
   civic practice. Finally, though, the move should be to promote deep,
   curriculum-level collaborations between artists, campuses, and communities. And this is probably the most difficult struggle of all (and, it
   is a struggle) because it means changing cultures and practices as they
   are commonly understood among these potential partners, cultures and
   practices that, so far, favor separation and not collaboration.

I'd like to return, for a moment, to Chinua Achebe and his concept of "imaginative identification": These are words that I like to hold in my mind as I work and
think about what it means to be an artist and a citizen in the world. "Imaginative
literature (Art) does not enslave; it liberates the mind. . . . Its truth is not like the
canons of orthodoxy or the irrationality of prejudice and superstition. It begins as
an adventure in self-discovery and ends in wisdom and humane conscience."[11]

Finally: Get out and Vote! And on that subject, here are some words by Amiri
Baraka that I also like to keep in mind. Baraka told me that he was inventing a
new African American form of poetry that is inspired by the Japanese Haiku.
It's called the Lowku. Here's one of my favorites:

The President
Introduces himself:
AM BUSH!

Notes

1. Michael Ignatief, "The Burden," *New York Times Sunday Magazine,* January 5, 2003, 1.

2. Jacob Needleman, "One: Our America," and "Seven: Slavery and the Story of America" in *The American Soul* (New York: Jeremy P. Tarcher/Putnam, 2002), 3–28, 237–68. My comments about interior life and outer world are a crude interpretation of Needleman's ideas on the subject of what he calls "the inner meaning of democracy." I was surprised to find so much useful thinking in his book because it is so steeped in metaphysical ideas and reverence for the wisdom of the "Founding Fathers."

3. Amiri Baraka, "Somebody Blew Up America," in *Somebody Blew Up America and Other Poems* (Philipsburg, St. Martin: House of Nehesi, 2003), 41–50.

4. Elaine Scarry, "The Difficulty of Imagining Other Persons," in *The Handbook of Interethnic Coexistence*, ed. Eugene Weiner (New York: Continuum, 1998), 40–62.

5. Ibid., 52.

6. "What Life Means to Einstein: An Interview by George Sylvester Viereck," *Saturday Evening Post,* October 26, 1929, 117.

7. Barbara Grizzuti Harrison, "Talking Dirty," *Ms.,* October 1973, 41.

8. William Carlos Williams, "Asphodel, That Greeny Flower," in *Asphodel, That Greeny Flower and Other Love Poems* (1938; New York: New Directions, 1994), 19.

9. Elaine Scarry, "The Difficulty of Imagining Other Persons," 40–41.

10. Chinua Achebe, *Hopes and Impediments* (New York: Doubleday, 1989), 153.

11. Ibid.

16

The Chance Project

John Jennings

As part of the *Brown v. Board of Education* Jubilee Commemoration at the University of Illinois at Urbana-Champaign, I organized the Chance Project, a national collegiate poster design competition. This essay examines the results of the competition, but it also reflects more broadly on my own experience of artistic education. In many ways my desire to create the Chance Project grew out of my personal encounter with education, and the results of the competition confirmed my own perceptions of both the positive aspects and inequalities informing art programs in the United States today. My journey through life has been partly a quest for balance. Balance shapes our universe. Balance in the form of social equality and justice has been an aspiration of our country since its foundation. However, balance has not always been achieved, neither in the scales of justice nor in equal access to fundamental resources, one of which is an education in the arts.

I attended a small, entirely African American school in rural Mississippi built on "Sixteenth Section" Land—public education trust land vested in the state—and housing grades one through twelve. I can recollect the weary faces of my overworked teachers as they worked to instill knowledge, dignity, and a sense of self-worth in us. I remember respecting them and studying hard to make good grades. My grandfather, who understood the value of a good education, reinforced these habits despite the fact he could neither read nor write himself.

I saw education as a way to achieve freedom from the small town of Flora. I wanted to see more than the cotton fields that surrounded me. I earned a chance to move further toward my goal with an academic scholarship to Jackson State University, a historically black university located thirty minutes south of my hometown. The journey wasn't far in physical distance, but the school seemed a million miles away to me. I used my time there to find my footing in an uncertain world and was able to earn a fellowship to the University of Illinois at Urbana-Champaign. My graduate studies started out in the field of art education and ended in the practice of graphic design. After earning both a master of arts and a master of fine arts degree, I returned to my native Mississippi and began to build a graphic design program at Jackson State University. I soon realized the extent of the inequities in funding, research opportunities, facilities, and virtually every other area that would help nurture and support a viable art and design program. Once again, I was faced with imbalance and I attempted to become the counterweight.

Teaching in the Art Department at Jackson State was very challenging. The budget was minute, the students unmotivated and undisciplined due to low morale. The university had let the Art Department become the "Art Appreciation Department," as there were very few actual art majors and an overabundance of students from other areas who simply needed to fulfill an art requirement for graduation. Despite immense difficulties, we were able to build the department into a relatively competitive and productive learning environment. After four years at JSU, UIUC invited me back to build the image-making area of the graphic design program there. Thus, I was again able to compare the two institutions.

As a graduate student at UIUC, the self-segregation of certain minority groups had bothered me, even in events that I enjoyed, such as the Black Congratulatory and the African American Homecoming. Because the student body at JSU is almost completely African American, I had not had the opportunity to experience such segregation there. At UIUC, on the other hand, students from a variety of backgrounds feel a need for representation and self-affirmation through student organizations rooted in race or ethnicity. I of course understand the feelings of isolation and loneliness that members of minority groups experience at UIUC, having experienced them firsthand. However, I have always felt that universities should be involved in the process of dismantling practices of segregation and provide a common, shared experience of higher education. Thus, when I returned to UIUC as a professor, I implemented a class project that called on students to create a series of posters against discrimination, segregation, and intolerance.

The university's call for projects to commemorate the *Brown v. Board* decision coincided exactly with these interests. Together with my former department chair, Professor Robb Springfield, I set into motion a nationwide collegiate poster design competition around the opportunities or "chances" afforded African Americans in this country by the decision. We asked entrants to use the phrase "A Chance to . . ." as a prompt for a slogan that could provide the basis for a poster ("A Chance to Grow," "A Chance to Dream," etc.). The students could also base their posters on totally original slogans or appropriate quotations if they so wished. We sent out a call-for-entries poster to an extremely diverse group of colleges and universities with graphic design programs. The entries were reviewed by three judges: Gabriel Chu Usadel, an art director for the advertising firm Ogilvy & Mather in Chicago; Noel Childs, who works in print and broadcast advertising for Fusion Idea Lab in Chicago; and William L. Brown, who currently heads the package design studio for the new retail division at Hallmark in support of product development for the Hallmark Gold Crown Channel.

The judges selected six winners, each of whom received two hundred dollars and had their posters displayed in the local mass transportation system for nine months. The posters were also distributed around the continental United States and throughout the school systems of Chicago and the state of Georgia.

The Chance Project confronted competitors with a number of unusual challenges. Most posters are oriented in a vertical manner and conform to the expectation, created by books and magazines, that one should read in the vertical format. Horizontal posters tend to be more static and flat and, in general, provide the designer with a greater challenge. The students in the competition had to use the horizontal orientation because of the spaces available in buses of the transportation system. The competitors also had to treat a delicate, complex subject in a clever, informative, and immediately understandable manner, yet it could not be unduly disruptive or aggressive, given the public and community-oriented nature of the transportation system. The poster had to "whisper" and "shout" simultaneously.

The six winning entries demonstrate the rich and diverse possibilities of the competition. Adam Gathman, a student from James Madison University, focused on an apple formed from halves of two different colors. The slogan "different skins, same core" (figure 16.1) serves as a powerful verbal statement of the central idea of the image. The judges admired the simplicity of the familiar form of an apple. The apple is also an obvious embodiment of students' appreciation for their instructors and is connected in the Bible to the hunger for knowledge. However, the "two-toned" apple and the slogan "different skins, same core" remind us of the ongoing significance attached to outer physical differences. The apple halves have two different light sources (note the highlights) that, despite their apparent joining, point up their difference. The colors chosen by Gathman also heighten the tension. Red and green are direct opposites on the color wheel and thus allude to the relationship of black and white in a racial context. Their inherent opposition also strengthens the intensity of each hue due to simultaneous contrast. One side depends upon the other. Overall, however, the unity and simplicity of the poster overcomes these internal contrasts.

Elizabeth Nelson, a University of Illinois student, won with an understated design that spoke volumes. The image focuses on a rusty red graphic of a desk from days gone by. The Malcolm Forbes quotation "education's purpose is to replace an empty mind with an open one" (figure 16.2) is reversed out on a plain pea-green background. The empty, isolated seat makes the viewer wonder who sat there and what did that person learn. The choice of an antiquated desk instead of a modern one suggests an even older question: when? The desk seems almost skeletal, with the complimentary green color of the background infiltrating

FIGURE 16.1.

Adam Gathman, *Different Skins, Same Core*, 2004. In the original, the left side of the apple is green and the right side is red. Digital print, 11" × 17". Courtesy of the artist.

FIGURE 16.2.

Elizabeth Nelson, *Education's Purpose Is to Replace an Empty Mind with an Open One*, 2004. Digital print, 11" × 17". Courtesy of the artist.

its emaciated form. Its transparent treatment gives it the appearance of an apparition. The rusty color connotes neglect and lack of care. The implication of an empty desk—wasted resources and wasted minds—provides a tension that greatly appealed to the judges.

Michael Lawson, a student at the Savannah College of Art and Design, depicted two industrial washing machines in a laundromat. One machine is labeled "WHITES" and the other "COLOREDS." The slogan "a chance for CHANGE" (figure 16.3) connects the machines. "50 years of mixing our colors" closes off the visual statement in the lower right hand corner. This poster was selected for its humor, craft, and unexpected complexity. The comparison of skin color to clothing raises the question of whether skin color and its associations are as arbitrary as those of clothing, and whether race is something that may be shed like clothing. "COLOREDS" is furthermore an old racial term for African Americans and seems outdated and not fit for our times. The labeling of the machines is also obviously a fiction—machines are never reserved for white or colored clothing—but this only points up the insanity of the days in which public facilities were reserved for either black or white people. Lawson also puns cleverly on the word "CHANGE," thoroughly exploring the possibilities of his laundry metaphor.

University of Illinois student Linda Brewster submitted a wonderful poster dealing with equality in education. The poster's stark background is that of an actual chalkboard common to almost any grammar school. The band of information at the edge of the image provides the frame for the board. The phrase "A Chance Too Learn" (figure 16.4) is written by two young hands. One is obviously African American, the other Caucasian. The misspelling of "Too" provides the hook in the image. Looking at the color of the chalk used by each student, we can see that the white chalk, in the white hand, has written the entire phrase "A Chance To Learn" and the "colored" chalk, in the black hand, has added the extra "o." The writing suggests, perhaps, that the white child has been there longer, and that the black student has only recently been included in the exercise. Yet the decision to change "to" to "too" also emphasizes inclusion: the idea that *Brown* provided black students with a chance to learn too, on the same terms as whites. Upon further examination we see that the writing occurs outside of the margins. It happens outside of the rules and guidelines. This adds a revolutionary or rebellious side to the image. It gives us the impression that this equality is happening on the fringes of the mainstream. Time is an important factor in this image also. The chance is happening right now. We can infer this because the writing isn't complete. We see the children in midstroke. They are in the moment of possibility even as we view the poster.

Blake Coglianese, also from the Savannah College of Art and Design, chose a playful approach for his winning entry. The judges were attracted to the directness

FIGURE 16.3.
Michael Lawson, *A Chance for CHANGE,* 2004. Digital print, 11" × 17". Courtesy of the artist.

FIGURE 16.4.
Linda Brewster, *A Chance Too Learn,* 2004. Digital print, 11" × 17". Courtesy of the artist.

and bright colors of the poster depicting four children of different ethnicities holding hands around the iconic red schoolhouse. It is intended for a younger audience but appeals to the very complex and necessary principle of unity. The encircled children gaze at one another but also at the schoolhouse. They are focused on education and its preservation. Their circle both protects the schoolhouse and creates for it a nimbus radiating energy. The phrase "A Chance to Learn Together" (figure 16.5) suggests a desire for education but also for inclusion. The circle denotes infinity, completion, and strength. The design of this poster conveys a simple message in a playful and visually arresting manner.

Another UIUC student, Donovan Foote, submitted a winning entry that relies on a field of beautifully vibrant colors. Yellows, blues, reds, and oranges dance fervently in the background. In the foreground the chalklike outlines of raised hands seem to wave to the viewer in salutations. The phrase "A CHANCE TO QUESTION" (figure 16.6) is superimposed on the image. Foote's poster grabs the viewer immediately with its mix of menace and playfulness. The abstract background creates a dreamlike atmosphere, while the flurry of raised hands of various colors conjures up the vision of enthusiastic, integrated students eager to engage. The phrase "A CHANCE TO QUESTION" looms in the foreground

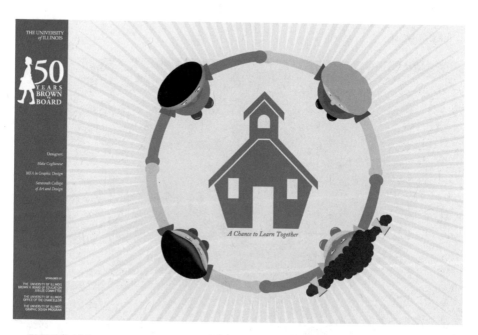

FIGURE 16.5.

Blake Coglianese, *A Chance to Learn Together*, 2004. Digital print, 11" × 17". Courtesy of the artist.

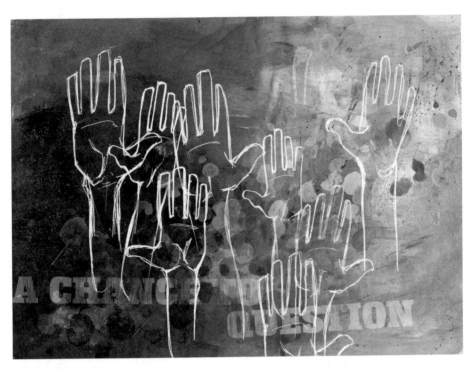

FIGURE 16.6.

Donovan Foote, *A Chance to Question*, 2004. Digital print, 11" × 17". Courtesy of the artist.

like a ghost, suggesting that education is not simply about students' reception of knowledge, but also an opportunity for them to interrogate it. This poster begs for answers for which we are still searching and sings of the hope that we may find them together.

Despite the overall success of the Chance Project, one aspect of it left me unsatisfied: no students from historically black colleges and universities (HBCUs) entered. We sent packets to the Tuskegee Institute, Howard University, and virtually every black college or university with a graphic design or art program. I had hoped that African American students and professors would take part in our contest because of its unique and worthy theme. This disparity prompted me to contact the journal *Black Issues in Higher Education,* which published an article investigating this aspect.[1]

One reason that no students from HBCUs participated may be the poverty of graphic design and art programs at such institutions. The irony, I suppose, is that *Brown v. Board* dealt with the balancing of the scales of education to include everyone. Yet there seems to be a serious lack of investment in the arts at many historically black institutions and grammar schools across the country. In fact, this deficit may reflect a general weakening in the curriculum at black educational institutions.

The journey isn't over. There are still gaps that need to be filled. One thing I asked in my classes here at UIUC during the discrimination project was if students were aware of such notable African Americans as Sojourner Truth, Dr. Charles Drew, or Crispus Attucks. I am sure my present readers would be alarmed at how many students simply don't know who these people were and how much they contributed to American history. I truly love this country. However, the truth is that love sometimes comes coupled with disappointment. There is still so much we need to do to strengthen and reform our educational system. I have to wonder what our students are learning. I have to question the system and the decisions of what gets taught to our children. I have to. This is America and everyone deserves that balance, that equality . . . that chance.

Note

1. "Brown Celebration Inspires Design Contest, Reveals Disparity," *Black Issues in Higher Education* 21, no. 8 (June 17, 2004): 2–3.

17

What Was Always There

Ralph Lemon

"You got to come along with me. You'll never find your way back if you don't and that's the truth."

Without a shortcut, we drive through a tangled landscape of dirt and graveled pig trails, under a canopy of live oaks, the road shaped by that filtered sunlight, sheltered green. And then the other Deep South of bare wooden bridges, rain-fed ponds, cotton field railroad crossings. Way before, I imagine, for a long time, only wild fertile landscape. Then antebellum. A battleground, then reconstruction. The Deep South. A battleground. A growing national mythology continues. The Delta, specifically, hill country. The country, a wild fertile landscape and its old American secrets.

"Look at it! Comin' from the big city, bet you can't believe that there's still untouched country like this. And people live out here!" Jimmy drives, smiling, "Been a long while since I've been out this way."

Jimmy drives these narrow dirt roads as if not a stretch or bend has been forgotten. And, yes, people live out here, in this "untouched country." A giant working farm, a little lived-in shack, a giant working farm, the unkempt hills and dense forest delta obliterating the difference.

Ninety-five-year-old Mr. Walter Carter, the oldest known resident of Bentonia, Mississippi, looks like he could be in his late sixties, a small man. He's waiting outside a simple brick house, in front of his screen door, dressed for an outing. A tan Homburg, a dark blue jacket, tan creased slacks, a yellow plaid shirt, and dark brown snakeskin cowboy boots. "Thirty-five minutes late," he barks.

After a few requisite photos in front of the house, a lineup of Carter, his wife, and her three grinning grown-up nieces, we pile back into the truck and drive back to the Blue Front. Along the way, another point of view, Mr. Carter gives commentary, on houses and yards of past friends and relatives, a yelling tour guide, with perfect vision and almost deaf. "I've outlived everybody," he brightly bellows.

Not far from Yazoo City and Robert Johnson's presumed third gravesite, outside Greenwood, is the quaint but oddly trendy hamlet of Bentonia, Mississippi, official population 390. A railroad crossing. Trendy because it has one of the few remaining juke joints in the Delta, the Blue Front Cafe. It's famous on most blues maps. Hometown of Nehemiah "Skip" James, Henry "Son" Stuckey, Jack Owens, and Buddy Spires, who still lives there, and holds the Bentonia blues lineage. Along with Jimmy "Duck" Holmes, who has owned the Blue Front since 1976. Yes, a real, alive juke joint, in how it has survived and continues to function. In the mid-'50s the Blue Front was a mini-mart. The juke in the front, and in the back of the front room, against the wall, one could buy fruit, vegetables, shoes, and clothing. In the back room was a kitchen for hot dishes, and in the very back room was a barbershop. More recently, when Levi's filmed Jack Owens for a commercial in 1995, the director made sure all the Coke signs were removed, and the soiled ceiling and half-painted walls stayed in place, immaculately authentic, to a history that has not stayed in place.

Jimmy's house, a white, one-story ranch, resting on a wide grassy lot, right off Highway 49, part of what had once been his father's sixty-acre farm, sits right next door to the original Blue Front Cafe, owned by his father. Later becoming the tiny whitewashed shotgun house of Henry Stuckey.

Jimmy remembers being five or six when he first held the giant guitar that belonged to Stuckey. Later, sitting in the front room of the house, taking lessons on his bright yellow plastic guitar. "I told him I wanted to sing like Elvis Presley, but Son Stuckey, he said, 'naw, that's white folks. I want you to sing like me.' Stuckey taught me the Bentonia style, the same style he taught Skip James. You know, he had nine kids, something like that, and not a single person related to him knows a thing about his music. You talk to them and they don't remember nothing."

It is part of Jimmy's mission to explain over and over, as best he can, the difference between Stuckey and James and Owens. How Owens and James became famous and how there's not a single photograph of Stuckey anywhere, that anyone knows about.

The original Blue Front is now mute and exposed. Weather-washed of color. Inside, rooms, sort of, free to the whole, with fallen clouds of yellowed insulation, and then an openness, free of critters, because it's too cold, an openness holding on to skeletons of tables and faded upholstered chairs, a sink, a tattered reproduced painting of a bouquet of flowers, still hanging on a leaning wall, barely, irreversible.

Jimmy parks. Mr. Walter Carter hops out of the truck and practically jogs to the porch of the Blue Front, anxiously waiting for Jimmy to unlock the door. "The pulse of this town," says Jimmy. "If it weren't for this place there'd be no place, no town and that's the truth."

We enter and sit in white plastic chairs, in the foreign afternoon darkness of the Blue Front. Jimmy offers us Cokes.

"Now, you've got to yell so he can hear you," Jimmy reminds me.

• • •

I had prepared a few simple questions for Mr. Carter. Sitting inches away from him, I yell so that he can hear.

What has kept you alive all these years?

Don't know. All my friends are dead.

"He's got more energy then most folks I know," Jimmy shouts from behind the bar.

I don't have much appetite but I eat when I need to eat. Doctor gave me some medicine to make me hungry, cost fifteen dollars and didn't do nothin', fifteen dollars and didn't do nothin'.

I'm sorry to hear that, I say, and then I try again.

What makes you happy?

Bein' around people, laughin' and talkin'. Jokin'. Lookin' at the TV. The soaps. *Guiding Light*'s my favorite.

How 'bout before? Do you remember or did you ever see Amos and Andy?

That was good. I liked that show. You can't get no good ones on TV now, gotta have cable.

Were those characters very different from the people you knew, grew up with?

No, not that much. I liked 'em.

They were New Yorkers you know?

Oh, didn't know that.

How 'bout movies, what's your favorite movie?

Don't watch movies. You need cable for that. All the good stuff's on cable.

I mean in a movie theater.

Never been to a movie theater.

How 'bout music? What do you like to listen to?

Oh, I like any music.

Did you ever play guitar?

Oh boy, no!

"He played with the women," Jimmy laughs.

Did you know Skip James? Jack Owens? Henry Stuckey?

Yeah, yeah, I knew Skippy James. Skippy James. He was different from most folks. He was a preacher for while. Then he'd play music, then he'd preach. Made a couple records, two or three. Jack I knew, a musician too. He stayed right up the road here. Went across the water to play. He and I was almost the same age. Stuckey, a musician too. A fisherman, fished all the time, everyday. Used to live right off 49. He would give a juke and we'd go to his place to frolic, when I was eighteen, nineteen stay all night. He died over there in Satartia. They was all farmers.

Frolic?

Frolickin', jukin', dancin', havin' a good time.

Jukin'?

Dancin'. The waltz . . . the one-step . . . two-step . . . the slow drag.

The one step, the slow drag? Do you remember any of them?

I don't know, it been so long. Well . . . yeah, I reckon so.

He gradually stands, unexpected, surprising everybody. Standing still for a few seconds, outside of remembering, and then he starts to move, mostly his legs, sliding, without bending any limbs, announcing and then moving from step to step. First the one-step, then the two-step, then the slow drag. His body thin as a rail and light, stiff, shinning. Arms rounded. Hat tilted to the side. His cowboy boots scratching out music on the sandy concrete floor, surprising himself. Then he stops, places his hands on his chest, coughing, smiling. A revelation.

• • •

"Did you see that? See that rhythm his feet got? I didn't know he could do that." Jimmy shouts, clapping. "That's old, partner, that's old. I been knowin' him all my life and never known he could do that."

We were all clapping.

I ask if he would do the slow drag again, the side step with the weird rhythm? It was remarkable. He demonstrates it again, a little puzzled this time, stepping and now forgetting. After a few seconds he stops and sits, crosses his arms, unfazed. We were all clapping.

A train roars by, suspending the interview and time. Until Mr. Carter mentions something about a young boy in Jackson who lost his legs recently, playing too near the tracks. It confused him. I bet he crawled up under that thing while it wasn't runnin', he says.

Jimmy nods. The whistle seems to go on forever, a long freight; maybe five minutes goes by before I can ask my next question.

Did you ever have any problem with white people, a long time ago?

No, not really. I knowd what you had to do to get along with them. You had to say "yessir" and "no sir." You couldn't just say "yes" and "no." You couldn't say you couldn't do what they asked. You had to try and do it.

Was that hard for you?

Oh, yeah. He laughs. It was hard.

Did you ever see a lynching or know someone that was lynched?

Well, hmm . . .

He pauses. And uncrosses his arms.

They hung Gary, hung him, when I was a chap. He was goin' with Miss Lilly Wallace, Gary was. Her husband was dead. Miss Taylor, her sister, stayed with her that night, with Miss Wallace and saw Gary sneakin' by the window and turned him in. Because of the rain they tracked him. Brought him over to Captain Taylor's place. Captain Taylor told Gary if he told him the truth they wouldn't bother him. Gary told the truth and Captain hollered, "Come and get him boys!" Gary was stupid, believin' Captain Taylor like that, "Come and get him boys!" They hung him from an ol' plum tree, over there cross the tracks that we chilluns used to play in. We called it gator limb, us chilluns, played up under it every day. That's why they hung him there, I believe. Big ol' tree set over side of the dirt road. They left him hangin' there till a white woman came down the road the next day, in a buggy and horse and got scared, made the black folks take him down.

Was Lily Wallace a white woman?

Yeah. She and Gary was goin' together. Secret.

Is the tree still there, the plum tree?

Oh man, no! No, man, no! That was a long time ago.

What was Gary's last name?

I don't remember.

Six months earlier, I had danced in the Blue Front. I'd gone south, again, this time to research what might be left of the environment of the Delta blues and to dance in the living rooms, yards and available spaces, of those surviving friends, children and grandchildren, along a slice of Mississippi's back roads, encountering some of the haunted ones. A personal project, a counter-memorial, a meditation.

• • •

I was thinking about this one in particular, one that didn't take place in Mississippi.

Knoxville East Tennessee News.
February 3, 1921
Camillia, Ga. Feb. 1, 1921, "Jim Roland, Negro, was lynched near here yesterday after shooting Jason I. Harvel, a white man, who had held a pistol on him and ordered him to dance.

Both men were well-to-do farmers. Each was standing with friends of his own race in front of a country store. Harvel pulled out a gun and ordered the colored man to dance for the amusement of himself and his white friends. Roland grabbed for the gun and it went off, killing Harvel.

Roland fled but was soon found by a posse which riddled him with bullets. Before doing so, the posse leader commanded Roland to dance. He refused."

How poetic, that one seemed.

I remember, every morning I'd stretch and warm up in the narrow space between the double beds of a Days Inn or a Comfort Inn, or a Motel 8 or 6, sometimes a Hampton Inn, from Memphis to New Orleans, in preparation for an opportunity to dance for someone. Sometimes it happened, sometimes it didn't. There was magic in this spontaneity. There was also preparation for this spontaneity, making myself available for a conversation, where both parties are saying, yes.

For instance: Here, I want to show you something that comes from the big city. And here, I want you to hear something from down here that you already know about that I discovered back east, in the big city. Or, here, I want to give you something that is about both places and possibly beyond, up there and down here.

And then you say, "Although I'm not quite sure what it is you're doing here, yes, I accept. And you can even photograph this moment. Sure, why not?"

"Welcome is every organ and attribute of me," sings the *Leaves of Grass*, Whitman.

And then I say, yes, why not? I can assure you, I know a lot about creative formality, in conversing with society, and can afford to bring some artificiality to these grassroots convergences, making the scared mundane more vivid.

Now, if that sounds interesting, let's get on with it.

So, Buddy Spires, of Bentonia, Mississippi, the blues harp partner of Jack Owens, told Jimmy "Duck" Holmes, over the phone, that if his visitors wanted to hear him blow the harmonica it would cost us twenty dollars. Five dollars extra to video.

Mr. Holmes pointed out Buddy Spires's yellow shotgun house from the Blue Front, across the railroad tracks, told us we had to pick him up and bring him back to the Blue Front.

Buddy Spires was putting on pomade, greasing his hair back. Wearing huge black sunglasses.

How long you been playing the harp, Buddy?

Since I was five, a gift from Santa.

Do you miss Jack Owens?

God yes. We had such good times, so many experiences together. Been two years. I try to keep my mind in the present but then I'll start to think about him and . . .

Didn't think what we was doin' all those years was anything, but people come around and wanted to hear us play. We been to California, twice, New York, once, Chicago, once, and where is it where it's really cold? Not Iowa, been there, once. Iowa weather is cool, not too cold.

Minnesota? Wisconsin? Canada?

Nope, been to those places, all once. I can't remember where, but Jack and I arrived in short-sleeved shirts and it was so cold the producer had to buy us some coats.

Buddy still finds this incident funny and laughs. Being blind, Buddy will tell this story over and over. He doesn't have to remember a face, voices come and go, and it seems handshakes don't count. Doesn't matter to him who's heard it once or twice or three times. It's a good story.

Did you ever play guitar, Buddy?

I tried but couldn't get the hang of it. Jack use to say, "don't worry about the guitar Buddy, I'll take care of the pickin', you just blow the harp."

I asked if there was anything special about Bentonia harp music, and he said no. Said he trained himself and just happened to be living in Bentonia, in that way his music had a Bentonia style. Later he mentioned, as though it wasn't very important, his awesome father, Arthur "Big Boy" Spires, who lived and played the blues in Chicago.

We drove Buddy back to the Blue Front. I bought him a beer and he sat and waited, telling jokes, about preachers, the devil, and rabbits, while Jimmy plugged in his electric guitar and a couple microphones. (Jimmy prefers the acoustic guitar, his "Baby," but it was missing a string. Jimmy, who was a student of Jack Owens, said Owens only played acoustic. Owens did at times play an amplified guitar. But I knew what Jimmy meant.)

"After Son Stuckey, Jack was my guru," Jimmy announced. "Whenever anyone asked Jack where his blues came from he'd say from working in the cotton fields or behind a mule. 'What else you'd expect a man would think about, workin' like that?' he'd say. You know, the most amazing thing about the old blues musicians? Something no one ever talks about? They were all illiterate. Couldn't read or write a lick! Would make their songs up in their heads, in cotton fields, behind mules, sometimes before going to bed, and the next morning they'd have the song. Ready to play."

Bentonia blues, open E, high wailing. "Nobody knows how the tuning got this way, but this is what makes Bentonia style so compelling," Jimmy continued, almost ready to play. (Actually, I'd read that Stuckey discovered the open E-minor tuning while a soldier in France during World War I, from soldiers he took to be Bahamians.)

A baleful sound. Startling, in how it refuses to entertain. And then that high-pitched singing, James had it, Owens had it, and Jimmy replicates it, "Son Stuckey, too, had a real tenor voice, you had to, no amplifiers in those days."

Buddy just blows the harp, a precise and muddy rage, without style, in complete love, in between beers.

In between trying to decipher a music that I could not decode, practically stomping my feet, and restoring Buddy's empty beer bottles, I sat, if one could call this sitting, and waited for something fast, upbeat. It never came. What's left of the environment of the blues. What was always there.

So I waited and then said, fuck it, and didn't wait for an opportunity, for the music to say, yes, come join us.

I did anyway, got up from my plastic chair and began to move, for a song, a boisterous dirge, like the rest of the music. A dance that had no steps or shape, like the music. No longer research. I disappeared, rhythmically, without discrimination. But not in the way I had dreamed. I danced, with bended knees. An intelligent moving body breaking down into a very hard floor, and Jimmy and Buddy played, Hard Time Killin' Floor Blues, oblivious to my dancing, while the onlookers, smiling, sitting around tables that propped up untidy ashtrays and cans of Budweiser, watched and nodded, acknowledging how my body was losing an opinion, in the bottomless soul of this place.

I stopped, sat down, no one clapped, no one said yes, nothing became more vivid, the music continued. And I was the only one surprised.

I remembered something Jimmy said. "Once, when those folks were shooting the Levi's commercial, one of the camera crew, a boy from England, somewhere like that, walked in to the place and fell to his knees and wept, howling, that he'd heard of juke joints all his life but never thought he'd ever see a real one."

A few days later, I thought how presumptuous I had been, dancing there, trying to experience something, trying to make something happen, forcing a complex event, even though private, there, in a place where there was absolutely no reason for irony, no discernable reason. Instead, what I found was perfect absence, a complete refusal to occupy a space I could never understand, because it keeps changing. Very unpoetic, this realization.

And a perversity of fate, I yell.

And in this is irony. Like Gary's story, whose last name Mr. Walter Carter couldn't remember, or maybe never knew. (Gary is now just Gary, and in the end that is his history.)

Mr. Carter, arms crossed, legs out stretched and crossed, continues to listen, if now showing a little exhaustion.

I then try to explain the particular absence I had experienced, without once using the word *history*. I also leave out the words, dancing and dying, in an attempt to make a more spiritual point. Ultimately, Mr. Carter doesn't understand, or doesn't hear my queries, has nothing to say. He doesn't ask me to dance, again, so that he can see for himself.

And I have no more questions for him. We sit facing each other in silence, listening, like the rest of the Blue Front community, to R&B music from a jukebox that now blasts through the juke joint, until Mr. Carter falls asleep.

The pulse of the town? Six AM to 10 PM, normal hours, modern hours, and no dirt floor, not this time. The whole town does seem to wander in and out of the Blue Front, kids, teenagers, adult men, women, and seniors. All black, but for the occasional European or Japanese. This is not an all-black town, by the way, absolutely not.

After a few minutes Mr. Carter wakes and suddenly shares a story, as if he thinks I've asked another question, or as though it were a dream he just had, about a big black buzzard-like bird, a prophecy bird, that flew over his house when he was a small boy, a bird he'd never seen before and never saw again, and how the next day his uncle was murdered, had his brains blown out with a shotgun.

Mr. Carter, wide awake now, then boasts about how he doesn't need a "stick," at ninety-five and how amazing that is. Says before he retired he was a gardener, for a long time. Says he's been retired for a long time. Says he has to jog around his house, his simple one-story brick house, every night, right before bed, otherwise he can't sleep.

Note

An excerpt of this story was published in *Dance, Human Rights, and Social Justice: Dignity in Motion,* ed. Naomi Jackson and Toni Shapiro-Phim (Lanham, Md.: Scarecrow Press, 2008), 156–65.

18

Art and Integration

An Interview with Carrie Mae Weems

*Carrie Mae Weems
and David O'Brien*

Q: When did you decide to become an artist?

A: When I was a child. I knew that I would be an artist. I dreamt of being an artist.

Q: So you were an artist before you were formed politically?

A: Yes, though while I don't come from an avidly political household, I did grow up with people who talked about ideas. Early in my life the idea of ideals was important. Ideas about rights and ideas about humanity. My father was such a great, great person in that way. He spoke so eloquently to me. From the time I was a child at his knee he spoke to me about my rights as a person. My rights as a person. To be and to do. To be a part of. That, then, came out of a very serious and early upbringing. We were looking out and questioning what was going on. My first May Day was with my mother and father. These men going off to this demonstration, and these women going to frolic in the park.

Q: They were union members?

A: They were all in the union. My father worked in hide houses and steel houses. My uncles were working the steel yard and in steel mills. So I come out of that kind of family—not a political family, but certainly a politicized family. And maybe that has to do with who we were, as black people living at that time (figure 18.1).

Q: You have referred to the *Brown* decision from time to time in your work. It is obviously a landmark civil rights decision, but do you have any personal experience of segregation or desegregation in education that has made the decision important for you?

A: No, not in the way that I think you are looking for. I grew up in Portland, Oregon. I went to school beginning in, say, 1959, and I went to a school that was mixed, and that was just the way it was. Being from a northern city—Portland wasn't necessarily a progressive town—but I never had a

FIGURE 18.1.

Carrie Mae Weems, *Carrie and Dad,* from *Family Pictures and Stories,* 1978–84. Silver Print, 13 × 8½". Photo courtesy of Carrie Mae Weems.

sense as a child that there was a real problem with my going to school with white children.

I had really amazing teachers throughout, and they were primarily white. I remember Ms. McCoy, my seventh-grade teacher, showing us a film on Nazism, and she showed it to us five or six times. She kept saying "Didn't you hear anything in that that upset you?" and we'd say "No," and she'd play it again and say "Didn't you . . . ?" And finally she said, "This man just said that black people were animals, and equated you to . . ." She ran this whole thing down. We said, "We don't know about that, but we know it's not true."

Q: What about integration in museums? What do you think have been the most important successes and failures over the last fifty years for integrating the museum?

A: It's a very interesting question and a dynamic problem. There was a moment in the '80s, in particular, when so much was happening. All kinds of artists were stepping up. There seemed to be a huge shift in the popular imagination about voice and broad participation, a belief that seminal voices were being left out and crippling us all, because we didn't know something and weren't privy to some significant forms of expression, because black artists, women artists, and minority artists generally speaking had been left out. There was a group of historians, collectors, curators, and artists who were all championing the need to redress this. That was a very important time, and some headway was made. Then there was a countermovement of anti–political correctness that reared its head and sent a lot of people scurrying for cover. I think we are still attempting to recover from that moment. And so what started as a strong, progressive movement has really since dissipated in a significant and obvious way, across the board. Black art, for the most part, is thought of as second-rate, and [many people now believe] that the voices that were seminal and important have been included, for the most part, and nothing else is really quite going on, and now we can turn our attention back to the boys' club, and that's where we are. The work of the Guerrilla Girls is still very much apropos to our moment. The system is still very much dominated by white men and is fairly closed because it moves according to who one knows and who one feels most comfortable working with.

Q: I agree that the late '70s and '80s was a progressive moment; however, looking back now, efforts to include minorities and women into the museum seem problematic in various ways. For example, one problem that confronted artists of color then and still confronts them today is that when they treat subjects pertaining to race, that's all that is seen in their work.

A: There could be any series of expressions, emotions, or ideas, and the work is always reduced to an expression of race and a question of class, and that becomes an easy, quick shorthand for dismissing it or not engaging with it as serious art.

Q: Or even if it is engaged seriously on the level of race, it does not have the same purchase it should have because the many other aspects of life it addresses are ignored. Its full range of expression is robbed from it.

A: It may be dealt with seriously in terms of race, but the work is limited by how the writer or curator engage with it. Ultimately, they do in fact dismiss it; they don't deal with the full complexity of the work.

Q: So how, as an artist, does one deal with this situation?

A: I am always trying to figure out how to negotiate that situation. No matter how much I push to talk about the other aspects of the work—formal considerations, emotional dynamics—I am often sidetracked back into this question of race.

The recent works that I've made—for instance, the video pieces, Meaning and Landscape, where everything exists behind shadow [laughs], was a strategy to push the conversation to another arena. It doesn't mean I am not interested in these questions [of race], but it does mean that I am endlessly limited in the ways in which the work is discussed.

Q: Your early work seemed grounded in your immediate, local experience—it explored, for example, issues of family life and your own family's migration from the South. Your more recent work seems far more globally situated and international: for example, the Africa series is set in Africa, and Ritual and Revolution refers to the Holocaust, the genocide in Cambodia, and the Irish potato famine (figure 18.2). Also, you engage with grand historical narratives and famous historical events. What prompted this change?

A: It's not a change. My interest in history was always there. My interest in human struggles internationally has always been there, and I've always sought to place my subjects in that larger context. It's another strategy to push the work beyond the narrow confines of race.

Q: Did the fact that you traveled so much in the '90s help you to contextualize your work in a more international narrative?

A: I'm not absolutely sure. Travel broadens us all, and so there is no way that I can live in Paris, or Germany, or Rome, or wherever, and not have that play a part in the way I engage with and think about the world. I wouldn't say that I made work directly in response to travel, but I am certain that travel has had a deep impact in the way I raise certain kinds of questions or problematize certain historical information.

Q: In the Sea Island series [which explores the Gullah culture on the coast of the Carolinas and Georgia (figure 18.3)] I was struck by the fact that you focus more on the material culture than on the people, and that in the photographs we never see the faces of people. I felt that you were suggesting that there is a certain opacity to cultures that should be respected—that the photographer must be respectful and sensitive when exposing a people or culture to public scrutiny.

A: The Sea Islands was for me a wonderful segue into entering a world of cultural

FIGURE 18.2.

Carrie Mae Weems, Installation view of *Ritual and Revolution* at Rhona Hoffman Gallery, 1998. Digital photographs on muslin, color pigment, audio component, size variable: smallest 71 × 74", largest 117 × 71". Photo courtesy of Carrie Mae Weems.

FIGURE 18.3.

Carrie Mae Weems, *Shells* and *McIntosh Shouters,* 1992. Diptych from the *Sea Island Series,* silver gelatin prints, 37 × 24". Photo courtesy of Carrie Mae Weems.

description that is not only found in the Sea Islands. Folk beliefs and superstitions are international in some respects, and very local in other ways.

In the early '90s I didn't like the idea of running into a place and photographing people. I felt that there was something really wrong with that. I didn't like that history of documentary photography. You know, you show these "suffering poor people." So for me it was about trying to find an elegant way to describe the meanings of a culture, without having to have an individual face stand in as the representation of that thing. And the same thing is true in the Africa series. And perhaps in other bodies of work as well. For instance, in the Louisiana project, where you never see the face, you are never allowed to engage with the subject as the representation of a type of person who lives in the place. What you are able to do is follow a

FIGURE 18.4.
Carrie Mae Weems, *Happiness,* from the *Missing Link* series, Iris Print, 41 × 29".

kind of muse, a kind of spirit that stands for much more than any individual person ever could.

Q: When the subject of diaspora comes up, it's often treated as a subject of identity—that is to say, the emphasis is placed on the similarities shared by the members of a diaspora. But in practice, diasporas are always communities in which identity and difference are very much in negotiation.

A: It's interesting that you say this, because when I showed the Sea Island series in the Johannesburg Biennial in South Africa, everybody there thought it was about South Africa. People asked me how I knew so much about South Africa. In one way it belies the underlying assumption that there are ways in which people of the diaspora recognize their cultural essence in the work, and at the same time, it's really also about what they bring to the work— their own personal beliefs. And if you showed the work in Portugal, they would see themselves in it as well.

It's been in these ways that I have tried to cut across this narrow band of race that I find so limiting. It's not completely useless, but not always useful. It doesn't allow for a broader expression on the part of the curator and art historian, who ultimately write about the work. They need to know that the work speaks outside of that narrow box of race—that they don't have to completely abandon the trusted handle of their own system of understanding.

19

Social Studies

Eight Artists Address *Brown*

David O'Brien

This essay emerges out of the exhibition *Social Studies: Eight Artists Address Brown v. the Board of Education,* which opened at the University of Illinois's Krannert Art Museum in April 2004, as part of the university's commemoration of the *Brown* decision, and subsequently traveled to the Spencer Art Museum at the University of Kansas. The exhibition was also part of an ongoing series of shows staged under the auspices of Social Studies Projects, a nonprofit organization directed by Carrie Mae Weems that provides opportunities for artistic collaborations addressing the struggle for social justice. For the exhibition at Illinois, I selected works by eight artists who address issues at the center of the *Brown* decision; in addition to Weems herself, these artists were Dawoud Bey, Sanford Biggers, Brett Cook-Dizney, Virgil Marti, Gary Simmons, Pamela Vander Zwan, and Jennifer Zackin.[1] Politically and artistically these artists are only loosely affiliated, but all of them seek to combine aesthetic ambitions with an exploration of pressing social and political concerns. The works in the exhibition focused on issues of identity and tolerance, particularly as they relate to desegregation and education today. In this essay I wish to explore the ways in which the work relates to the *Brown* decision and then reflect briefly on the potential of art today to advance our understanding of the issues at the center of the landmark case.

An exhibition devoted to the *Brown* decision must confront the fact that artists are seldom called on today to comment on important historical issues, even one with such broad significance for a multiracial, democratic society. For some time, the art forms most championed by museums and critics have, far more often than not, set themselves off from the everyday political culture, cultivating new, difficult, and often esoteric viewing practices, and leading many to consider the visual arts a marginal, even elitist arena for creativity. At the very time when the *Brown* case was making its way through the courts, the art historian Meyer Schapiro wrote that "Artists today who would welcome the chance to paint works of broad human content for a larger audience, works comparable in scope to those of antiquity or the Middle Ages, find no sustained opportunities for such an art; they have no alternative but to cultivate in their art the only or surest realms of freedom—the interior world of their fancies, sensations, and feelings, and the medium itself."[2]

The 1960s and 1970s witnessed a significant repoliticization of art, yet it remains a common and justified complaint that the main institutions devoted to the collecting and display of art ignore or suppress overtly political work, particularly that related to the subject of race. It may come as some surprise, then, that a number of ambitious young artists would use their work to explore such pragmatic issues as integration and tolerance in education. Perhaps it is even more surprising to find a substantial iconography in contemporary art devoted to students, classrooms, and schools. That is, however, precisely what characterized the art in *Social Studies*. Significantly, the work in the exhibition was not created specifically for the *Brown* commemoration; rather, it was selected from preexisting bodies of work or grew organically out of the artists' current artistic pursuits. This simple fact testifies to the ongoing importance of the issues at the core of the *Brown* case, both within advanced artistic practice today as well as more generally within American society. If *Brown* seems like an unlikely subject for an art exhibition, this may have more to do with the institutions governing artistic practice than with the interests of practicing artists.

Most of the artists in the exhibition had, at some point in their careers, created an important body of work devoted explicitly to the subjects of education and integration, and this is what drew my attention to them. Such was the case, for example, with Dawoud Bey. He had just completed the Chicago Project, a collaboration with Dan Collison and Elizabeth Meister, who made audio recordings accompanying Bey's photographs.[3] Three works from the Chicago Project figured in the exhibition. Each consists of a large photograph of a student from a school in or around the Hyde Park neighborhood of Chicago and a recording of the same student reflecting on issues of identity that arise in their everyday lives (figure 19.1).

The photographs are remarkable for the ways in which they capture the sitters in a moment of apparent calm, staring deeply into the lens: they seem to offer direct access to the students. Yet the students' recorded thoughts concerning questions of identity—which touch on subjects as varied as race, ethnicity, physique, and gender—reveal a complexity and individuality that could never be determined from the picture alone. On one recording, for example, we hear a young black man with a gentle voice recall an instance in which he was the victim of racial profiling by the police. On another recording, a young white woman argues that, as a member of a racial group that is in the minority in her high school, she deserves the right to apply to minority programs. In still another, a student wonders whether, against her father's advice, she should indicate she is Iranian on her college application. The words spoken by the students on the audio component immediately complicate the impression left by the photographic portrait. Taken together, the visual and verbal portraits point up the inability of any one representation to fully encapsulate an individual. They remind us of the limitations of representation and the dangers of settling on fixed and confining views of people's identities, even as they provide captivating insights into the experience of today's youth.

Education is also an explicit theme in the art of Gary Simmons. He has worked in a wide variety of media, from photographs, to multimedia installations, to erased drawings, but throughout his career he has repeatedly returned to images drawn from the world of pedagogy. He is perhaps best known for his smudged and partially erased drawings on chalkboards. Early in his career he used this medium to explore stereotypes and images linked to racial oppression, but his more recent work is far more ambiguous and treats race less directly.

Simmons contributed three photographs to the exhibition, all of which focused on classrooms or other spaces devoted to learning at a variety of institutions, from poorly funded public schools to wealthy private universities. As with much of Simmons's work, the human figure is conspicuously absent, its presence only implied by the environment that has been constructed for it. We normally think of such spaces as filled with activity: learning, discipline, concentration, and distraction. Indeed, the aura or ghost of such activities seems to hang about these spaces. Yet the emptiness of the space ultimately calls attention to the intangible and fleeting nature of the act of learning. Despite the apparent banality of their subjects, the photographs possess a powerful presence, partly as a result of the auratic presence of learning, but also as a result of their formal properties: impressive scale, symmetric compositions, and simple, rectilinear shapes. In *503–509* (figure 19.2), for example, Simmons offers an image of large swinging wooden doors that might come from any number of older educational buildings, yet he manages to imbue this simple image with great significance, partly through its pared-down, monumental geometry and partly through the effect of the glowing light emanating from the opaque windows, partially occluding the surrounding doorframe. An image that at first seems banal reveals unexpected significance, perhaps as a metaphor of education as a source of enlightenment, as a gateway or passage to knowledge, or more abstractly as a source of aesthetic or spiritual pleasure.

Education is also a prominent theme in the work of Brett Cook-Dizney. He has explicitly addressed the implications of desegregation on education in his *[De]Segregation* (2001), which combined portraits and quotations of a professor, a staff member, and a student at Harvard University's Graduate School of Education into three large paintings displayed on the street outside the school's library. As with much of his work, this project was the result of a community-based collaboration. The sitters and their friends helped to transfer their own images onto canvas by tracing projected drawings, made from photographs, onto the canvas. The final paintings, completed in spray paint by Cook-Dizney, were displayed on the street outside the School of Education. Through the use of accompanying texts, the work drew particular attention to new segregating practices in education today, such as vouchers and the privatization of education.

For *Social Studies,* Cook-Dizney contributed one of a series of installations he has created, all of which combine images of himself as a boy with various objects from his youth. *Documentation of American Cultural Capital* (1999) pictures the artist as an adolescent in an enormous portrait on plywood, again done in the artist's signature spray-paint style (figure 19.3). His likeness is surrounded by various objects—toys, a graduation cap, a drawing of pilgrims, a daily chores chart, academic records, standardized test scores—all of which speak to the processes of cultural reproduction and socialization we all undergo as we grow up.

The rituals of childhood and its processes of socialization are equally apparent in *a small world . . .* (1999–2001), an installation that resulted from a unique collaboration between the artists Sanford Biggers and Jennifer Zackin (figure 19.4). In this installation, excerpts taken from home movies of the artists as children appear side by side. The movies play in a room decorated in the manner of a middle-class family den, complete with wood paneling, a shag rug, and full-sized couch. Viewing the movies, it quickly becomes apparent that they are stunningly similar, despite the fact that one is about a white Jewish girl and the other is about a black Christian boy. Both movies are composed of scenes of grilling, piano lessons, birthday parties, religious celebrations, and vacations to places like Disneyland. The video suggests that, despite differences in race, religion, and gender, the children share remarkably similar habits, manners, and rituals. Yet, at the same time, the worlds of blacks and whites exist in almost total separation, with one side of the screen populated almost entirely by whites, and the other almost entirely by blacks. The collaboration between Biggers and Zackin is a spur for us to reevaluate the significance of those markers and beliefs that divide us even in the face of a broadly shared common culture.

Issues of race, education, and equal rights are treated in a more symbolic fashion in the work of Pamela Vander Zwan and Carrie Mae Weems. *Plessy v. Ferguson* (2003), the result of a collaboration between Vander Zwan and Weems, refers to an important legal predecessor to *Brown.* The *Plessy v. Ferguson* case resulted from the arrest of an African American man, Homer Plessy, for sitting in the "white" car of a train in New Orleans. The Supreme Court ruled in 1896 that states had the right to separate the races, so long as the facilities provided to them were equal. The decision was not reversed until the *Brown* case reached the Supreme Court in 1954. Vander Zwan and Weems's piece dramatizes this history by picturing the two artists attempting to occupy a single seat (figure 19.5). It allegorizes the conflict behind the Court decision as a competition for limited resources and reminds us that our judicial system has not always promoted integration and equality of racial groups.

Vander Zwan takes up some of the underlying political issues relating to the *Brown* case in *Shedding Light* (2004), an installation consisting of a variety of objects and images. Resting on a shelf are Braille versions of three central documents of American society—the Declaration of Independence, the Constitution, and the Bill of Rights—and a deck of flash cards, each of which displays a single letter of the alphabet, in both print and Braille, as well as well as a particularly loaded word beginning with the letter. The letter "I," for example, is accompanied by the word "Include." On the wall above the shelf are four prints that juxtapose a written word or phrase with a word in Braille. All of the words carry a strong ideological charge: "Department of Defense," "Diversity," and "Traitor," and "Disciplinary Segregation" (figure 19.6). If the viewer takes the time to decode the Braille words using the cards, she discovers that they differ from the written words in provocative ways: while the paired words are synonyms, political debates have rendered one of them unpalatable or unacceptable. "Disciplinary Segregation," for example, translates as "Solitary Confinement," and "Diversity" translates as "Affirmative Action." Finally, on the wall above the prints are photographs of people from various walks of life—an art dealer, deli owners, and a mother and child—in their everyday environments. All except the child and a customer in the deli wear woolen blindfolds. The piece encourages us to consider who is truly blind in our society and to what extent we see the world and understand language through the veil of ideology. Forthrightly critical of the contemporary political status quo, Vander Zwan asserts that a conservative hegemony pervades the terms of public discourse, endangering the possibility of rational, open debate and change. She mocks the language games of the political Right and calls for vigilance regarding the manner in which the issues at the core of cases like *Brown* are discussed and remembered.

Among the artists in the exhibition, Weems is by far the most established. Throughout her career she has used her art to draw attention to the pernicious effects of racism. For example, in the 1980s she examined such things as the persistence of racism in American jokes (Ain't Jokin' series, 1987–88) and the significance of skin color within African American life (Colored People, 1989–90). More recently her work has taken on a more global perspective, relating African American experience to a larger African diaspora and linking civil rights abuses in America to larger social catastrophes such as the Holocaust, the Irish potato famine, and genocide in Cambodia. It must be observed, however, that race is just one of many themes taken up in Weems's work: too many accounts of the artist make it appear as though this were her one and ever-present subject. She is justly praised for keeping discussion of such issues as racism and civil rights at the center of American artistic practice for over two decades—and this is why she was an obvious choice as a visitor during the *Brown* jubilee celebration at Illinois—but she has also brought her art to bear on subjects as varied as family relations and American material culture.

Weems was represented in the exhibition by four plates from her Commemorating series (1991), which pays homage to the efforts of black leaders to combat racism in America (figure 19.7). Weems has repeatedly used commemorative plates in her work. For example, in her Sea Islands series she used them to draw attention to the survival of African culture in the Gullah society of the coastal Carolinas and Georgia. But whereas the plates in that series were modestly crafted and decorated with Africanizing border designs, in accord with the folk culture of the Gullah, the plates in the Commemorating series are elegant and gold-rimmed, retrospectively bestowing the respect and honor that have usually been denied to the individuals cited in them. One plate in the exhibition paid homage to *Plessy* in the following words:

Commemorating
Plessy
who challenged Ferguson's
separate but equal
bull-shit

Another was inscribed with the names of various plaintiffs whose cases were consolidated with the *Brown* case before the Supreme Court (and consequently subordinated to *Brown* in public memory):

Commemorating
Harvey Briggs, Jr., Ethel Belton
Dorothy Davis, Linda Bona and
Spotswood Bolling
for challenging the Board of Education

This last plate is proof positive of Weems's longstanding interest in *Brown* and the central place she gives it in the civil rights struggle.

Weems also exhibited *For Rosa, for Daisy,* a triptych of photographs from a series entitled May Days Long Forgotten (2003) (figure 19.8). The piece forgoes the imagery of struggle in favor of a pastoral iconography of flowers and children. The series focuses on girls with elegant coiffures and dresses adorned with floral prints. In some photographs the girls lounge decorously on lawns; in others they pose for tightly cropped portraits. The round or oval frames and the convex protective glass, in combination with the setting and costume, suggest the pictorial conventions of an earlier period. They offer a private, idyllic world of innocence, beauty, and repose that contrasts with a public record too often characterized by strife and oppression. Yet the work is more than a simple record of pastoral idyll. On the one hand, the work may exhibit a certain nostalgia for Weems's own days as a girl: she participated in May Day celebrations in which the men went off to march in labor demonstrations while the mothers dressed up their daughters and brought them to the park. On the other hand, Weems was inspired to create the piece by her encounters with two girls in her hometown of Syracuse, New York, who live in difficult circumstances and have discovered a completely different image of themselves through their encounter with Weems.[4] Most viewers will, of course, not view the image with this knowledge, but it can nonetheless serve to remind us that art confronts us with a world of imagination and fantasy. Weems's work often engages many of the most difficult problems confronting society today, but it can also provide us with a world of uncompromised beauty that inspires in a completely different fashion.

While much of the work in the exhibition was selected in order to address the issues of racial integration and education, I wanted to establish also that the fight against bigotry and the acceptance of difference in public education are not solely limited to the question of race. Thus the exhibition included Virgil Marti's *Bullies* (1992), a work that loudly, but humorously, draws attention to these same issues as they relate to homosexuality (figure 19.9). This garish, flocked wallpaper includes high-school yearbook portraits of the boys who mistreated Marti, calling him a "sissy" and a "faggot" for behaviors that he would later associate with his gayness. The portraits are set against a fluorescent background and framed by garlands of flowers that form strong diagonals across the wall. The stunning fluorescent colors, illuminated by black lights, bring to mind male adolescent culture of the 1970s, yet the flocked, pseudo-velvet texture and garland pattern recall the efforts of many middle class households to acquire the opulence and grandeur of the upper classes of the nineteenth century. Marti jokingly exacts his vengeance on his former persecutors by integrating their likenesses into a decorative design that carries strong associations of femininity and vulgarity. In the process, he reminds us that public education still needs to be reformed not simply to integrate races, but also to foster acceptance of various sexualities.

• • •

In an essay on vernacular African America photography, the cultural critic bell hooks speculated that racial desegregation has had specific effects on African American visual culture:

> In part, racial desegregation—equal access—offered a vision of racial progress
> that, however limited, led many black people to be less vigilant about the

question of representation. Concurrently, contemporary commodification of blackness creates a market context wherein conventional, even stereotypical, modes of representing blackness may receive the greatest reward. This leads to a cultural context in which images that would subvert the status quo are harder to produce. There is no "perceived market" for them. Nor should it surprise us that the erosion of oppositional black subcultures (many of which have been destroyed in the desegregation process) has deprived us of those sites of radical resistance where we [African Americans] have had primary control over representation.

Continuing on, hooks laments "the utter loss of critical vigilance in the arena of image making" and "a relinquishment of collective black interest in the production of images."[5] She is particularly concerned that African Americans may have abandoned vernacular photography as a means to define an identity in opposition to the oppressive images provided by a white-supremacist society, but she also indicates that African American artists are implicated in this process as well.

One would expect concerns over racial self-representation to ease in an integrated society, just as one might hope for the abolition of race itself, but hooks draws our attention to a largely unexamined risk of the integrationist position: if race persists, and if the struggle for African American self-definition is abandoned in the effort to integrate, what representations will come to define blackness? And what representations will be forgotten or lost? For hooks, the issue of representation takes precedence over desegregation:

> The history of black liberation movements in the United States could be characterized as a struggle over images as much as it has also been a struggle for rights, for equal access. To many reformist black civil rights activists, who believed that desegregation would offer the humanizing context that would challenge white supremacy, the issue of representation—control over images— was never as important as equal access. As time has progressed and the face of white supremacy has not changed, reformist and radical blacks would likely agree that the field of representation remains a crucial realm of struggle, as important as the question of equal access.[6]

This statement will strike many as being overly pessimistic about the results of the civil rights struggle and desegregation. Perhaps, too, it is pointless to weigh the relative importance of rights versus the control of images—both are essential—but hooks is surely correct to emphasize the continuing importance of the struggle in the field of representation.

In this regard, *Social Studies* offers clear evidence that artists are still fully engaged in that struggle. It challenges the dehumanizing, restrictive definitions of identity that have allowed discrimination and intolerance to exist in our edu-

I go to Kenwood Academy and Kenwood is 90% black and . . . 3% Asian and . . . basically the rest white. I've always been, like, the minority at my school so it doesn't bother me, unless it becomes an issue with other people—then it bothers me. I guess some people assume that I'm different when I'm not necessarily, because usually I'm the only white person in the class and I guess they think that I don't wanna to talk to them or something, but . . . I'm sort of quiet in class. They assume that maybe I have something against *them,* but they really don't have any reason to think that. I don't know, they ask me if I would ever, like, be friends with black people and I'm like—I *have* black friends. You just don't *know* who I'm friends with and . . . People have asked me if I would ever date black people and stuff like that. I said, that yeah, I would and I *have* dated black people and I *have* plenty of black friends. Not only am I like one out of very few white people with blacks, but I'm also not exactly too wealthy . . .

So, like, I don't know, that's affected me a lot when it comes to, like, being able to do things, like, um, there was one thing I wanted to do. Um, it was a paleontology thing over the summer. It was with the University of Chicago. I don't know where they went, but they went, they went away for like a month and, it sounded really cool. And it was for minorities *only,* yet, I felt that I was a minority. So I was upset. I said I was going to apply anyways, but . . . I didn't.

FIGURE 19.1.

Dawoud Bey, *Simone, Kenwood Academy High School,* 2003. Chromogenic print. Courtesy of the artist, Rhona Hoffman Gallery, and Gorney Bravin + Lee.

FIGURE 19.2.

Gary Simmons, *503–509,* 1998. Cibachrome, 75 × 57″. Unique. Courtesy of the artist and Metro Pictures.

FIGURE 19.3.

Brett Cook-Dizney, *Documentation of American Cultural Capital*, 1999. Spray enamel, mixed media with personal objects on wood and plexiglass, 96" × 144". Courtesy of the artist and P.P.O.W. Gallery, New York.

FIGURE 19.4.

Sanford Biggers and Jennifer Zackin, *a small world . . . ,* 1999–2001. Multimedia installation with split screen video projection, 6 minute loop, dimensions variable. Courtesy of the artists.

FIGURE 19.5.

Pamela Vander Zwan and Carrie Mae Weems, *Plessy v. Ferguson,* 2003. One of a suite of five chromogenic prints, each 24" × 24". Courtesy of the artists and P.P.O.W. Gallery, New York.

FIGURE 19.6.

Pamela Vander Zwan, *Shedding Light,* 2004. Multimedia installation, dimensions variable. Courtesy of the artist.

FIGURE 19.7.

Carrie Mae Weems, *Untitled* from Commemorating, a series of twenty-three plates, 1991. Ceramic, 10" diameter. Courtesy of the artist and P.P.O.W. Gallery, New York.

FIGURE 19.8.

Carrie Mae Weems, *For Rosa, for Daisy,* 2003. Triptych from May Days Long Forgotten, 2003. Three chromogenic prints, wood and convex glass; center panel: 34" diameter; side panels: 34" × 28". Courtesy of the artist and P.P.O.W. Gallery, New York.

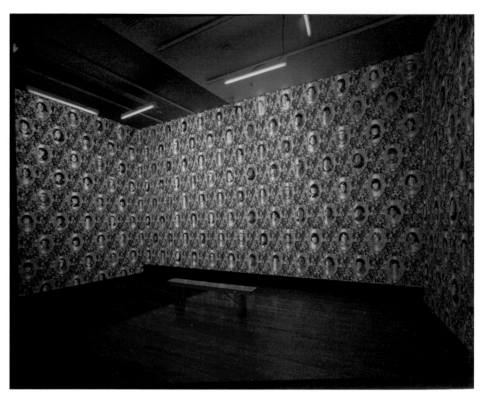

FIGURE 19.9.

Virgil Marti, *Bullies,* 1992. Fluorescent ink and rayon flock on Tyvek illuminated with black lights, dimensions variable. Courtesy of the artist. Handprinted at the Fabric Workshop and Museum, Philadelphia. Photo by Richard Loesch.

cational system. At a time when many of the government programs introduced to redress the past discrimination in education are in danger of being eliminated, these artists remind us of the long struggle for equal rights in America and the continuing problems we face today in achieving a just, tolerant, and equitable society. They demonstrate that the issues and values driving the *Brown* decision are very much alive in artistic practice today, and they spur us to think about these issues in new and compelling ways. Perhaps most importantly, they offer us inspiration as we work to secure and expand the achievement of the 1954 Supreme Court decision.

Notes

1. The exhibition showed at the Krannert Art Museum in April and May of 2004, and at the Spencer Museum of Art in October and November of 2004. In addition to numerous reviews in local publications, the exhibition was featured by *Newsday* on its Web site in a survey of activities across America commemorating *Brown*. I wish to acknowledge here the assistance of Pam Vander Zwan, who played a major role in identifying work for the exhibition, and Carrie Mae Weems, who generously offered to include it in the Social Studies Projects series. I also wish to thank Ted Gournelos for his help as a research assistant.

2. Meyer Schapiro, "The Introduction of Modern Art in America: the Armory Show," in *America in Crisis: Fourteen Episodes in American History*, ed. Daniel Aaron (New York: Knopf, 1952), 241.

3. The Smart Museum in Chicago organized the collaboration, and all the students in these portraits attend schools in the neighborhood surrounding the museum. The project has been published as Dawoud Bey et al., *Dawoud Bey: The Chicago Project* (Chicago: David and Alfred Smart Museum of Art, 2003).

4. Weems provided this information in a MillerComm Lecture at the University of Illinois on May 5, 2004.

5. bell hooks, *Art on My Mind: Visual Politics* (New York: New Press, 1995), 58.

6. Ibid., 57.

Section IV

Illinois and *Brown*

The commemoration offered the University of Illinois at Urbana-Champaign an opportunity to reflect not only on the national significance of *Brown*, but also on its ramifications closer to home. The essays in this section demonstrate the impact of the court case at the university, in the towns of Champaign and Urbana, and in the state of Illinois. Joy Ann Williamson Lott's essay allows us to appreciate both the achievements of black student activists in changing university policies and institutions in the era of Black Power, but she also demonstrates the enormity of the opposition they faced and the costs of their struggle. In some ways, Chancellor Richard Herman answers Lott's account of the university in the 1960s with his own essay about how diversity and immigration have helped shape greatness in American education; Herman articulates the need to welcome all new arrivals who invigorate both education and democracy. Kathryn Anthony and Nicholas Watkins document the place of black students in the university's architecture program, noting how this has been affected by the *Brown* decision and the policies that followed in its wake. Nathaniel Banks offers a frank assessment of his experience as a student and administrator in the public and private schools of Champaign. And James Loewen discusses the grim and largely unexamined history of sundown towns in Illinois.

20

A Legacy of Firsts

African Americans in Architecture at the University of Illinois at Urbana-Champaign

*Kathryn H. Anthony
and Nicholas Watkins*

Despite the gains made by the historic *Brown v. Board of Education* court decision in the past half century, the number of African Americans in architectural education and practice has remained astonishingly low, particularly in comparison to their counterparts in professions such as law and medicine. In 1997 noted scholar Lee Mitgang, coauthor of a landmark study of architecture education nationwide, called for an end to "apartheid in architecture schools," and argued that "the race record of architectural education is a continuing disgrace, and if anything, things seem to be worsening."[1] Mitgang was referring in part to a disturbing pattern of racial segregation in architectural education. Out of 1,313 African American students enrolled in architecture schools in North America, 45 percent were students at the seven historically black schools with accredited architecture programs—Florida A&M, Hampton, Howard, Morgan State, Prairie View A&M, Southern, and Tuskegee—while the remainder were enrolled at the other ninety-six schools of architecture.[2]

In fact, architecture has been all too slow in diversifying its ranks. As of academic year 2006–7, national statistics show that out of 14,707 full-time students enrolled in accredited bachelor of architecture degree programs in the United States, 6.2 percent (915) were African American; out of 2,601 graduates of these programs, 3.5 percent (90) were African American. That same year, out of 2,953 full-time students enrolled in accredited master of architecture programs in the United States, only 3.4 percent (99) were African American; out of 1,284 graduates of these programs, only 2.1 percent (27) were African American. In 2006–7, out of 2,076 full-time architecture faculty, only 3.4 percent (71) were African American.[3] In terms of architectural practice, as of 2008, only 1.1 percent (741) members of the American Institute of Architects (AIA), the leading professional organization in the field, were African American, and only 106 of these were women.[4]

At UIUC's School of Architecture, 2008 enrollment figures showed a total of 22 African American students, including 18 undergraduates and 4 graduates.[5] Figures 20.1 and 20.2 show the enrollment numbers of African American undergraduate and graduate students since 1980. No African American currently serves full time on the tenured or tenure-track faculty.

It might come as a surprise, then, to learn that the University of Illinois at Urbana-Champaign has contributed significantly to the education of African American architects around the United States, perhaps more so than any other public university with the exception of historically black schools with accredited architecture programs.

This essay documents the history of African American architecture alumni at the University of Illinois at Urbana-Champaign. Our research used various methods to identify African American architecture alumni and track their careers.[6] Results led to a Web site with lists of alumni, interviews, and examples of notable work, and to an exhibit accompanying the opening of the April 2004 National Organization of Minority Architecture Students (NOMAS) annual symposium. This

FIGURE 20.1

African American Architecture UIUC Undergraduates

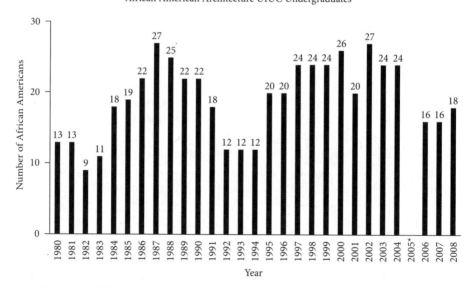

* Data not available.

Statistics based on enrollment on the tenth day of class. Note that the number has never exceeded thirty in any academic year. Based on a graph created by Nicholas Watkins. *Source:* University of Illinois at Urbana-Champaign, Division of Management Information, www.dmi.uiuc.edu/stuenr.

FIGURE 20.2

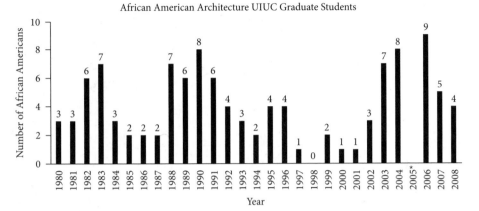

* Data not available.

Statistics based on enrollment on the tenth day of class. Note that the number has never exceeded ten in any academic year. Based on a graph created by Nicholas Watkins. *Source:* University of Illinois at Urbana-Champaign, Division of Management Information, www.dmi.uiuc.edu/stuenr.

event drew students of color from across the Midwest to the Urbana-Champaign campus for a weekend of scholarly presentations and design activities. The exhibit was displayed for African American History Month in February 2005. The Web site was part of an interactive display at Chicago's Museum of Science and Industry, a component of its "Architecture: Pyramids to Skyscrapers" exhibit in 2006, which drew crowds of visitors.

A Brief History

The architecture program at the University of Illinois at Urbana-Champaign began in 1870. It was the second academic architecture program in the United States and was originally part of the College of Engineering.[7] By the start of the twentieth century, under the direction of department head Nathan Clifford Ricker, it was recognized as one of the nation's top programs.[8]

Walter T. Bailey (1882–1941) was the first African American to graduate with a bachelor of science in architectural engineering at UIUC in 1904 (figure 20.3). In 1910 he received an honorary master's degree in architecture from UIUC. Bailey hailed from Kewanee, Illinois, where he attended Kewanee High School. He arrived on campus in 1900. Following his graduation, he worked briefly for Harry Eckland, an architect in Kewanee, and for Spencer and Temple, an architectural firm in Champaign. During that time he assisted in planning Colonel Wolfe School in Champaign (1905). That same year, he was appointed Head

FIGURE 20.3.
Walter T. Bailey (1882–1941) was the first African American to graduate with a Bachelor of Science in Architectural Engineering at UIUC in 1904. Photo taken 1904. Credit: University of Illinois at Urbana-Champaign Archives.

of the Mechanical Industries Department at Tuskegee Institute in Tuskegee, Alabama, where he also supervised the planning, design, and construction supervision of all new campus buildings. While at Tuskegee he designed White Hall (1908), a women's' dormitory, as well as two churches in Montgomery, Alabama (1910, 1912). He remained at Tuskegee until 1916, when he opened an office on Beale Street in Memphis, Tennessee, a street nicknamed "a main street of Negro America."[9]

The Knights of Pythias, a large national fraternal order of African Americans formed in the post–Civil War era, was a significant client for Bailey. The organization provided programs for recreation, racial and social advancement, life insurance, and death benefits, as well as aid to the sick, persons with disabilities, the elderly, orphans, and widows. During Bailey's career in Memphis, he designed the Mosaic State Temple Building (1922) and the Pythian Theater Building (1922–23), both in Little Rock, Arkansas. He also designed the Pythian Bath House and Sanitarium in Hot Springs, Arkansas (1923), a recreational facility exclusively for African Americans (figure 20.4). Ironically, although many

Pythian Bath House, Sanitarium and Hotel

FIGURE 20.4.

Exterior view of the Pythian Bath House, Sanitarium and Hotel in Hot Springs, Arkansas (1923), a recreational facility exclusively for African Americans designed by Walter T. Bailey. It boasted then-modern amenities such as telephone service, cold and hot water for each room, two parlors, a roof garden, and an ornate lobby with marble trim. Source: "Souvenir Folder of the Pythian Baths" (1923). Credit: University of Illinois at Urbana-Champaign Archives.

African Americans served as laborers in Hot Springs' elaborate bath houses, they were prohibited from using them. The Pythian Bath House provided a respite from the oppressive world of Jim Crow.

In 1924 Bailey moved his practice to Chicago, site of two of his major projects: the National Pythian Temple (1927) and the First Church of Deliverance (1939). Both served as icons of African American achievement and power on Chicago's South Side, a region then commonly referred to as Bronzeville or Black Metropolis and a destination for those escaping the South during the Great Migration. When it was completed, the National Pythian Temple, an eight-story building with a steel frame, yellow brick facing, and decorative terra cotta reliefs, was one of the tallest buildings in the area. It provided an auditorium for large gatherings, commercial and office space for African American businesses, as well as residential apartment units. Bailey's design for the First Church of Deliverance expansion, also on Chicago's South Side, became an Art Moderne landmark. The church was known for its gospel music and radio broadcast ministries, and its architectural style was a reflection of these new religious mediums. In response to its radio broadcasts, the congregation swelled and needed a larger facility.

Bailey died of pneumonia in 1941. Although his work was overlooked for decades, he was rediscovered as the subject of a 2002 master's thesis and was one of two UIUC African American architecture alumni featured in the 2004 publication *African American Architects: A Biographical Dictionary 1865–1945*.[10] The second was Beverly Greene (figure 20.5).

Thirty-two years after Bailey paved the way for African American men, Chicagoan Beverly Greene (1915–57) was the first African American woman to graduate with a bachelor of science degree in architectural engineering from UIUC in 1936. She also received a master's degree in city planning from UIUC in 1937 as well as a master's degree in architecture from Columbia University in 1945. She was hired by the Chicago Housing Authority in 1938, a milestone for a woman—and particularly a woman of color—at that time. At age twenty-seven in 1942, Greene was the first African American woman to receive her license to

FIGURE 20.5.

Beverly Greene (1915–57) was the first African American woman to graduate with a Bachelor of Science in Architectural Engineering at UIUC in 1936. Greene is believed to be the first African American woman to receive her license to practice architecture in the United States. During her short career, she produced valuable designs for the Chicago Housing Authority and the UNESCO United Nations Headquarters in Paris. Source: *The Illio* (1936), 73. Credit: Illini Media Company.

practice architecture in the United States. After relocating to New York City she worked for Isadore Rosefield and specialized in design for healthcare facilities and hospitals. In 1955 she began work for Marcel Breuer on the UNESCO United Nations headquarters in Paris (1958) as well as the New York University campus (1956). In 1956 she collaborated on the design of the Christian Reformation Church in New York City. She died prematurely from cancer at age forty-one.[11]

Champaign-Urbana had its share of racism and segregation throughout much of the twentieth century. While activities at the School of Architecture proceeded as usual, and the insular design studios dominated students' everyday lives much as they do today, school archives reveal that at least some architecture students were concerned about racial issues. For example, in 1953, the editor of *The Bannister,* the school's newsletter, urged architecture students to protest the exclusionary policies at local barbershops. An editorial in the paper read as follows:

> DISCRIMINATION. Recently a sheet of paper was passed out before a foot-ball game. The subject was discrimination against colored people in the local barbershops. Maybe you aren't aware that Negroes cannot get a haircut in a local shop, but whether you are or are not, it is the truth. This ghastly absurd thing is taking place in a democracy.
>
> The barbers are not the only offenders in this terrible crime, and I for one would like to see a little action on the part of the students. Here are some suggestions.
>
> 1. Picket the barbershops that practice discrimination.
> 2. Refuse to get a haircut in any shop that will not treat everyone as an equal, regardless of race, color, creed, or religion.
> 3. Let our hair grow in protest.
> 4. Go to neighboring towns for haircuts.
> 5. Cut your own.
> 6. Any one or all of the above.
>
> The barbers are dependent upon the school trade, as is everything else in the Twin Cites, and with a slight amount of pressure from us they have to treat everyone as equals or go out of business.
>
> Anyone interested in this crusade for democracy, please use the suggestion box on the second floor of the Arch. Bldg.[12]

Another article appeared in 1964 in the *Ricker Reader,* a student newsletter. Entitled "The Segregated City Beautiful: A Delusion," it discussed controversial proposed legislation to prohibit Illinois property owners from refusing to rent or sell on grounds of race.[13] The newsletter's editor, Jeffrey Marx, presented both sides of the February 1964 debate between Arthur F. Mohl, vice president of the

Illinois Association of Real Estate Boards, and Leon M. Despres, alderman for Chicago's Fifth Ward and member of the Chicago City Council in City Planning, Housing, and Urban Renewal. Mohl favored the continuation of existing laws, claiming that proposed changes would be "undemocratic."[14] Despres argued in favor of passing new legislation on the grounds that Chicago's housing segregation was effectively a "visible prejudice; segregated schools, segregated churches, a segregated mentality, and segregated health, both mental and physical."[15] Marx followed up with an interview of Robert O. Bowles, executive director of the Champaign County Urban League, discussing the proposed urban renewal project for the northeast neighborhood. Other than these few examples, however, it appears that the tempestuous political climate of the civil rights era was only rarely reflected in the School of Architecture.

Sparked by the civil rights movement and the assassination of Martin Luther King, the university created the Special Educational Opportunities Program (SEOP) in 1968. One of the program's major accomplishments was Project 500, an effort to recruit at least 500 students of color, especially African Americans, in fall 1968. Consequently, the late 1960s and early 1970s saw increased participation by African Americans as architecture students. Organizations such as the Black Architecture Students Association (BASA, established in 1970) and the Community Advocacy Depot (CAD, established in 1969) became venues within which African American architecture students could find solidarity. Andrew McGlory (BS 1973, MArch 1976), one of BASA's founding members, recalls:

> BASA was started in response to a growing number of Black Students in the Department of Architecture who felt the need for an organization which would serve as an instrument for mutual development and offer a concerted voice on their behalf. One of the first requests from BASA to the Department was to have a place where we would be able to socialize and study together. The Department responded by giving BASA a room in a house at 911 South Sixth Street that was primarily being used as a studio for architectural graduate students working on special projects. After several weeks, the graduate students abandoned the house except for one Australian student named Paul. Upon graduating, Paul also left the house. During Paul's stay at the house, he was a great mentor to BASA members.
>
> The house at 911 South Sixth Street became officially the BASA House in 1971. We were able to use this house for the next five plus years. In 1976 we were told that we no longer would be able to stay in the house and were given a room in Noble Hall (Room 404). During the five plus years in the house we used the second floor as studio space where we would have from two to three students in each of the four rooms on the second floor. Upper classmen and graduates used the studio spaces. Also we had our own darkroom, library study, and fellowship rooms for socializing and the housing of our first two annual BASA Spring Symposiums in 1973 and 1974.[16]

Through CAD, architecture students collaborated with community members, the Champaign Housing Authority and the Champaign Park District. Students created housing designs for low-income persons of color in the Champaign-Urbana community.

Ernest Clay (BArch 1969, MArch 1970), the school's first full-time, tenure-track African American faculty member, was hired in 1970 as an instructor and rose to the rank of associate professor before retiring in 1999. In 1978 Clay formed the University of Illinois chapter of NOMAS. Following Clay's appointment was that of Carl Lewis (BS 1991, MArch 1992), the school's second full-time, tenure-track African American faculty member, who served as assistant professor from 1992 to 1997. He currently works as an academic advisor and continues teaching at UIUC. Lewis distinguished himself through his appointment to the United States Architectural and Transportation Barriers Compliance Board in 1996. Two other African Americans, John Gay (BS 1988) and Ira Jones (MArch 2000), have also served briefly as visiting faculty, Gay in 1996–97 and Jones in 2000–2001. David Franklin (MArch 1996) and Nikolas Hill (BS 2001) have served as visiting critics on reviews in design studios.

The East St. Louis Action Research Project (ESLARP) began in 1987 as an effort to improve the standard of living among African American neighborhoods in East St. Louis, Illinois, one of the nation's most economically depressed cities. ESLARP has grown into a collaborative effort of students and faculty from a variety of disciplines across campus, including architecture, landscape architecture, and urban and regional planning. Often these collaborations have occurred in joint studio settings where students from all three disciplines are combined. Among the many design studio projects in which students and faculty have engaged in East St. Louis are housing, a light rail transit system, a farmers' market, and the redevelopment of a park. Scores of others can be found on the ESLARP Web site.[17] Over the years several architecture faculty have participated in these projects, including Michael Andrejasich, Kathryn Anthony, Osman Ataman, Ernest Clay, Lynne Dearborn, Carolyn Dry, and Robert Selby. Some alumni of ESLARP studios have pursued careers in the development of low-income housing.

Following in the footsteps of BASA and CAD, NOMAS provides support for current African American students and other students of color. Each year, NOMAS hosts a symposium and sends several of its members to the national conference of the parent organization, NOMA. The organization has received substantial financial support both from the university and from the school. In 2002 NOMAS had its first all-woman slate of officers with Dawntaya Rodgers (BS 2003) as its president.

Several alumni have enhanced the stature of African Americans in the profession through their involvement with the National Organization of Minority

Architects (NOMA). They have included Ernest Clay, Drake Dillard, Nikolas Hill, Sharon Samuels, and Tebogo Schultz. In 2002 Schultz (BArch 2000) served as national student representative for NOMA. In 2003 Samuels (BS 1998) served as chair of the NOMA International Congress and Exposition in Chicago, and Drake Dillard (BArch 1973) served as president of NOMA (figure 20.6). Samuels is conducting research along with her colleague Katerina Ruedi to document the accomplishments of all African American women architects, tentatively entitled "133 and Rising"; the number 133 reflects the total number of such women in the United States at the time the study began.

A number of African American alumni have been elevated to Fellows of the American Institute of Architects, one of the highest honors in the profession. Among them are David Lee (BArch 1967), Roger Margerum (BArch 1956), Karl Thorne (BArch 1969), and Jack Travis (MArch 1978). Several have worked on high-profile projects, such as the United States Air Force Academy in Colorado Springs (Margerum), Boston's Big Dig (Lee), and the 1991 film *Jungle Fever* (Travis). Short biographies of these and other alumni are included in the appendix at the end of this chapter.

FIGURE 20.6.
Drake Dillard (BArch, 1973) served as the 2003 President of the National Organization of Minority Architects. He currently practices in Los Angeles. Photo taken in 2002. Credit: Kathryn H. Anthony.

Reflections

Our research revealed a significant "legacy of firsts": Walter T. Bailey as one of the first African Americans to graduate from an architecture school, Beverly Greene as the first African American woman to receive her license to practice architecture in the United States, Ernest Clay as the first African American tenured faculty in the school, and Jack Travis's book *African American Architects in Current Practice* as the first of its kind. Although being the "first" earns all these individuals a place in the history books and distinguishes them as trailblazers, there is no doubt that for some of these individuals it was also at great personal cost. For serving as a minority of one, perceived as the lone ambassador of your race, must have been a lonely position indeed—and that is still true today.

The School of Architecture continues to struggle with issues of diversity. So, too, the profession of architecture continues to lag behind professions like law and medicine that have been much more successful in diversifying their ranks. This challenge has been well documented in numerous publications, including Kathryn H. Anthony's book, *Designing for Diversity*.[18] In the early 2000s, the American Institute of Architects has launched a major campaign to promote diversity. In 2003 it revived its diversity conference, which had not been held for several years. In 2008 the AIA convened a diversity plenary, Multiformity '08 (architects embracing diversity), in St. Louis, which drew sixty-three invited participants representing AIA leadership and members, students, collateral organizations, large and small firms, professional affinity groups, and experts outside the profession. The outcome was a document called the Gateway Commitment, leading to the development of a multiyear action plan to have an impact on the recruitment, matriculation, retention, and promotion of talented, diverse individuals in architecture. The AIA's 2009 national convention theme was "The Power of Diversity: Practice in a Complex World."

In 2000 the school adopted its first diversity plan, outlining several target areas for improvement.[19] The school's diversity committee has monitored the plan periodically. One of the plan's goals has been to stress diversity in the school's extracurricular activities. The school has been somewhat successful in achieving this goal by inviting more women guest lecturers to speak in the school lecture series. Yet other than at the annual NOMAS symposia, African American speakers continue to remain rarities. In response to its diversity plan, the school can claim modest success in increasing the numbers of African American visiting critics on design studio reviews, both throughout the semester and during the prestigious Earl Prize awards reviews held at the end of each semester.

The school has had one of the strongest student representations at the annual NOMA convention, even including those from historically black colleges and universities. One should note that many architectural schools are not even represented at this event. The student organization resource fee, a campuswide resource that supports activities and programs of registered student organizations, coupled with funds from the School of Architecture, has supported as many as ten to twelve NOMAS students each year to travel to the convention. Many of these students, although not all, are African American; others are Latino/a and Asian-American. Both the university and the school have displayed a strong commitment to NOMAS, probably more so than many other universities.

Since 1991 the school has offered a seminar on gender and race in architecture, one of the few courses of its kind, taught by Kathryn H. Anthony.[20] It focuses on the roles of women and persons of color as critics, creators, and consumers of the built environment, and it includes historical and contemporary contributions of African American architects. Field trips have included visits to African American–owned firms in Chicago, such as Heard and Associates, Smith & Smith Associates, Inc., and Nia Architects. In 2004 the seminar drew among the highest percentages of African American students of any course in the school. At that time, Assistant Professor Carla Jackson, then of Tuskegee University, served as a guest speaker, as did David Franklin (MArch 1996). Yet because it is currently offered only as an elective to ten to twenty students, its impact across the school has been minimal. And the fact remains that the vast majority of students graduating from the school are still hard-pressed to name even one African American architect, either past or present. In this sense, one questions the extent to which the school is offering a truly comprehensive architectural education. Unfortunately, the same is likely the case at most other schools of architecture across the country. In the era of our first part–African American president, Barack Obama, it is hoped that this will change.

The school continues its efforts to recruit African American students. As minority student scholarships have increased, more students from historically black colleges and universities such as Florida A&M, North Carolina A&T, and Tuskegee University have chosen to attend Illinois for graduate school. Overall, however, the numbers of African American students continue to remain low. Surprisingly though, it appears that the numbers of African American students at UIUC have still outnumbered those at our sister school, University of Illinois at Chicago, where the resident population of African Americans is much higher.

In retrospect, what was the impact of the *Brown v. Board of Education* decision on the UIUC School of Architecture? Prior to 1954, only eight African Americans had graduated from the school; the remaining graduates all came afterwards. Prior to the 1968 SEOP and Project 500, only twelve had graduated. One can argue that compared to *Brown v. Board*, Project 500 was even more influential in opening the doors to African American students on the UIUC campus. As a result of Project 500, the first wave of African American architecture students, a total of nineteen, graduated in the 1970s. Although only ten African American architecture students graduated in the 1980s, a second wave of thirty-nine graduated in the 1990s. Yet the reality is that Project 500 would have been unlikely without *Brown v. Board*. Furthermore, the location of African American architecture alumni as of 2004 revealed that while thirty-one were in Chicago and twenty-one were elsewhere in Illinois, the remainder, over forty-five, were out of state. Hence the impact of our alumni—and on our built environment—can be felt not only in Chicago and Illinois but also nationwide.

Finally, what was the impact of the *Brown* Jubilee Commemoration Committee on the School of Architecture? The exhibit of African American architecture alumni proved to have an unanticipated yet successful outcome.[21] In fact, while the exhibit was not part of our original research proposal, it turned out to be one of the most valuable components of our research. Although compared to an exhibit a Web site has potential to reach a much larger audience and can be much longer lasting, its impact is more nebulous and thereby not as appealing to some. Exhibits are a significant component of the culture of the architectural profession. Architects have always enjoyed opportunities that afford public recognition of their work, and exhibits have traditionally achieved this purpose. In our case, the exhibit provided a unique venue where African American architects of the past and present could speak to those of the future through images and written testimony.

The interactive display of our African American architecture alumni Web site at Chicago's Museum of Science and Industry in 2006 provided a special, highly visible opportunity to promote the accomplishments of our alumni to a wide audience. This would never have happened were it not for the *Brown* Jubilee and the committee's support of the project. Numerous children from the Chicago public schools visited this exhibit as part of their class field trips. Members of national organizations of minority architects from across the country saw the exhibit. And visitors from Chicago and around the world were able to learn about the impact of African American architects from the University of Illinois and elsewhere. In 2008 Kathryn Anthony and Leeswann Bolden updated the Web site and presented it at a conference called "Race, Diversity, and Campus Climate at the University of Illinois at Urbana-Champaign," an event sponsored by the UIUC Center for Democracy in a Multicultural Society.

What other impact has the *Brown* Jubilee had on the school? Most importantly, the history presented here had never been documented before. As such, it provides a new set of lenses from which to view the school. And from what we can ascertain, ours appears to be one of the only studies of its kind. So despite its concentration on one school and one set of alumni, it serves as a unique case study—another important "first"— pioneering a route for other schools to follow.

Appendix: Selected Biographies

A few UIUC alumni and their professional accomplishments are spotlighted here.

Alicia Belton (BSAS 1960, MArch 1992) opened her Minneapolis-based architecture and construction-management firm, Urban Design Perspectives, in 1999. The firm's projects include residential, office, entertainment/recreation, and religious buildings. Among them are Club Three Degrees Christian Nightclub in Minneapolis and Rondo Lofts in St. Paul. In 2008 Belton's firm was selected as part of the team to design the University of Minnesota's new Urban Research and Outreach/Engagement Center in north Minneapolis. Belton and her designs have been featured in the magazine *Homes of Color.*[22]

David Franklin (MArch 1996) also received an MS in real estate development finance from Columbia University in 1991 and a BS in construction technology from Purdue University in 1986. In his capacity as president of Domain Architects in Indianapolis, Indiana, Franklin is involved in project programming, design, planning, and construction administration. He has served on the board of directors of the Indianapolis chapter of the American Institute of Architects and as a delegate to the Indiana state chapter board of the AIA. He has also taught at Indiana State University in Terre Haute, Indiana. His firm has received numerous awards including four in 2004 for such projects as the IRMSDC Business Center in Indianapolis.

Andrew Heard (BArch 1962). Founded in 1967 in Chicago, Heard & Associates, Ltd.'s projects range from the design of medical facilities to public facility rehabilitation; from large multifamily housing to the restoration and preservation of architectural landmarks; from high-security penal institutions to multimodal transportation facilities. The firm's public buildings include fire stations, libraries, and courtrooms as well as specialized industrial and recreational facilities.[23] Heard's firm designed the new library at Chicago State University (2004), a four-story signature building at the entrance to its campus. Its architecture was inspired by sixteenth- to eighteenth-century geometric designs on baskets and pottery in the Museum of African Art in Washington, D.C., and it resembles a distinctive jeweled African crown reflecting the cultural link from Africa to America.[24]

David Lee (BArch 1967) is a partner at Stull and Lee, Incorporated, an architecture, urban design, and planning firm in Boston.[25] His firm is noted for its research-oriented and client-centered design approach, and its portfolio includes correctional facilities, stations and other transit facilities, and multifamily housing and residences. Stull and Lee has received numerous design awards, including the 1999 Boston Society of Architects Honor Award for Excellence in Architecture, Citation for Research and Planning, for its design of the Boston Police Headquarters. Lee was elevated to Fellow of the American Institute of Architects and is an adjunct professor at the Harvard Graduate School of Design.

Roger Margerum (BArch 1956) graduated from Chicago's Crane Technical High School in Chicago and later from UIUC at age twenty-five. He became a registered architect in Illinois, Michigan, and Tennessee. As an intern at Skidmore, Owings and Merrill in the 1950s, he worked on the design of the United States Air Force Academy in Colorado Springs (figure 20.7). After working in Chicago, he moved to Detroit, where he continued his career at Smith, Hinchman and Grylls (now Smith Group). Later with his firm, Roger Margerum, Inc. Architect, based on Woodward Avenue in Detroit, he designed numerous projects including schools, office buildings, a small riverside pavilion shelter at Ambassador Bridge, and the Sain Auditorium and Performing Arts Center in Detroit. He served as president of AIA Michigan in 1983. Margerum was elevated to Fellow of the American Institute of Architects and was one of the founders and charter director of NOMA. His unconventional house design was featured in a 2007 article in the *Detroit Free Press*.[26]

Andrew McGlory (BS 1973, MArch 1976), a graduate of Chicago's Roosevelt High School, decided to become an architect in the eighth grade. He is senior project architect in the Facility Planning Department at Saint Paul Public Schools in Saint Paul, Minnesota. In that capacity he managed projects up to $50 million and oversaw

FIGURE 20.7.

While an intern at Skidmore, Owings and Merrill, Roger Margerum (BArch 1956) worked on the design of the world renown United States Air Force Academy in Colorado Springs, Colo. Credit: National Park Service, "The United States Air Force Academy: Founding a Proud Tradition," http://www.cr.nps.gov/nr/twhp/wwwlps/lessons/114airforce/114visual3.htm.

design consultants and engineers from the pre-design through the post-occupancy stages. He is involved in both the planning of new buildings and modifications to existing buildings. As vice president of Andrews Architecture Ltd. in Minneapolis, he has been involved in urban planning and real estate development. He has served as Midwest Region Vice President of NOMA.

Damona Smith Strautmanis (BS 1990, MArch 1993, MBA 1993) is principal at Jormida Consulting LC—a real estate development and design and construction project management consulting firm in Silver Spring, Maryland. Ms. Strautmanis is the owner/developer of office, retail, and residential projects. Prior to launching Jormida Consulting, she was employed with the Peterson Companies and served as project director of design and construction for the $300 million downtown Silver Spring redevelopment project.

Karl Thorne (BArch 1969) also received a Master of Architecture degree from the University of Pennsylvania in 1970 where he studied under Louis Kahn. In 1972 Thorne returned to his native Jamaica as senior architect/planner of the Urban Development Corporation of Jamaica. He has served on the faculty of the University of Florida's School of Architecture since 1978, where he holds the rank of professor. In 1980 he established his own firm, Karl Thorne Associates, Inc. Architects/Planners, a practice focusing on educational architecture. Projects include the design of the George C. Kirkpatrick Jr. Criminal Justice Training Center at Santa Fe Community College in Gainesville, Florida; and at Florida A&M University in Tallahassee the Frederick G. Humphries Science and Research Center, the School of Journalism and Graphic Communication, and a museum addition to the historic Carnegie Library. The museum houses the largest collection of African American artifacts and memorabilia in the Southeast. Thorne has served on numerous national committees for NOMA and AIA, and as a member of the Florida Building Commission from 1996 to 2004. In 1998 Thorne was the recipient of the Florida Association of the American Institute of Architects Anthony Pullana Memorial Award for Distinguished Service to the Profession. In 1998 he was elected to the AIA College of Fellows.

Jack Travis (MArch 1978) received his bachelor's degree in architecture from Arizona State University before arriving at UIUC. Born in Newellton, Louisiana, he attended Bishop Gorman High School. He is the editor of *African American Architects in Current Practice*, the first volume of its kind to include biographical profiles and sample professional design projects from a wide array of architects nationwide.[27] He also served as the consultant to film director Spike Lee on his groundbreaking film *Jungle Fever* (1991), which featured the lead character Flipper Purify, an architect modeled somewhat after Travis himself. As principal and founder of Jack Travis Architects in New York City, he has been active in the New York Coalition of Black Architects. In 2004 he was elevated to Fellow in the AIA. Among his more notable projects are the Armani Boutique (1989) located in New York City's Flatiron District and the Saunders residence (2000) in Hasting-on-Hudson, N.Y., modeled after an African compound (figures 20.8–20.9).

FIGURE 20.8.

Interior view of the Holt Residence in New York, designed by architect Jack Travis (MArch 1978), which features a small hut within a compound. Travis edited the groundbreaking book, *African American Architects in Current Practice* (1991) and served as consultant to film director Spike Lee on his film *Jungle Fever* (1991). Credit: Jack Travis, FAIA.

FIGURE 20.9.

Exterior view of the Saunders residence, Hasting-on-Hudson, N.Y., designed by Jack Travis (MArch 1978). Fashioned after an African compound, it combines an existing structure with a children's play room, a four-car garage, and an African sculptural garden. Credit: Jack Travis, FAIA.

Notes

We were grateful to receive funding from the *Brown* Jubilee Commemoration Committee for this research. Thanks are due as well to Rodney Howlet and Leeswann Bolden for their valuable assistance with the Web site, and to Jason Zoss for assistance with the graphs.

1. Lee D. Mitgang, "Saving the Soul of Architectural Education: Four Critical Challenges Face Today's Architecture Schools," *Architectural Record* (May 1997), 125.

2. Bradford C. Grant and Dennis Alan Mann eds., *The Professional Status of African American Architects* (Cincinnati: Center for the Study of Practice, School of Architecture and Interior Design, University of Cincinnati, 1996), 3–4, 11.

3. National Architectural Accrediting Board 2007 Statistical Report, http://www .naab.org/accreditation/statistics.aspx (accessed April 5, 2009).

4. Correspondence from Yvette Morris, "AIA Membership Statistics," American Institute of Architects (February 6, 2009).

5. School of Architecture Student Records, University of Illinois at Urbana-Champaign, Undergraduate and Graduate Office, 2008.

6. The research methodology for this project involved two phases. For phase 1, an attempt to uncover the "lost history" of African American architecture alumni, we analyzed School of Architecture archives, student newsletters, and other school publications. We also reviewed academic and professional literature searching for mentions of UIUC architecture alumni.

Phase 2 was an effort to learn more about both living and deceased alumni, their experiences as students, and their professional accomplishments since graduation. We worked with the School of Architecture alumni office to identify a total of 87 African American alumni. Since that time even more were identified; as of 2004, the number of alumni is approximately 105.

We used self-reported information to locate each of their addresses and invited all living alumni to participate in our project. We sent an invitation packet in October 2003, including a cover letter, an agreement form, two short-answer questionnaires, and a self-addressed stamped envelope. The packet included endorsement letters from then-chancellor Nancy Cantor, who initiated the *Brown v. Board of Education* commemoration, and Drake Dillard (BArch 1973), 2003 President of the National Organization of Minority Architects (NOMA). It provided the address for the African American Architecture Alumni (AAAA) UIUC Web page. The Web page provided respondents the option to fill out questionnaires electronically. The first questionnaire asked alumni to provide demographic information about age, sex, marital status, schools attended, mentors, degrees earned, and places of residence. The second questionnaire asked alumni to select questions that interested them and to describe milestones in their careers, challenges they encountered, and both positive and negative experiences while students at UIUC. Two follow-up reminder postcards were sent.

Altogether, 15 alumni sent agreement forms and responses via postal mail. Ten alumni completed either one or both questionnaires. More participants were included in 2005 when the Web site was updated. We analyzed the data through a content analysis.

7. University of Illinois, *The Alumni Quarterly and Fortnightly Notes,* 2, no. 2 (June 1916): 346.

8. Christopher J. Quinn, "Nathan Clifford Ricker: Translator and Educator," *Arris* 11 (2000): 40.

9. George Washington Lee, "Poetic Memories of Beale Street," *West Tennessee Historical Society Papers* 28 (1969): 65.

10. Mikael David Kriz, "Walter T. Bailey and the African American Patron" (MA thesis, University of Illinois at Urbana-Champaign, 2002); Tim Samuelson, "Walter Thomas Bailey," in *African American Architects: A Biographical Dictionary 1865–1945,* ed. Dreck Spurlock Wilson (New York: Routledge, 2004), 15–17. See also Lee Bey, "Black Designer All but Forgotten," *Chicago Sun-Times,* February 9, 1998.

11. Roberta Washington, "Beverly Loraine Greene," in *African American Architects,* ed. Wilson, 175–76.

12. "Discrimination," *The Bannister,* November 11/December 2, 1953, 3.

13. Jeffrey Marx, "The Segregated City Beautiful: A Delusion," *Ricker Reader,* April 27, 1964, 23–28.

14. Ibid, 23.

15. Ibid, 24.

16. Correspondence from Andrew McGlory (October 27, 2004).

17. *East St. Louis Action Research Project,* College of Fine and Applied Arts, University of Illinois at Urbana-Champaign, http://www.eslarp.uiuc.edu (accessed January 5, 2009).

18. Kathryn H. Anthony, *Designing for Diversity: Gender, Race, and Ethnicity in the Architectural Profession* (Urbana: University of Illinois Press, 2008).

19. See *School of Architecture Diversity Plan,* University of Illinois at Urbana-Champaign, http://www.arch.uiuc.edu/about/diversity/diversityplan (accessed February 12, 2009).

20. See Architecture/Gender and Women's Studies 424: Gender and Race in Contemporary Architecture, School of Architecture, University of Illinois at Urbana-Champaign, http://www2.arch.uiuc.edu/kanthony/arch424fa07/ (accessed February 12, 2009).

21. In hindsight we discovered that certain individuals were more enthusiastic about responding to our request for information about them to include in the school exhibit than they were to our request to respond on the Web. This surprised us.

The responses to both the questionnaire and to the exhibit were insightful. Some architects sent us not only excerpts from their published work but also veritable scrapbooks of their lives. Paired with the questionnaire responses, this material provoked rich narrative possibilities for the format and composition of the exhibit. Not only could we display the narratives of selected participants, but also we could contextualize these individual narratives within the broader history of the university.

22. Quintin Chatman, "Lasting Impression: Minneapolis Architect Alicia Belton," *Homes of Color,* July/August 2005, 20–24.

23. See Heard & Associates Ltd. Web site, http://www.halrktec.com/index.htm (accessed April 10, 2008).

24. Paul and Emily Douglas Library, Chicago State University, http://library.csu .edu/news/newlib.htm (accessed October 21, 2004).

25. Stull and Lee, Inc.—Architecture and Planning, http://stullandlee.com (accessed April 10, 2008).

26. John Gallagher, "45–Degree Angle: Detroit Architect's First Home Turns Corner on Modern Design," *Detroit Free Press,* November 11, 2007. See also the Urban Design Perspectives Web site at http://www.urbandesignperspectives.com (accessed February 12, 2009).

27. Jack Travis, ed., *African American Architects in Current Practice* (New York: Princeton Architectural Press, 1991).

21

Reflections on the *Brown* Commemoration from a Champaign Native

Nathaniel C. Banks

For many years now, I have been ambivalent regarding the lofty notion of desegregation and integration. Because of this, I find that the *Brown v. Board of Education* commemoration helped me to clarify the reasons for that ambivalence and to solidify the origin of some of those jangling thoughts. First, I must admit that I had never given much serious reflection to the 1954 Supreme Court decision regarding desegregation. I was six years old when the decision was handed down. Although I spent part of my kindergarten year in a segregated school, the entire rest of my academic life was spent in "integrated" educational institutions. This experience provided me with a schema that was rather unusual in the 1950s and '60s.

My experiences in those desegregated environments profoundly affected my thinking when it comes to race and education. The *Brown* commemoration activities allowed me to reflect on those experiences. As I listened to the individuals my age and the age of my parents speak of their contributions to and struggles with the notion of desegregation on local and national levels, I was able to identify with their stories and to put my own into a much larger context. I could see how all of those individual and local stories contributed to the tapestry of racial justice on a national level. I was also able to see how my experiences in Champaign-Urbana mirrored those of families at the head of the struggle. Additionally, the commemoration allowed me to see more clearly the thinking that drove the decisions made by my own community leaders: decisions that I have often criticized, because of what I perceived as negative outcomes of desegregation and integration in the Champaign schools.

Now that I am in my sixties, and I am much more reflective, this seems a fitting time to place the notions of integration and desegregation in proper perspective. As a child growing up in the 1950s, I remember hearing adults talking about square pegs and round holes. When I think of my experiences in our local schools, it seems that this analogy is an apt description of my experiences as well as those of other African American children. Based on national achievement statistics, our local struggles mirror those nationally. To slightly modify the metaphor regarding integration and desegregation, our current public educational system is a square hole, and black students are round pegs that we are striving to fit into that hole. With that analogy as a starting point, I offer the following reflections on the impact of *Brown* on my life.

To begin with the positive, I believe that *Brown* helped facilitate significant increases in the numbers of blacks receiving the benefits of public education, thus enabling larger numbers to utilize their education to rise into higher income brackets. I believe that people from low-income working-class families like mine were the primary beneficiaries of the *Brown* decision, and it has allowed us to develop personally and professionally because of the organizing and work that culminated in the *Brown* decision. I also believe that our community leaders had our welfare in mind when they pushed so diligently for desegregation and integration.

Brown, however, was not able to neutralize the underlying problem that made it a necessity. This brings us back to the square hole/round peg metaphor. White supremacy has and will be, at least through my lifetime, the undercurrent that caused the need for *Brown* and that also neutralized much of its intent. Unfortunately, it extends into present-day society. The desire of many whites to be superior and preeminent permeates every aspect of our society, including the educational system. The superiority of one group always comes at the expense of another group. In this country the other group has been and always will be black people. Much of the policy-making in this nation has been and is driven by the shortsighted notion that white supremacy cannot survive if black people are allowed to compete equally in society. The school system has suffered from this way of thinking.

In the Champaign community, or "up south" as we in the black community call it, the promotion of white supremacy has always been accompanied with a smile and is best described as systemic, institutional racism. It is this infrastructure that has produced the Champaign schools' millennium version of *Brown* called the Consent Decree. Regardless of how often and how long we work on the "problem" of a gap in achievement, the underlying assumption is that black children and their families are primarily at fault for their inability to fit into the system. Thus, again the square hole/round peg syndrome. Square and round imply two different cultures and value systems. As long as the round pegs must be forced into the square holes, there will be perpetual conflict.

My experiences in integrated schools led me to hate myself, fear success, eschew challenges, and run from responsibility. In the "integrated" educational system from first grade through a master's degree in college, I have had to learn and live as an outsider. The institutional racism that I and most other black people experienced affected us in different ways. Three stand out for me. For some, it strengthened the inner desire to succeed. For others, it created a desire to do just the opposite of the goals and purposes of our educational institutions. So if the institutions valued success, we embraced failure. If the institution rewarded hard work, we valued not working at all. If the institutions valued participation, we valued disconnectedness. A third reaction to white supremacy and institutional racism includes a combination of the first two.

That is the reaction that I and many of my peers took. We were the ones who were told by our parents "you have to be twice as good to get half as far." Some of us embraced that notion and became twice as good. Many of us decided that the burden of constantly striving to meet unattainable standards was a burden not worth bearing. We wondered to ourselves, Why can't I just be who I am: an average person wanting to live a decent life? Why do I have to work to please people that could care less about me in the first place? Many of us with this reaction went on to have children and grandchildren. Our progeny inherited those deep-seated feelings and frustrations.

One of the by-products is what we now describe as the "achievement gap."[1] The phenomenon, however, is not new, nor has it been overlooked by scholars. My experiences and the experiences of many African American children are well known to scholars and have been described by many writers. Recently Janice E. Hale summarized the views of a number of scholars whose findings echo my own experience: "Ray McDermott defines African Americans as being a pariah group in American society. F. Barth says that they are actively rejected by the host population because of behavior or characteristics positively condemned by group standards. V. P. Franklin has noted that African Americans are considered pariahs because whites no longer need their labor. McDermott's structural inequality thesis holds that the host population works to defeat the efforts of the pariah child to beat the cycle of degradation that is his birthright."[2] Collectively, these authors indicate that the square hole/round peg paradigm is deliberate and an integral part of the American society.

Because our society operates in a square hole/round peg way, one might ask whether the lot of black people is hopeless. I would contend that the answer is no. It does, however, mean that institutional racism must be taken into account in order to understand our ability to embrace and succeed within the educational system. We need to be diligent in imagining and building social structures and institutions free of racism in order for us to live productive and meaningful lives. Many African Americans have unrealistically concluded that the *Brown* decision and other civil rights initiatives would lead to general social acceptance, as if we would just be able to force our round pegs into the square holes of integration and desegregation. We have mistakenly reasoned that we would be accepted and valued if we could just sit in physical proximity to white students. So, whether we are looking at the issue of busing, neighborhood schools, reading programs, parental involvement, or other issues, we as black people have been viewing our success or lack thereof from a round peg perspective. I am not suggesting that all of our issues stem from unrealistic expectations of desegregation and integration. I am, however, saying that we in the black community need to do a major readjustment in our thinking and reevaluate our focus if we want to benefit in meaningful ways from the legacy of *Brown*.

As a Christian, an artist, a parent, and an educator, issues of justice, kindness, love, and respect for human life have guided and directed my personal and social development. I have learned that those issues also play a huge role in the development of our children into citizens of this society. In order for children to become productive adults, certain things need to happen during their formative years. For instance, I believe that in order for children to develop properly, it is essential for them to be and feel nurtured. When we as adults create positive, nurturing learning environments, it is more possible to educate our youth and more likely that they will succeed.

I would not use the word "nurturing" to describe my own personal experiences with the integrated public schools. My experience was closer to alienation. This was especially true once I was of middle and high school age. As a result, my potential as a student in that system was limited to the confines of that environment. Fortunately for me, I had a strong family and community background from which to draw my sense of self and well-being. To be fair, there was also a handful of teachers who took educating all of their students seriously. In my eighteen years of educational experiences, I can think of approximately four people that fit the description. I responded to the positive environments in their individual classrooms. Most of the time, however, I found very little support in the school system.

My negative experiences in the public schools had a lasting affect on my outlook toward educational systems in general and our local schools in particular. Those experiences have affected me socially. For instance, I have never been to a high school reunion and have no desire to ever attend one. My reasoning was and is simple: why would one want to reunite with bad experiences? That same mindset stayed with me through my college interactions as well: I would never think of attending a reunion of my college. I have, however, attended reunions sponsored by former college classmates who, like me, felt alienated from the larger university. These negative experiences with public education usually happen to African Americans in integrated or desegregated environments. I can remember conversations with students who attended predominately black primary and secondary schools and colleges where they expressed fond memories of their school days, their teachers, and their classmates. In general, those former students seemed to be more satisfied with their lives and more able to create and develop a purpose for themselves than many students like myself who attended integrated schools.

Rather than let these negative feelings fester, I chose to run for a seat on the local school board to help address this issue of alienation from a policy and systems perspective. Even today, as a public school board member, I see regularly how disconnected the black students are in our system. Although I am deeply saddened by this, I fully understand why our students feel as they do. I am committed to promoting policies that will change the culture of alienation with which so many of our students struggle.

The children of today are the grandchildren of those who were in school when *Brown v. Board of Education* was delivered. It is apparent to me that the contemporary responses of African American children to their educational environment, although more extreme than ours, are still rooted in the same sense of alienation from a culture that is hostile to their educational achievement. The system of education, regardless of all of the rhetoric and outward changes, has not changed the square hole/round peg culture. It shows no real inclination to change in the foreseeable future. The "square hole" of white supremacy and institutional racism is still alive and well. One can't help but wonder how much further we or our offspring might have gone if most us had been educated in an educational system where love, nurturing, and high expectations were the rule rather than the exception.

So what should be done? Unfortunately, we cannot look merely to national leadership to facilitate the kind of change needed. When it comes to equity and achievement, the national solutions seem to be focused on punishing round pegs for being round. We are, however, still blessed with the notion that the education of our children needs to happen primarily on the local level. I submit that our local community needs to change itself radically on the preschool and elementary level. We must work to establish nurturing and supportive environments that increase the numbers of children in that first category. We should make the school systems flexible enough to allow for the creation of smaller, nurturing schools. Those schools should be controlled by the community they serve. The educational research clearly indicates that schools showing success with black children are small and nurturing. They have teachers who are able to identify with the students, and the students are able to identify with them. They have strong support from families. And finally, they utilize the surrounding community as a resource.

Locally, we are not without positive models. Several notable examples give me hope that there are modest gains being made in changing the culture of indifference toward children of color. Two are from the local public schools and two from private environments. In each case, the keys to success lie in the quality and commitment of the staff, the vision and competence of the leadership, and the attitude of staff toward the children's families. One exemplary program can be found at Canaan Academy. At Canaan children at the preschool level are learning to count to a hundred in at least four languages. They also learn logic and ethical behavior. At Stratton and Booker T. Washington Elementary Schools in Champaign, children are being taught in an environment that respects bilingual and foreign language backgrounds. At the Nia Nation Freedom School Summer Program, students are encouraged to have deep discussions about their reading materials. Their reading materials also reflect their own cultural frames of reference. All of these educational environments have teachers who know their students' learning styles and their families. These few local programs can serve as examples to others schools in our local public school systems. They give me hope that ultimately *Brown* was, in fact, more positive than negative in addressing needs of access to the benefits of the educational system. In the fifty years since *Brown v. Board of Education,* would I have preferred to see more progress in Champaign-Urbana? I would have to answer yes to that question. One thing is certain: those families and social institutions responsible for *Brown v. Board of Education* exhibited a determined and focused commitment to justice for African American families. In our current multicultural world, those same qualities are still needed. Their diligence inspires me to continue their legacy by remembering and acting on it within my own context, and to encourage as many young people as will listen that they must do the same.

Notes

1. Douglas N. Harris and Carolyn D. Herrington, "Accountability, Standards, and the Growing Achievement Gap: Lessons from the Past Half-Century," *American Journal of Education* 112, no. 2 (2006): 209–38; Jaekyung Lee, "Racial and Ethnic Achievement Gap Trends: Reversing the Progress toward Equity," *Educational Researcher* 31, no. 1 (2002): 3–12; Richard Rothstein, *Class and Schools: Using Social, Economic, and Educational Reform to Close the Black-White Achievement Gap* (Washington, D.C.: Economic Policy Institute, 2004).

2. Janice E. Hale, *Unbank the Fire: Visions for the Education of African American Children* (Baltimore: Johns Hopkins University Press, 1994), 155.

22

Reform in the Black Power Era

Joy Ann Williamson Lott

The black freedom struggle of the mid-twentieth century suffers from steriliza-
tion in the collective American memory. It is treated as a relic, a long-ago era
that finally brought legal precedent in line with American ideas on democracy,
freedom, and equality. Sanitizing history in this manner ignores the difficulty
of the reformation process and minimizes the costs that activists paid when
attempting to make the American Dream a reality. This piece seeks to human-
ize the reforms of the Black Power era at the University of Illinois at Urbana-
Champaign (UIUC). It is not a discussion of the intricate nature of reform, but
the climate in which the reforms occurred. In the late 1960s campus administrators and black students clashed on the kinds of reforms necessary to make
UIUC a hospitable learning environment and valuable campus experience for
black students. While they engaged in careful deliberations, both administrators and black students were under siege from a variety of internal and external
sources admonishing them to focus on the business of education. Under these
conditions, the reform process was intensely stressful. The point of this piece is
to remind us of the price UIUC constituents, particularly black students, paid
to make the reforms a reality.[1]

Champaign, Illinois, was a southern town in its attitude toward and treatment
of black residents well into the twentieth century. By the 1930s the city maintained a firm pattern of residential and educational segregation. Commercial
sites like barber shops, theaters, and restaurants maintained segregated service
policies until the early 1960s. UIUC supported similar regulations by barring
black students from residence halls, maintaining all-white sports teams out of
courtesy to "a Big Ten understanding," and allowing white student organizations
to have racially restrictive covenants.[2] The increased demand for democratic
rights at the end of World War II and the liberal attitudes of certain administrators, faculty, and students influenced university policy in the mid-1940s, but the
university took only small and measured steps toward creating a hospitable campus climate for the small number of black students. University officials opened
residence halls to black students in 1945, but only did so after being shamed in
the black Chicago press and by a public campaign spearheaded by a black state

representative. Even then, the university allowed only two black women to move into university housing and forced them to live together—the university refused to assign black and white women to the same room.[3] The university devised nondiscriminatory policies and allowed black men to participate on sports teams in the mid-1940s, but administrators refused to take action against white student organizations that refused to remove racially exclusive language from their charters. Administrators kept the university aloof from societal concerns and remained cautious in changing the racial dynamic in Champaign.

Administrators at UIUC responded to pressure from its constituents and federal initiatives in the early 1960s. The burgeoning civil rights movement of the early 1950s attracted liberal students and faculty at UIUC. They organized a variety of clubs and organizations, including a branch of the National Association for the Advancement of Colored People (NAACP), and worked to equalize opportunities and put an end to the racial hierarchy in central Illinois. In fellowship with their southern civil rights counterparts, campus activists held fundraisers for southern civil rights campaigns, initiated attacks on segregated facilities in the Champaign community, stepped up the attack on racially exclusive student organizations, and criticized the university for its passive role in societal reform.[4] Federal incentives also pushed the university to act. The 1954 *Brown v. Board of Education* decision did not have a direct impact on UIUC, but it provided a psychic boost to activists fighting for equal opportunity and questioning university complicity in the perpetuation of a racial hierarchy. The 1964 Civil Rights Act required a census of all postsecondary institutions and dramatized the low number of black students. It also threatened to withhold funding from institutions found in noncompliance with nondiscriminatory statues. The 1965 Higher Education Act created a variety of financial aid programs to help low-income students afford college. The act did not restrict funding to black students, but African Americans benefited most from the newly created programs. UIUC administrators were not opposed to the notion of equal opportunity, but pressure from the bottom up and from the top down forced university officials to respond in a more active manner than in the past.

University officials decided that a recruitment program aimed at black students could be a first step in inserting the university in social reform. Administrators discussed how to increase the number of black students on campus as early as 1963. According to a faculty committee report: "It is not sufficient simply to affirm the principle of nondiscrimination in all aspects of the University's undertakings. Instead it is urgent to develop an affirmative action program to help overcome handicaps stemming from past inequality so that all shall have equal opportunity to develop their talents to their fullest capacity."[5] But university attempts were uncoordinated and met with limited success. University-wide committees prodded administrators toward creating target enrollment numbers and an aggressive recruitment program. By 1967 UIUC had only 223 black under-graduates, making up 1 percent of the student population, a negligible increase from previous years. In March 1968, UIUC administrators devised a cohesive plan to admit 200 black high school seniors for the 1968–1969 academic year, more than doubling the average number of black freshmen in recent classes.

The university's plans coincided with black student concerns. Before 1967, the few black undergraduates on campus remained relatively quiet in their criticism of the university. The expansive campus layout meant they rarely interacted with any other black students during the school day. They created organizations like fraternities and sororities through which they received social sustenance, but most recounted feeling isolated and intensely lonely. As the civil rights movement and its organizations became popular, black students began to entertain the formation of a political action group to serve their specific needs as black students at a predominantly white institution. By the mid-1960s, black students decided that the campus NAACP chapter was inef-fective and outdated and instead created a campus chapter of the Congress of Racial Equality (CORE) in 1966. Initially, CORE maintained integrated membership, but a few months after its inception black students ousted whites from the organization.[6] Their action mirrored a shift in the larger black freedom struggle, its mission, and its tactics. After decades of attempting to force their way into the existing social order only to meet intense white resistance and repression, many African Americans, including youths, became disillusioned with the goal of integration to the point of disdain. The murders of black youth activists, doubts about the federal government's dedication to improving the conditions of African Americans, and suspicions of the extent to which whites could be considered true allies produced a shift in ideas on the proper tactics and means to gain black liberation. Many African American youths, including those at UIUC, grew frustrated with the slow pace of change and demanded more power, real power, Black Power.

The Black Power movement called for African Americans to recognize and be proud of their heritage, build a sense of community, define their own goals, and control their own institutions. To accomplish these tasks, blacks were called to unite. Black UIUC students embraced the Black Power movement's militant form of grassroots protest based on an ethic of black self-determination and translated it into meaningful action at UIUC. A small group organized the Black Students Association (BSA) in late 1967 as a way to create a structured and legitimate power base to force change at UIUC. The campus CORE chapter dissolved, as CORE members became BSA members. In part, BSA became an advocacy organization through which students discussed grievances with the administra-tion. The organization also fulfilled a more immediate purpose: the alleviation of psychological stress and frustration. The small number of black students on campus was a constant source of anxiety, and BSA offered black students an opportunity to meet, socialize, and devise solutions to their concerns.

BSA, like the UIUC administration, devised ways to increase the enrollment of black students. BSA took up the task "due to a lack of initiative of the University" and because "the black students here would be able to relate much better to the other blacks, thus making our efforts more successful."[7] University officials agreed that black students could be effective recruiters, and with university sanction, BSA representatives visited eleven predominantly black Chicago high schools during the winter break of 1967. They spoke about BSA and UIUC, encouraged those interested to apply, and distributed applications. The lack of a real commitment and strategic plan on the part of the university hindered their efforts, however, and the number of black students admitted for the 1968–69 academic year barely increased. Disappointed but undeterred, BSA focused on strengthening the continuing-student community and directed its attention toward campus issues. In particular, the organization sought to unite the black student population divided by Greek-letter affiliations, physical separation on campus, political proclivities, and apathy. BSA also devised a political agenda and entertained direct confrontation "with any institution within or outside the University" and the use of "any tool necessary" in the fight for Black liberation.[8]

The April 4, 1968, assassination of Dr. Martin Luther King Jr. created a sense of urgency for both black students and university administrators. For black students, it provided one of the catalysts in increasing Black Power sentiment and promoting black student unity. Liberal administrators considered it a violent reminder that the university had a role to play in societal reform. Pressured by BSA, segments of the campus community, and the attitudes of liberal administrators, UIUC scrapped the original recruitment program to enroll two hundred black freshmen and devised an even more aggressive program.[9] The university presented its new plan to the public in a news release May 2, 1968—less than one month after King's assassination: "Working in close cooperation with the Black Students Association, the Chancellor announced that substantial efforts will be made to increase the program to hopefully enroll at least 500 students for September 1968."[10] The university used knowledge gained from previous efforts to cleave together the Special Educational Opportunities Program (SEOP). Due in large part to the efforts of BSA recruitment staff, UIUC enrolled 565 students through SEOP, a remarkable increase from previous years. By admitting such a large number of students, SEOP became one of the largest affirmative action programs initiated by a predominantly white university to attract low-income black high school students. Clarence Shelley, the black director of an economic opportunity program in Detroit, was recruited and appointed dean of the program in July.

The new SEOP students arrived on campus in early September, one week prior to the beginning of the academic year, for an extended orientation program.[11] Illinois Street Residence Hall (ISR), a new and highly coveted residence hall, hosted the students. A state of total confusion existed when the freshmen arrived, however. Miscommunication between BSA recruiters and SEOP students regarding financial aid and admission requirements exacerbated the fact that the university was unprepared for the number of students who accepted offers of admission. Many arriving students had not taken the appropriate placement tests, had no dormitory assignments, and found that the financial aid promised them was nonexistent. Nonetheless, a sense of camaraderie between freshmen and BSA members alleviated some of the tension produced by the academic, financial, and housing uncertainties. The students spent an entire week on campus prior to the arrival of the general student body, which meant that UIUC felt like a black college to many students. As the orientation week came to a close, black students expressed optimism about the upcoming academic year, though BSA members worried about how to maintain the sense of cohesiveness and community fostered during orientation.

Before moving to their permanent rooms on campus, several women visited the residence halls to which they were assigned. They complained that the rooms were too small and demanded that they be allowed to choose their roommates rather than be assigned to one through university channels. Twenty women refused to remove their luggage and vowed to stay in ISR until a satisfactory conclusion was reached. Financial aid concerns heightened anxieties for all of the incoming freshmen, and inadequate funding became an additional flashpoint. BSA executive staff, Dean Shelley, and housing staff met repeatedly over the next few days to resolve the issues. On September 9, 1968, students gathered outside ISR to hear the results of the most recent meeting. As the number of students grew, BSA members suggested the group convene outside the Illini Union. BSA officers and university administrators moved their meeting to the third floor of the Union, where BSA officers reiterated the female students' complaints, described the financial aid situation as unacceptable, and demanded that Chancellor Jack Peltason come and address their grievances. Rain forced the group of students awaiting the results of the meeting to move inside the union to the South Lounge.

After the meeting with BSA officers, administrators went to the South Lounge of the Illini Union to address the group at 12:30 AM—half an hour after the union's closing time. Administrators explained that they were doing everything possible to remedy the situation, but the students refused to leave. With rumors of property damage, theft, and physical assaults on white passersby, administrators decided that it would not be safe for Chancellor Peltason to come to the union, and they continued to negotiate with the students. By 2:00

AM, a few individual students had gone home but most remained for a variety of reasons, not all of which had to do with political consciousness and a desire to confront the university. Many students chose to stay for the sake of unity and to support the women protesting their room assignments. Some of the women were afraid to walk home so late at night and doubted they could get into their residence halls after curfew. In response to rumors of a growing police presence, many students feared they would be injured by billy clubs or dogs if they left the security of the lounge. Some actually thought the chancellor was going to arrive at any minute to address the group. Others were not aware of the fact that they were violating university regulations by remaining in the union after closing hours. Some students remembered being coerced into staying by BSA members, nonstudents, and older students. Some students simply were asleep. By 3:00 AM, it was apparent that most students had resolved to remain in the union, for whatever reason, until some action was taken on the part of the administration.[12]

Meanwhile, several administrators and staff gathered at the Student Services Building, one block from the union. Clarence Shelley remembered that "they were trying to decide what to do, arrest them, make them leave, or let them sit all night until they got tired."[13] Administrators established that the students violated university regulations by remaining in the union after closing. Reports of property damage and attacks on white students precipitated their decision to arrest the students. Chancellor Peltason described the decision as difficult, but he said he felt compelled to take action: "As much as one hates to call the police the alternative was to let them stay there for a week. Then the State will be breathing down our neck, the program will be in trouble, and everybody will say, 'you shouldn't have done it.' So, let's clean it up."[14] At 3:03 AM, university officials called ninety Urbana, Champaign, state, and university police to the scene. The police moved in quickly and the students, after being assured they would not be injured, left peacefully. By the early morning hours of September 10, 1968, the Illinois campus was inaugurated as the scene of the first student "riot" of the 1968–69 academic year. Police arrested almost 250 black students on counts of mob action and charged them with "being an inciter, leader or follower of an alleged unauthorized mass demonstration."[15] Nineteen of the arrested were continuing students, three were SEOP transfer students from the University of Illinois at Chicago, but most, 218, were SEOP freshmen. All students were released from jail on bond with considerable help from the black community in Champaign—concerned community residents guaranteed the bonds of the students who did not have the money to post it themselves.[16]

The arrests terrified many SEOP and continuing students. Many advocated Black Power, but they wanted to get a college education not simply spend their time spreading Black Power principles to central Illinois. The incident left many students in a state of disbelief and completely stunned. They had been on campus only one week, and the beginning of the academic year was still another week away, when they were arrested, charged with mob action and unlawful assembly, faced with legal hearings, and confronted by possible dismissal from the university.

News of the September 9, 1968 incident spread across the country. In the *New York Times,* the headline read, "Classes to Begin at U. of Illinois: Tension Pervades Campus after Monday's Protest"; in the *Wall Street Journal,* "Black Student Revolt: Colleges' Bid to Enroll 'Disadvantaged' Brings Problems and Protests; Feeling Strange at Illinois"; in the *Los Angeles Times,* "College Plan for Negroes Passes Test; But 'Project 500' at Illinois U. Meets Obstacle"; in the *St. Louis Globe Democrat,* "300 Negro Students Charged in U of I Row"; in the *St. Louis Post Dispatch,* "Illinois University Officials Meet Negro Group's Housing Demands"; and in bold letters in the local campus newspaper, the *Daily Illini,* "Blacks Occupy Illini Union." The articles chronicled the goals of SEOP, the students' arrival on campus, the fact that whites were barred from the South Lounge where the black students met to discuss their grievances with the administration, the vandalism of the Illini Union, and the number of black students arrested.

The *Chicago Tribune,* under the headline "Negroes Riot at U of I; Negroes Go on Rampage after Row," painted a particularly vivid but grossly incorrect image of the student sit-in. The article described "the wave of violence" and nature of the "rampage" precipitated by the black women's refusal to leave ISR. Citing police officials, the article estimated the damage at $50,000, a figure far exceeding official estimates of $4,000. For those unfamiliar with the nature of SEOP, the newspaper offered a false representation of the financial assistance they received, a representation that increased resentment toward SEOP participants: "The students, most of them Negroes from Chicago and East St. Louis—but some of them from as far away as Philadelphia—were to receive free tuition and free room and board."[17] A *Tribune* editorial published the same day corroborated the article's representation and went further, using racist imagery to describe the sit-in. The editorial claimed that "black students and outside supporters went ape" and "swung from chandeliers in the lounges of the beautiful Illini Union." The editorial characterized such behavior as unconscionable and lamented that these "slum products" responded to the benevolence of the university and Illinois taxpayers "by kicking their benefactors in the groin."[18]

Tension had not subsided between the black students and the administration, and the sentences from their involvement in the September 9, 1968 incident had yet to be handed down when BSA delivered an ever-growing list of demands to the administration on February 13 and 14, 1969. The demands included dropping all criminal charges against those who participated in the Illini Union incident;

establishing "a Black Cultural Center large enough to accommodate all Black people which will be run by the Black Students Association"; hiring fifty black residence hall counselors by September 1969, including 15 percent blacks in the incoming graduate student class; hiring 500 black faculty within a four-year period, beginning with 150 by September 1969; establishing an autonomous Black Studies Department with a major emphasis on Afro-American and African studies; and fulfilling the university's financial commitment to the SEOP students. Demonstrating their link to the black Champaign community, of the thirty-five demands published in the February 18, 1969 issue of the *Black Rap,* twenty dealt with student issues while the others dealt with Champaign resident issues and included eliminating the high school diploma as a requirement for employment at the university, forming a committee to assist in increasing employment of black residents, and extending access to university buildings such as the Illini Union and the Intramural Physical Education Building to Champaign residents. Though BSA demands centered around black students and black Champaign residents, they also recognized the value of certain white allies and explicitly included white Champaign employees of the university in their demand for a wage increase.[19]

Tension permeated the campus atmosphere throughout the 1968–69 academic year. Administrators felt under siege from the Illinois legislature, which curtailed student freedoms and tied the university's hands while administrators dealt with student protests, from black students who continually provoked university officials, from white students who initiated aggressive and disruptive Vietnam War protests, and from an angry citizenry who wrote letters to the board of trustees, President David Dodds Henry, and Dean Shelley imploring them to "start cracking some heads, as that is what is wrong with this country."[20] Black students also felt under attack. They faced angry parents unconvinced that activism and academics could coexist; white students who described BSA demands as irrational, discriminatory, and dangerous; racists who described them as "black apes," "black pigs," "dregs of society," and "hoodlums"; lawsuits and possible university sanction; and a divide in the black student community about how to proceed with negotiations with the university.[21] This environment aggravated both the opposition between BSA members and the university administration and the tension between blacks and whites.

Some faculty, administrators, and students exacerbated racial tensions on campus by openly doubting the black students' ability to compete at Illinois. They claimed that the black students' increasing activism reflected their academic frustrations. This view reached a national audience in a letter written by an Illinois professor of psychology, Lloyd Humphreys, and published in an October 1969 issue of the journal *Science.* Dr. Humphreys never mentioned SEOP by name but did identify his university affiliation and noted a "crash recruitment program" begun in 1968. In the article, he stated, "recent events at my own university have produced in me a strong pessimism about the future." He then characterized "Negroes" as less intelligent than "Caucasians" and attributed the difference to biological factors and "deficiencies in the home and neighborhood." His main point was that affirmative action programs brought intellectually unqualified blacks to campus and had a negative impact on student quality. He then connected their academic difficulties to their activism on campus: "A group of young people who are newly imbued with pride in race are placed in a situation in which they are, by and large, obviously inferior. . . . The causal chain from [*academic*] frustration to aggression is well established. A large ability difference as a source of aggression cannot be ignored. The universities are damned if they don't admit more Negroes, but they are also damned in another sense if they do."[22] Humphreys's sentiment was far from universal on campus, and his statements were countered by other faculty members who supported the black students' rights to attend Illinois.[23] However, anecdotal evidence suggests that black students encountered a markedly hostile environment inside and outside the classroom. Even if some claims of racism were exaggerated, many black students stated to the university ombudsman that that their psychological well-being had been deeply affected.[24]

The link Humphreys made between poor academic performance and aggressive campus activism was completely spurious.[25] The majority of SEOP students met standard qualification requirements. Though they received lower GPAs and graduated at a lower rate than white students, SEOP students consistently outperformed administrator expectations and succeeded more often than they failed. Moreover, white student activities, not black student protest, had brought the National Guard to campus on two occasions, caused more than $20,000 in damage to the university and nearby campustown, and precipitated the need for a Rumor Center through which the university could control and correct misinformation during times of campus unrest.[26] The black student sit-in at the union and the $4,000 worth of damage paled in comparison. If violence and campus activism were related to academic difficulty, it appeared that, according to Humphreys's logic, white students were even less academically fit than black students.

It was in this context that the Afro-American Cultural Program, Afro-American Studies and Research Center, Office of Minority Student Affairs, and a variety of race-based organizations and support programs for underrepresented students came to exist at UIUC. The victories were hard won as black students and administrators battled each other and their critics over the nature of reform. Focusing on the results and ignoring the difficult process through which change occurred diminishes the role of black students and implies that a consensus existed on the worth of particular educational reforms and black student demands. Administrators were not uninterested in equal opportunity, but they were pushed in a particular direction and forced to act more quickly by the activist black student community. Black students kept the university's feet to the fire and paid a price. Former student activists are proud of their accomplishments, but many left with psychological and emotional scars. UIUC was an important battleground in the black freedom struggle in Illinois, and its constituents paid a heavy price to improve the campus experience for all UIUC students.

Notes

1. For a detailed discussion of the reforms at UIUC see Joy Ann Williamson, *Black Power on Campus: The University of Illinois, 1965–1975* (Urbana: University of Illinois Press, 2003).

2. "Negro Students at the University of Illinois: An Outline of Their Enrollment, Graduates, Activities, History, and Living Conditions, 1934–1935," 4, Arthur Cutts Willard Papers, General Correspondence, Box 2, Folder: Colored Students, University of Illinois, University of Illinois at Urbana-Champaign Archives (all archival material was gathered from the University of Illinois Archives unless otherwise noted).

3. "Just Like Dixie: No U of I Dorms for Negroes," *Daily Defender,* August 4, 1945; A. C. Willard to Charles Jenkins, August 2, 1945, Arthur Cutts Willard Papers, Box 92, Folder: Housing for Colored Students; and "Negro Students at the University of Illinois."

4. See various signed affidavits, Harry M. Tiebout Papers, Box 3, Folder: SCIC Dissolution and Reorganization, 1951; and Harry Tiebout to NAACP, August 26, 1961, and Herbert L. Wright to Claudia Young, April 4, 1960, Harry M. Tiebout Papers Box 4, Folder: Restaurants.

5. University Committee on Human Relations and Equal Opportunity, Preamble, "Interim Report by the University Committee on Human Relations and Equal Opportunity," 30 November 1964, 1, University Committee on Human Relations and Equal Opportunity Papers, Box 1.

6. "University of Illinois Undergraduate Student Organization Record," Student Organization Constitutions and Registration Cards File, Box 7, Folder: CORE formerly NAACP.

7. William Savage, "Retention and Recruitment," *Drums,* March 1967, Black Student Association Publications.

8. "Goals Are Black Unity and Black Consciousness," *Drums,* November 1967, Black Student Association Publications.

9. Illinois administrators attributed their swift action in part to the pressure from BSA ("University of Illinois-Urbana, Special Educational Opportunities Program," attachment in Charles Sanders to Emerson Cammack, February 21, 1969, Educational Opportunities Program File, Box 1, Folder: Proposals, 1968–69).

10. Press Release, May 2, 1968, Special Educational Opportunities File, Box 1, Folder: SEOP Feb.–July 1968.

11. Not all SEOP students were African American. Also, not all black freshmen were in SEOP. Some were admitted to UIUC prior to the initiation of SEOP.

12. The accounts of September 9, 1968, were taken from "Security Office Report of Events, Illini Union, September 9 and September 10, 1968," Clipped Article File of Clarence Shelley.

13. Clarence Shelley, interview with author, Champaign, Ill., August 29, 1997.

14. Jack Peltason, interview with author, Irvine, Calif., June 28, 2001.

15. "Report of Proceedings by Subcommittee A of the Senate Committee on Student Discipline," April 1969, Educational Opportunities File, Box 6, Folder: Union Incident.

16. "Security Office Report of Events."

17. John O'Brien, "Negroes Riot at U of I; Negroes Go on Rampage after Row," *Chicago Tribune,* September 11, 1968.

18. Editorial, *Chicago Tribune,* September 11, 1968.

19. "We Demand," *Black Rap,* February 18, 1969, Black Students Association Publications.

20. Legislative actions include Public Act 1583, 76th Cong., 2d sess. (September 26, 1969); Public Act 1582, 76th Cong., 2d sess. (September 26, 1969); and Public Act 1580, 76th Cong., 2d sess. (September 26, 1969). The quote is from M. Theodore Engeln to Clarence Shelly, September 10, 1968, Clipped Article File of Clarence Shelley.

21. White student sentiment is represented in Mary Kathryn Fochtman, "Complaint," *Daily Illini,* September 13, 1968; Dale A. Law, "The Masses," Letters to the Editor, *Daily Illini,* February 20, 1969; and Name Withheld, "Get with It," Letters to the Editor, *Daily Illini,* February 21, 1969. The racist remarks are from Engeln to Shelley, September 10, 1968.

22. Lloyd Humphreys, "Racial Differences: Dilemma of College Admissions," *Science* 166 (October 10, 1969): 167.

23. See Harry Triandis to Lloyd Humphreys, October 7, 1969, Vice-President for Academic Affairs Correspondence, Box 9.

24. The university questioned black students about the psychological stress they experienced. See "Audiotapes," [1965], Ombudsman's Subject File.

25. Patricia Gurin and Edgar Epps found that the individual achievement goals of black students and their activism were unrelated, that grade performance was not related to activism, and that nationalist ideology was almost always unrelated to how well students performed in college (Patricia Gurin and Edgar Epps, *Black Consciousness, Identity, and Achievement: A Study of Students in Historically Black Colleges* [New York: John Wiley and Sons, 1975], 346, 350).

26. For materials concerning white student protests see President David D. Henry General Correspondence, Box 221; *Illinois Alumni News* 49, no. 4 (1970); Ombudsman's Subject File, Box 2, Folder: Demonstrations 1969–70; and "Strike: The Student's Voice," March 4, 1970, Ombudsman's Subject File, Box 2, Folder: Demonstrations 1969–70.

23

Lest We Forget

Richard Herman

In the largest wave of immigration in our history between 1890 and 1914, some fifteen million immigrants made the journey from Europe to the United States. They came from Turkey, Lithuania, Hungary, Austria, Greece, Italy, and Romania. They also came from Russia, part of a mass exodus of Jews escaping the pogrom in that country.

In the early 1900s my mother's parents also sailed to America. They decided to risk their lives on a dangerous sea voyage to America rather than face the murderous campaign against Jews in Russia at that time. When they arrived at Ellis Island, America was approaching a historic high-water mark for the percentage of foreign-born residents. Between 1910 and 1915 fully 15 percent of America's population was from somewhere else. In Chicago four out of five residents were new arrivals.

They were not welcomed with open arms. In the prestigious *Atlantic Monthly,* Francis Walker wrote, "The problems which so sternly confront us today are serious enough without being complicated and aggravated by the addition of some millions of Hungarians, Bohemians, Poles, south Italians, and Russian Jews."[1] Walker's complaint came at the crest of a wave of anti-immigration sentiment. If you know your Chicago history you will remember Haymarket Square, where in 1886 a bomb exploded during a labor rally organized by immigrants. The Haymarket bombing triggered a national wave of fear; foreign birth was equated with terror. Sound familiar?

In Chicago hundreds of socialists, anarchists, and other radicals were rounded up. Eight anarchists, all but one of them German immigrants, were indicted for conspiracy, though none was charged with throwing the bomb. After a conspicuously biased trial, seven were hanged; the eighth was given a long prison sentence.

I often try to imagine how disoriented my grandparents must have felt in their first years in America. But I more often think about the excitement they must have felt, too. For it was not just a new country with a new culture and language, it was a payoff on the promises of new opportunities. Whatever dreams my grandparents already had, the first sight of America must have created new ones.

Today, a new wave of immigration is washing over the United States. Eleven percent, or thirty-five million people living in this country, were born elsewhere. If the current rate of immigration continues, we will certainly surpass the record of 15 percent foreign-born set a hundred years ago. Believe me—this is a good thing.

Lady Liberty's Lesson

There is a three-hour evening boat ride you can take every evening from Brooklyn's Sheepshead Bay to the Statue of Liberty. I highly recommend it. The boat is usually filled with our newest immigrants. It's a boisterous cruise, filled with the often dissonant sounds of many languages competing for space. There is no shortage of beer and cigarettes and frivolity. But all that changes as the boat chugs into New York Harbor. There the music is turned off, the captain kills the motor, and everyone stops talking. It's the moment everyone has been waiting for. The tourist boat bobs in front of the Statue of Liberty. Ellis Island is off to the right, that great destination for my grandparents and millions more. In the pitch-black stillness families line up for pictures. Flashbulbs spark, lighting the darkness, and for a second you can see the uncontrolled joy on the faces of these newest immigrants. You will never forget this scene. The smiles. The relief. For this is a benediction. A final blessing from Lady Liberty, the lights of Manhattan glittering in the background. No matter where they are from—Turkey, Armenia, Sudan, Colombia, Haiti, Mexico—these newest American citizens know what that statue represents.

But do we still know what it represents?

Two decades after my grandparents first saw Lady Liberty's torch in New York Harbor, Congress passed the Immigration Act of 1924. Though the act encouraged immigration from much of western and northern Europe, it placed strict quotas on the numbers of Italians, Irish, Jews, Japanese, and people of other ethnicities that many white Protestant Americans considered inferior. Much of the debate centered on questions of national identity, race, and ethnicity. In California, voters passed a law forbidding Japanese land ownership.

In Georgia, candidates won national office by railing against the evils of Catholicism. Wealthy businessmen launched a national propaganda campaign against Jews. Mobs in Illinois stoned Italian immigrants and burned their homes. And the Ku Klux Klan again reared its ugly head.

In the 1930s, immigration slowed to less than a trickle, not because of the passage of the Immigration Act of 1924, but because of the Great Depression. With no jobs available, people simply stopped coming to the United States. In fact, during this period, more people left America than came.

During World War II, America became a safe haven for many of Europe's intellectual elite—people like Albert Einstein—who were fleeing Nazism, Communism, and war. The contributions of these immigrants cannot be overstated. Many joined the faculty of our nation's leading universities, pursuing fundamental research, sharing their knowledge with American students and elevating American universities to unprecedented levels of prestige.

Former president of Harvard James Conant led the charge to pull American academia out of its parochial stasis and tap into the rich intellectualism and talent of postwar Europe. From that point forward the United States began to have world-class universities.

Citizens of the World

Recently, I gave a memorial for a longtime faculty member, Ladislav Zgusta. This great scholar was born in Czechoslovakia and survived two occupations of his native country, including by the Nazis. While I was delivering remarks for this memorial I could not help but think that Professor Zgusta came to the University of Illinois, to this campus and community, with his stories, sorrows, scholarship, and hopes.

And I thought about my grandparents.

Professor Zgusta's story is the ultimate immigrant's story, the eternal story all of us in the United States share, through our own lives and those who came before us. And, as is well-noted by now, that influx of immigrants, that scattering of seeds in the wind, if you will, that came to our shores after World War II, took our universities to the premier level they hold today.

Yet, if you will allow me a lament, this seems to be a time when many in our country do not want to remember and celebrate all that others have brought to this nation and continue to bring. And that saddens me greatly. For if we forget Professor Zgusta's story then we forget our own story, too. And we cannot afford to do either. This is the reason we must continue to keep our doors open and welcome the many international students and faculty members who come here today temporarily, or permanently, seeking their future on our campus, while enriching us with their very presence. We are—and we must remain—a global campus.

That is also the reason we encourage our students, your sons and daughters, to study abroad through our Global Studies Program and programs such as the Center for International Business Education and Research. Mary McKenna, a recent student of ours at Illinois and a member of our Global Studies Initiative, juggled a triple major of English literature, Spanish, and international studies. But what changed her life was a year spent abroad in Ireland and in Spain. After that life-transforming experience, she now believes the future depends on us being informed global citizens. Mary says, "It means being conscious not only of your own country or your own little area. Everything we do affects someone else across the world." No surprise that she plans a career in international human rights law. Being out in the world changed Mary's life, increased her possibilities, and sparked her idealism.

We must prepare our students to be citizens of the world. Students like Gray Mateo, the first in her family to go to college here in the United States. I know Gray's parents are beaming with pride in their daughter. We are, too, Gray.

That's what we do so well at Illinois. We prepare our students for the new landscape—the "flat world" as the *New York Times* columnist Thomas Friedman penned it, where, as Friedman says, "It is now possible for more people than ever to collaborate and compete in real time with more other people on more different kinds of work from more different corners of the planet and on a more equal footing than at any previous time in the history of the world."[2]

Newcomers developed many of the technological innovations that have driven our economy during the last two decades. And they continue to do just that. Many of these foreign-born entrepreneurs came here to study at American universities and decided to stay. Jerry Yang, one of the cofounders of Yahoo, emigrated from Taiwan. Google co-creator Sergey Brin was born in Russia. Hotmail cofounder Sabeer Bhatia was raised in India.

Our own Illinois graduate and inventor of the revolutionary online payment service PayPal, Max Levchin, was born in Kiev, Ukraine. When the Soviet empire broke apart, Max's parents moved the family to the city of broad shoulders, Chicago. Would Max have been able to reach his amazing potential in Ukraine?

At one time these people would not have been allowed to immigrate to America. And we would have been the poorer for it.

Illinois continues to be a mecca for international study. Our university—your university—is one of the leaders in the country in numbers of international students who study at the graduate level. They help fill this country's paucity of graduate students in science, math, and technology. Our universities are still the best in the world but, globally, our fifteen-year-olds are tied for twenty-first place in average academic performance.

In 2003, American eighth graders ranked fourteenth in math and eighth in the world in science. Somewhat as a result, great universities across the nation continue to rely on these students to do research and help solve global problems in areas such as energy and the environment. But we must make it easier, not harder, for these students to study and work in the United States. Without these bright, talented and creative minds, America is in danger of losing its economic and technological edge.

Thomas Friedman recently wrote about attending a graduation ceremony at Rensselaer Polytechnic Institute, one of our great science and engineering universities. He watched as student after student received their newly minted PhDs. He wrote that he could not help but notice that their names were Hong Lu, Tao Yuan and Fu Tang. There is, of course, nothing wrong with that except for the fact that this new crop of foreign-born graduates would probably return to their native countries, to help those booming economies, because our Immigration and Naturalization Service had made it very hard for them to stay here. He wrote, "I think any foreign student who gets a PhD in our country—in any subject—should be offered citizenship. I want them. The idea that we actually make it difficult for them to stay is crazy."[3]

At Illinois, as with most great research universities in this nation, we educate vast numbers of international graduate students at fundamentally the expense of the federal government and then we tell them they have to go back. Friedman is right.

Across the New Silk Road

In the summer of 2007 my wife, Susan, and I traveled the world—from the Silk Road to Rio to the Gaza Strip. Two scenes left indelible impressions. In northwestern China I stood at the western gate of the Silk Road near Dunhuang. This is where the Great Wall ends its six-thousand-mile traverse and where ancient traders once exchanged their goods. Out there in the barren Gobi Desert is also where I toured the Mogao caves, which date back to 366 AD. These Buddhist shrines with their wall paintings and artifacts left me breathless. I had never seen such well-preserved frescos depicting hunters, dancers, musicians, and miniature icons of Buddha. I did not expect such riches in a desert.

Just a few years earlier it might have seemed odd for me, the chancellor of a major land-grant university, to be standing on the clay-colored landscape of the Gobi Desert. But that summer, when I also traveled to Israel, Cyprus, and Brazil, it made perfect sense. I knew I had to be there.

Consider the symbolism. In the midst of trying to internationalize this university that sits in the heart of the American Midwest I was standing at one of the most historical junctions on the most famous of trade routes—the Silk Road. A place where East meets West. A place Marco Polo visited at the age of fifteen in the 1200s. He was so taken with China he stayed for the next twenty years.

These were the seeds of what we now routinely, and sometimes disparagingly, call globalization. Our exchanges are no longer impeded by sandstorms. We may not be using camels to travel anymore—although I did see them in the Gobi—and we may not be trading spices and silk for gunpowder and paper, but the same principles still apply—ideas transcending political boundaries. Knowledge shared between people who may not even share a common language. An unquenchable thirst for understanding in this complex world we all share, whether it is in 600 AD or in the twenty-first century.

The booming economies of India and China now compete with our own.

Not just for oil and steel and food. But for brainpower, too, the world's best and brightest. Last year China graduated 4.1 million college students, 800,000 of them in the fields of science and technology. India graduates 2.7 million students each year. The United States graduates 1.3 million students.

The combined growth of India and China during the past two decades has cut the portion of the world living in extreme poverty from 40 percent to 20 percent. India's government has calculated that if it can keep the economy growing at 8 percent a year for the next decade, it will lift 350 million people out of poverty. This is great news for all of us and here at Illinois. We want to help with that trend through education, partnerships, and tech transfer.

That summer, I also traveled to Israel. I learned you can only experience the Middle East by going there. The visit changed my life. The juxtaposition of tradition and modernity, the religious and the physical, is almost beyond words. Most of what we read about the Middle East is about endless war and failed peace. Every day it seems we are witness to images of irreversible hatred and heartbreaking carnage. Yet on the streets of Haifa and in the classrooms of the Technion and Hebrew universities, there is cause for optimism, the hope that education always brings.

At the Women's Center in the Bedouin community of Lakia, I heard what it means in terms of education to be a minority within a (Jewish) majority that itself is a minority within a region that has an Arab majority. And while the disparities were apparent, optimism and passion were also in the air. The same hopeful spirit resides in Al-Qasemi College, the first institute of Islamic higher education in Israel and a key lifeline that reaches out to local Arab women in an effort to educate them as citizens of the world. We need to hear about these brave steps toward commonalities, too. They are a balm against fatalism.

In between discussions on tech transfer, potential partnerships, the challenges to Israeli and Palestinian higher education, and the related issue of the future of Jewish settlements, I stood at the lookout point of Nebi Mari and looked out at Gaza. I imagined a world without walls and checkpoints, suicide martyrs, and child coffins. In this holy place with olive trees as old as ancient Rome I was reminded of my obligation as an educator and as a human being. I was reminded that I—the chancellor of a great university and son and grandson of Russian immigrants—I, too, am a citizen of the world.

Remembering

Allow me one final story.

My past came back full circle when our daughter got engaged and needed a dress. Now this is typical New York: my wife, Susan, knew a friend of a friend of a friend, who knew a tailor who made dresses for Vera Wang. We got this particular wedding dress for a song—wholesale—because just like Woody Allen has famously remarked, "In my family, it was a crime to buy retail."

When we arrived at his loft, the tailor turned out to be an eighty-year-old Holocaust survivor. All of a sudden it was forty years earlier, when my grandfather had been a tailor and I had been sent to lofts in New York to get clothing from relatives—wholesale, of course. All the memories with my late grandparents came rushing back to me with great vividness.

One of the great mysteries of our short lives is that we can never prepare for these moments, these sensory-filled triggers to our past.

What set me back in time were the dust particles in the slant of the light through the loft windows, the way the tailor was bent over at his work, the yellow tape draped over his back, pieces of chalk dust on his fingers, his glasses balanced on his nose, and the concentration. The staccato whirl of the sewing machine competing with the sounds of the city outside. Stacks of raw fabric. Scraps of my family's history. In fact, everything in that tailor's tiny loft.

On that day, I stood there with my wife and my daughter, and I remembered where I came from. I remembered my courageous grandparents—may they rest in peace—landing at Ellis Island, the two of them not knowing what awaited them across New York Harbor. Not knowing but trusting in America's great promise. I remembered living with my grandparents in the Bronx. The time when I was sixteen watching the Perry Como show with my grandmother and out of the blue she remarks, "He can park his shoes under my bed any time." The holiday meals. The births and bar mitzvahs. The deaths. The celebrations.

The grieving.

This life.

I went to buy a dress for my daughter and, instead, I came away with this inescapable thought—I am forever the grateful grandson of immigrants. I am forever an American. And, because of all of that, I am forever the luckiest person in America, as are all of you.

Notes

1. Francis A. Walker, "Restriction of Immigration," *Atlantic Monthly* 77 (June 1896): 822–29.

2. Thomas Friedman, *The World Is Flat: A Brief History of the Twenty-First Century* (New York: Farrar, Strauss, and Giroux, 2005), 8.

3. Thomas Friedman, "Laughing and Crying," *New York Times*, May 23, 2007.

24

Enforcing *Brown* in Sundown Towns

James W. Loewen

Fifty years after *Brown,* the United States is still marred by sundown towns—communities that do not allow African Americans to spend the night. They dot the United States from Connecticut to Washington, Florida to California. Historically, many of these towns posted signs at their city limits that usually read, "Nigger, Don't Let The Sun Go Down On You In Pana," or whatever the town name. Some of these communities remain all white today. Their existence raises questions about how *Brown* was enforced and whether Supreme Court decisions make a difference in our society.

In 1954, after all, the U.S. Supreme Court stated that people could not be kept out of a school because of their race. The right literally to live in a town—not the right to go to a desegregated school but simply to live—is surely a basic human right. Yet when *Brown* was decided in 1954, thousands of towns denied this right to African Americans, and scores denied it to Jewish Americans or Chinese Americans. Surprisingly, however, for the next half century and more, the nation has continued to tolerate entire communities that do not allow African Americans to live in them.

Historical Background

The predecessor of *Brown* was *Plessy v. Ferguson* in 1896, of course. It was symbolic of the "nadir of race relations," that period from 1890 to about 1940 when African Americans, Native Americans, and some other groups lost civil and voting rights.

The nadir can be dated to 1890 for three reasons:

American Indians lost the last shards of independence at the Massacre at
   Wounded Knee.
Mississippi passed its new state constitution, "legally" disfranchising black
   voters, defying the Fourteenth and Fifteenth Amendments, and the
   federal government did nothing about it.

After failing narrowly in the Senate to pass the Federal Elections Bill,
which would have given Republican voters in the South—black and
white—some hope of fair elections, Republicans offered a new response
to the usual Democratic charge that they were "nigger lovers." They
denied it—abandoning the struggle for black rights. Since Democrats
had always opposed black rights, this change in Republican ideology
signaled the end of an era.

During the nadir, thousands of sundown towns formed across the United
States, except in what might be called the traditional South. Whites in the traditional South would never expel their maids, janitors, or agricultural laborers.
Elsewhere—the Ozarks, the Cumberlands, the Midwest, Oregon, the suburbs
of cities from Boston to Los Angeles—sundown towns were more the rule than
the exception.

The Extent of Sundown Towns in Illinois

The case of Illinois, a focus of my research, is especially instructive. In 1890
African Americans lived in every Illinois county. By 1930, six counties had none,
while another eleven had fewer than ten African American residents. Exclusion,
not free choice, underlies these numbers. In Illinois and elsewhere, entire counties developed and enforced the policy of keeping out African Americans. Oral
history from long-term residents, occasionally confirmed by written sources,
confirms ten of these seventeen counties as exclusionary by 1930, and I suspect
all seventeen were. Several other counties in Illinois allowed no African Americans except in one or two isolated locations.

Malcolm Ross of the U.S. Fair Employment Practices Commission became
aware of the practice in Calhoun County, along the Mississippi River north
of St. Louis, during World War II, because it affected employment in war
industries in the St. Louis metropolitan area. "Calhoun County is recorded
in the 1940 census as '8,207 whites; no Negroes; no other races,'" he wrote.
"This is not by accident. Calhoun people see to it that no Negroes settle there."
Ross was shocked at the practice and called Calhoun "an earthly paradise for
those who hate Negro Americans." He would surely be shaken to learn that
sixty years later the 2000 census recorded not a single black household in the
county, and in 2009, residents suggested it would not be prudent for African
Americans to try.[1]

Other counties had no outside observers like Ross, but the practice can still
be confirmed via oral history. According to an eighty-three-year-old lifelong
resident of Mason County, north of Springfield, the sheriff "would meet [blacks]
at the county line and tell them not to come in." I don't believe that he literally

met them at the line, but I do believe that the resident is correct in communicating that the sheriff enforced the sundown policy. Despite its location between Springfield and Peoria, both with large African American populations, and on the Illinois River, an important trade route, Mason County's black population declined from 29 in 1890 to 0 by 1930. A more recent resident of Havana, the county seat of Mason County, confirmed that African Americans "were not welcome to purchase or live in our town." This was "a wide known fact amongst [*sic*] the community." More research is needed to be sure, but like Calhoun, Mason County does not show a single black household in the 2000 census.[2]

Sundown towns are far more widespread than sundown counties. Macon County, in the center of the state, was certainly never a sundown county; its county seat, Decatur, has long had a sizable black population. But these ten towns in Macon County show no or almost no black residents in census after census: Argenta, Blue Mound, Long Creek, Macon, Maroa, Mount Zion, Moweaqua, Niantic, Oreana, and Warrensburg. In these towns, oral history supports with some detail that five—Blue Mound, Maroa, Mount Zion, Moweaqua, and Niantic—mounted formal or informal prohibitions against African Americans. About Niantic, for example, two longtime residents told me that they understood that Niantic had passed an ordinance that blacks had to be out by sundown. One added that when the Wabash Railroad work train was in Niantic, employees took care to pull it into the main yard in Decatur for the night, since section hands slept on the work train and that would violate Niantic's ordinance. Two retired Wabash employees confirmed that the railroad did follow that policy. I believe that researchers on site in the other five towns could quickly amass similar information.

"Sundown suburbs" formed later, mostly between 1900 and 1968. Most of them were all-white "legally" from the start, having required restrictive covenants in all residential neighborhoods as they formed. Joseph Sears, developer of Kenilworth, the richest suburb of Chicago, incorporated the restriction "Sales to *Caucasians only*" into his village's founding documents.[3] When needed, however, suburbs too resorted to coercion and violence to stay white. In 1992, for example, threats, arson, and other bad behavior drove a black family from a neighborhood of Berwyn, a western suburb of Chicago, after they had moved in. As he departed, the father and husband explained, "When we realized that we had no official support for being in Berwyn, we felt like outside intruders." Thus Berwyn still acted as a sundown suburb in 1992.[4] Many Chicago suburbs not only excluded blacks, but also Jews.

In 1970, when sundown towns were probably at their maximum, Illinois had 621 towns larger than 1,000, ranging from Wyanet (population 1,005) to Chicago.[5] Of these, 448, or 72 percent, were "all white" (I use quotation marks because some sundown towns made an exception for one black household, even as they posted signs or otherwise acted to keep out any others). In addition, 55 hamlets smaller than 1,000 came to my attention because of evidence confirming them as sundown towns. Thus my universe of Illinois towns totaled 676. Of these 676 towns 503, or 74 percent, were all white. Of these 503, I collected information as to whether blacks were allowed to live within 219 communities in past decades, and of these, 218 proved to be sundown towns or suburbs, or 99.5 percent! We can predict that about 99.5 percent of the remaining towns would also turn out to be sundown towns, there being no good reason to suppose that the next towns will be different from those we know. Therefore, our best single estimate is that about 500 of the 503 were all white on purpose—a clear majority of all Illinois communities. Confirmed Illinois sundown towns ranged in size from hamlets of just a few hundred people to Cicero, a Chicago suburb that in 1970 had 67,058 residents, and Pekin, an independent city in central Illinois with 31,375 and another 3,500 in its suburbs.

Many sundown towns passed ordinances—or think they did—prohibiting African Americans from spending the night or buying or renting property. Other towns never bothered with laws, confident that their reputations, secured by decades of hostility toward occasional black visitors, guaranteed that no African Americans would dare to "intrude." In 1978, for instance, when a black family moved into Arcola, Illinois, near Champaign-Urbana, the town's only real grocery store refused to sell to them. At least as late as 2004, residents of Anna, in southern Illinois, did not think that a single black family lived in Anna or adjacent Jonesboro. Anna residents, as well as residents of nearby towns, know Anna to be an acronym for "Ain't No Niggers Allowed," which implies that Anna remains all white on purpose.[6]

The Impact of *Brown*

Even before the *Brown* decision, sundown ordinances were illegal. In the early years of the twentieth century, city after city in southern and border states passed "segregation ordinances." Such laws were allegedly race-neutral, prohibiting the sale of residential property to a black if most residents in the neighborhood were white and vice versa. In practice they were invoked only by whites against blacks. Moreover, even had they been enforced in a "race neutral" manner, like *Plessy* they were all about race, having been devised by the dominant race to avoid contact with the subordinate race. Soon they would have prompted residential apartheid in every city that passed them. In 1917 *Buchanan v. Warley*, a case challenging the ordinance in Louisville, Kentucky, went to the U.S. Supreme Court. In that year, at the nadir, no plea for black rights alone would have been likely to prevail. The Court ruled segregation ordinances illegal because a *white* right was at stake: the right of a white seller to sell property to the highest bidder, even if that person happened to be black. Residential segregation ordinances thus "destroyed the right of the individual to acquire, enjoy, and dispose of his property," in violation of the due process clause of the Fourteenth Amendment. Although *Buchanan* ruled unconstitutional a law intended to create sundown neighborhoods, there can be no doubt that as a precedent, it would also invalidate ordinances intended to create sundown towns, which did not hide their explicit antiblack intentions behind even a gloss of fairness.[7]

Nevertheless, whites continued to pass residential segregation ordinances as well as plain sundown ordinances. In Villa Grove, Illinois, a few miles south of Champaign-Urbana, city officials mounted a siren on the municipal water tower some time after 1914 and sounded it at 6 PM every night to warn African Americans to leave town before dark. For the same reason, whistles sounded in several other towns in Illinois, Indiana, and Ohio. In Minden and Gardnerville, Nevada, the 6 PM whistle told Native Americans to be gone.

Residents in many towns, including public officials, believed their sundown ordinances were still in force even after *Brown*. In the summer of 1984 or 1985, for example, the town of New Market, Iowa, hired a little band called Westwind from a nearby college to play at a street dance. One member of the band was African American. After they had played for an hour or two, it started to get dark. During a break between sets, the member of the city council who had engaged the band came over and said, "Hey, we almost had an incident here. The sheriff reminded me that it was against city ordinance for a colored person to be in town after dark and that we were about to break the law. So, since most of the members of the city council are here, we held a special meeting of the council and voted to suspend the law for the night."

The next day, presumably, the ordinance went right back into effect. It may still be, informally, for the 2000 census showed no African Americans in New Market; indeed, the entire county showed not a single black household. Many residents of central Illinois sundown towns still believed their ordinances were in effect at least as late as the 1990s. The Villa Grove siren sounded until about 1999.[8]

Enforcing *Brown*

Neither *Brown* nor the ensuing civil rights movement made much difference to these practices, because the federal government did not really enforce *Brown* or such post-*Brown* federal laws as the 1964 Civil Rights Act. Instead, at best the government enforced the rights of African Americans to enforce *Brown* and these later acts. Black pioneers tested restaurants and motels across the South, sat wherever they wanted on buses, and sometimes got beaten or killed for their trouble, forcing the government to act. Where African Americans did not take such actions—including where African Americans did not exist—*Brown* and subsequent decisions and laws went unenforced.

Having no black children, sundown towns had no black students to desegregate their schools after 1954. Having no black populations, these towns had no African Americans to test their public accommodations after 1964. Members of the St. Louis chapter of the Student Nonviolent Coordinating Committee did announce to the media that they were going to test restaurants and motels in Williamson County, Illinois, shortly after passage of the act. Almost every community in Williamson County and adjoining Franklin County was a sundown town then, including Benton, Carterville, Christopher, Herrin, Johnston City, Mulkeytown, Royalton, Sesser, West Frankfort, and Ziegler. The Williamson County sheriff talked with local motel owners and restaurant owners and told them they had two choices, according to former resident Jim Clayton: "Either they could accommodate them, and they'd all go back to St. Louis, or they could refuse, and all hell would break loose." They complied. Afterwards they put their signs back up—"White Only" or "Management Reserves the Right to Refuse Service to Anyone"—and Williamson and Franklin counties disobeyed the law for another two decades. The persistence of sundown towns after *Brown* surely offers support to the theory that laws in and of themselves make no difference.

At least two towns in the United States and probably several whole counties went sundown—pushed out their entire African American populations—in response to *Brown*. Shortly after the 1954 edict came down from the Supreme Court, the all-white Sheridan, Arkansas, school board voted to comply. Sheridan had been operating an elementary school for African Americans but was busing its black high school students to adjacent counties. The decision to desegregate led to a "firestorm of protest" in the white community, in the words of a Sheridan native, which prompted the board to reverse itself. At this point, Jack Williams, the owner of the local sawmill and the sawmill workers' homes, made his African American employees an extraordinary offer: he would *give* them their homes and move them to Malvern, twenty-five miles west, at no cost to them. This turned out to be a proposition they couldn't refuse, for if a family would not move, he would evict them and burn down their home. Not unreasonably, blacks "chose" to accept the buyout and leave Sheridan in response to this ultimatum. A few other African Americans lived in Sheridan—not in Williams's employ—but what could they do? The preacher, the beautician, the café owner suddenly found themselves without a clientele. They left too.

After 1954 the African American population of at least five counties in Kentucky, Missouri, and Tennessee also declined abruptly. Perhaps the black families in these counties moved away voluntarily, but the example of Sheridan raises suspicion. Historian Mary Waalkes has uncovered an account from one of the five, Polk County, Tennessee, saying that *Brown* prompted whites to force black families to sell their farms, "to rid the county of school children who would have to be integrated into the Polk County system." The number of African Americans in Polk County—which had been 566 in 1890—fell from 75 in 1950 to just 28 ten years later, including only 4 of school age, among 12,160 inhabitants. Unlike much milder responses to *Brown*, such as the riots in Little Rock or Clinton, Tennessee, which did not attack the black community at large, nothing has ever been done by civil rights lawyers or the federal government about these expulsions.[9]

Also in 1954, residents of Vienna, Illinois, drove out Vienna's small black community, which had existed since the Civil War. In the 1950 census, African Americans numbered thirty-four; additional black families lived just outside Vienna's city limits. Then in the summer of 1954, two black men beat up a white grandmother and allegedly tried to rape her teenaged granddaughter. The grandmother eventually died, and "every [white] man in town was deputized" to find the culprits, according to a Vienna resident in 2004. The two men were apprehended; in the aftermath, whites sacked the entire black community. "They burned the houses," my informant said. "The blacks literally ran for their lives." The *Vienna Times* put it more sedately: "The three remaining buildings on the South hill in the south city limits of Vienna were destroyed by fire about 4:30 o'clock Monday afternoon." The state's attorney and circuit judge later addressed a joint meeting of the Vienna city council and Johnson County commissioners, "telling them of the loss sustained by the colored people." Both bodies "passed a resolution condemning the acts of vandalism" and promised to pay restitution to those who lost their homes and belongings. Neither body invited the black community to return, and no one was ever convicted of the crime of driving them out. In the 2000 census, Vienna's population of 1,234 included just 1 African American. As far as I can tell, Vienna's action was not in reaction to *Brown*, although most southern Illinois towns operated tiny segregated elementary schools for African Americans (grades 1–8) and then tried to discourage them from attending high school.[10]

Impact of Sundown Towns

Unlike much milder responses to *Brown*, such as the riots in Little Rock or Clinton, Tennessee, which did not attack the black community at large, nothing has ever been done by civil rights lawyers or the federal government about these expulsions in Arkansas, Illinois, Kentucky, Missouri, or Tennessee.[11] Action against sundown towns is necessary, however, because sundown towns undo *Brown*, segregate society, and foment racism. The white townspeople of Sheridan, for instance, were probably no more prejudiced than residents of many other Arkansas towns until 1954. Indeed, they may have been *less* racist than many, since their school board briefly voted to desegregate Sheridan's schools in response to *Brown*, a step taken by only two towns in Arkansas. After all blacks left in 1954, however, Sheridan's notoriety grew. As their thinking shifted to justify what they had done, eliminating African Americans came to be deemed a constructive step. As two Sheridan residents said in separate conversations in 2001, "You know, that solved the problem!" If "the problem" was blacks, the residents were right, but if the problem was racism, the residents were dead wrong. Incidents of harassment increased until African Americans wouldn't stop in Sheridan for gas, even during the day. Long after non-sundown towns in Arkansas desegregated their schools, Sheridan fans maintained a reputation for bigotry at athletic contests with interracial high schools.

Sheridan was hardly unique. Residents of sundown towns and suburbs are generally more racist than residents of biracial towns. Sundown towns collect white racists from the outside world who are attracted by their lack of diversity. They also create racists, for living in an all-white community leads many residents to defend living in an all-white community.

Sundown towns also affected the *Milliken v. Bradley* decision, the 1974 case in which the Supreme Court upheld Detroit's suburbs' right to run overwhelmingly white schools because they were legally separate from Detroit.[12] Most of these suburbs had been overwhelmingly white on purpose. For decades, government officials played key roles in keeping Dearborn white. African Americans repeatedly tried to live in Wyandotte; repeated acts of violence by Wyandotte residents and formal acts by its city government kept them out. A similar series of violent and nonviolent actions performed or condoned by city governments kept African Americans from living in Grosse Ile, Grosse Pointe, and other suburbs in the Detroit area. Little of this information about Detroit's sundown suburbs, however, including the explicit actions over the years taken by their governments to stay all white, was considered by the Supreme Court.[13] In its absence, five of the nine justices held that residential exclusion was not open to remedy by litigation. In turn, school segregation resulting from residential exclusion was also not open to remedy. So long as a sundown suburb avoided segregating its handful of zero to nine black students into a majority black school, it was operating lawfully. Thus, because the suburbs had been so bold as to exclude African Americans almost totally, their school systems were declared not racially segregated.

Looking backward, the importance of *Milliken* is obvious. This ruling largely ended the efforts of federal courts to desegregate school systems in the North, following the promise of *Brown*. In effect, this decision signaled suburbs that they could continue to be all white, so long as they did not openly say they were. The consequences were further white abandonment of Detroit (and some other central cities), continued resistance to African American newcomers in the suburbs, and further mystification of the sundown process. Thus *Brown* did not change sundown towns, but sundown towns did change *Brown*.

Postscript: Change in Sundown Towns

That last sentence is perhaps too pessimistic. Sundown towns and suburbs have been in retreat since about 1980. There has been a shift in the zeitgeist, the spirit of the times. The rise of admired black figures like Jackie Robinson and Ella Fitzgerald, later Bill Cosby and Alice Walker, and still later Michael Jordan and Oprah Winfrey, helped white Americans accept an African American family on their block. This change was achieved indirectly by the civil rights movement, triggered in turn partly by the 1954 decision. Although the 1964 Civil Rights Act made little impact on residential segregation, other laws, notably the 1968 Federal Housing Act, passed in the wake of the murder of Martin Luther King Jr., did make it harder to keep out African Americans.

Even though the movement rarely addressed northern sundown towns and suburbs directly, its success in the South did help to undercut the rationale for sundown towns in the North, thus affecting sundown towns indirectly. The televised images of black young people peacefully picketing and sitting in and getting beaten or jailed in the process jolted white northerners. These scenes made clear that white misbehavior—not alleged black inferiority—was the source of America's racial problem. As African Americans no longer came to be seen as the problem, colleges and universities welcomed and even recruited black students, while the sundown suburbs and neighborhoods from which so many white college students came still discouraged and even barred African American residents. Now whites who argued for sundown towns and suburbs found themselves on the defensive. Indeed, the proportion of whites who openly favored the racial segregation of neighborhoods declined nationally to just 15 percent by 1994.

America's increasing multicultural complexity has also helped to undermine sundown towns. Hispanics and Asians live throughout the United States. Their presence in most sundown towns may weaken white resistance to African Americans. The rush of Mexican and Asian Americans into Cicero and Berwyn, Illinois, for example, has loosened those adjacent suburbs' ban on African Americans. By 2000, Cicero had 956 African Americans in 275 households, 54 of whom owned their homes; Berwyn had 588 in 221 households, 81 of whom owned. As we have seen, such numbers would have been inconceivable in 1991. Meanwhile, Cicero's 85,616 population was almost 80 percent Hispanic in 2000, and Berwyn's was almost 40 percent and rising.

These hopeful signs come just in time. "To separate [children] . . . solely because of their race generates a feeling of inferiority as to their status in the community that may affect their hearts and minds in a way unlikely ever to be undone," wrote Chief Justice Earl Warren more than half a century ago.[14] To bar families from living in a place solely because of their race generates a feeling of superiority among *white* residents as to their status in the community that may affect their hearts and minds in a way unlikely ever to be undone.

Even today, most municipalities are unlikely to change by themselves, which is why residential segregation remains our nation's most intractable civil rights problem. States and the federal government need to act to end America's remaining sundown towns and suburbs. Every sundown town needs to be asked to admit that they excluded, apologize for it, and state that they do not discriminate any more. The third statement must be backed by changed actions. Every family entering the real estate market needs to choose a home with the goal of ending residential segregation in mind. Only when it becomes impossible to evade school desegregation by moving to overwhelmingly white jurisdictions will the promise of *Brown* become real.

Notes

1. Malcolm Ross, *All Manner of Men* (New York: Reynal and Hitchcock, 1948), 66; author interviews with two residents and a former resident in January 2009.

2. Author interview with Mason County resident, April 2000; Kelly Burroughs, 1988 graduate, Havana High School, post to Classmates.com, November 27, 2002 (accessed November 2002). V. Jacque Voegeli says that five African Americans had been forced out of Mason County much earlier, during the Civil War (*Free but Not Equal* [Chicago: University of Chicago Press, 1967], 89), but between 1864 and 1890, sensing new opportunities, African Americans went everywhere in the United States, including Mason County.

3. Colleen Kilner, *Joseph Sears and His Kenilworth* (Kenilworth, Ill.: Kenilworth Historical Society, 1990), 138, 143, her italics.

4. Alex Kotlowitz, "How Regular Folks in Berwyn, Ill., Tried to Fight Prejudice," *Wall Street Journal*, June 3, 1992.

5. This figure is approximate. I may have overlooked a town or two that exceeded 1,000 in 1970 but not in adjoining censuses; I also omitted most "census designated places."

6. Anna was named for a white woman in 1854. In 1909 residents drove out its black community, and Anna has been a sundown town ever since.

7. *Buchanan v. Warley*, 245 U.S. 60 (1917).

8. John D. Baskerville, e-mail message to the author, July 2003.

9. Mary Waalkes, e-mail message to the author, July 2002.

10. Vienna city employee, interview with author, February 2004, confirmed by two other residents; "Three Negro Homes Burned Here Monday," *Vienna Times*, September 9, 1954.

11. Personal interviews by the author in Sheridan and Vienna; Mary Waalkes, e-mail message to the author, July 2002.

12. *Milliken v. Bradley,* 418 U.S. 717 (1974).

13. Evidence of racial residential exclusion committed or condoned by suburban governments was in the trial transcript, but the appeals court didn't consider it because the court found evidence of school segregation policies sufficient to decide the case in favor of the plaintiffs. The Supreme Court reversed that finding but then failed to consider the trial court's evidence on residential exclusion!

14. *Brown v. Board of Education,* 347 U.S. 483, 494 (1954).

Section V

Public Intellectuals and *Brown* and Its Legacy

This last section groups together essays by a variety of public intellectuals—a political leader, a university president, and two journalists—who have used their talents as writers and speakers to bring the message of *Brown* and other major civil rights events and figures to a wide audience. Their essays in this volume rely on a range of emotions, experiences, and forms of address that rarely figure in academic research. In his assessment of the last fifty years of the civil rights movement, Julian Bond relies on impassioned political commentary to indict the Bush administration's policies regarding racial equality. Chris Benson's heart-wrenching account of Emmett Till's lynching makes the cruelty and horror of that event palpable again. At the same time, Benson reflects on how the story itself, when picked up by the mass media, made the civil rights struggle urgent to many formerly apathetic Americans. In an epilogue to Juan Williams's highly acclaimed biography of Thurgood Marshall, Williams and Christopher Teal reflect on the many lives that Marshall's work directly affected and the continued significance of his work today. Freeman Hrabowski draws on his personal experiences, both as a student and as a university administrator, to reflect on the nation's progress in providing equal access to education since the *Brown* decision and to suggest a path forward.

25

Civil Rights

Now and Then

Julian Bond

I want to talk about a subject many think about but few actually discuss—the subject of race and racial discrimination.

For many, the mere mention of the word—or even descriptions of the various races that make up our society—is divisive, setting us apart, setting neighbor against neighbor. The truth is that most Americans of different races are not neighbors—they tend to work and live and study apart. They do so because of a long history, and without an understanding of that history, of our past, there can be no common understanding of our present, no common understanding of the role race has played and continues to play in creating an already divided society, and no common understanding of the common effort required of us all.

Over fifty years ago, in April 1954, Martin Luther King Jr. preached his first sermon as the new pastor of Montgomery's Dexter Avenue Baptist Church. He was twenty-five years old. One month later, on May 17, 1954, the United States Supreme Court unanimously declared in *Brown v. Board of Education* that segregated schools violated the Constitution's promise of equal protection. As we commemorated the fiftieth anniversary of that landmark decision, it is easy to cast a cynical eye on the status of school desegregation in America today—or the sorry state of race relations—and minimize the significance of *Brown*. That is a grave mistake, for *Brown,* by destroying segregation's legality, gave a nonviolent army the power to destroy segregation's morality as well.

Thus it is no coincidence that in 2004 we also celebrated the fortieth anniversary of the passage of the 1964 Civil Rights Act—the most sweeping civil rights legislation before or since, and our democracy's finest hour. So 2004, as we have commemorated these anniversaries, was a time to examine our present in relation to our past. And, as we prepare for and engage in national elections, 2004 was a time for an examination of our present in relation to our future.

We look back on the years between *Brown* and the passage of the 1964 Civil Rights Act with some pride.

Martin Luther King's first national address was at a 1957 Prayer Pilgrimage on the third anniversary of *Brown* at the Lincoln Memorial.

In 1963 alone, the year that King—fresh from the battlefields of Birmingham—told the nation of his dream at the March on Washington, there were more than ten thousand demonstrations against racism. King was the most famous and best known of the modern movement's personalities, but it was a people's movement. It produced leaders of its own, but it relied not on the noted but the nameless, not on the famous but the faceless. It didn't wait for commands from afar to begin a campaign against injustice. It saw wrong and acted against it; it saw evil and brought it down.

Those were the days when women and men of all races and creeds worked together in the cause of civil rights. Those were the days when good music was popular and popular music was good. Those were the days when the president picked the Supreme Court and not the other way around. Those were the days when we had a war on poverty, not a war on the poor. Those were the days when patriotism was a reason for open-eyed disobedience, not an excuse for blind allegiance. Those were the days when the news media really was "fair and balanced" and not just stenographers for the powerful.

But those were not "the good old days."

In those days, "[t]he law, the courts, the schools, and almost every institution . . . favored whites. This was white supremacy."[1]

Martin Luther King described it in 1962. He said then:

When you have seen vicious mobs lynch your mothers and fathers at will and drown your sisters and brothers at whim; when you have seen hate-filled policemen curse, kick and even kill your black brothers and sisters; when you see the vast majority of your twenty million Negro brothers smothering in an airtight cage of poverty in the midst of an affluent society; when you suddenly find your tongue twisted and your speech stammering as you seek to explain to your six-year-old daughter why she can't go to the public amusement park that has just been advertised on television, and see tears welling up in her eyes when she is told that Funtown is closed to colored children, and see ominous clouds of inferiority beginning to form in her little mental sky, and see her beginning to distort her personality by developing an unconscious bitterness toward white people; when you have to concoct an answer for a five-year-old son who is asking: "Daddy, why do white people treat colored people so mean?" . . . when you are harried by day and haunted by night by the fact that you are a Negro, living constantly on tip-toe stance, never quite knowing what to expect next, and are plagued with inner fears and outer resentments; when you are forever fighting a degenerating sense of 'nobodiness'—then, you will understand.[2]

In those days, you would understand that most southern blacks could not vote. They attended inadequate, segregated schools, if they went at all, and many attended only a few months each year. Most could not hope to gain an education beyond high school. Most worked as farmers or semiskilled laborers. Few owned the land they farmed or even the homes in which they lived.

This was a massive system of racial preferences, a vast affirmative action plan for whites—enforced by law and terror. It had one name and one aim: to crush the human development of a whole population. It began with slave-catching in Africa, and it continues on to the present day. Only by acknowledging the name, nature, and scope of the problem can we measure the magnitude of our success—and the costs of our failures.

When the Supreme Court announced in May 1955 that the white South could make haste slowly in dismantling segregated schools, I was a year older than Emmett Till. His death three months after *Brown II* was more immediate to me than the Court's decision had been. We were nearly the same age when he was murdered, in Money, Mississippi, for whistling at a white woman. His death and the black newspapers that came into my Pennsylvania home—the *Pittsburgh Courier* and the *Baltimore Afro-American*—had created a great sense of vulnerability and fear of all things southern in my teenaged mind, and when my parents announced in 1957 that we were relocating to Atlanta, I was filled with dread.

Emmett Till's death had frightened me. But in the fall of 1957 a group of black teenagers encouraged me to put that fear aside. These young people—the nine young women and men who integrated Central High School in Little Rock, Arkansas—set a high standard of courage and grace under fire as they dared the mobs who surrounded their school. Here, I thought, is what I hope I can be, if ever the chance comes my way.

The chance to test and prove myself did come my way in 1960, as it came to thousands of other black high school and college students across the South. First through the sit-ins, then in Freedom Rides, and then in the voter registration and political organizing drives in the rural South, we joined an old movement against white supremacy that had deep, strong roots; for many of us young people, however, it was the recent *Brown* decisions that had created the opportunity for us to play active roles, to seize and share leadership in the movement for social justice.

Brown was the movement's greatest legal victory. It changed the legal status of black Americans, and ironically made it possible to challenge the established movement's narrow reliance on legal action. As Richard Kluger has written: "Not until the Supreme Court acted in 1954 did the nation acknowledge *it had been blaming the black man for what it had done to him.* His sentence to second class citizenship had been commuted; the quest for meaningful equality—equality in fact as well as in law—had begun."[3]

I believe in an integrated America—jobs, homes, and schools. I believe in it enough to have spent most of my life in its elusive pursuit. I think it is a legal, moral, and political imperative for America—a matter of elemental justice, simple right waged against historical wrong. I not only have spent most of my life in the cause of integration, but in 1947—when I was seven years old—I was also a plaintiff in a lawsuit in rural Pennsylvania against segregated schools. It never came to trial. The school board had segregated schools by giving students achievement tests that all blacks failed and all whites passed, but when the two dumb sons of the local white political boss failed the test, they closed the black school, and all of Lincoln University Village's children went to a one-room school together.

Last year I visited Berea College in Kentucky, opened by abolitionists as an integrated school in 1855. It was closed by the Civil War, but opened again in 1866 with 187 students—96 blacks and 91 whites. It dared to provide a rare commodity in the former slave states—an education open to all—blacks and whites, women and men.

One of those early students was my grandfather, James Bond. Like many others, I am the grandson of a slave. My grandfather was born in 1863, in Kentucky; freedom didn't come for him until the Thirteenth Amendment was ratified in 1865. He and his mother were property, like a horse or a chair. As a young girl, his mother had been given away as a wedding present to a new bride, and when that bride became pregnant, her husband—that's my great-grandmother's owner and master—exercised his right to take his wife's slave as his mistress. That union produced two children, one of them my grandfather. At age fifteen, barely able to read and write, he hitched his tuition—a steer—to a rope and walked across Kentucky to Berea College, and the college took him in.

My grandfather belonged to a transcendent generation of black Americans, a generation born into slavery, freed by the Civil War, determined to make their way as free women and men. From Berea, he studied for the ministry, married, and had six children—one of them my father, Horace Mann Bond. My father graduated from Pennsylvania's Lincoln University and earned a doctorate in education from the University of Chicago. For him, too, education was a means to a larger end—the uplift of his people and the salvation of his race. How fitting, then, that he would be asked to help the NAACP in its legal campaign against school segregation—the campaign that culminated in *Brown v. Board of Education*.

There can be no mistake: those fifty years since *Brown* have seen the fortunes of black America advance and retreat, but the decision is always cause for sober celebration, not impotent dismay. We celebrate the brilliant legal minds who were the architects of *Brown v. Board*; we celebrate the brave families who were its plaintiffs; and we celebrate the legal principle that remains its enduring legacy—that, in the words of Chief Justice Earl Warren, "the doctrine of separate but equal has no place."[4]

That the quest for meaningful equality—political and economic equity—remains unfulfilled today is no indictment of past efforts. It is testament to our challenge.

When my grandfather graduated from Berea, in 1892, the college asked him to deliver the commencement address. He said then:

> The pessimist from his corner looks out on the world of wickedness and sin, and blinded by all that is good or hopeful in the condition and progress of the human race, bewails the present state of affairs and predicts woeful things for the future.
>
> In every cloud he beholds a destructive storm, in every flash of lightning an omen of evil, and in every shadow that falls across his path a lurking foe.
>
> He forgets that the clouds also bring life and hope, that lightning purifies the atmosphere, that shadow and darkness prepare for sunshine and growth, and that hardships and adversity nerve the race, as the individual, for greater efforts and grander victories.[5]

"Greater efforts and grander victories." That was the promise made by the generation born in slavery more than 140 years ago. That was the promise made by the generation that won the great world war for democracy six decades ago. That was the promise made by those who brought democracy to America's darkest corners four decades ago, and that is the promise we must all seek to honor today.

We meet as our nation is engaged in an unwise war of occupation in the Persian Gulf, war without reason or necessity, war whose primary rationale morphed from weapons of mass destruction to "weapons-of-mass-destruction-related-program activities," and a retroactive justification of concern for human rights.

The NAACP opposed unilateral war against Iraq, but we are as one with all Americans in supporting our fighting forces. We commend the bravery and sacrifice of our women and men in uniform, who represent all races and faiths. We pray for a swift return of our fighting forces to America's shores and a just and lasting peace at home and abroad.

When Martin Luther King spoke out against the war in Vietnam in 1965, he was revolted at the hypocrisy of America's claims for bringing freedom overseas when blacks enjoyed few freedoms here. War abroad, he said, stole from Americans at home. "The pursuit of widened war," he said in 1966, "has narrowed domestic welfare programs, making the poor, white and Negro, bear the heaviest burdens at the front and at home."[6] How sadly true those words ring today.

We know America's twin towers—freedom and justice—are still standing. It is our job to keep upright what others would weaken and destroy. America is strongest when she is just; she is fiercest when her people are free.

Less than a week after the September 11 attacks, President George W. Bush went to the Washington Islamic Center. Standing in his stocking feet, the president vowed to prevent hate crimes and discrimination against Arabs and Muslims in the wake of the attacks. He renewed this vow on the first anniversary of the attacks. The president's stated goals—retaliation against terrorists abroad and promotion of tolerance at home—are reminiscent of the Double V campaign waged by blacks during World War II, which at the time symbolized victory against fascism abroad and racism at home. With the events of September 11, we realize we have not achieved either victory—not yet against tyranny abroad, not yet against racism here at home. Just as this enemy—terrorism—is more difficult to identify and punish, so is discrimination a more elusive target today. No more do signs read "white" and "colored." The law now requires the voters' booth and schoolhouse door to swing open for everyone. No longer are they closed to those whose skins are black.

But despite impressive increases in the numbers of black people holding public office, despite our ability to sit, eat, ride, vote, and go to school in places that used to bar black faces, in some important ways nonwhite Americans face problems more difficult to attack now than in the years that went before. To mention but one—a most important one—let me quote at length from the October 21, 2004, issue of *The Black Commentator*. They write:

> The bottom fell out of Black wealth accumulation in the deep recession of 2000–2001, a downturn that hurt all ethnic groups, but from which whites and Hispanics rapidly rebounded. Whites recouped their losses from the recession and fattened their holdings by 17 percent between 1996 and 2002. Hispanics boosted their meager household wealth to about $7,900 during that period—still only one eleventh of white households, but almost fully recovering the 27 percent loss they suffered at the turn of the 21st century. Blacks also lost 27 percent of their net worth in 2000–2001, but got back only 5 percent in 2002. These African American losses appear near-permanent, the result of the deindustrialization of the United States—the destruction of the Black blue-collar workforce.[7]

Hispanics, clustered in the low wage service sector, suffered less lasting effects. However, for African Americans, the worst news just keeps on coming, the legacy of slavery and Jim Crow discrimination. As Roderick Harrison, a researcher at the Joint Center for Political and Economic Studies, told the Associated Press: "Wealth is a measure of cumulative advantage or disadvantage. The fact that black and Hispanic wealth is a fraction of white wealth also reflects a history of discrimination."[8]

It is a "reflection" in the American mirror that whites don't want to see, believing in the vast majority that their privilege and wealth has been earned—and at no one else's expense. In truth, as Harvard social demographer Dr. Michael A. Dawson puts it, "The racial structures in the United States continue to this day to produce wealth disparities." Today, these structures are working feverishly to dislodge Blacks from their precarious perches in the middle class. Yet whites remain implacably opposed to engaging in even a discussion of reparations, while continuing to profit from "the inherited gift that keeps on giving." . . .

Surfing through the recession with their assets largely intact, white America pretends that some malady of "culture"—rather than the crimes of a nation—is what holds African Americans back. And some Black fools believe them.

"There were several members of the Congressional Black Caucus who took the position that the racial wealth disparity was due to the misbehavior of Black folks," says Dr. William "Sandy" Darity, recalling events at the 2003 Black Caucus Week, in Washington. Several silly Black lawmakers theorized that wealth disparities could be eliminated if only African Americans would engage in less impulse buying and save more money, said Darity, a Professor of Public Policy Studies, African and African American Studies and Economics at Duke University. He continued: "In fact, if you control for income, the Black savings rate is at least as high as the white savings rate. There is some evidence to suggest that it might be higher."

By Darity's calculations, African Americans would have to go without food, shelter, clothing and all other expenses *en masse* "for well over a decade" to save enough to achieve wealth parity with whites. "So I would say, there is no way that you can catch up by systemic and careful savings. If African Americans saved all of their income—that is, if we didn't eat, pay any bills, but saved every cent of income—we could not close the wealth gap," said the professor, who also teaches economics at the University of North Carolina, Chapel Hill.[9]

So when we are asked why the NAACP doesn't focus on social service, and why we don't surrender to the great tutorial instinct so prominent among blacks in the middle class, to instruct our less fortunate brothers and sisters and their children in the proper way of doing things, we respond that we are an organization that fights racial discrimination. We believe that racial discrimination is a prime reason why the gaps between black and white life chances remain so wide. And we believe that to the degree we are able to close these race-caused gaps, we will see the economic and educational lives of our people increase and their prosperity increase. We believe when our people have social justice, they won't need social service.

The NAACP, whose board I chair, has always been nonpartisan, but that doesn't mean we're noncritical.

The passage of the Civil Rights Act of 1964 and the Voting Rights Act of 1965 marked the beginning of the dependence of one of our political parties on the politics of racial division to win elections and gain power. By playing the race card in election after election, they've appealed to the dark underside of American culture, to the minority of Americans who reject democracy and equality.

They preach racial neutrality and practice racial division. They celebrate Martin Luther King and misuse his message. Their idea of reparations is to give war criminal Jefferson Davis a pardon. Their idea of a pristine environment is a parking lot before the lines are painted in. Their idea of equal rights is the American and Confederate flags flying side by side. Their idea of compassion is to ask the guests at the millionaires' banquet if they want an extra helping and a second dessert. They've tried to patch the leaky economy—and every other domestic problem—with duct tape and plastic sheets. They write a new Constitution for Iraq and try to rewrite the Constitution here at home. They draw their most rabid supporters from the Taliban wing of American politics.

Now they to want write bigotry back into the Constitution; they want to make one group of Americans outsiders to our common heritage. They want to do what has never been done before—to amend the Constitution to create a group of second-class citizens. The Constitution is the last hope of freedom; it cannot become a carrier of prejudice and intolerance.

And what about the opposition party? Too often they're not an opposition; they're an amen corner. With some notable exceptions, they have been absent without leave from this battle for America's soul. When one party is shameless, the other party cannot afford to be spineless.

Our economic imbalances not only mean difficult times for many, they also undermine democratic values. The danger is that plutocracy will prevail over democracy, and the free market will rule over the free citizen.

The reason for the current deficit and the vanished surplus can be placed squarely on the tax giveaway to the rich. To make up for just the initial tax cuts, we would have to cut spending by five billion dollars five days a week for over a year. That was the whole point—to further enrich the already wealthy and to starve the government, making it unable to meet human needs, signing a death warrant for social programs for decades to come.

The nation lost more than 2.5 million jobs between 2001 and 2004. In George W. Bush we had a president who talked like a populist and governed for the privileged. We were promised compassionate conservatism; instead, we got crony capitalism. We had an attorney general, John Ashcroft, who is a cross between J. Edgar Hoover and Jerry Falwell. We had a senate majority leader, Bill Frist, who voted consistently against labor rights, against civil rights, and against women's rights. And he's the one who replaced the bad guy!

Only one senator—Russell Feingold of Wisconsin—voted against the first hastily prepared and ill-considered terrorism measure proposed after September 11. He explained his vote this way: "If we lived in a country that allowed the police to search our home at any time for any reason; if we lived in a country that allowed the government to open your mail, eavesdrop on your phone conversations, or intercept your email communications; if we lived in a country that allowed the government to hold people indefinitely in jail based on what they write or think, or based on mere suspicion that they are up to no good, then the government would no doubt discover and arrest more terrorists. But that probably would not be a country in which we would want to live."[10]

Nor do we want to live in a country that permits infiltration and surveillance of religious and political organizations. Yet, the new FBI guidelines proposed by J. Edgar Ashcroft do just that. Just as we remember J. Edgar Hoover, we remember his counterintelligence program, called COINTELPRO. And whose intelligence did they want to counter? In a program called "Racial Matters", the FBI tried to disrupt the civil rights movement. They tried to smear Martin Luther King Jr. They not only wanted him discredited, they wanted him dead. They threatened him with the release of damaging information if he did not take his own life. We thought we had put a stop to Hoover's programs of spies and lies in the 1970s after these abuses were exposed. Now, under the guise of fighting terrorism, the FBI is going back to spying on law-abiding citizens.

War and fear often cause hasty mistakes, costly both in economic and human terms. We need to remember what we are fighting for. In the summer of 1918, on the eve of America's entry into World War I, one of the NAACP's founders, W. E. B. Du Bois, urged blacks to "forget our special grievances and close ranks shoulder to shoulder with our fellow citizens and the allied nations that are fighting for democracy."[11] The criticism he faced then was immediate and loud. He quickly reversed his position and realized then—as we must now—that calls for a retreat from our rights are always wrong. He understood then—as we must now—that when wars are fought to save democracy, the first casualty is usually democracy itself. That is why we must be vigilant against the steady erosion of American values and the basic rights we cherish.

We ought to remember the words of President Theodore Roosevelt, who said in 1918, "To announce there must be no criticism of the President, or to stand by the President, right or wrong, is not only unpatriotic and servile, but is morally treasonous to the American public."[12] And the words of Ohio senator Robert Taft, who said two weeks after Pearl Harbor had been attacked: "I believe there can be no doubt that criticism in time of war is essential to the maintenance of any kind of democratic government."[13]

The FBI and the CIA kept files on me in the 1960s; they may be keeping files on me today. While they were watching and following and photographing and wiretapping those of us working nonviolently in the freedom movement, a wave of white terrorism was sweeping across the South unchallenged. It has taken forty years and more to bring a pitiful few of those terrorists to justice. And it has taken forty years and more to put in place a framework for civil rights enforcement, now threatened on several fronts.

The administration's judicial nominees are hostile to the basic principles of civil rights law and civil rights enforcement. They oppose the core constitutional principle of "one person, one vote." They've supported federal funding for racially discriminatory schools. They've tried to rewrite antidiscrimination laws from the bench, and they've eroded congressional authority to pass laws that protect civil rights.[14] Among those staffing the Voting Rights Section of the Justice Department is a lawyer who helped run the purge of Florida's voting rolls before the 2000 election. Another is a former senior counsel for the misnamed Center for Equal Opportunity, founded to fight laws requiring racial justice in America.

Organizations dedicated to overturning the gains of the civil rights movement are now dictating public policy. They will not rest until white preferences are restored. Their very names are fraudulent, and their aims are frightening. They have already stolen our vocabulary, and they want to steal the just spoils of our righteous war. Sophisticated and well funded, over the past decade they have won several victories in the plot to dismantle justice and fair play. For more than a decade, they have waged ideological war against moderation in the federal judiciary and then squealed the loudest when the extremists they support are rejected. Now they have ascended to unprecedented positions of power within the federal government.

There is a right wing conspiracy, and it controls the administration, both houses of Congress, much of the judiciary, and a major portion of the media. They want to make any government consideration of race illegal, and thereby do away with our rights and much of the legacy of the civil rights movement, including affirmative action. They say they believe in a color-blind America, where race doesn't count. Sadly, in America, equal opportunity is color-coded. What they really want is a color-free America, and they think they'll get there by not counting race. But as long as race counts, we've got to count race.

Affirmative action was created to fight what Supreme Court Justice Sandra Day O'Connor has called "the unhappy persistence of both the practice and the lingering effects of racial discrimination."[15] Affirmative action has been under attack not because it has failed but because it has succeeded. It created the sizeable middle class that now constitutes one-third of all black Americans. In the late 1960s the wages of black women in the textile industry tripled. From 1970 to 1990 the number of black police officers, lawyers, and doctors doubled. Black electricians and college students tripled; black bank tellers more than quadrupled.

Its opponents keep telling us affirmative action carries a stigma that attaches to all blacks—as if none of us ever felt any stigma in the days before affirmative action was born. Why don't they ever make this argument about the millions of whites who got into Harvard or Yale because Dad was an alumnus? Or what about those who got a good job because Dad was president of the company—or president of the United States? You never see them walking around, heads held low, moaning that everyone in the executive washroom is whispering about how they got their jobs. Most of our elite professions have long been the near-exclusive preserve of white men. I seriously doubt if a single one of these men is suffering low self-esteem because he knows—everyone knows—his race and gender helped him win his job.

Look at it this way—it is the fourth quarter in a football game between the black team and the white team. The white team is ahead 145 to 3. They own the ball, the uniforms, the field, the goalposts, and the referees. All of a sudden the white quarterback, who feels badly about things that happened before he entered the game, turns to the black team and says: "Hey fellows, can't we just play fair?" Of course, playing fair in this game is double-speak for freezing the status quo in placing, permanently fixing, inequality as part of American life.

Affirmative action is not about preferential treatment for blacks; rather, it is about removing the preferential treatment whites have received for centuries, giving equal treatment to people denied equality in the present and the past. Without it, both white and blue collars around black necks would shrink, with a huge depressive effect on black income, education, home ownership, and life chances.

In 2003 the Supreme Court upheld the legality of affirmative action in two cases from the University of Michigan.[16] In doing so, the Court gave legal sanction to what we knew to be morally, socially and educationally correct.

As quiet as it is kept by those who declare themselves "colorblind" in his name, Martin Luther King supported affirmative action. He said in 1963: "It is impossible to create a formula for the future which does not take into account that society has been *doing something special against the Negro* for hundreds of years. How then can he be absorbed into the mainstream of American life if we do not do *something special for him now,* in order to balance the equation and equip him to compete on a just and equal basis?"[17]

President Bush chose Martin Luther King's birthday in 2004 to unilaterally elevate Charles Pickering to the federal bench—Pickering's hostility to civil rights and leniency to cross burners notwithstanding.[18] President Bush chose Martin Luther King's birthday in 2003 to announce that, even though he admits society continues to do something special *against* racial minorities, his administration would not do anything special *for them*; he opposed the University of Michigan's efforts to promote diversity among its student body.[19] That is so ironic—after all, the Bush family has enjoyed three generations of preferences at Yale University: preferences for first daughter, for her father before her, and for his grandfather before him.

The Bush Administration liked to use Secretary of State Colin Powell and National Security Adviser and later Secretary of State Condoleezza Rice as human shields against any criticism of its record on civil rights. After all, Bush is proud of boasting, his administration is more diverse than any in history—except the one that preceded it. But the day after the administration filed its brief in the Michigan cases, Rice issued a rare statement on a domestic issue, saying, "[I]t is appropriate to use race as one factor among others in achieving a diverse student body."[20] And Rice has acknowledged that affirmative action was responsible for her employment at Stanford University.[21] Powell, for his part, has long been an outspoken advocate for affirmative action and specifically said he hoped the University of Michigan would prevail in court.[22]

The Civil War that freed my grandfather was fought over whether blacks and whites shared a common humanity. Less than ten years after it ended, the nation chose sides with the losers and agreed to continue black repression for almost a hundred years. The freed slaves found that their former masters once again controlled their fate.

American slavery was a human horror of staggering dimensions, a crime against humanity. The profits it produced endowed great fortunes and enriched generations, and its dreadful legacy embraces all of us today. As John Hope Franklin writes:

> *All* whites . . . benefited from American slavery. *All* blacks had no rights they could claim as their own. *All* whites, including the vast majority who owned no slaves, were not only encouraged but authorized to exercise dominion over *all* slaves, thereby adding to the system of control. . . . [E]ven poor whites benefited from the legal advantage they enjoyed over *all* blacks as well as from the psychological advantage of having a group beneath them. . . .
>
> Most living Americans do have a connection with slavery. They have inherited the preferential advantage, if they are white, or the loathsome disadvantage, if they are black; and these positions are virtually as alive today as they were in the 19th century.[23]

Two hundred and forty-six years of slavery were followed by a hundred years of state-sanctioned discrimination, reinforced by public and private terror, ending only after a protracted struggle in 1965. Thus, in 2004, it has been only a short thirty-nine years that *all* black Americans have been allowed to exercise the full rights of citizens, only thirty-nine years since legal segregation was ended nationwide, only thirty-nine years since the right to register and vote was universally guaranteed, only thirty-nine years since the protections of the law and Constitution were officially extended to all. And now some are telling us those thirty-nine years have been enough. To believe that is the victory of hope over experience. To believe that is the victory of self-delusion over common sense.

The removal, over the decades since the 1960s, of the more blatant forms of American apartheid, has made it too easy for too many to believe today that all forms of discrimination have disappeared. Opinion polls reveal that a majority of whites believe that racial discrimination is no longer a major impediment for people of color. In one study, 75 percent of whites said that blacks face no discrimination in obtaining jobs or housing even as such discrimination becomes more severe. In another poll, two-thirds of whites said they were "personally satisfied" with the way black Americans are treated in society. Polls show that most white Americans believe equal educational opportunity exists right now, even as our schools become more segregated, not less, across the country.[24]

The successful strategies of the modern movement for civil rights were litigation, organization, mobilization, and coalition, all aimed at creating a national constituency for civil rights. Sometimes the simplest of ordinary, everyday acts—sitting at a lunch counter, going to a new school, applying for a marriage license—can have unforeseen results. It can change the universe, it can challenge the way we think and act. The movement marched and picketed and protested against state-sanctioned segregation, and brought that system crashing to its knees. Today's times require no less, and in fact insist on more. Now as we find ourselves refighting old battles we thought were already won and facing new problems we have barely begun to acknowledge, we ought to take heart. If there is more to be done, we have more to do it with, much more than those who came before us and who brought us along this far.

As a nation, we have a history of aggressive self-help and voluntarism, in churches and civic clubs and neighborhood associations, providing scholarships, helping the needy, promoting social service. But volunteering for social service alone does little to change the status quo. Creating change requires challenging power. It is never enough *just* to ignore evil. It is never enough *just* to do good. It is never enough *just* to feed the hungry and house the homeless, as commendable as these deeds are.

It may be helpful to think about our task in this way: Two men are sitting by a river and see, to their great surprise, a helpless baby floating by. They rescue the child, and to their horror, another baby soon comes floating down the stream. When that child is pulled to safety, another baby comes along. As one man plunges into the river a third time, the other rushes upstream. "Come back!" yells the man in the water. "We must save this baby!"

"You save it," the other yells back. "I'm going to find out who is throwing babies in the river and I'm going to make them stop!"

I recently heard Professor Lani Guinier say that minorities are like the canaries that miners used to carry to warn them when the underground air was becoming too toxic to breathe.[25] But too many people want to put gas masks on the canaries instead of eliminating the poison in the air. Too many want to put life preservers on the babies instead of stopping them from being thrown into a treacherous, dangerous flood.

We have a long and honorable tradition of social justice in this country. It still sends forth the message that when we act together we can overcome. And we have a revitalized NAACP prepared for the challenges that lie ahead.[26] We have no permanent friends, and no permanent enemies, just permanent interests, and those interests are justice and freedom. It is a serious mistake—both tactical and moral—to believe this is a fight that must be waged by black Americans alone. That has never been so in centuries past; it ought not to be so in the century unfolding now. Black, yellow, red, and white—all are needed in this fight. All of us are implicated in the continuation of inequality—it will require our common effort to bring it to an end.

A civil rights agenda for this new century must include continuing to litigate, to organize, to mobilize, forming coalitions of the caring and concerned, joining ranks against the comfortable, the callous and the smug. It must include:

> fighting discrimination, wherever it raises its ugly head—in the halls of government, in corporate suites, or in the streets.
> ensuring every citizen registers and votes and guaranteeing the irregularities, suppression, nullification, and outright theft of black votes that happened on Election Day 2000 never, ever happen again.

In the pre-1965 one-party south, voter intimidation, often lethal, was the exclusive handiwork of the nearly all-white Democratic Party. When he signed the Voting Rights Act into law, President Lyndon Johnson was prescient when he told an aide, "We are delivering the South to the Republicans for a generation."[27] After the act's passage and initial application, as resistant whites fled the Democratic Party and found a sympathetic home in the Republican Party and newly enfranchised blacks joined the Democrats, these menacing and threatening practices became the exclusive province of Republicans. The NAACP and People for the American Way released a report before the 2004 election that documented these practices over decades, up to and including the present day.[28] Those opposed to voter rights have posted armed guards and real and make-believe policemen at the polls. They have told voters they could cast their votes on alternative days, even after the election was over. They have demanded forms of identification not required by law. They have told voters that outstanding warrants or unpaid utility bills would prevent them from voting. They have said immigration officials would haunt the polls, checking on voters' immigration status. They have constructed phony purge lists that included the names of longtime legitimate voters. They have loosed the FBI and state police on elderly voters. They have set up so-called "ballot security" and "ballot integrity" programs, based on the racist presumption that minority voters are inveterate Election Day cheaters, and they have harassed and intimidated those voters at will.

John Ashcroft owed his political success and eventual demise in Missouri to opposition to civil rights.[29] As governor, he vetoed bills that would have promoted voter registration in St. Louis, a black political stronghold.[30] As attorney general, Ashcroft launched the "Voting Access and Integrity Initiative" in 2002.

The emphasis is on "integrity," which means intimidation of minority voters in the guise of preventing fraud in the voting process.[31] Now the Department of Homeland Security has even gotten into the act, attempting this month to ban a nonpartisan voter registration operation outside a naturalization ceremony in Florida.[32]

We must demand fair treatment for people with HIV/AIDS, especially for people of color. This disease strikes African American women more than any other group. It doesn't happen to "others"—it happens to all of us.

We must demand that "criminal justice" cease being an oxymoron. We know race, more than any other factor, determines who is arrested, who is tried and for what crime, who receives what length of sentence, and who receives the ultimate punishment—and we are determined that it stop.

And we must demand that the unceasing open season on our people by police come to a stop, and the criminals in uniform be punished.

And we must ensure that our children—in inner city and suburban and rural schools—receive the best education, an education that prepares them for the century just begun.

There is much more—none of it easy work, but we have never wished our way to freedom. Instead, we have always worked our way.

By the year 2050 blacks and Hispanics together will be 40 percent of the nation's population.[33] Wherever there are others who share our condition or concerns, we must make common cause with them. In the NAACP, we believe colored people come in all colors—anyone who shares our values is more than welcome. The growth in immigration and the emergence of new and vibrant populations of people of color hold great promise and great peril. The promise is that the coalition for justice has grown larger and stronger, as new allies join the fight. The peril comes from real fears that our common foes will find ways to separate and divide us. It doesn't make sense if blacks and Latinos fight over which group has less power; together we can constitute a mighty force for right.

Racial justice, economic equality, and world peace—these were the themes that occupied King's life; they ought to occupy ours today.

We live in a small world. If we could shrink the earth's population to a village of 100 people, with existing ratios remaining the same, the world would look like this:

there would be 57 Asians, 21 Europeans, 14 from the Western Hemisphere, both north and south, and 8 Africans.

52 of the 100 would be female. 70 would be nonwhite. 70 would not be Christians.

6 of the 100 people would own 59 percent of all the wealth in the world and all 6 of these would be from the United States.

80 of the 100 would live in substandard housing. 70 would be unable to read or write. 50 would suffer from malnutrition.

Only 1 would own a computer. Only 1 would have a college education.

Looking at the world in this way, we are reminded of our mutual dependence and mutual responsibilities.[34]

We know our world and our lives changed on September 11. We don't know how much even yet. But we know we have a job to do at home as much as abroad. When I started working four decades ago, there were five workers paying into the national retirement system for every retiree. I can't possibly know who my five were, but their names could easily have been Carl, Ralph, Bob, Steve, and Bill. When I retire, there will only be three workers paying into the retirement system—their names could easily be Tamika, Maria, and Jose. We need to provide them with the best schools, the best health care, the best jobs, and the strongest protections against discrimination we possibly can.

Notes

1. John Hope Franklin and Alfred A. Moss Jr., *From Slavery to Freedom: A History of African Americans,* 8th ed. (New York: Alfred A. Knopf, 2000), 155.

2. Martin Luther King Jr., Letter to Alabama clergymen, Birmingham, April 16, 1963, http://www.africa.upenn.edu/Articles_Gen/Letter_Birmingham.html (accessed June 26, 2007).

3. Richard Kluger, *Simple Justice* (New York: Alfred A. Knopf, 1976), 748, emphasis added.

4. *Brown v. Board of Education,* 347 U.S. 483, 495 (1954).

5. James Bond, "Commencement Address," *Berea College Reporter* (June 1892).

6. Martin Luther King Jr., "The Casualties of the War in Vietnam," public speech, Los Angeles, February 25, 1967, http://www.stanford.edu/group/King/publications/speeches/unpub/670225-001_The_Casualties_of_the_War_in_Vietnam.htm (accessed June 26, 2007).

7. This section can be traced back to an Associated Press article: Genero C. Armas, "Wealth Gap Grows for Minorities." *CBS News,* October 18, 2004, http://www.cbsnews.com/stories/2004/10/18/national/main649831.shtml (accessed June 26, 2007).

8. Ibid.

9. Editorial, "Wealth of a (White) Nation: Blacks Sink Deeper in Hole," *Black Commentator,* no. 110, October 21, 2004, http://www.blackcommentator.com/110/110_cover_white_wealth.html (accessed June 26, 2007).

10. Senate, Russell Feingold of Wisconsin speaking against *The Uniting and Strengthening America by Providing Appropriate Tools Required To Intercept and Obstruct Terrorism (USA Patriot) Act of 2001,* H.R. 3162, *Congressional Record* (October 25, 2001), 147, no. 144, S11020, http://frwebgate2.access.gpo.gov/cgi-bin/

waisgate.cgi?WAISdocID=27239037012+0+0+0&WAISaction=retrieve (accessed June 27, 2007).

11. W. E. B. Du Bois, "Close Ranks," *The Crisis* (July 1918): 111.

12. Theodore Roosevelt, Editorial, *Kansas City Star,* May 7, 1918, http://www
.theodoreroosevelt.org/life/quotes.htm (accessed January 9, 2009).

13. Robert Taft, public speech to the Executive Club, Chicago, December 19, 1941, in *The Papers of Robert A. Taft,* ed. Clarence E. Wunderlin (Kent: Kent State University Press, 2001), 2:303.

14. Civilrights.org, Fact Sheet, November 8, 2002, "The 2002 Election and the Threats to Civil Rights in the 108th Congress," http://www.civilrights.org/library/fact-sheets/the-2002–election-and-the-threats-to-civil-rights-in-the-108th-congress.html (accessed January 9, 2009). Cf. list of nominations during Bush Administration at the U.S. Justice Department Web site: http://www.usdoj.gov/olp/nominations.htm (accessed June 27, 2007); Kwame Holman, "Race and Justice," *Online NewsHour,* May 8, 2001, http://www.pbs.org/newshour/bb/race_relations/jan-june01/justice_05–08.html (accessed June 27, 2007); Jim Lobe, "Civil Rights Groups Blast Bush Court Nominee," *OneWorld on Yahoo News,* October 27, 2003, http://us.oneworld.net/article/view/71337/1/> (accessed June 27, 2007); Charles Babington, "Acrimony over Bush Judicial Nominations Resurfaces," *Washington Post,* May 3, 2006, http://www.washingtonpost.com/wp-dyn/content/article/2006/05/02/AR2006050201536.html (accessed June 27, 2007).

15. *Adarand Constructors, Inc. v. Peña,* 515 U.S. 200 (1995).

16. *Gratz et al. v. Bollinger et al.* 539 U.S. 244 (2003); *Grutter v. Bollinger et al.* 539 U.S. 306 (2003) 288 F.3d 732.

17. Martin Luther King Jr., *Why We Can't Wait* (New York: Harper and Row, 1963), 146, emphasis added.

18. The White House, press release, "President's Statement on Appointing Judge Charles Pickering to Fifth Circuit Appeals Court," January 16, 2004, http://www
.whitehouse.gov/news/releases/2004/01/20040116–19.html (accessed June 27, 2007).

19. The White House, remarks, "President Bush Discusses Michigan Affirmative Action Case," January 15, 2003, http://www.whitehouse.gov/news/releases/2003/01/20030115–7.html (accessed July 1, 2007).

20. Neil A. Lewis, "Bush Adviser Backs Use of Race in College Admissions," *The New York Times,* January 18, 2003.

21. "Dr. Rice said, 'I am myself a beneficiary of a Stanford initiative that took affirmative action seriously, that took a risk in taking a young PhD from the University of Denver,' referring to her arrival on the campus in 1981" (Stuart Silverman, "Rice Considered a Centrist on Affirmative Action at Stanford," *Los Angeles Times,* January 25, 2003).

22. On the Michigan case: David Firestone, "From 2 Bush Aides, 2 Positions on Affirmative Action," *New York Times,* January 20, 2003. See also Nicholas Lehmann,

"The Three-Cushion Shot That Won Colin Powell's Support for Affirmative Action in Higher Education," *Journal of Blacks in Higher Education* 26 (Winter 1999–2000): 102–4.

23. John Hope Franklin, letter to the editor, *Duke University Chronicle,* March 29, 2001, http://media.www.dukechronicle.com/media/storage/paper884/ news/2001/03/29/UndefinedSection/Letter.Horowitzs.Diatribe.Contains.Histori- cal.Inaccuracies-1454140.shtml (accessed July 1, 2007), emphasis added.

24. Erica Frankenberg, Chungmei Lee, and Gary Orfield, *A Multiracial Society with Segregated Schools: Are We Losing the Dream?* (Cambridge, Mass.: Harvard Uni- versity Civil Rights Project, 2003). Gallup Poll News Service, "Race Relations," Opin- ion Poll, January 4, 1997, to February 28, 1997, http://brain.gallup.com/documents/ questionnaire.aspx?STUDY=GNS97–RACE> (accessed July 2, 2007); Charlotte Astor, "Gallup Poll: Progress in Black/White Relations, but Race Is Still an Issue," in "Toward One America: A National Conversation on Race," in "Commentary: Race in America: Perceptions and Parameters," *U.S. Information Agency* 2, no. 3 (1997), http://usinfo.state.gov/journals/itsv/0897/ijse/gallup.htm (accessed July 2, 2007; site now discontinued).

25. Lani Guinier and Gerald Torres, *The Miner's Canary: Enlisting Race, Resisting Power, Transforming Democracy,* new ed. (Cambridge, Mass.: Harvard University Press, 2003), 11.

26. A 1993 leadership study by Brakeley, John Price Jones, Inc., showed 75 per- cent of blacks believed the NAACP was the leader among groups with civil rights, social justice, and race relations agendas. In this study, 75 percent of all respondents believed the NAACP adequately represented the black community. An October 1995 *U.S. News and World Report* poll reported 90 percent of blacks supported the NAACP. In an April 1998 poll conducted by the Foundation for Ethnic Understand- ing, 81 percent of blacks reported a favorable opinion of the NAACP. The NAACP is profoundly democratic: "Nationally, the NAACP (of all black civil rights/political organizations) is governed by its individually based membership" (Adolph Reed, *Class Notes* [New York: The New Press, 2000]).

27. Clay Risen, "How the South Was Won," *The Boston Globe,* March 5, 2006, http://www.boston.com/news/globe/ideas/articles/2006/03/05/how_the_south_ was_won/?page=1 (accessed July 3, 2007).

28. People For the American Way Foundation and the National Association for the Advancement of Colored People, *The Long Shadow of Jim Crow; Voter Intimida- tion and Suppression in American Today,* available for download at http://site.pfaw .org/site/PageServer?pagename=report_the_long_shadow_of_jim_crow (accessed January 9, 2009).

29. OnTheIssues.org, "John Ashcroft on Civil Rights," http://www.ontheissues .org/Celeb/John_Ashcroft_Civil_Rights.htm (accessed July 4, 2007).

30. Institute for Public Accuracy, "New Concern of Ashcroft Record: Discrimina-

tory Voter Registration," press release, January 15, 2001, http://www.accuracy.org/newsrelease.php?articleId=751 (accessed July 4, 2007).

31. Attorney General John Ashcroft, Prepared remarks, Voting Integrity Symposium, October 8, 2002, http://www.usdoh.gov/archive/ag/speeches/2002/100802b allotintegrity.htm (accessed July 4, 2007).

32. Harold Meyerson, "Blocking the Latin Ballot?" *Washington Post*, September 22, 2004, http://www.washingtonpost.com/wp-dyn/articles/A40122–2004Sep21 .html (accessed July 4, 2007).

33. Jennifer Cheeseman Day, "National Population Projections," *U.S. Census Bureau*, http://www.census.gov/population/www/pop-profile/natproj.html (accessed July 4, 2007); U.S. Census Bureau News, press release, "Census Bureau Projects Tripling of Hispanic and Asian Populations in 50 Years; Non-Hispanic Whites May Drop To Half of Total Population," March 18, 2004, http://www.census.gov/Press -Release/www/releases/archives/population/001720.html (accessed July 4, 2007).

34. David J. Smith, *If the World Were a Village* (Hong Kong: Wing King Tony Company, Ltd. 2002).

26

Reflections on America's Academic Achievement Gap

A Fifty-Year Perspective

Freeman A. Hrabowski III

The fifty years since *Brown* represent essentially my lifetime so far. In fact, I was three years old when the decision was rendered and started kindergarten that September, at age four. As we look at the developments after *Brown,* much of the substantive progress began almost ten years later, in the early to mid-1960s, when a number of us went to college and when my university, the University of Maryland, Baltimore County, was founded. Consequently, while most of our students can relate to this period as history, many of us see it as our story.

The following quotation from Henry Louis Gates captures the thinking of many African Americans, and others, about the status of blacks after decades of progress. (While Gates's point of reference is the death of Dr. King, we know that the *Brown* decision is considered one of the precursors of the civil rights movement, of which Dr. King is the most visible symbol.)

> When I was growing up in the fifties, I could never have imagined that one of Harvard's most respected departments would be a Department of Afro-American Studies and that twenty professors would be teaching here at the turn of the century. Our experience at Harvard is just one instance of a much larger phenomenon. Since the death of Dr. Martin Luther King in 1968, individual African Americans have earned positions higher within white society than any person black or white could have dreamed possible in the segregated 1950s. And this is true in national and local government, in the military and in business, in medicine and education, on TV and in film. Virtually anywhere you look in America today, you'll find black people. . . . [W]ho can deny that progress has been made? In fact, since 1968, the black middle class has tripled, as measured by the percentage of families earning $50,000 or more . . . [but] this expanding middle class even now includes only 17 percent of all black Americans. . . . At the same time—and this is the kicker—the percentage of black children who live at or below the poverty line is almost 35 percent, just about what it was on the day that Dr. King was killed. Since 1968, then, two

distinct classes have emerged within Black America: a black middle class with "white money," as my mother used to say, and what some would argue is a self-perpetuating, static black underclass.[1]

The fiftieth anniversary of *Brown* is reason enough to reflect on the decision's significance and the nation's progress since 1954. But the Supreme Court's 2003 ruling on the University of Michigan affirmative action case heightens *Brown*'s importance. That ruling reaffirmed the importance of diversity by allowing the "narrowly tailored use of race in admissions decisions to further a compelling interest in obtaining the educational benefits that flow from a diverse student body."[2]

In the decision, Justice Sandra Day O'Connor issued a powerful statement on the value of diversity, asserting that "In order to cultivate a set of leaders with legitimacy in the eyes of the citizenry, it is necessary that the path to leadership be visibly open to talented and qualified individuals of every race and ethnicity."[3] She also expressed the expectation, however, that "twenty-five years from now, the use of racial preferences will no longer be necessary."[4] This assertion troubles anyone who looks carefully at today's academic achievement gap between minority and white children, and in particular at the reading and math skills of minority children in relationship to the requirements of the nation's No Child Left Behind Act. In fact, half a century after *Brown*, patterns of segregation continue for most black and Latino children, many of whom attend schools that are underfunded, underachieving, and unequal. But even in wealthy school districts, the majority of black and Latino children lag dramatically behind their white classmates.

To assess how far the nation has come since 1954—and to predict how far the nation can progress in the next quarter-century—it may be helpful to look back at the climate and events surrounding and following *Brown*; to consider the influence of these events and *Brown* on both K–12 education and the nation's colleges and universities; to examine where we are today regarding educational opportunity and the academic achievement gap; and finally, to suggest how we can increase the number of minority students who succeed academically, both broadly and at the highest levels. Unlike America in the 1950s and '60s, when the civil rights movement involved primarily African Americans, twenty-first-century America is focused on the challenge of educating not only black and white children, but also millions of other children of color—largely Latino, American Indian, and Asian.

Changes in the Wind: 1950s and 1960s

Writing about the *Brown* decision in his book *Simple Justice,* historian Richard Kluger asserts that "Probably no case ever to come before the nation's highest tribunal affected more directly the minds, hearts, and daily lives of so many Americans."[5] Indeed, the Supreme Court's decision on May 17, 1954, was both a legal and moral formulation overturning its 1896 decision in *Plessy v. Ferguson,* which had given legal legitimacy to the bogus ideas and policies of "separate but equal." This doctrine, the Court asserted, "has no place in the field of public education."[6] Interestingly, the arguments used by the lawyers for the plaintiffs were based largely on interdisciplinary work in the social sciences, rather than simply on legal theory. Through *Brown,* then, the Court not only provided the means by which to rectify decades of educational inequality (reflected, in part, by shameful funding disparities between schools for blacks and whites and irrational commuting requirements imposed on black children), but it also dramatically challenged the nation's conscience. Until that time, some states spent two to three times as much, if not more, on schooling white children. Barely one year later, however, in its follow-up ruling on *Brown,* the Court qualified the mandate it issued in 1954 with its famous "all deliberate speed" stipulation,[7] which had the effects of calling into question the interpretation of its 1954 decision and of slowing school desegregation. In short, those states and local jurisdictions that sought to be defiant now could delay action.

In fact, the *Brown* decisions became precursors of the nation's civil rights movement, leading ultimately to federal legislation insisting on equal opportunities. At times during this turbulent period, progress was stymied by serious, even tragic setbacks—from the 1955 murder of fourteen-year-old Emmett Till in Mississippi and the 1956 expulsion of Autherine Lucy from the University of Alabama (just days after she enrolled as the first black graduate student there), to the 1963 bombing of the Sixteenth Street Baptist Church in my hometown of Birmingham, Alabama, which killed four black girls, and the 1968 assassination of Dr. King in Memphis, Tennessee. At other times, though, progress was steady and clear—from the Montgomery, Alabama, bus boycott in 1955, the federally enforced school desegregation in Little Rock in 1957, and the Birmingham children's march in 1963 in which I participated, to the Civil Rights (1964), Voting Rights (1965), and Fair Housing (1968) Acts.

Reflections on Birmingham

Naturally, my perceptions of this period are heavily influenced by my own background as a "Negro" or "colored" child growing up at the time in Birmingham. In the African American community there, as in other cities and towns, adults worked hard to counter for their children the message from the larger, outside, white world that we were second-class citizens. Nevertheless, I remember inescapable messages reinforcing our second-class status—from schools, water fountains, restaurants, hotels, movie theaters, and amusement parks for

"Whites Only," to seeing only whites as positive role models on television and in positions of responsibility downtown (from businessmen and policemen to even sales clerks). Perhaps no practice was more degrading to me than receiving used, worn books from white schools. These messages had an immeasurable impact on the psyches of young African American children, and the 1954 *Brown* decision took direct aim at segregation's psychological impact. Writing for the Court, Chief Justice Warren asserted that "To separate [black children] from others of similar age and qualifications solely because of their race generates a feeling of inferiority as to their status in the community that may affect their hearts and minds in a way unlikely to be undone."[8]

In response to segregation's psychological harm, the black community of my youth constantly worked to balance the negative messages we received from the outside world—from constructive guidance in the home and neighborhood, to moral lessons taught in the church, to inspirational stories in the black newspapers, to constant encouragement by black teachers who told us we were special. The message we received in our world was that we would have to be twice as good as others in order to overcome life's unfair obstacles. Moreover, for many of the children, academic work took on an added dimension. From our exposure to local leaders like Reverend Fred Shuttlesworth, and to national leaders like Dr. King and Reverend Andrew Young, both of whom came to Birmingham in 1963, when I was twelve, we learned that these leaders were often educated, knowledgeable people, and that knowledge was power. As they prepared the children to march peacefully in protest demonstrations, they served as extraordinary role models, demonstrating their ability to think clearly, speak eloquently, and act confidently. In so doing, they reinforced what our families and teachers had been telling us all our lives—that education makes the difference between success and failure. In the process, many of us became more committed than ever to becoming the best.

Recently, I had dinner in Washington, D.C., with several childhood friends from my neighborhood in Birmingham, including a former director of the International Monetary Fund, a former CEO of a major financial institution in New York, and the former National Security Advisor and Secretary of State Condoleezza Rice. While we may have held different opinions on a variety of issues, what we shared was a common understanding of the impact of growing up in the '50s and '60s in a segregated neighborhood that supported its children and valued education.

My memories of Birmingham in 1963 are vivid. As a ninth-grade student, I listened to adults questioning the idea of encouraging children to march as a tactic in the civil rights struggle. But participate and march we did. My memories of the events that unfolded are particularly clear. I recall seeing big dogs and fire hoses as I led my line of children—singing freedom songs, "Ain't going to let nobody turn me 'round"—with the goal of kneeling on the steps of city hall and praying for our freedom. My heart was pounding, and I have never been more afraid. Before we could reach the steps, however, we were stopped by Birmingham police commissioner "Bull" Connor, who asked me, "What do you want, little Niggra?" As I replied, "We want our freedom," he spat on me, and the police shoved us into the paddy wagons in a moment of confusion. I spent five days of confinement thinking about the meaning of freedom, while constantly supporting the kids for whom I was responsible and worrying about my own personal safety. It was one of the most frightening experiences of my life; yet, we learned many lessons—the importance of group support, what it means to stand up for your beliefs, the power of individual choices.

After being released, I was devastated to learn that I could not return to school. In fact, the local board of education had suspended all children who had participated in demonstrations and used this approach to discourage others from doing so. I distinctly remember worrying that, even as an A student, I might not be able to finish school, or that I might miss so much schoolwork that I would be unable to excel. I will never forget our jubilation when we learned that a federal judge in Atlanta ordered the school system to return the child protesters to school. And so it was that in this community and environment, during tense and often terror-filled times that gripped the nation, my friends and I grew up as children.

Changes in Higher Education

Throughout the 1960s, as integration came slowly to public schools in the South and elsewhere in the country, important changes also were taking place in previously segregated colleges and universities, and the experiences of black students moving into these institutions ranged from peaceful integration to being met with resistance and violence. In recent years, I have spoken at anniversary events marking the desegregation of Clemson University and the medical schools at Duke and Vanderbilt, where the transitions were reasonably smooth. Such experiences were in sharp contrast to the response in 1963 by Alabama governor George Wallace, who, on national television many of us recall, stood defiantly in the doorway, blocking the admission of black students to the University of Alabama in Tuscaloosa.

Just three years later, in 1966, as I entered Hampton University in Virginia, the University of Maryland, Baltimore County (UMBC) opened its doors to approximately seven hundred students—black and white—and became Maryland's first predominantly white postsecondary institution that, from its inception, admitted any student qualified to attend, regardless of race. (Today, in fact, we refer to ourselves as a "historically diverse" university.) Unlike UMBC, however, most of the nation's colleges and universities were founded long before court rulings outlawing segregation. Many of those in the South admitted their first blacks in the early 1960s. Others, like my graduate alma mater, the University of Illinois at Urbana-Champaign, had admitted a few before this period but initiated major desegregation efforts in the mid- to late 1960s. Over time, these efforts have resulted in the movement of substantial numbers of African American college students from historically black colleges and universities (HBCUs). In 1954 the vast majority of black college students were enrolled in HBCUs; by 1980, however, fewer than 20 percent were studying at HBCUs; and today, more than 85 percent are enrolled in predominantly white institutions, and these institutions award more than three-quarters of all bachelor's degrees earned by blacks.[9]

1970s and 1980s

With the influx of black students onto campuses where they had previously been excluded, American colleges and universities began grappling with the challenge of helping these students to succeed. The focus shifted with time from simply admitting these students—what some called a "revolving door" phenomenon—to their academic performance. My own observations and experience as a graduate student at the University of Illinois are illustrative.

In 1968 the university established Project 500, an experiment in affirmative action that presented challenges for both the administration and students. Among the five hundred black undergraduate students admitted, a few thrived academically because of strong backgrounds, but many were not prepared to handle college-level work and therefore struggled simply to pass or left discouraged. In retrospect, it is remarkable that some of these students succeeded, given the university's lack of experience with black students and the students' weak academic preparation. Working with these students as a graduate student helped me to understand what often happens to minorities and others whose academic preparation is significantly below that of most students and in climates that lack successful experience in educating minorities. We find that the environment, or their experience there, often shakes their confidence and leaves them feeling like victims, unable—and sometimes even less motivated—to overcome obstacles.

The UMBC Experience

The UMBC experience over the past several decades is especially instructive. On arriving at UMBC in 1987, two decades after its founding, I found a complicated situation involving the campus's black students, especially those in science and engineering. During my first week as vice provost (on April Fool's Day, in fact) I walked onto the tenth floor of the administration building and found the entire floor occupied by hundreds of black students and television cameras. The students were protesting what they saw as racism on campus. A staff member assured me, though, there was no cause for concern. "Don't worry," she said. "This happens every spring." I immediately thought back to the last time I had seen a major student protest—it had been at Hampton in the 1960s, and I had participated in it. My second thought was that, ironically, I had become "The Administration."

We quickly learned that the primary reason for the protest—beyond a number of obvious racial incidents in the residence halls—was the students' sense of isolation, perhaps resulting, at least in part, from their poor academic performance, especially in science and engineering. When we examined data on black students' grades and retention rates, we found that their mean grade point average was slightly below 2.0, and substantially below those of whites and Asians. In short, many of the black students who expressed disappointment about the campus climate, were, in fact, also not doing well academically. Many simply lacked the academic background needed to succeed—not only in terms of high school preparation, but also study habits, attitudes about course work, and a willingness to accept advice about balancing school work, outside interests, and part-time employment. While the university had been successful in preparing blacks in the social sciences and humanities for graduate programs and especially law school, few black students were succeeding in science and engineering—a national trend. In addition, like other institutions, the university had not developed an adequate support system for these and other students, especially in science and engineering.

We responded to the problem by working with focus groups of faculty, staff, and students, several of whom showed considerable interest in understanding this issue and helped develop strategies for supporting students. We found that many of the challenges that minority science students were experiencing were being experienced by all science students, and that we needed to look carefully at both admission standards and the level of support we were giving students (e.g., tutorial efforts, academic advising, freshman-year experience) in order to improve their performance and increase retention among all students. Within this broader context, and with support from philanthropists Robert and Jane Meyerhoff, we created in 1988 the Meyerhoff Scholars Program. The program has become a national model for excellence and diversity in science and engineering.

Today at UMBC, unlike at most universities, no academic achievement gap exists between minority and white students across disciplines. At other institutions, we find that underrepresented minority students, even those with strong academic preparation, often do not persist at rates similar to those of their white counterparts (often, the research points out, because these students face negative stereotyping and low expectations).[10] UMBC has become a model for what is possible regarding minority high academic achievement, and this is why representatives from other universities, foundations, federal agencies, and companies with interests in this area visit the campus regularly. In fact, *Science* magazine has identified the Meyerhoff Program as one of the nation's leading higher education initiatives for "training minorities and women scientists," specifically citing "institutional leadership" as one of the program's strongest components.[11] That leadership refers broadly to department chairs and leading faculty and staff, in addition to central administration; and the involvement of research faculty with minority undergraduates is precisely what makes UMBC one of the exceptions in the country. In this light, fifty years after *Brown,* the question is how much progress has the nation made in eliminating the achievement gap in schools, colleges, and other areas of society? The results, we find, are mixed.

Fifty Years Later: Where Are We Today?

Unquestionably, changes in American society resulting from *Brown* and other landmark developments of the civil rights movement have made it possible for African Americans to participate freely and fully in all walks of American life. Those changes also have enabled high-achieving blacks to excel and become national leaders—from former secretary of state Colin Powell to Brown University president Ruth Simmons and Johns Hopkins neurosurgeon Ben Carson, for example.

Persistent Disparities

While serious disparities continue to persist between blacks and whites in education, Census Bureau data show that the percentages of African Americans and whites attending school and graduating from high school and college are much higher now than at the time of *Brown,* and that the gap between the two groups has narrowed over time. The percentage of blacks twenty-five years old and over with high school diplomas increased dramatically between 1957 and 2002, from 18 percent to about 80 percent, and the percentage of whites the same age earning high school diplomas increased from 43 percent to almost 90 percent.[12] But high school completion rates are only one measure of achievement. Perhaps an even more important question to ask is how well prepared today are minority students who are graduating from high school? Unfortunately, the answer is not encouraging. The National Assessment of Educational Progress report showed heartening gains by African American schoolchildren in the 1970s and early 1980s and a narrowing of the achievement gap, but by the late 1980s, that gap had stopped narrowing.[13] Most alarming, in the nation's high schools today, the achievement gap is distressingly wide, with African American and Hispanic twelfth graders performing at the same level as white students in eighth grade.

School Resegregation and *No Child Left Behind*

In addition, we are seeing the steady "resegregation" of America's minority school children, particularly African Americans, especially in the nation's urban areas. We know that the majority of children in our country attend schools where most of the children are the same race. Between 85 and 95 percent of the students in many of the largest school districts in the country—New York, Los Angeles, Chicago, Miami, Houston, Washington, D.C., Detroit, Baltimore—are black and Latino children.[14] Georgetown University law professor Sheryll Cashin provides evidence of this disturbing development, even in cities cited as models of desegregation, in her book *The Failures of Integration*:

> Take Charlotte-Mecklenburg [school district], North Carolina, for example. By the early 1980s, the school district had come close to fulfilling a court order to eliminate its system of dual education. . . . By the late 1980s [however], . . . the number of racially identifiable schools began to grow and then in the early 1990s began to accelerate. By 1999, the school system was resegregating rapidly, even though the district's demographics were relatively stable . . . and Mecklenburg County as a whole was more residentially integrated than it had been thirty years earlier. Whereas roughly 19 percent of black students had attended racially identifiable black schools in 1991, by 1996, the count had risen to 23 percent; by 2000, that percentage had risen to 29 percent, and by 2001, the number jumped to 37 percent. In the 2002–2003 school year, fully 48 percent of the black students in the Charlotte-Mecklenburg school system attended racially identifiable black schools.[15]

Commenting on school resegregation more generally, Cashin notes that

> A similar fate befell many, if not most, school districts throughout the country that serve significant numbers of minority children. Black and Latino public school students are now more separated into racially identifiable schools than at any time in the past thirty years. Nowhere are the effects of this retreat more palpable than in the South. Court-ordered desegregation of African American students in the late 1960s and 1970s resulted in the South becoming the region with the most integrated schools. By 1988, the South reached a high point of 43.5 percent of black students attending majority-white schools, up from a mere 0.001 percent in 1954. But by 2000, marking a twelve-year and continuing process of resegregation, only thirty-one percent of black students in the South attended majority-white schools.[16]

In fact, many of the nation's poorest black children live in "'hypersegregation'—a demographer's term for segregation along several dimensions that translate into a deep wall of isolation and concentrated poverty."[17] Such isolation has a profoundly adverse impact on children's education, which was well documented in sociologist James Coleman's famous 1966 study, *Equality of*

Educational Opportunity.[18] Moreover, Abigail Thernstrom, coauthor of *No Excuses: Closing the Racial Gap in Learning,*[19] recently highlighted the implications of the achievement gap among American school children and concluded that the federal government's No Child Left Behind Act falls far short as a remedy for narrowing the gap, "with its unfunded mandates, its tendency to drown schools in data . . . and its dream deadline of 2014 for 100 percent of students to be achieving at the proficient level."[20] Elsewhere, Thernstrom has written:

> Unequal skills and knowledge are the main source of ongoing racial inequality today. And racial inequality is the nation's great unfinished business, the wound that remains unhealed. . . . It's true that, after decades of disgraceful silence in the public square, the federal government has finally addressed the situation. The central aim of the 2001 No Child Left Behind Act is . . . "to close the achievement gap." . . . [But] students radically disengaged from school need radical intervention . . . [and] the standards-based testing and rather weak accountability measures in . . . No Child Left Behind . . . are . . . insufficient steps down the road to closing the gap. More is needed, especially for the country's most disadvantaged youngsters.[21]

According to Cashin, No Child Left Behind "provides more in the way of mandates for testing than it does resources for the most challenged schools to meet the new standards. . . . [T]he Bush administration reneged on its promise to provide an additional $5.8 billion in funding for the poorest schools to meet the act's tough performance requirements."[22] At the very least, closing the achievement gap will require sustained efforts and resources to support new and experienced teacher preparation, strong after-school and summer academic programs, ongoing parental education, and, perhaps most important, a critical shift in the thinking of both policy-makers and the public about the complexity of this issue.

College Preparation and Changing Demographics

Despite the challenges at the K–12 level, at the higher education level, the percentage of blacks age twenty-five and over with college degrees grew from a miniscule 2 percent in 1957 to 17 percent in 2002, while the percentage of whites the same age earning college degrees grew from 8 percent in 1957 to 29 percent in 2002.[23] On the other hand, however, what stands out is that many of the underrepresented minority students today are ill-prepared for college work. In fact, one study of minority freshmen in California's public colleges and universities determined that nearly three-quarters of all black freshmen and almost two-thirds of all Hispanic freshmen needed developmental mathematics courses, while over 60 percent of both black and Hispanic freshmen required developmental English education.[24] Now, more than ever, colleges and universi-

368 · **Freeman A. Hrabowski III**

ties should be involved in K–16 education not only for moral reasons, but also for self-interest. Enlightened universities are connecting proactively to school systems. The list of such initiatives at UMBC is long and impressive.

Minority student achievement has become a major issue throughout the nation's school systems. African American, Latino, and American Indian children trail significantly behind their white and Asian American counterparts in academic achievement, including high school completion, college participation, and college graduation rates.[25] These and other disparities are of growing concern especially because of the nation's overall growth and its dramatically increasing diversity. We know, for example, that Hispanics are the fastest growing ethnic group in America; in fact, we expect that before 2050, one of every four Americans will be Hispanic. By that time, 10 percent of the population will be Asian American, and 14 percent will be black. In other words, essentially one of two Americans will be of color. Former university presidents Derek Bok and William Bowen, in *The Shape of the River,* capture the essence of this compelling issue: "The reasons why diversity has become so important at the highest levels of business, the professions, government, and society at large are readily apparent. . . . [A] healthy society in the twenty-first century will be one in which the most challenging, rewarding career possibilities are perceived to be, and truly are, open to all races and ethnic groups."[26]

Emphasizing High Academic Achievement

Ultimately, the critical question is how do we increase the number of minorities prepared to enter and excel in leadership positions across sectors of society? *Reaching the Top,* the College Board's 1999 report on high academic achievement among minorities, points out that

> Credentials play a gate-keeping role for entry into most professions. In many fields, from engineering to school teaching, a bachelor's degree is the minimum credential. Advanced degrees are required for entry into many desirable professions, such as law and medicine. In some areas of scientific research, postdoctoral study is increasingly essential. . . . [I]t is undeniable that high academic achievement helps people gain access to high quality advanced education and, subsequently to top-notch career options. Unsurprisingly, many people who excel in their studies later excel in intellectually demanding professions.[27]

The academy is a primary example, where fewer than 3 percent of all full-time, tenured faculty at Carnegie Doctoral Research/Extensive institutions are African American.[28] While we have made progress in the production of black PhDs, the actual numbers and percentages are still small. Regarding PhD productivity, in the early 1950s before *Brown,* fewer than 150 African Americans with doctoral degrees were employed in the nation, and the number was fewer than 600 fifteen years later.[29] Moreover, by 1975, blacks accounted for less than 4 percent of all doctoral degrees (1,056 of 28,796),[30] and by 2001, the percentage was virtually the same (1,604 of 40,744).[31] In this light, the College Board report focuses on the need not only for broadly addressing the achievement gap, but also for concentrating on increasing the numbers of minority students who achieve at the highest levels so that more will pursue graduate and professional degrees.

What is distinctive about UMBC's vision is that we are increasing the number of high-achieving minorities at "the top," creating a cadre of well-prepared minority students who will become leading researchers and professionals. To the surprise of some, one of the greatest examples of long-term success in diversity on this campus involves African American social sciences and humanities graduates who have become leading attorneys, judges, and policy-makers. Among recent examples are the first black woman speaker pro-tem of the Maryland House of Delegates and three others who graduated from the University of Maryland Law School, including the first black president of the Maryland Bar Association, the first black secretary of higher education in the state, and the first black woman circuit court administrative judge in Baltimore. Universities might be well served to identify broad success stories and practices that can provide lessons for replication.

One of the campus's most recent success stories involves the Meyerhoff Program and its emphasis on ongoing evaluation. My colleagues and I have learned a great deal in our research on how these high-achieving students were raised—including especially the roles of parents and families, the significance of peer pressure, and the importance of supplemental education.[32] At the same time, what we have learned from our ongoing evaluation of the undergraduate and graduate experiences of these students can be applied at colleges and universities nationwide to prepare many more minority, and majority, research scientists and engineers.

• • •

On the fiftieth anniversary of *Brown*, Americans have tended to focus more on minority students' deficiencies than on their strengths, and much of the discussion in education has been about addressing the achievement gap. We can, however, find inspiring exceptions. Several years ago I had the pleasure of speaking at the celebration of the first one hundred minority PhD recipients (many in the social sciences and humanities) who participated in the Mellon-Mays Undergraduate Minority Fellows Program. Like the Mellon-Mays program (which has produced many more PhDs since that celebration), the Meyerhoff Program, which started the same year, stands out—it has produced from the undergraduate program more than fifty PhDs and MD/PhDs and more than one hundred physicians. With hundreds of Meyerhoff graduates now in graduate and professional programs throughout the country, we expect to average ten or more PhDs per year. It also is significant that we have started a major initiative to produce minority PhDs across disciplines here. Our success is rooted in an idea that the African American scholar W. E. B. DuBois referred to a century ago as "The Talented Tenth." While some considered this notion elitist, I am convinced that, more than ever, when the popular culture suggests to minority children that it is not "cool" to be smart, American society needs to increase substantially the numbers of blacks and other minorities who excel academically—and we in universities have a special responsibility in this regard. In his much heralded 1903 treatise, *The Souls of Black Folk,* DuBois wrote,

> Can the masses of the Negro people be in any possible way more quickly raised than by the effort and example of this aristocracy of talent and character? . . . [I]t is, ever was, and ever will be from the top downward that culture filters. The Talented Tenth rises and pulls all that are worth the saving up. . . . This is the history of human progress. . . . How then shall the leaders of a struggling people be trained and the hands of the risen few strengthened? There can be but one answer: The best and most capable of their youth must be schooled in the colleges and universities of the land. . . . A university is a human invention for the transmission of knowledge and culture from generation to generation, through the training of quick minds and pure hearts, and for this work no other human invention will suffice.[33]

Notes

1. Henry Louis Gates, *America behind the Color Line: Dialogues with African Americans* (New York: Warner Books, 2004), 1.

2. *Grutter v. Bollinger et al.,* 539 U.S. 306 (2003).

3. Ibid.

4. Ibid.

5. Richard Kluger, *Simple Justice: The History of Brown v. Board of Education and Black America's Struggle for Equality* (New York: Knopf, 2004).

6. *Brown v. Board of Education,* 347 U.S. 483 (1954).

7. *Brown v. Board of Education,* 349 U.S. 294 (1955).

8. *Brown v. Board of Education,* 347 U.S. at 494.

9. William Harvey, *Minorities in Higher Education 2002–2003: Annual Status Report* (Washington, D.C.: American Council on Education, 2003), 6, 60, 67.

10. Claude M. Steele, "A Threat in the Air: How Stereotypes Shape Intellectual Identity and Performance," *American Psychologist,* 52, no. 6 (1997): 613–29; Elaine Seymour and Nancy M. Hewitt, *Talking About Leaving: Why Undergraduates Leave the Sciences* (Boulder, Colo.: Westview Press, 1997); Walter Recharde Allen, "The Color of Success: African American College Student Outcomes at Predominantly

White and Historically Black Public Colleges and Universities," *Harvard Educational Review* 62 (Spring 1992): 45–65.

11. *Science* 301 (August 22, 2003): 1030. The article looks at the report by BEST (Building Engineering and Science Talent, a consortium of education, government, and corporate leader), "A Bridge for All: Higher Education Design Principles to Broaden Participation in Science, Technology, Engineering, and Mathematics," officially released in April 2004.

12. *Educational Attainment*, U.S. Census Bureau, April 5, 2006, http://www.census .gov/population/www/socdemo/educ-attn.html (accessed April 10, 2008).

13. National Assessment of Educational Progress, http://nces.ed.gov/ nationsreportcard/naepdata (accessed April 10, 2008).

14. Sheryll Cashin, *The Failures of Integration: How Race and Class Are Undermining the American Dream* (New York: Public Affairs, 2004), 219.

15. Ibid., 217.

16. Ibid., 217–18.

17. Ibid., 96. "Hypersegregation" is a term coined by sociologists Douglas Massey and Nancy Denton in *American Apartheid: Segregation and the Making of the Underclass* (Cambridge, Mass.: Harvard University Press, 1993).

18. James S. Coleman et al., *Equality of Educational Opportunity* (Washington, D.C.: U.S. Dept. of Health, Education, and Welfare, Office of Education, 1966).

19. Abigail Thernstrom and Stephan Thernstrom, *No Excuses: Closing the Racial Gap in Learning* (New York: Simon and Schuster, 2003).

20. Editorial, *Baltimore Sun*, August 26, 2003, A-14.

21. A. Thernstrom, "Schools Are Responsible for the Main Source of Racial Inequality Today," *Los Angeles Times*, November 13, 2003.

22. Cashin, *The Failures of Integration*, 229.

23. U.S. Census Bureau, http:/www.census.gov/population/socdemo/education/ tabA02.pdf.

24. R. Roach, "Remediation Reform," *Black Issues in Higher Education* 17, no. 12 (2000): 16–23.

25. Harvey, *Minorities in Higher Education*, 49–50, 55–56.

26. William G. Bowen and Derek Bok, *The Shape of the River: Long-Term Consequences of Considering Race in College and University Admissions* (Princeton: Princeton University Press, 1998), 11–12.

27. College Entrance Examination Board, National Task Force on Minority High Achievement, *Reaching the Top: A Report of the National Task Force on Minority High Achievement* (New York: The College Board, 1999), 4.

28. *Integrated Postsecondary Education Data System* (Washington, D.C.: National Center for Education Statistics, 2001).

29. James E. Blackwell, *Mainstreaming Outsiders: The Production of Black Professionals* (Dix Hills, N.Y.: General Hall, 1987).

30. National Science Foundation, *Women, Minorities, and Persons with Disabilities*

in Science and Engineering: 2000 (Washington, D.C.: Division of Science Resources Studies, Survey of Earned Doctorates, U.S. Government Printing Office, 2000).

31. Harvey, *Minorities in Higher Education,* 66.

32. Freeman A. Hrabowski III, Kenneth I. Maton, and Geoffrey L. Greif, *Beating the Odds: Raising Academically Successful African American Males* (New York: Oxford University Press, 1998); Freeman A. Hrabowski III, Kenneth I. Maton, Monica L Greene, and Geoffrey L. Greif, *Overcoming the Odds: Raising Academically Successful African American Young Women* (New York: Oxford University Press, 2002).

33. W. E. B. DuBois, "The Talented Tenth," in *The Souls of Black Folk* (Chicago: A. C. McClurg and Co., 1903), 193.

27

Just Because of the Color of His Skin

The 1955 Lynching of Emmett Till

Christopher Benson

It is significant and it is appropriate that we come together in January, the month we celebrate the birth of Dr. Martin Luther King and remember the death of Mamie Till-Mobley—the mother of Emmett Till.

Clearly, a time of transition. And connection. But it also is a month of reflection during a year of such reflection. Janus, the Roman god for whom January is named—the god of portals and passageways—Janus is represented by the two faces, one looking back, one looking ahead. But since the Romans adopted—some would say, *appropriated*—so much from other ancient cultures, we must also take a moment in this context to recognize Sankofa, the African symbol of the same principle. The bird who reflects on what has been and on what is yet to be, even as it spreads its wings.

We are poised at that magical moment. Just before taking flight. Time to take a moment—a *Sankofa* moment—to take stock of where we've been, where we're going.

As I thought about this visit, I was struck by a memory of about six years ago. I was in town visiting my family and generally catching up on this and that. I had the chance to speak with one of my nieces, who was about five at the time, and she wanted to tell me the latest of the family business—especially the news about her eighteen-year-old brother, who had just started at the University of Illinois.

"And, oh, yeah, Uncle Chris, Dino went away to college . . . or something."

"Really?" I said, as if this really was the first time I had ever heard it. "So how's he doing?"

"Oh, great. He's getting straight A's."

"No kidding."

"Yeah. Straight A's. No crooked ones."

Now I could probably get a lot of mileage out of that crooked-A payoff. But

I prefer to take this in a different direction. Because I believe there is something of a lesson in that anecdote for a five-year-old, for her eighteen-year-old brother, indeed, for all of us. Guidance in considering what lay ahead, what we have left behind.

What could be better for a five-year-old to learn? Hard work nets rewards, no matter how symbolic. And let's face it, avoiding those yucky crooked A's has got to be worth the effort. For an eighteen-year-old, what could be more satisfying than seizing a wondrous opportunity—like the first-class education of this university—what could be better than being determined enough to take advantage of that opportunity? Making it work, making it pay dividends. And for all the rest of us, what could be more encouraging than the confirmation—the affirmation—that we can achieve what we conceive when we are committed to our goals? When we reach that deep awareness of the world of possibilities created by living a purposeful life.

These are important points to consider. Not only in connection with the celebration of the birth of Dr. Martin Luther King Jr., but also because the year 2004 was special. It was in this year that we reflected on the meaning of a number of significant historical milestones.

Looking forward. Looking back.

At the end of 2005—December—we commemorated the fiftieth anniversary of the beginning of the yearlong Montgomery Bus Boycott. The event that launched the public career of Dr. King.

May 2005—May 31 to be exact—marked the fiftieth anniversary of *Brown v. Board of Education,* the second of two Supreme Court rulings in that landmark case, with the implementation order: "With all deliberate speed."

Between these two events—on August 28, 2005—the fiftieth anniversary of the lynching of Emmett Louis Till.

Not only does Emmett's murder come almost exactly at the midpoint between *Brown* and Montgomery, but in an important way, I believe it also is *central* to the other two. Only recently have we begun to fully appreciate the profound connection among these important historical events. Events that still have relevance, still have meaning to us, and to an eighteen-year-old just starting college, and to a five-year-old just gaining a level of consciousness about the larger world and a sense of purpose, a sense of personal worth, value, meaning in that world.

It is vitally important for us to reflect on all this—how we got here—to this place, at this point in time, to reflect on all the sacrifices that got us here and the level of commitment needed to carry us forward.

To consider our own responsibility. That is not to suggest a guilt trip. But to say that we all have to assume responsibility—responsibility for our moment. That is the debt we owe history. It is the investment in our future. That's what it means to live a purposeful life, as our forebears have taught us.

When the Justice Department announced on May 10, 2004, that it would open a new investigation into the nearly fifty-year-old lynching of Emmett Till, there was a deep feeling that justice already had been done. Finally, powerful people were hearing the gentle voice of Emmett's mother, Mamie Till-Mobley. A voice that resonated through her public statements, through her speeches, and, of course, through her book.

She was determined. She was committed. She would never let us forget.

That distinctive, unwavering voice tells the compelling story that has meant so many things to so many Americans. It has generated headlines. It even has sparked a congressional resolution, introduced by Mother Mobley's congressman, Bobby Rush.

Mother Mobley's story is the story of courage and determination. The story of a mother's love. And the hate crime that changed America. The story of a lifetime. How one person really can make a difference in the world. It is the story of a journey to justice. And the redemption that faith in justice can bring. Ultimately, this is a story that illuminates the soul. And lifts the spirit.

Even though it doesn't start out that way.

Emmett Till was fourteen years old in the summer of 1955 when he traveled from his Chicago home to tiny Money, Mississippi. Excited about his two week vacation. Mississippi Delta. Wide open spaces. As far as the eye could see. Cotton season had just started. And when you don't have to do that back-breaking work for a living, it can seem like fun to do it for just a minute. Days in the field picking with his cousins. Afternoons fishing or swimming in the Tallahatchie River nearby. It was to be the adventure of a lifetime.

Emmett. A bright, fun-loving Chicago kid. Two hundred percent boy. A natural leader among his friends. The center of everybody's universe. Living the life. A life with no restrictions. Unbounded ambition.

He never even realized just how the boundaries had begun to close in on him as soon as he stepped off that train in the Delta.

A week after Emmett arrived, white racists came for him. Banging on the door of his relatives. Two in the morning. Calling him out. He was taken away. And then, over the course of the next several hours, he was beaten, tortured, killed. His body dumped in the Tallahatchie River with a seventy-five-pound gin fan tied around his neck with barbed wire.

Now, Emmett is said to have whistled at a white woman. At Bryant's Grocery and Meat Market. The uptown hangout. The store with a mostly black clientele, where there always was that checker game on the front porch and some candy and soda pop inside waiting for Emmett and his cousins and their friends after working all day in the fields. The store was owned by twenty-four-year-old Roy Bryant and his twenty-two-year-old wife, Carolyn, who was tending the store alone that Wednesday evening when Emmett and his friends dropped by. Emmett bought two cents worth of bubble gum. For Mother Mobley, exactly what took place after that was never completely settled. Several versions of the events have emerged.

As usual, on the front porch, there was a checker game going on around seven that evening. When Emmett whistled—a prolonged wolf whistle—one of the friends who was there says he thought he was whistling at a slamming checker move. A couple of Emmett's cousins have said that he whistled at Carolyn Bryant as a joke, a prank, never realizing what that would mean in the Mississippi Delta in 1955. Then there is the story Mother Mobley believed until her dying day. The week after Emmett's murder, one of his cousins was quoted in the *Chicago Defender* as saying that Emmett sometimes made a whistling sound when he spoke. Something shifted in Mother Mobley when she heard that one. Emmett had triumphed over polio as a six-year-old. Miraculously, there was no permanent muscle damage to his legs. But there was a mark. His vocal cords. He was left with a stutter. To help him overcome it, Mother Mobley taught him to whistle when he got stuck on words beginning with *b* and *m* and *p* and the like. Just whistle, she told him. Steady your breathing. Then speak.

Bubble gum would have been a sticking point for a boy with Emmett's stutter. And Mother Mobley went to her grave with the tension that only a mother could experience. Wondering whether the one thing she taught her son to help him have a better life, may in the end have cost him his life. Whatever happened, this is what she carried with her.

Emmett's body—like so many other bodies dumped in the Tallahatchie River—was never supposed to be found. But three days after his death, he rose. His knee was spotted sticking up just above the surface.

Emmett was so badly beaten that he was unrecognizable except for one thing. A ring that had been left to him by his father. A ring that his killers somehow had overlooked when they stripped him and left him.

Now, this story would have ended right there at the banks of the river where Emmett's body was recovered. So many lynching stories ended that way. Right there in the immediate area of the lynching. Just as they were intended to do. After all, the point of a lynching was to send a message to blacks in the immediate area. Know your place. Stay there. Don't even think about it.

Mamie Till-Mobley was not willing to stay in her place. This was different. Mother Mobley was different. During a powerful moment of transformation, she began to take charge. And she wound up making three critical decisions that affected hundreds of thousands of people, and the course of events that followed. She insisted that her son's body be returned to her in Chicago. She insisted on inspecting his body to make a positive identification. She insisted on having an open casket funeral.

Now these might not seem like remarkable decisions. But in context, we can see how important they were. First, Mississippi authorities ordered that Emmett be buried right there in Mississippi. Immediately. Somebody wanted this ugly event to be covered up for all time. Mother Mobley said no. Send my boy home. And the family moved heaven and earth to get it done. Second, the body was only released under an agreement that the shipping box would not be opened. It was locked and carried the seal of the State of Mississippi that was not to be broken. Mother Mobley said no. She hadn't signed anything. Let them come to Chicago and sue me, she said. I dare them to sue me for looking upon my son one more time. Third, it was unheard of for a body as mutilated as Emmett's to be put on display. It shocked everyone around Mother Mobley when she insisted on this. She was urged to reconsider. She stood her ground. She said no. I want the world to see what I have seen.

These decisions were so important because, obviously, if Emmett had been buried in Mississippi, we never would have known what happened to him. If his mother hadn't gone through the horrible step-by-step process of identifying his body, then we would have been left with uncertainty. And in the four days that Emmett's body lay in state in Chicago, an estimated one hundred thousand people filed by him. Jesse Jackson has called it the largest civil rights demonstration to occur up to that point. Photos of the body in *Jet* Magazine and in the *Chicago Defender* carried the image around the country.

People were horrified by what they saw. They were outraged. Mother Mobley wanted that. But she also wanted them to be moved by it—to be moved to action. She recognized that she and so many others had been complacent about the course of events and the nature of race relations in America. Like so many others, she believed she had escaped the horrors by getting out of Mississippi, only to find that the worst of Mississippi race hatred had followed her. She wanted people to know that the race problem in America was not just the problem of people in Mississippi or Alabama or Georgia. The race problem in America was the problem of people in Chicago and Detroit and Champaign, too. As Malcolm X would say so many years later: the Mason Dixon line is the Canadian border.

So people *were* horrified and they *were* moved to action. The line was drawn. They were coming after our kids now. It all had to stop. And the message took hold. Roy Wilkins, executive secretary of the NAACP issued a blistering statement: "Mississippi has decided to maintain White supremacy by murdering children." There were more than five thousand documented lynchings in the years following Reconstruction. You can see now why Emmett Till is the one name everyone remembers.

In response to all this—this public outcry—two men were arrested and charged with Emmett's murder. Roy Bryant, Carolyn's husband, and J. W. Milam,

Roy's half-brother. They immediately admitted that they had taken Emmett from the house of his relatives, but claimed they had let him go. He had walked back home, they said. Some three miles. In the dead of night.

Bryant and Milam were brought to trial within a month of Emmett's murder. Now, that might sound like a good thing. It is not. Even in the Mississippi Delta of the 1950s, this was unreasonable. When the Framers provided for the right to a speedy trial, this was not exactly what they had in mind. I mean, let's face it, they spend more time building a case on *Law and Order*. Right? Half the show each week is devoted to, what? The *investigation*. You have to research. You have to prepare to go to trial. It's like going off to war. You wouldn't even *think* about going off to war without a strategy, without a plan, without preparation. Right? Well, all right, maybe *some* people would. But we know differently. We know that the only justifiable war, the only moral war, is a winnable war, and to win a war you have to be prepared, and to be prepared you have to do your groundwork, and if a trial is like warfare, then you don't go to trial without the groundwork. A full and complete investigation.

The point is that a murder case takes a lot longer than a month to prepare for trial, even when you have all the investigative resources to work with. And that was not the case here.

The trial was a huge event. About a hundred reporters, photographers, and television crew people from all over the country and as far away as Europe descended on tiny Sumner, a town that boasted it was a "Good Place to Raise a Boy." The total population of the town was fewer than six hundred people. But it would swell to more than a thousand during the five days of the trial—a trial that seemed at times like a carnival. Someone said it was bigger than the Bruno Hauptmann trial, the Lindberg baby kidnapping case. David Halberstam, who covered the trial as a young reporter, would say later that this was the first big media event of the civil rights movement.

Of the one hundred or so reporters who covered the trial, twelve were African American. There was a press table set up in court. And then there was a special place for the African American reporters. The Jim Crow table, where Mother Mobley often was seated right next to *Jet* writer Simeon Booker, a former Nieman Fellow, acclaimed investigative reporter Alex Wilson of the *Defender*, Jimmy Hicks of the *Baltimore Afro American*, and on and on.

Interestingly—sadly—the highest ranking official to attend the trial was a member of Congress, Charles Diggs of Detroit, who happened to be black. He also had a special place. At the Jim Crow table. When Diggs first presented his card to get into the court as an observer, one deputy turned to another and said: "A nigger congressman? That ain't possible. It ain't even legal . . . is it?"

The sheriff of Tallahatchie County had insisted that there would be no integration in his courtroom. And, yes, the courtroom was his. Just about everything in the county was his. Or, at least, under his jurisdiction. Sheriff H. C. Strider was exactly the man that Central Casting would send out for the role of, well, H. C. Strider. The stereotypical bigoted southern white sheriff. Each day, he'd greet the group there at the Jim Crow table by saying simply: "Morning . . . niggahs." Strider—the man who was supposed to put all his resources to work for the prosecution of a murder case—wound up working for the defense. He helped screen potential jurors who were likely to acquit. Jurors he knew. It was his business to know everybody in the county. And he knew where they lived. He collected their taxes. He was a wealthy man. A powerful man. A plantation owner. In fact, as Halberstam notes, if you wanted to find Strider in the local telephone directory, you had to look under *P*—for plantation. He was reported to have hidden a couple of star witnesses in jail to make sure they couldn't testify. It appears that Strider even lied on the stand—under oath. He was called as a witness—for the defense. He said he couldn't tell whether the victim recovered from the river was black or white. He doubted whether even the victim's own mother could identify him. And he denied signing a death certificate. This was on September 22. But on September 1, Strider already had signed a death certificate. One that identified Emmett by name, specified his race, and even listed his mother's name. That document was officially certified on September 16, before the trial began. But it was not delivered to Mother Mobley until well after the trial had ended.

Apart from Strider's testimony, there were a number of dramatic moments during the trial. Of course, Mother Mobley testified and went through the painful process of describing the mutilated body she had identified as her son at the funeral home. Under cross-examination she was accused of faking Emmett's death to collect on his life insurance policy.

Moses Wright, Emmett's great uncle, testified about the night of the kidnapping when the two white men came into his home, threatened him and his family and took Emmett away. Promising to bring him back if he wasn't the right one. Moses Wright also testified that he heard a voice from inside the truck the men drove—a woman's voice—identifying Emmett.

In probably the most dramatic moment in the proceedings, Moses Wright stood and raised his hand to finger the defendants. No one could remember a case where a black man stood in open court and even accused a white man of a crime, let alone pointing him out.

Now just to put this moment in context, it was an offense in the South during this period for a black man simply to look a white person in the eye. Or to forget to say sir or ma'am. Or to forget to step aside on the sidewalk, or step off the sidewalk. A black man could be beaten—or worse—for simply gazing upon a white woman in a movie poster. There was a rigid system of racial apartheid that existed in this country, and it was violently enforced.

Then there was the testimony of Willie Reed. He was eighteen years old, a sharecropper, and had never been out of Mississippi even though his mother had moved to Chicago. Willie had seen something on the morning of Emmett's murder and he went into hiding. There were things you were just not supposed to see in the Mississippi Delta in 1955.

But the black reporters and Medgar Evers and other NAACP activists found out about it. They enlisted the help of a couple of friendly white reporters and a county sheriff who had a tug of conscience, and they mounted a search of the cotton fields in the area—including high-speed chases down the local roads—until they found Willie. Persuaded him to come forward.

Willie Reed actually saw Bryant, Milam, a couple of other white men, and two black men with Emmett at the Sheridan Plantation. He testified about all this. He also testified about what he heard. Violent beating and screaming coming from a shed attached to the barn. Willie told me that he felt he had to come forward. He felt he owed that to Emmett's mother. He was not that much older than Emmett and would have wanted someone to do it for him—for his mother—if he had been Emmett.

Immediately after his testimony, Willie was relocated to Chicago, where he had a nervous breakdown. Now, he tells me, he thinks about the whole thing all the time. Every day. Especially as he drives to work in Chicago. Down Emmett Till Road.

Then, of course, there was the testimony of Carolyn Bryant. She claimed that Emmett grabbed her, made lewd suggestions, and, of course, whistled at her.

Fortunately, the jury was dismissed during this testimony, and it ultimately was not allowed in. It simply did not provide a justification under the law for beating and shooting someone. For murdering someone. But the law and custom were two different things in Mississippi. And, unfortunately, this testimony was all presented in open court. Everybody in town heard about it. Of course, there was no way to keep all that from the jury.

People I talked to, people Mother Mobley talked to—people who were there at the store with Emmett—say he wasn't even in the store long enough to have done any of that. One of his cousins actually stood in the door most of the time—keeping an eye out for him to make sure he didn't get into trouble. He denies that Emmett ever touched the woman. In any event, the jury deliberated a little more than one hour. They stretched it out by taking a Coke break. They wanted to make it look good before coming back to render the verdict they had decided on long before the evidence had been presented.

Not guilty.

Within a month of their acquittal, Bryant and Milam granted an interview to *LOOK* Magazine. Their highly detailed account of how they murdered Emmett. It was published in February. They couldn't be tried again for murdering

Emmett, so they spoke very freely. Emmett had to be taught a lesson, they felt. He was an uppity Negro from the North. They saw him as defiant. They wanted to use him to send a message that black folks had better not step out of line. Stay in your place. For their published confession, they were paid about four thousand dollars. In essence, a bounty.

The real point here, though, is that message they wanted to send. It is key to understanding the nature of this crime. There was a debate going back and forth for a while during the pretrial period. The NAACP asserted that Emmett's killing was a lynching. Mississippi powerfolk got their feathers ruffled, arguing, no it was just murder. It might sound silly at first, because well, someone is dead. Brutally killed. What difference does it make what we call it? But it is highly significant. And here is where we connect to *Brown*.

Murder is bad. No question about it. But a lynching is much worse. There a number of factors to weigh in determining a lynching, but the critical difference for our purposes is in causation. Any number of factors can lead to a murder and there will be a number of normal defenses that are set in motion. But the key to a lynching—among all the other factors—is that it is a race crime. A hate crime. And, in this case, a crime against a child. That was the last thing Mississippi officials wanted transmitted all over the country. They already had their hands full.

The first part of *Brown vs. Board of Education* had been decided one year earlier, in May 1954. The decision struck down "separate but equal" in public education as unconstitutional. The second part of *Brown* came down in May 1955, ordering desegregation with all deliberate speed. A symbolic more than a real immediate victory. Over the course of 2004, we were engaged in a retrospective on *Brown* and whether it achieved its goals, what with the resegregation of public schools and the hostility toward affirmative action in higher education in some sectors.

Whether or not *Brown* has had an enduring effect in education in the last fifty years, it certainly had not changed anything in its first year. That is not to say that *Brown* had no effect. It did. It redefined the legal relationships of blacks and whites. Important. Historic. Precedent-setting.

But the Supreme Court doesn't have a police force. It doesn't have troops to dispatch when it comes to making sure its orders are carried out. The white opposition, however, had a great deal of power. And people to champion the fight against the Supreme Court. From the very top. Senator James O. Eastland. Down to the county sheriffs like H. C. Strider. And even lower on this racist food chain—the bottom-feeders, the thugs, the enforcers on the front lines—people like Roy Bryant and J. W. Milam.

Now, while African Americans applauded the *Brown* decision at the time, there was no immediate mass movement—no groundswell—to push for implementation of the decision. Not surprisingly, it would take years to see that effect. It's important to keep two points in mind. One, *Brown* redefined our legal relationships—black and white—for all time. Two, even though there was no immediate practical effect of *Brown* in that schools were not desegregated overnight, there was an immediate reaction that set so many other things in motion. There was brutal and violent white backlash throughout the South. It was cold-blooded. Particularly in Mississippi. Most especially in the Mississippi Delta, where Emmett was visiting.

Whites were up in arms. "Massive Resistance," they called it. And the battle was fought on two fronts. White Citizens' Councils were formed. Business and political leaders who—among other things—would compile lists of African Americans who pressed for their voting rights or signed petitions calling for desegregation.

These lists were published, and the people who signed those petitions were hit hard. Economic reprisals. That was Level 1 of the Massive Resistance. Loans were denied. Employment was terminated. Mortgages were foreclosed. Farmers were denied seed and equipment. People were driven out of their homes. Out of their businesses. And it was irreversible. Even if you turned around and tried to remove your name from a petition. There was no mercy. It wasn't about you. It was about all those people who might try to emulate you. It was about sending a message. The NAACP tried to help and set up a special fund at the Tri-State Bank of Memphis. Some three hundred thousand dollars was raised to provide low-interest loans to ease the pain.

So, Level 1 of the backlash. Economic reprisals. Orchestrated by the White Citizens' Councils. Groups somebody called the KKK in business suits. Groups that had been formed with the help and support of powerful Mississippians like Senator Eastland.

Level 2 was the bloody enforcement. Physical violence, up to and including murder. People like Bryant and Milam were the enforcers—wittingly or unwittingly. But they were all given encouragement in a climate of white hot hostility where people like Eastland vowed to fight integration to the death. And urged others to follow his example. Which is why the NAACP's Roy Wilkins felt justified in charging that Emmett's murderers "felt free to lynch him" because of the racist climate that state leaders there had accepted and, to a large extent, encouraged. No wonder, then that people like Bryant and Milam came to believe that they could get away with murder.

There were two other cases that provided aid and comfort to this belief. The very summer Emmett arrived in the Delta. First there was Reverend George Lee of Belzoni—not far from where Emmett would visit in August. In May of that year, Reverend Lee—an NAACP organizer—was found dead in his wrecked car. The county sheriff determined that it was a car accident. Well . . . yeah . . .

the car was wrapped around a light pole on the side of the road, but that part happened shortly after the shotgun blast that took him out. And, those shotgun pellets that were pulled out of Reverend Lee's face? The sheriff said they were dental fillings.

Two weeks before Emmett arrived in the Mississippi Delta, Lamar Smith, a successful black farmer and war veteran, was passing out election literature on the town square in Brookhaven. Again, not far from where Emmett would visit. Three white men approached Smith and shot him. They were so brazen, they didn't even bother to put on the white sheets and hoods. They just walked right up and blew him away. High noon. Broad daylight. Plain sight. Right there in the town square in front of so many witnesses—who never saw a thing. They called it "a reign of terror." If Homeland Security had been on the case back in 1955, the African American communities in the state of Mississippi would have been on Code Red. This was the world that Emmett stepped into. A bright, self-assured boy from Chicago. Drawn to Mississippi at that time, it seems, for a purpose he couldn't possibly have understood.

In a way, Emmett's very presence threatened the status quo. After all, his confidence and independence just might have been contagious. Best to snuff it out. So he was murdered. Lynched. Executed. Not because of all those things that were claimed. Whether or not they even happened. No, not for any of that. But just because of the color of his skin.

But, still, why? What were people so afraid of? As with the backlash itself, the anxiety in Mississippi operated on two levels. First, with people like Bryant and Milam, there was an irrational fear of integration, which itself operated on two levels. It all basically boiled down to sex and superiority.

The first part was probably best articulated—if that's the most suitable word for it—by none other than President Dwight D. Eisenhower who, as an apologist for the white southern anxiety, reportedly explained in words to this effect: "You have to understand the White Southerner's position. He just doesn't want some big overgrown Negro sitting next to his little school girl."

The concern apparently was that if you allowed little black and white kids to sit next to each other on the first day of school, the next day they'd be running off to get married.

As a footnote, Eisenhower's response to the early push for civil rights, or his lack of response, was very interesting when you see it from our vantage point. The Southern Strategy that was so important to Richard Nixon's presidential campaigns in 1968 and 1972 actually seemed to be percolating back then in the '50s.

Nixon served as Eisenhower's vice president. Southern Democrats were ripe for Republican plucking. No wonder, Eisenhower's Justice Department turned a deaf ear to the pleadings of Mother Mobley and others on her behalf—people like the newly elected Mayor Richard J. Daley. Daley the first.

So, there was the sex thing. And then there was the second prong of poor white anxiety. The superiority part. The one thing poor whites had, it seems, was the feeling that, no matter how bad things got, there was somebody who was lower than they were. So, the one power they had was the one they held over blacks. Their sense of superiority was their capital. If blacks were equal, then poor whites would have nothing. And they never took time to realize that they were being gamed. That they actually had more in common with blacks than not. That they needed to turn their anger on those who were exploiting them, not those who also were being exploited.

That leads to the interest that the white power structure had in fighting desegregation and voting rights. It was all about the numbers. The bottom line. And you could begin measuring it all on the voter rolls. Start with Tallahatchie County, where the murder trial was conducted. In 1955 there were roughly thirty thousand people living in Tallahatchie County. Nineteen thousand blacks and eleven thousand whites. Blacks held a nearly two-to-one edge over whites, yet not a single black was registered to vote.

Obviously things would have been dramatically different in Tallahatchie County, Mississippi, in 1955 if African Americans had been allowed to register to vote. Maybe there would have been a different sheriff. One who respected the rule of law. One who investigated murder cases rather than working to set killers loose. Maybe.

Certainly, the jury pool would have had a different . . . *complexion.* Maybe the very experience of power sharing would have produced a whole different attitude in the Mississippi Delta.

Blacks were not in the majority everywhere in Mississippi or even throughout the Delta, for that matter, but in many counties, the population figures were significant enough for blacks to hold the balance of power. If they had been allowed even a modicum of power.

So, the case that came out of Money, Mississippi, ultimately was about money. And power. Poor and working class whites found some commonality with the business and elite classes, and together they circled the wagons to defend against the onslaught of the outside agitators—the people who threatened their way of life.

I don't want to diminish the significance of race hatred in Emmett's lynching. This was a hate crime. Racism is at the very heart of this murder. But the point I'm making is that race hatred itself was exploited by people who helped to set a context that made this crime possible. And made whites in Mississippi really believe that they could indeed get away with murder.

In a way, the white power structure in Mississippi was worse than the lower classes, even though it was the poor whites who were doing the heavy lifting. The dirty work. The rednecks were just stupid. Which is no excuse, of course.

But the elite was diabolical, cynical, manipulative. These are people who could have led, and chose instead to incite. People who could have condemned hate crimes and chose instead to condone them. People who could have cleaned up the mess that had been made of race relations. Ultimately, they are the ones who were left with blood on their hands. But, while they may have won the battle, they lost the war.

Everything changed as a result of the murder of Emmett Till and the acquittal of his murderers. Within three months of the end of the murder trial, Rosa Parks was arrested on that bus in Montgomery. A yearlong bus boycott began and a bold new leader emerged to inspire us. To move us forward. Many years later, after Rosa Parks and Mother Mobley became close friends, Mrs. Parks would reveal that she was thinking about Emmett that fateful day on the bus. She was thinking about what they had done to that poor boy, and she would not be moved.

Coretta Scott King also has said that the murder of Emmett Till and the quiet grace and dignity of his mother and the courage of so many others who had taken a stand in Tallahatchie County—people like Moses Wright, who stood tall in that courtroom and never flinched as he challenged two white men and an entire white community and an entire system—that all of that helped to embolden the people of Montgomery, Alabama, only three months later.

They said in Montgomery that if they could do it over in Tallahatchie County, Mississippi, we can do it here. They did it for us. We have to do it for the next in line. And so on and so on. If the chain goes unbroken, then we will break this thing down.

And so it began.

I have met so many people and have read about so many more who say they were Emmett's age when he was killed. They attended his funeral or read about him in *Jet* or the *Defender*. They saw the picture. They were horrified. They felt vulnerable. For at least a generation, black kids were exposed to the Emmett Till story in what would become a rite of passage. They were deeply moved by it.

It stripped them of the protection of their childhood. That sense of innocence. For so many the story of Emmett Till became the introduction to race relations in America. Little black kids have grown up learning that there are people out there—white people—who can cause them harm, kill them, for no other reason than the color of their skin. There would no longer be a safe place to hide from a dangerous reality—and a realization. Everybody had to take responsibility for what we had become. Anyone who had done anything to cause the problem. Anyone who had done nothing to stop it from happening.

There no longer could be any innocent bystanders.

For an entire nation, the murder of Emmett Till marked the death of innocence.

386 · **Christopher Benson**

So, *Brown* redefined the legal relationships between blacks and whites. Emmett's lynching moved people to want to fight for the change promised by *Brown*. And Montgomery provided the strategy of nonviolent, public demonstrations and boycotts.

The rights . . . the motivation . . . the plan.

And so many of those kids who had been Emmett's age when he was killed and who were moved by that event, became involved in the civil rights movement when they came of age. It was a movement, after all, that was characterized by its youth. Foot soldiers. And later leaders and activists in social service and in politics and business.

There were other effects.

NAACP recruitment and fundraising. In the year after Emmett's murder, membership and contributions spiked. I saw a report indicating that the organization took in roughly two hundred and fifty thousand dollars that year. A considerable increase. For a short period, Mother Mobley was out on a lecture tour supported by the NAACP, and she would address crowds and churches and rallies where thousands of people would fill barrels and trash cans with what they called "fighting dollars" for the NAACP.

Out of Montgomery came the Southern Christian Leadership Conference, which, under Dr. King's leadership, defined the nonviolent movement for social justice.

Legislation. Ultimately, the principle of *Brown* was given meaning and real effect in areas outside education by laws that were passed. The Civil Rights Act of 1964 and the Voting Rights Act of 1965. These laws were most directly affected by the mass movement and the relentless lobbying of the civil rights leadership—particularly Dr. King.

But the Civil Rights Act of 1957 helped to pave the way. This was the first civil rights law enacted since the end of the Civil War and created the post of Assistant Attorney General for Civil Rights and the U.S. Commission on Civil Rights. During the congressional hearings leading to the act, a number of witnesses testified about Emmett Till, pointing to the need for the protection the law envisioned.

The media. The black press already was energized and motivated to cover the struggle for social justice. But the critical thing that developed out of the events surrounding the murder of Emmett Till was that mainstream media discovered a story.

First, this was the beginning of the television age. The civil rights movement provided great visuals. Many, as we know, would come later. Fueled by police dogs and fire hoses. Images that were said to have moved President John F. Kennedy to begin making a serious effort to move civil rights legislation on the national agenda. But early on, it was clear this was a story that lent itself to pictures. And the picture of Emmett—the brutal effect of race hatred—was seared into our national consciousness.

Second—and in that connection—Emmett Till's murder and trial did something for civil rights coverage that *Brown* couldn't do. It took the complex issue of legal rights, civil rights, and social justice, and put a human face on them. That continued into Montgomery with Rosa Parks and Dr. King and on into Little Rock with nine courageous high school kids and the college students of the sit-ins, the children of Birmingham, and on and on.

As scholars of the period have recognized, white reporters, many from the South who had fought against totalitarianism in World War II, suddenly had to face the stark contradictions that existed in their own home region.

Interestingly, the civil rights leadership also became very sophisticated in dealing with the media. They came to appreciate that whoever controlled the story ultimately would win the day. The racists in Little Rock, Arkansas, and Anniston, Alabama, and Oxford, Mississippi, and Selma and Birmingham . . . well, they never did get it.

Many people have said over the years that Emmett Till's brutal murder helped to galvanize the civil rights movement. In commenting on the fortieth anniversary of the 1963 March on Washington, the Reverend Jesse Jackson told Tavis Smiley that there would have been no March on Washington—which took place on the 28th of August, eight years to the day from Emmett's murder—had it not been for Emmett Till and the courage of his mother.

In doing my research and in working closely with Mother Mobley on *Death of Innocence: The Story of the Hate Crime that Changed America* (New York: Random House, 2003), I came to fully appreciate that assertion. Indeed, in making the decisions that she made, in exposing the horrors of race hatred to the world, Mamie Till-Mobley became the bridge between the way we were and the way we are. It is because of her that we will never be the same again.

There are so many moving passages in Mother Mobley's book. One comes to mind in this context.

I have discussed the anniversaries of *Brown* and Montgomery that we commemorated in 2005. But there is another important anniversary. The fortieth anniversary of the Voting Rights Act, which was signed into law in August 1965. And one sure measure of the effectiveness of that law is on the bottom line in Mississippi, where, as I mentioned, blacks had been killed and driven from their homes for attempting to register to vote. According to a recent statistical summary issued by the Joint Center for Political and Economic Studies in Washington, in 2001, there were 892 black elected officials in the state of Mississippi. Eight hundred and ninety-two. More than any other state in the South. More than any other state in the country.

Now, while there was a tremendous amount of lobbying on the part of Dr. King and others for the Voting Rights Act, there was one single event that moved this issue front and center in the national consciousness. And the national agenda. Bloody Sunday. The police riot on the Edmund Pettus Bridge as demonstrators were brutalized at the beginning of the Selma to Montgomery March. This year, in the month of March we will commemorate the fortieth anniversary of that event.

But the moving moment—the Mother Mobley Moment I mentioned—takes us back to the year 2000. The thirty-fifth anniversary. That year, there was a reenactment of the march. So much had changed by this time. Black Alabama troopers were on hand now. Saluting the marchers instead of beating them. Urging them on instead of stopping them cold. Coretta Scott King was there on the front line. So was John Lewis, the black congressman from Atlanta, who had been beaten bloody on that same bridge in 1965. Reverend Jesse Jackson was there. And so was a white southerner. On the front line. Helping to lead the march. President Bill Clinton. Also there was Mother Mobley. She hadn't been at the first march and so she felt she had to be there for the reenactment. Even though she would have to make the crossing in a wheelchair. Her health was failing terribly. So was that of her husband, Gene, who had suffered a stroke and needed assistance walking across the bridge.

There were so many people there that day. A logistical nightmare. Just as the march got started, there was a huge squeeze onto the bridge, and Mother Mobley—in the second row, just behind President Clinton and Reverend Jackson—was getting stuck in the crush of humanity. She cried out: "Reverend Jackson, please, I need your help. The Red Sea is closing in on me." At that moment, President Clinton turned and stopped the whole march and said: "Let this mother through." And the Red Sea parted and she was wheeled to the other side, where she watched the crossing.

Mother Mobley clearly moved so many people during her lifetime. It's the story. Powerful in its simplicity. In effect, the book *Death of Innocence* is a trinity of intersecting stories. At its heart, *Death of Innocence* is the story of a very special relationship between a mother and son. The body of the story turns on Emmett's brutal lynching and the profound historical significance of this tragic event. The soul is Mother Mobley's journey—the journey of a lifetime, one that carries her from the brink of suicide to the self actualized, spiritually energized person she was destined to become.

Mother Mobley stands as a metaphor for the African American experience. Although she might have had her moments of doubt and disappointment, she remained resolute in her faith. She suffered great injustice, but still believed in the justice system. She suffered the worst abuses and indignities of Jim Crow, but still believed that the promise of full equality would one day be kept. She was slowed by the great obstacles placed in her path, but she was never stopped.

Hers is a story of empowerment and love and redemption; of bringing hope from despair, joy from anguish, forgiveness from anger, love from hatred. Even though death is at the core of this story, it ultimately is life affirming. One of the truly amazing things to me is that Mother Mobley never harbored any bitterness for the confessed killers of her son. Not that this satisfies our sense of justice, but it seems that Roy Bryant and J. W. Milam never really had very happy lives following the trial. Blacks—their main clientele—boycotted the stores they ran in the Delta. Whites ostracized them. Never forgave them for drawing all that negative attention to Mississippi and then turning around and confessing. They left Money, moved out of and then back into Mississippi. Milam was in and out of financial trouble for years. Bryant lost most of his eyesight trying to learn the welding trade. I saw a report somewhere that he actually served as a sheriff's deputy for a brief period. Which I guess only makes sense in the topsy turvy world of Planet Mississippi, existing in that strange parallel universe where innocent people are executed and the guilty are exonerated. And given a badge. Ultimately, their wives left them and, it seems, Bryant and Milam died very lonely and bitter men. I base that conclusion in part on a telephone conversation Mother Mobley told me about. She was able to listen in as a radio talk show host interviewed Bryant in 1994, not long before his death. Bryant said he didn't want to talk about Emmett Till. Unless he got paid. He said Emmett Till ruined his life. *His* life.

And still, Mother Mobley was not bitter.

She had the heart of a saint. The soul of an angel. She believed that every soul deserved the chance at redemption. She was opposed to capital punishment. She never wanted these killers to be executed. She only wanted them to live long enough to be sorry for what they had done.

In the end, it seems, she was denied even that.

Even so, she never wavered from her opposition to capital punishment. The last public event of her life was in December 2002. A conference of murder victims' families against the death penalty. There she called on then-governor George Ryan to end capital punishment in Illinois.

On January 11, 2003—the day of Mother Mobley's funeral—Governor Ryan cleared Death Row. In making his announcement, citing so many factors, including his commission report, he included the following statement: "Mamie's strength and grace not only ignited the civil rights movement—including inspiring Rosa Parks to refuse to go to the back of the bus—but inspired murder victims' families until her dying day." Mother Mobley showed, in the purposeful way she lived her life, just how one person can make a difference in the world. And that's what she wanted for all of us. That is how she wanted us to honor her son.

Looking back . . . finding that purpose . . . in moving ahead. She mined her grief for a mission. She said: "God told me He would take one child, but would give me thousands in return." God keeps promises.

Mother Mobley taught for twenty-three years in the Chicago Public Schools, often handling the most difficult students. Even gang members. She became that teacher we all remember. The one who made a difference. The one who changed our lives. She made a point of finding in each one of her kids that extraordinary gift she believed we all have. She lived the kind of committed life she believed every person in this country should live. She had come to see the value—the true value—in life itself, but most especially in her life and in every life she encountered. And she worked with all her kids to teach them the important lessons you can only teach when you've lived the life she lived. As Mother Mobley expresses in the book: "Every choice you make comes at the expense of so many choices you *could* have made. We must be careful to consider all our choices, and what they will cost us." She believed . . . she believed very deeply . . . that we all have a purpose. It flows from that very special gift we have. The one she found in every child she touched. That thing—that one thing—that sets us apart from every other person on the planet.

I happen to write. That's what I do. Not to put too fine a point on it, but that's my gift. That's my purpose.

Yours might lie in a petri dish or on the bottom line of a ledger or through a hoop. Yes, there is a purpose in that. Certainly, there is purpose and there is meaning in the life Michael Jordan has lived. Michael Jordan and Michael Jackson and Jesse Jackson and Jesse James and James Van Der Zee and Gloria Vanderbilt . . . and on and on and on . . .

The point is that you must find your gift—your purpose—ask what you can do with the time you have been given. It may be in the area of social service or public service. Certainly, President Barack Obama stands tall as an example of the purpose-driven life. And there clearly is a need for this kind of dedication. So many challenges we still face. Fifty years after the murder of Emmett Till.

The "Whites Only" signs have been removed. And . . . yeah . . . that's a good thing. But in far too many situations, these days, that simply means there is no warning of the dangerous attitudes that lay in wait. The Southern Poverty Law Center in Montgomery is currently tracking some seven hundred hate groups across the United States. We still have some serious problems.

It is important to note that we cannot adequately address the problem of hate crime without addressing the problem of self-hate crime. Black-on-black violence. We have to teach kids to have respect for life. But how is that done, really? How can a black kid value the life of another black kid when he sees no value in his own life? When he feels that society is showing him no respect.

There still are some serious problems we need to address. But you don't have to work in social service to be of service. Use what you have to make a difference. That's what Monica Haslip did in Chicago, with the Little Black Pearl Workshop. Monica's background is in marketing, and she also is an artist. She found a way to merge her professional training and artistic talent to help get black kids off the street and to give them some hope. She learned about grant-writing and fundraising and has recently opened the doors to a new multimillion dollar art and design center on 47th Street in Chicago. Kids learn arts and crafts. They make and sell their work. But they also learn about business. They learn to organize. They learn to cooperate. They learn to see value in themselves and in each other. They move on with a whole new attitude about life.

These are the kind of stories that give us hope.

Same with Mother Mobley. She didn't become an activist until later in life. After retirement. But we were all well-served by what she did as a teacher. Among so many other things, she taught kids the speeches of Dr. King. They expanded their intellect. They learned their history. They learned values. They developed a sense of industry and confidence. They took their act on the road and inspired so many others.

Mother Mobley called each class of student speakers the Emmett Till Players, and they recently celebrated their thirtieth anniversary. It was such a joy to see how many had gone on to become ministers and lawyers and motivational speakers and business people.

Mother Mobley believed that what she was doing was every bit as important as what people in the movement were doing. After all, what good are the opportunities that are created by the rights we secure if we do not have the skills and the wherewithal to seize those opportunities?

One of Mother Mobley's favorite speeches by Dr. King was one that had been inspired by Dr. Benjamin Mays, his mentor and the longtime president of Morehouse College. In effect it advised us to be the best at whatever we are. If you are a street sweeper, then sweep streets the way Michelangelo sculpted marble. In the end, people will say, there lived a great street sweeper.

God bless Mother Mobley. She certainly swept her job well.

And then . . . then there is the hip-hop community. A number of artists are paying tribute to Emmett Till in their work, and that is a good thing. It is a reminder. In a language that coming generations will listen to.

Some go even further than just rapping. Last year, the rap artist Fifty Cent formed a book club. And the first selection was *Death of Innocence*. Fifty bought twenty-five hundred copies of the book and passed them out free to high school students in his native Queens. Now that might have been good enough, but the students were invited to participate in a writing competition. They wrote essays about their impressions of the book, the significance of it, the characters who had the most meaning for them. I've read a number of the essays and I have to say, they renew our hope for the next generation. If we can just reach out. Educate. Enlighten. Inspire.

So we all have something to contribute. Something to share in this remarkable story we are living.

We are a rich, diverse nation. Many different cultures. Many different backgrounds. Many different interests and motivations. One of the most important things that we all have in common is the great American narrative that is unfolding even as we meet here. We might have dramatically different views on the important issues of the day. Whatever our views are on moral values, or affirmative action, or social security, the very fact that we engage in the discourse is the point of convergence. The point of connection. We are contributing to the narrative—together—in the way we live our lives. And what a story it is.

I live in Hyde Park in Chicago. There are train tracks that I can see running all the way south from twenty-two floors up. Standing there, gazing out toward the horizon, you feel that you can see Kankakee and Champaign and Cairo. Cairo, where only fifty years ago Negroes would have to get up from their seats all over the train.

At the station in Cairo, they'd have to do this. They'd move to the front car. The one directly behind the engine. The one that caught all the soot and heat and pollution from the engine. The one that made them cough. But they would have to move there at Cairo . . . before crossing over into Kentucky. They knew their place. They choked on it.

I can see that as I gaze out toward the horizon. Cairo and Kentucky and Memphis and Mississippi. And I hear that train every night when it makes the trip south. Every morning when it comes back again. There are four different kinds of trains that pass my place. Two different kinds of commuter trains, freight trains, and then this one. The City of New Orleans.

You see, this is the train that Emmett rode down to Mississippi. The train that brought his body home again. I've learned to recognize this particular train. Even when I'm not looking, I recognize it. This train is different from the others. I know the sound of the wheels on the tracks. This train has a unique . . . footprint. You can track it over miles and days and months and years.

I know the sound of the horn. It's different from the others. It has a distinctive . . . voice. A voice that tells us stories about a mother and a son and a movement . . . a movement from there to here . . . from south to north . . . from then to now.

Every day I hear these stories. Great stories trumpeted on the horn of a train . . . a train with a long memory. Rich stories about a people who believe in America. We do believe in America. In the American dream. In the Americans who dare to dream and who have the courage to fight to make their dreams come true. People who know—who know from experience—what courage really means. Not necessarily living your life without fear. Courage—true courage—means moving beyond the fear you feel.

What a great story are we. The story of hope and determination and perseverance. The story of individual and collective strength. The story of how each one of us can make a difference. I have seen how Mother Mobley's great story has affected people. Franklin McMahon was the courtroom illustrator for *Life* magazine during the trial of Emmett's murderers. Inspired by what he saw during that time, he spent most of his professional life covering the civil rights movement and the protest movement and electoral politics. McMahon would also take his wife and his children along with him on assignment. The kids would march in the demonstrations while their father worked. He told me how they grew up—little white kids—knowing that the struggle for full equality in this country was their cause, too. So, you see, this is not just a black story.

President Clinton told the thousands who had gathered at the Edmund Pettus Bridge that he was grateful for the sacrifices they had made back in 1965—sacrifices that had set him free.

No, this isn't a black story. It is an American story. A magnificent narrative. And you are a part of that. The essential part of that. The writers of it. You are writing this story in the way you live your lives. Think about that. And decide. What is the story you will write with the life you live? The time—the precious time—you spend on this planet. Write your life. Live your story. Make it magnificent. A best seller. Write it. Write on. Write here. Write now. Write away. Don't waste any time. Don't keep us all in suspense.

I am very proud of the experience I had with Mother Mobley—the last six months of her life—helping to document the story she lived. The one that has touched each and every one of us—whether we knew it or not. I was too young to have been involved in the civil rights movement. But now, in a way, I feel that I was involved. And I feel so very blessed.

In the end, Mother Mobley was in terrible health. She suffered renal failure. She was on dialysis three times a week. Her eyesight was failing. But her vision was sharper than ever. She bore the wisdom of the ages. When you looked into her eyes, you could see forever.

What she saw way out on the horizon was justice. She had the patience of a person who has suffered so many disappointments over the years, but has never given up on her faith.

Because of her keen vision, because of her many lifetimes of experience, because of her resolve, she knew that change doesn't happen overnight. Change happens over time.

God bless her, she gave it all the time she was given. And then she left us.

In her teaching, Mother Mobley had so many pearls she shared with her students. Among them was this one from the book, the sense that "Good was not good enough. Better was just another step along the way . . . The key was to keep working, keep striving, keep pushing on. After all, how will you ever know that you have done your very best if you stop. Never be satisfied. Never settle. . . . If you believe that the horizon is the finish line, then you will keep moving forward." Looking out on the horizon . . . As I said at the beginning, this is a time of great reflection. As we commemorate the milestones of the movement this year, we must think about what happens after the party's over.

Is it going to be, "Okay, that was fun. Last one out, hit the lights?" Do we simply move on, or do we move forward? There is a distinction. Moving on suggests we leave behind so many pleasant memories. Moving forward suggests we are challenged by this moment to take on the unfinished business of the movement.

Dr. King's dream has not been fully realized. For one thing—and it is no small thing—we still see in our classrooms and our offices and our neighborhoods so many judgments that are being made about people just because of the color of their skin.

Mother Mobley came to learn something very important. That we are all interconnected. What happens to one of us affects us all. One of the lessons of the Emmett Till story is that you cannot simply ignore the serious problems of society and hope not to be affected by them. Our responsibility as fully functioning citizens in a democratic society demands more of us. Sooner or later, you will be confronted by the social problems of the day. They will come looking for you. When you least expect it. Two in the morning. Knocking.

The investigation into Emmett's murder is a good thing. An encouraging thing. It shows us first that we do have rights that others are bound to respect. It sends the signal that you cannot get away with murder in this country. Hate crime will not be tolerated. No matter how long it takes, you will be made to answer for these crimes.

Our hope is that the government will continue to be vigorous. Our duty is to continue to be vigilant.

A friend of mine said something to me recently. Something simple and profound all at once. Something that will be with me all year. His name is David Barr, an award-winning Chicago playwright. The person who introduced me to Mother Mobley. He is the only other person who worked with her in telling her story. It was in the form of a play. So, there I was with David, high atop the Hancock Building. Discussing a collaboration. Looking out at, like, forever. Lifting a glass or two . . . or four . . . and he said, "You know I want? Every night I want to go to bed exhausted." That hit me right away. For all the reasons it should have. So I adopted it. Every night, I want to go to bed exhausted. I want to spend everything I have in a given day, knowing that I will be renewed by my sense of purpose and I will able to do it all over again the next day. Using it all up.

So, in closing, that is what I want to wish for all of you. May you go to bed exhausted every night of your life. Because every day for the rest of your life, you will have used yourself up—spent every last ounce of everything you've got. Knowing that the next day you will be renewed . . . physically . . . spiritually . . . ready to start all over again . . . exhausting yourself.

Do that. Wear yourselves out. Seize the moment. Squeeze the moment. Get two hours of enrichment out of every hour you are given. And always, always live on purpose.

28

Thurgood Marshall's Vision

Juan Williams and Christopher Teal

Biography, by its very nature, focuses on a single life, but is worthless unless the story of that single life reflects the stories of many others. Thurgood Marshall, the black lawyer who stood before the Supreme Court to argue for racial equality in America, never stood alone. As special counsel for the NAACP Legal Defense Fund, he represented millions of people who faced the personal pain of living in a nation where the law and the government supported racism. In the ten years since the publication of *Thurgood Marshall: American Revolutionary* (New York: Times Books, 1998) the phone still rings several times a month with these very people on the other end of the line, people who want to go back to 1954. They want to talk about the *Brown* decision.

All these years later, many of the people are quite elderly. Some cry as they remember people who fought alongside them but are no longer alive. Before the entire generation is gone, these people want to personally share their role in the great drama of the *Brown* case. As the watershed decision rendered in *Brown v. Board of Education of Topeka* reaches its fiftieth anniversary they also have stories to tell, stories they want in the history books.

Their stories vary in the details, but they all circle around that one critical moment in American history like planets orbiting the sun—the momentous ruling in *Brown*. It was *Brown* that raised the possibility of integration becoming a reality in their minds, whether they were for it or against it; it was *Brown,* in a single ruling, that put the power of the federal government's judges, FBI agents, and even the U.S. military's force on the side of equal rights for all; it was *Brown* that made segregation not only immoral, but a crime.

In Prince Edward County, Virginia, the people who went to school with sixteen-year-old Barbara Johns want the world to know that she lit the fuse on the only student-led fight against school segregation that became part of the *Brown* case. The Virginians also speak with awe of Spottswood Robinson and Oliver Hill, the lawyers who helped Barbara Johns stand up against the fearsome power of segregation in a small, rural town.

The letters and phone calls from South Carolina speak to the pressure on black farmers, laborers, and preachers who dared to sign a petition in support of the lawsuit to end segregated schools. Black families working as sharecroppers on white-owned farms were thrown off the land they had worked for generations, because they supported Lawyer Marshall and the NAACP case. But the farmers and preachers held together to challenge the system.

Callers from Kansas are sometimes moved to tears of the power of Reverend Oliver Brown's dedication to school integration. Others want to be sure that history does not forget the surprising support of many white Kansans for opening school doors—including lawyers representing the state who are proud to have fought for integration. And the emotional testimonials from Kansas extend to NAACP lawyers Robert Carter and Jack Greenberg, who came west to represent "Little Linda" Brown, the reverend's daughter who wanted to go to the whites-only school near her house.

Time and again these testimonials come back to a man the old folks call Lawyer Marshall. Sometimes the boisterous big man stayed in their homes while working on a case. Once in a while the people calling about Marshall are the lawyers who worked with him or even against him on a case. A surprising number of people mention the sacrifice they made to get into a court to see him at work. Some still have receipts from the money they sent to the NAACP to support his work.

All of these personal acts of sacrifice and inspiration built to a crescendo with the May 17, 1954, decision. When Thurgood Marshall was at his best in a courtroom, he made his clients into real people suffering real damage from the laws of segregation. He told their stories—both as a legal argument for equal rights and as an appeal to the ideals and conscience of white Americans. At the time, some people condemned Marshall for using personal anecdotes and sociological evidence. The same critics condemned the high court for citing such evidence when they ruled in Marshall's favor in *Brown*. But while the facts, the law, and basic fairness were on Marshall's side, it may have been the power of those individual narratives that ultimately tipped the balance in the Supreme Court and the court of public opinion. Those stories were not just ornamentation, but gave the legal arguments the ineffable force of human justice.

• • •

Fifty years later a complex set of fresh challenges confronts us, and a new river of powerful and personal stories flows.

In 2003 minority students at the University of Michigan Law School had their own stories to tell the Supreme Court as they successfully fought to preserve the idea that race should be a legitimate factor when students are chosen for the nation's most selective schools. White students who had filed suits against affirmative action programs at the University of Michigan and University of Texas law schools also had stories to tell. Their stories are about the frustration of achieving the grades necessary to get into colleges or graduate schools only to be rejected in favor of minorities with lower test scores. In a way, their plight was also heard when the same Supreme Court struck down numerically based racial preferences in college admissions at the University of Michigan's undergraduate school.

Then there are the angst-filled stories from the generation who fought for academic integration but now see top universities allowing blacks, Hispanics, whites, and Asians to live in separate housing, dine separately, and even hold university-sponsored graduation ceremonies that are racially exclusive. The rationale of students and administration is that minority students at these white schools need the emotional support that comes with strong racial cohesion. But to the outside world it appears these schools are teaching students lessons on the value of separatism. In the Michigan cases of 2003 Justice Clarence Thomas, a polarizing figure on the Court when it comes to matters of race, harshly criticized affirmative action for generating just this kind of "aesthetic" diversity at elite institutions. It is a deeply ironic story that this voluntary separatism is a fact of life at institutions that advertise themselves as enlightened examples of racial diversity.

These modern-day stories seem to collide with the stories told by Marshall's generation, stories focused on the battle to improve education through integration. This new generation doesn't deny the validity of the stories told by Marshall and his peers. Instead they argue the relevance of those stories in light of the bitter reality they face fifty years after the *Brown* case: that America's schools are still very segregated, and the remedies devised in the past—including affirmative action—seem to have failed.

The impression of renewed segregation is borne out by statistics: a 2003 study by the Civil Rights Project of Harvard University found that the nation's twenty-seven largest school districts are "overwhelmingly" black and Latino and are segregated from white private and public schools—the study labeled them Apartheid Schools. And the trend is getting worse. As a result of a reversal that began in 1988, the percentage of white students attending public schools with black and Hispanic students "is lower in 2000 than it was in 1970 before busing for racial balance began." As a consequence, according to the report, "at the beginning of the twenty-first century, American public schools are now twelve years into the process of continuous resegregation."

Several key trends have contributed to the new segregation. First, a continuation of "white flight" to the suburbs and a series of setbacks on the Supreme Court during the 1970s have stopped efforts to fully achieve desegregation. For example, *San Antonio Independent School District v. Rodriguez* (1973) denied efforts to equalize spending between rich and poor school districts. And *Milliken v. Bradley* (1973) prevented busing between suburban and urban school districts in Detroit to achieve integration. Together these decisions effectively brought the era of active integration to a halt. In his dissent in the Detroit case, Marshall said that the ruling would allow the nation's cities to be divided into black and white enclaves, and as a result, the schools themselves would be segregated. "It is a course, I predict, our people will ultimately regret," he concluded.

A second key trend that has shifted the dynamics of race in America is immigration. Five years after the publication of *Thurgood Marshall: American Revolutionary,* one thing is clear—demographic changes have forever altered this new generation's stories about race in American society. The influx of immigrants from Mexico and Latin America, as well as from Asia, the Caribbean, Africa, and eastern Europe, has reached unprecedented heights in this nation of immigrants. The Hispanic population grew notably during the 1990s, and with over thirty-seven million Hispanics residing in the United States, this ethnic group now surpasses African Americans. For the first time in U.S. history, black people, whose numbers stand slightly more than thirty-six million, are not the biggest minority group. Though they do not yet have the political or economic clout that African Americans continue to exercise, these new voices are telling different stories about race relations and creating a new American reality of race.

In America's highly diverse population, the race question has transformed; it is no longer simply a matter of blacks making demands of the white establishment by pointing to the history of slavery, legal discrimination, and cultural bigotry. The new immigrant's story, whose starting point is usually a heroic effort to get to America, seen as a land of economic and political opportunity, stands in sharp contrast to traditional black narrative of slavery and racism. In this new America, where more than half of all public school students are minorities, school integration is not universally viewed as key to equalizing educational opportunities.

These new trends have created a new reality in which many judges, school boards, and parents have tired of race occupying the primary position in the discussion of school reform. Their refrain is that race is too divisive, and legal segregation is not the issue. Thurgood Marshall's critics have long contended that equality in education, not integration, should have been the goal of *Brown,* and must now be the goal of American leaders. The black middle class fled to suburban enclaves, and poor black children were left behind in failing neighborhoods and schools. Black children across the country continue to score lower as a whole on achievement tests. Hispanics remain at much greater rates of poverty, with higher dropout rates and higher segregation rates. Both groups remain far behind their Anglo and Asian-American counterparts on test scores. These facts, say Marshall's critics, must be addressed with better schools—not with more theoretical worries over integration. Are Marshall's remedies, particularly affirmative action, even relevant anymore?

From its inception, affirmative action has been under fire by critics who claim it unjustly rewards less-qualified individuals, and does nothing to address long-term problems of discrimination. But since Marshall left the Court in 1991, the slow whittling away at affirmative action programs across the nation has continued unabated. Circuit courts held, in cases such as *Hopwood v. State of Texas* (1996), that schools might be limited in their use of race to determine admissions. In a case that affected African Americans and Hispanics equally, the Fifth Circuit determined that the University of Texas had not given enough evidence that the Fourteenth Amendment permitted them to use race as a factor to benefit African Americans and Hispanics.

The high court also took a more direct control of affirmative action programs, In *Adarand Constructors, Inc. v. Peña* (1995), the Court held that when it came to set asides, affirmative action programs must meet strict scrutiny standards. This meant that the governmental program must meet "compelling" national interests and be narrowly tailored. This had the effect of greatly limiting many affirmative action programs.

In many ways the most visible opponent to Marshall has been his replacement on the Supreme Court, Justice Clarence Thomas. Previewing the turn away from race in a 1987 *Howard University Law Review* article, Thomas wrote: "*Brown* was a missed opportunity as was all of its progeny, whether they involve busing, affirmative action, or redistricting." Thomas concluded that the Warren Court made a mistake by basing its 1954 decision on stories about the damage that school segregation did to hearts and minds of black children. He wrote that by making "sensitivity the paramount issue," the Court lost sight of the Constitution and the Declaration of Independence, which call for liberty and equality for all citizens. Americans should be free, Thomas wrote, to rise above "petty squabbling over 'quotas,' 'affirmative action,' and 'race conscious remedies for social ills.'"

Thomas's stand is in keeping with his judicial philosophy as a strict constructionist and his laissez-faire justice when it comes to government intervention about race. He would have no problem with allowing the "market" to determine whether and how people segregate.

In other words, the future justice Thomas was one of the first to make a case that is widely accepted today—that Americans should be free to create public schools with students of any color as long as they are good schools. In that way of thinking, all-black schools can be just as good as all-white schools. And schools made up of poor children can be just as good as made up of rich children.

While Thomas's approach is strong in the American tradition that embraces individual rights, it could lead to rigid resegregation and catastrophe without some governmental oversight. And the truth is, despite all of these trends, the Marshall affirmative action view may be heavy-handed and clumsy at times in its efforts to overcome discrimination. But like the "trust-busters" of the last century, it recognizes the role that government must play to ensure that racial majorities— even if they are not racist but simply looking out for their best interest—do not impose a disadvantage on minorities. People can be free to associate, but they must not exclude. And the fact is that segregation has not gone away. While political leaders may not want to talk about race, America's neighborhoods are becoming more segregated, there is a greater divide between blacks and whites on standardized tests, and the upper echelons of corporate life remain exceedingly white for such a diverse nation. As the stories in the quivering voices of those that lived through Jim Crow can attest, segregation does nothing to positively affirm a person's sense of liberty, freedom, or racial pride.

• • •

All of these judicial actions and ongoing debates point to just how important Marshall's ideas and presence remain. The arguments in the 2003 Supreme Court case over the University of Michigan revolve around Marshall: Marshall's work in the 1978 *Regents of the University of California v. Bakke* decision to get Justice Powell to agree to consider race as a factor in admissions is the central issue at stake in the current affirmative action debate—it was Justice Powell's discussion of race in *Bakke* that was ambiguously confirmed in the Court's latest confrontation of the issue. Regardless of whether Thurgood Marshall's views have always won the day, one thing is very clear after a quick look at the nature of discussions taking place in contemporary life: one would have to say that Marshall remains very relevant.

Looking back at Marshall's work, one can take a different view of him in today's light. Previously he had been seen as a plodding legal mind, slowly working to overturn the Jim Crow system of segregation. He refused to make direct attacks on segregation as unconstitutional until after he had won some significant court decisions that he would use as a basis for the final blow. Even after his 1950 victory in *Sweatt v. Painter* desegregating the University of Texas Law School, he had to be pressed to abandon the legal strategy of insisting on equalizing separate facilities for blacks. Only after being repeatedly pushed did he use the direct attack—and argue that the very idea of school segregation was unconstitutional because it violated the idea of equal rights for all Americans.

This path was successful for him and his case. But even more than a methodical strategist, Marshall can really be seen as a visionary. His creative mind was molded by crucial experiences—his years of growing up in segregated, but racially mixed Baltimore; early brushes with great thinkers such as Langston Hughes and Charles Houston; an uncompromising view that segregation must be overturned. All of these factors led him to develop the notion that integration, and only integration, was the remedy that cured what ailed society. His notion that no legal barrier to interaction should exist between different racial groups was (and is) a powerful demonstration of an ideal. And despite growing rates of segregation, despite setbacks, Marshall as the visionary and the architect of race relations is indubitable.

Though the ongoing debate about affirmative action and the consequence of the desegregation decision flourishes, it is clear that *Brown* still ranks as one of the most significant legal decisions in U.S. history. Since the Supreme Court ruled that "separate facilities are inherently unequal," life for black Americans and other minority groups has improved by every measure—graduation rates, income, and home ownership to name just a few.

The importance of *Brown* is that it finally led to the complete dismantling of Jim Crow segregation throughout the country, and slowly but surely the nation has changed. Fifty years later, no state is permitted to enforce segregated schools. A once enslaved and isolated class of citizens has seen the political, economic, and social power rising over the past five decades.

History celebrates Marshall as a Supreme Court justice and as an attorney for the NAACP. But in fact it was his creativity and ideals that set him apart. This persistent vision—the promise of America as an open, fully democratic nation—could only become a greater reality with the possibility of a more integrated society. This was Marshall's goal in *Brown,* his life work and his legacy.

Fifty years after the *Brown* decision, Thurgood Marshall's role as its architect remains at the core of the never-ending, great debate about race in America. And in this debate, amid the millions of individual stories that harmonize and diverge, Marshall's voice still echoes loudest of all.

Epilogue

Brown's Global Impact

Mary L. Dudziak

In the years after the *Brown v. Board of Education* decision, the case did not slip quietly into historical memory. *Brown* became a cultural icon. It was embraced in the abstract, but controversy continued over just what *Brown* meant. This came to the surface in the Supreme Court itself in 2007, in a case that considered whether school districts could voluntarily take race into account in assigning students to maintain racially balanced schools. In *Parents Involved in Community Schools (PICS) v. Seattle School District No. 1,* the Court held plans like this to the highest constitutional standard, and struck them down as violating the equal protection clause. In his majority opinion, Chief Justice John Roberts went beyond the usual practice of interpreting a past case in a way that supported his holding. He drew upon the words of the litigants in *Brown* themselves to support his reading of the Fourteenth Amendment. Roberts quoted from the plaintiff's brief in *Brown*, along with the oral argument made by NAACP lawyer Robert Carter before the Supreme Court, implying that a rigid "colorblindness" theory of Fourteenth Amendment equality was what the plaintiffs themselves had sought in *Brown* in the first place. Carter, now a retired federal judge, strongly objected.[1]

As important as racial equality in education was, Justice Stephen Breyer's dissent suggested that *Brown's* importance went beyond disputes in American communities. According to Breyer, *Brown* "affected . . . deeply not only Americans, but the world." To support this point, he quoted from a Nigerian newspaper, one of the many reactions to *Brown* around the world. The *West African Pilot* had lauded the ruling, because the "United States should set an example for all other nations by taking the lead in removing from its national life all signs and races of racial intolerance, arrogance or discrimination."[2]

Breyer was right to point to *Brown's* global impact. But the worldwide significance of the case was not simply that it enabled others to find a positive model in American racial justice. Rather, *Brown* stemmed damage done to the nation's image around the world, which for years had been negatively affected by racial segregation. *Brown* was a case about American schools, but it also affected U.S. foreign relations.[3]

International concern about American race discrimination was not new during the 1950s. What was new was the nation's role as the Cold War "leader of the free world." Discrimination in the United States hampered the nation's ability to convince other peoples that American democracy was a better form of government than communism. If in the world's leading democracy schoolchildren were segregated by race and many African Americans were disenfranchised, some wondered why democracy was a good form of government for nonwhite peoples of the world. With many African and Asian nations soon to gain independence, racism threatened U.S. relations with these emerging countries.[4]

One of the reasons American equality was so important was that the cold war was cast as a battle between two systems of government: one that protected the rights of its people, and one that denied them. President Harry S. Truman described the conflict this way in 1947, warning the nation that Americans faced a cold war battle against an adversary that was evil because it denied rights to its own people. The Soviet Union "relies on terror and oppression . . . fixed elections, and the suppression of personal freedoms," he warned, while American democracy embraced "free institutions, representative government, free elections, guarantees of individual liberty, freedom of speech and religion, and freedom from political oppression." Many believed that to win the cold war, the United States needed to convince others that American democracy was superior to communism.[5]

But American racial problems frequently undermined efforts to construct a favorable image of American democracy for the world. Following World War II, some African American soldiers returned home to southern communities that wished to remind them of their "place." News of brutal beatings and killings of veterans appeared in the media in the United States, and quickly found their way into the world's newspapers. American allies as well as critics suggested that American racism was the nation's Achilles heel, and that if the United States hoped to spread democracy, it should begin by practicing it at home.[6]

The Soviet Union took advantage of this American weakness, using it extensively in anti-American propaganda. By the late 1940s, race in America had become a principal Soviet propaganda theme. American diplomats were told that readers who usually dismissed communist propaganda paid more attention to propaganda on American racism. The reason was simply that there was so much truth to it.[7]

Global interest in American racial problems gave the civil rights movement an important platform. Civil rights activists petitioned the new United Nations, arguing that American race discrimination violated the human rights of African Americans. The U.S. government responded, using overseas information programs to try to rehabilitate the image of American race relations, casting it as a story from slavery to freedom, and of enlightened progress under democracy. Ultimately, however, American leaders believed that only civil rights progress would dampen the negative effect of racial problems on U.S. foreign relations.[8]

U.S. Ambassador to India Chester Bowles emphasized this point in a 1952 speech at Yale University. Peoples of color in Asia and Africa "seldom think about the United States without considering the limitations under which our 13 million Negroes are living," he emphasized. They were "convinced that solely because of their color, many Americans are denied a full share in the life of the richest nation on earth, and in their ears this conviction gives our claim to world leadership a distinctively hollow ring." Rather than responding through information programs, it would be easier to respond to these concerns "if we have a better answer from home." Bowles told his audience, "I can think of no single thing that would be more helpful to us in Asia than the achievement of racial harmony in America."[9]

School segregation was especially damaging to U.S. prestige. Because of this, *Brown v. Board of Education* was both a threat and an opportunity. It was a threat because if the Supreme Court upheld segregation, the decision would be a major world news story, reinforcing negative views about race and American democracy. It was an opportunity because if the Court struck down segregation, it would be a major statement that racism was at odds with the U.S. Constitution, and the nation was overcoming its past practices of injustice.[10]

The Justice Department filed a "friend of the court" brief in *Brown* in 1952. This was just one of a number of civil rights briefs filed by the department since the 1948 housing discrimination case *Shelley v. Kraemer.* The brief supported the plaintiffs' argument that school segregation violated the constitution. It focused special attention on the District of Columbia, which was before the Court in one of the five cases consolidated in *Brown.* Washington, D.C., was "the window through which the world looks into our house," the brief suggested. Segregation in the nation's capitol was therefore especially embarrassing. It was "a graphic illustration of a failure of democracy." School segregation anywhere in the country was a problem, however, having "an adverse effect upon our relations with other countries. Racial discrimination furnishes grist for the Communist propaganda mills, and it raises doubts even among friendly nations as to the intensity of our devotion to the democratic faith."[11]

To support its cold war claims, the brief quoted extensively from Secretary of State Dean Acheson. According to Acheson, the damage to U.S. foreign relations from race discrimination was growing: "The United States is under constant attack in the foreign press, over the foreign radio, and in such international bodies as the United Nations because of various practices of discrimination against minority groups in this country." While some attacks were distortions, "the undeniable existence of racial discrimination gives unfriendly governments the most effective kind of ammunition for their propaganda warfare." School segregation in particular had been "singled out for hostile foreign comment." The impact of such practices on the international standing of the United States, in Acheson's words, "jeopardizes the effective maintenance of our moral leadership of the free and democratic nations of the world."[12]

The Supreme Court did not mention foreign relations in the *Brown* ruling, but members of the Court were well aware of the international impact of race discrimination, having encountered it on their travels overseas. When the ruling was issued, it was just what the State Department had been hoping for, and was immediately used in programming for foreign audiences. The Voice of America beamed the news around the world, especially to China and the Soviet Union, emphasizing that the issue of school segregation "was settled by law under democratic processes rather than by mob rule or dictatorial fiat."[13]

Brown was celebrated around the world. "At Last! Whites and Blacks in the United States on the same school benches," was the headline in *Afrique Nouvelle,* a newspaper in French West Africa (now Senegal). The decision was of special interest throughout Africa, reported the Nigerian *West African Pilot.* *Brown* would have a world impact, for abolishing racism in America "would be the greatest possible assurance of America's good faith and sincerity towards the establishment of a true world-wide democracy." The ruling was front-page news across India, with New Delhi's *Hindustan Times* noting that "American democracy stands to gain in strength and prestige from the unanimous ruling" since school segregation "has been a long-standing blot on American life and civilization." For the *Sydney Morning Herald,* an Australian newspaper, *Brown* would "go a long way toward dissipating the validity of the Communist contention that Western concepts of democracy are hypocritical." The global reaction to *Brown* was recognized within the United States and was seen as one of the ruling's great benefits. A *San Francisco Chronicle* article suggested that Brown would have an even greater impact overseas than on the American South, because it would restore the faith of other nations in American democracy. *Brown* would "stun and silence America's Communist traducers behind the Iron Curtain," the *Pittsburgh Courier* argued, for it would "effectively impress upon millions of colored people in Asia and Africa the fact that idealism and social morality can and do prevail in the Unites States, regardless of race, creed or color."[14]

Since the international impact of civil rights reform gave the civil rights movement important leverage, NAACP Executive Secretary Walter White wrote to U.S. ambassadors stationed in thirteen countries, inquiring about *Brown*'s impact in increasing "faith in the American democratic process and in the United States itself." He found the responses encouraging.[15]

"The Court's decision and the events following it have been watched with great interest by Italian public opinion," U.S. Ambassador to Italy Clare Boothe Luce wrote to White. "On balance, I think the result has been, not only to give Italians a fresh reminder of the meaning of American democracy, but also to cut the ground from under the anti-American propaganda put out by the Communists on this point." U.S. Ambassador to Israel Francis H. Russell also found that "the Supreme Court decision has done much to strengthen belief in the essential democracy of American life." Meanwhile, there was little coverage in the Soviet Union. For the paper *Izvestia, Brown* was simply one of America's "demagogic gestures intended for export." The Court's delay in implementing desegregation, according to the paper, showed that the Court's action had "a purely masking character and that it was taken only for propaganda purposes."[16]

As American diplomats had hoped, *Brown* dampened international criticism. When Carl Rowan traveled to India later in 1954, he was told by American diplomats that "I could expect less heat on the race question" than usual because *Brown* had been so well publicized in India. The National Security Council reported that "the decision is regarded as the greatest event since the Emancipation Proclamation, and it removes from Communist hands the most effective anti-American weapon they had in Black Africa."[17]

Although *Brown* made it easier for American diplomats to argue that the U.S. government supported civil rights, race in America would continue to be a major story in the world's newspapers. This meant that although *Brown* was an important milestone, more effort was needed. The civil rights movement raised the stakes in the early 1960s, as demonstrators took to the streets. Events in Birmingham, Alabama, in May 1963, when peaceful demonstrators were brutalized by police, generated especially harsh foreign criticism. The national and international reaction to Birmingham led President John F. Kennedy to call for a strong civil rights bill in the last months of his presidency. Ultimately, civil rights statutes and court cases helped ease global criticism, even though inequality in American communities remained.[18]

In more recent years, the nation has not been immune to the way rights violations can undermine U.S. international prestige. In the late twentieth century, as other nations came to view the death penalty as a human rights violation, executions in the United States led to international protests. It was not until after the terrorist attacks of September 11, 2001, however, that the U.S. government began to again take very seriously the way American actions affected U.S. prestige around the world. An outpouring of international criticism followed disclosure of the abuse of prisoners by Americans at the Iraqi prison Abu Ghraib, and the Guantánamo prison camp came under fire. The Bush Administration turned to public diplomacy, sending American athletes and others around the world to boost U.S. prestige. But there is a lesson for our own time in the story of *Brown*'s global impact: the most enduring way to improve the U.S. image is to live up to the ideals. Now, as during the cold war years, the nation is stronger as a world leader when it protects individual rights.[19]

Notes

1. *Brown v. Board of Education*, 347 U.S. 483 (1954); *Parents Involved in Community Schools v. Seattle School District No. 1*, 551 U.S. 701, 127 S.Ct. 2738 (2007); Adam Liptak, "The Same Words, but Differing Views," *New York Times*, June 29, 2007.

2. *Parents Involved in Community Schools (PICS) v. Seattle School District No. 1*, 127 S.Ct. at 2822–23 (Breyer, J., dissenting). Breyer's source for the *West African Pilot* was Mary L. Dudziak, "*Brown* as a Cold War Case," *Journal of American History* 91 (June 2004): 32–42. The original article appeared in *West African Pilot* (Lagos), May 22, 1954, 2.

3. Mary L. Dudziak, *Cold War Civil Rights: Race and the Image of American Democracy* (Princeton: Princeton University Press, 2000), 94–114. On *Brown v. Board of Education*, see James Patterson, *Brown v. Board of Education: A Civil Rights Milestone and Its Troubled Legacy* (New York: Oxford University Press, 2001); Robert J. Cottrol, Raymond T. Diamond, and Leland B. Ware, *Brown v. Board of Education: Caste, Culture, and the Constitution* (Lawrence: University Press of Kansas, 2003).

4. Melvyn Leffler, *A Preponderance of Power: National Security, the Truman Administration, and the Cold War* (Stanford: Stanford University Press, 1992); Thomas Borstelmann, *The Cold War and the Color Line: American Race Relations in the Global Arena* (Cambridge, Mass.: Harvard University Press, 2001), 45–84; Dudziak, *Cold War Civil Rights*, 18–46.

5. President Harry S. Truman, Address before a joint session of Congress, March 12, 1947, *Public Papers of the Presidents: Harry S. Truman, 1947*, at John T. Wooley and Gerhard Peters, The American Presidency Project, http://www.presidency.ucsb.edu/ws/?pid=12846 (accessed April 6, 2009).

6. Dudziak, *Cold War Civil Rights*, 18–39.

7. Ibid., 43–56.

8. Carol Anderson, *Eyes off the Prize: The United Nations and the African American Struggle for Human Rights, 1944–1955* (Cambridge: Cambridge University Press, 2003), 58–112; "The Negro in American Life," (circa 1950), folder 503, box 112, series II, Chester Bowles Papers, Manuscripts and Archives, Yale University Library, New Haven, Conn.; Dudziak, *Cold War Civil Rights*, 26–39, 43–56.

9. Chester Bowles, "Racial Harmony—How Much Does It Matter in World Affairs?" 1952, folder 540, box 115, series 2, Chester Bowles Papers, Manuscripts and Archives, Yale University; Dudziak, *Cold War Civil Rights*, 77–78.

10. Ibid., 101.

11. Brief of the United States as Amicus Curiae, *Brown v. Board of Education*, 347 U.S. 483 (1954), 4–8; Dudziak, *Cold War Civil Rights*, 91–102.

12. Brief of the United States as Amicus Curiae, *Brown v. Board*, 6–8; Dudziak, *Cold War Civil Rights*, 96–102.

13. *New York Times*, May 18, 1954, p. 1; Dudziak, *Cold War Civil Rights*, 102–7.

14. U.S. Consul, Dakar, French West Africa, to Department of State, May 26, 1954, RG 59, 811.411/5–2654, Records of the Department of State, National Archives, College Park, Maryland; *West African Pilot* (Lagos), May 22, 1954, p. 2; "A Great Decision," *Hindustan Times*, May 20, 1954 (found in Supreme Court—School Case— Foreign Press—1952–May 1954, box A619, General Office Files, Group II, National Association for the Advancement of Colored People Papers, Manuscript Division, Library of Congress, Washington, D.C.); *Sydney Morning Herald*, May 22, 1954, p. 3; *San Francisco Chronicle*, May 18, 1954, p. 18; *New York Times*, May 18, 1954, p. 2 (quoting *Pittsburgh Courier*); Dudziak, "*Brown* as a Cold War Case."

15. Walter White to Horace A. Hildreth, September 16, 1954, Folder: Supreme Court—School Case—Foreign Press—June–December 1954, box A619, General Office Files, Group II, National Association for the Advancement of Colored People Papers (Manuscript Division, Library of Congress, Washington, D.C.).

16. Clare Boothe Luce to Walter White, Sept. 24, 1954, Folder: Supreme Court— School Case—Foreign Press—June–December 1954, box A619, General Office Files, Group II, NAACP Papers; Francis H. Russell to White, October 18, 1954, Folder: Supreme Court—School Case—Foreign Press—June–December 1954, box A619, General Office Files, Group II, NAACP Papers; Charles E. Bohlen to White, October 9, 1954, Folder: Supreme Court—School Case—Foreign Press—June–December 1954, box A619, General Office Files, Group II, NAACP Papers; S. Kondrashov, "Judges and Governors: International Notes," *Izvestia*, June 23, 1954 (U.S. Embassy translation), Folder: Supreme Court—School Case—Foreign Press—June–December 1954, box A619, General Office Files, Group II, NAACP Papers.

17. Carl T. Rowan, *The Pitiful and the Proud* (New York: Random House, 1956), 19; National Security Council, "Status of the United States Program for National Security as of June 30, 1954," NSC 5430, *Foreign Relations of the United States, 1952–1954* (Washington, D.C.: Government Printing Office, 1984), 11:7777, 1785–86; Dudziak, *Cold War Civil Rights*, 107–9.

18. Ibid., 208–48.

19. Michelle Brown, "'Setting the Conditions' for Abu Ghraib: The Prison Nation Abroad," *American Quarterly* 57 (September 2005): 973–97; Amy Kaplan, "Where Is Guantánamo?" *American Quarterly* 57 (September 2005): 831–58.

Kal Alston is Associate Provost for Academic Administration at Syracuse University, where she also serves as Professor in Cultural Foundations of Education and Women and Gender Studies. Her research has focused on race and gender in the social practices and discourses of philosophy, education, youth culture, and the media. During her sixteen years on the faculty in Gender and Women's Studies and Educational Policy Studies at the University of Illinois at Urbana-Champaign, she served as Chair of the Chancellor's Committee on the Status of Women and as Director of Gender and Women's Studies. She also occupied leadership roles on the Graduate College Executive Committee, the Diversity Planning Committee, the Athletic Board, and the University Senates Conference.

Margaret L. Andersen is the Edward F. and Elizabeth Goodman Professor of Sociology at the University of Delaware. She has authored and coauthored numerous books focusing on the sociology of race and gender, including *Race and Ethnicity in the United States: The Changing Landscape, Thinking about Women: Sociological Perspectives on Sex and Gender,* and *Race, Class, and Gender: An Anthology,* and a forthcoming biography, *Living Art: The Life of Paul R. Jones, African American Art Collector.* In 2006 she received the Jessie Bernard Award from the American Sociological Association, given annually to the scholar whose works have expanded the horizons of sociology to include the study of women. She has also won two awards for excellence in teaching at the University of Delaware, and is the president of the American Sociological Association.

Kathryn H. Anthony is Professor and former Chair of the Design Program, and former Chair of the Building Research Council in the School of Architecture at the University of Illinois at Urbana-Champaign, where she also serves on the faculty of the Department of Landscape Architecture and the Women's Studies Program. Her book *Design Juries on Trial: The Renaissance in the Design Studio* won the Creative Achievement Award from the Association of Collegiate Schools of Architecture. She is the author of numerous articles and books, including *Designing for Diversity: Gender, Race, and Ethnicity in the Architectural Profession,* a text that has earned a number of awards, including the Collaborative Achievement Award from the American Institute of Architects and the Achievement Award from the Environmental Design Research Association, and was selected as an honor book by the Chicago Book Clinic. Professor Anthony has served on the editorial boards of *The Journal of Architectural Education* and *Environment & Behavior.*

Lifelong Champaign, Illinois, resident **Nathaniel C. Banks** is Director of the Campus Community Interface Initiatives at the University of Illinois, where he received his bachelor's degree in trumpet performance and masters in music education. He has served as director of the Bruce D. Nesbitt African American Cultural Center, and director of the Upward Bound College Prep Academy through the Office of Minority Student Affairs. Banks helped to found the Judah Christian School, where he also was an administrator. As a community activist he has served on the Champaign-Urbana Area Project and the Champaign Police Community Relations Committee, and has chaired the Champaign-Urbana Charter School Initiative, which targeted at-risk students. He is currently a member of school board for the Champaign Community Unit School District 4 and is cofounder of Mo' Better Music, an instrumental music program for low-income youth. Banks has written for local publications and has contributed to the book *Black Culture Centers: Politics of Survival and Identity.*

Bernice McNair Barnett is Associate Professor in the Departments of Sociology, Educational Policy Studies, and Women and Gender Studies at the University of Illinois, Urbana-Champaign, where she is also a national board advisor for the Center on Democracy in a Multiracial Society. She is a founding member of the American Sociological Association's Race, Gender, and Class section and former Midwest Regional Director of the Association of Black Women Historians. Her research interests include women's civil rights leadership; gender, race, and class inequalities; and social movements of the 1960s. Professor Barnett is author of "Invisible Southern Black Women Leaders in the Civil Rights Movement: The Triple Constraints of Gender, Race, and Class" (in *Gender & Society*) and "Black Women's Collectivist Movement Organizations: Their Struggles During the 'Doldrums'" (in *Feminist Organizations: Harvest of the New Women's Movement*). She is completing an in-depth study, "Women of *Brown v.*

Board: A Gendered Analysis," based on life-history interviews with the widow and daughters of Reverend Oliver Brown and other plaintiffs in the *Brown* case.

Associate Professor of African American Studies and Journalism at the University of Illinois, **Christopher Benson** focuses on the convergence of media and social issues, and on techniques of magazine article writing. With a background as a writer and lawyer, he served as Washington editor for *Ebony* and contributed to *Jet, Chicago, The Crisis,* and the *Washington Post.* Benson's documentary *Paper Trail: 100 Years of the "Chicago Defender"* was broadcast by PBS in 2005. As vice president of Johnson Publishing Company, he oversaw the development of *Ebony South Africa.* He also has worked as speech writer for several Washington politicians and authored *Special Interest,* a Washington-based suspense thriller. Benson has written and published short stories and was coauthor of Mamie Till-Mobley's memoir *Death of Innocence: The Hate Crime That Changed America,* which won the 2004 Blackboard Nonfiction Book of the Year Award and a Robert F. Kennedy Book Award. He has also won two Midwest Emmys and a Peter Lisagor Award for exemplary journalism for his work on *Paper Trail.*

Ed Blankenheim is noteworthy as one of the original thirteen Freedom Riders who risked his own safety to protest racial segregation in the South. Blankenheim helped mobilize riders nationwide and was a passenger on a bus that was firebombed in Anniston, Alabama. In 1961 the Freedom Riders boarded buses, trains, and planes to test the 1960 Supreme Court ruling outlawing segregation in all interstate public facilities and transportation. "People were on fire. They wanted to change things and they did," said Blankenheim. "It was the freedom ride notion itself—riding for freedom—that changed the civil rights movement." As the riders were beaten and arrested along the way, national attention rose and hundreds joined the campaign. Retired from his life vocation as a carpenter, Blankenheim passed away on September 26, 2004.

Julian Bond, Director of the Southern Poverty Law Center, has served more than twenty years in the Georgia General Assembly. As a writer, teacher, and lecturer, he has been on the cutting edge of social change since he led college demonstrations in Atlanta in 1960. A graduate of Morehouse College, Bond is currently Professor of History at the University of Virginia. He holds numerous honorary degrees and awards and has been a powerful advocate and leader in organizations targeting human rights and desegregation. In 1995 Bond was elected to his fourth term on the National Board of the NAACP and has served as chairman since 1998. A collection of Bond's essays has been published under the title *A Time to Speak, A Time to Act.* His poems and articles have appeared in national publications such as the *New York Times, American Negro Poetry,* and the *Los Angeles Times.*

Orville Vernon Burton is Professor of History and Sociology and Senior Research Scientist at the National Center for Supercomputing Applications (NCSA) in Champaign, where he is Associate Director for Humanities and Social Sciences and an affiliate of the Afro-American Studies and Research Program. He has served as Director of the College of Charleston's Program in the Carolina Lowcountry and as president of the Agricultural History Society. Professor Burton has authored more than a hundred articles and eight books, including *The Age of Lincoln* and the Pulitzer-nominated *In My Father's House Are Many Mansions: Family and Community in Edgefield, South Carolina,* and has received prestigious teaching awards from esteemed institutions such as the Carnegie Foundation and the American Historical Association. His research, which crosses the humanities and social sciences, focuses on race relations, community, family, politics, and religion in the American South.

Jason Chambers is Associate Professor in the Department of Advertising at the University of Illinois at Urbana-Champaign. Dr. Chambers has presented his research into the African American consumer market both nationally and internationally. His work has been published in books and journals in the United States, Asia, and Europe. The University of Pennsylvania Press published his first book, *Madison Avenue and the Color Line: African Americans in the Advertising Industry,* in early 2008. This penetrating work examines the employment and entrepreneurial experiences of blacks in the advertising industry and their fight to diversify both the industry and advertisements.

Constance Curry is a writer, civil rights activist, and Fellow at the Institute for Women's Studies, Emory University. Curry authored three books based on leaders she met while working in Mississippi for the freedom movement in the 1960s, the award-winning *Silver Rights, Aaron Henry: The Fire Ever Burning,* and *Mississippi Harmony,* and coauthored and edited *Deep in Our Hearts: Nine White Women in the Freedom Movement.* Her documentary film *The Intolerable Burden,* based on *Silver Rights,* won the John E. O'Connor Award from the American Historical Association.

Curry's current work addresses resegregation in American schools and its role in tracking youth of color to prison. Most recently, she cowrote Robert Zellner's memoir *The Wrong Side of Murder Creek*.

Joseph A. De Laine Jr. is the son of the Reverend Joseph Armstrong De Laine, who is credited for his leadership role in the first challenge to the "separate but equal" doctrine. This legal challenge in Clarendon County, South Carolina, *Briggs v. Elliott*, led to the 1954 *Brown v. Board of Education* Supreme Court decision. Joseph De Laine Jr. received his BS degree from Lincoln University and did graduate work at New York University, after which he pursued scientific research at three major research institutions in New York and New Jersey. At Hoffman LaRoche, Inc., he served as Director of Diagnostic Product Marketing, Director of Corporate EEO, Pharmaceutical Promotions Manager, Director of Sales Planning, and Employee Health Services Manager. De Laine represented South Carolina on the *Brown v. Board* Fiftieth Anniversary Presidential Commission. He is also a member of the Board of Directors of the Briggs-De Laine-Pearson Foundation.

Mary L. Dudziak is the Judge Edward J. and Ruey L. Guirado Professor of Law, History and Political Science at the University of Southern California. Her publications include *Cold War Civil Rights: Race and the Image of American Democracy* and *Exporting American Dreams: Thurgood Marshall's African Journey,* and two edited collections: (with Leti Volpp) *Legal Borderlands: Law and the Construction of American Borders* and *September 11 in History: A Watershed Moment?* Her work has been supported by fellowships from the Guggenheim Foundation and the American Council of Learned Societies, and in 2007–8 she was a Member of the School of Social Science at the Institute for Advanced Studies in Princeton, N.J.

Joe R. Feagin is the Ella C. McFadden Professor of Liberal Arts at Texas A&M University. His primary research interests concern the development and structure of racial and gender prejudice and institutional, systemic discrimination. He has authored forty-eight books, including *Systemic Racism, Racist America, Social Problems: A Power-Conflict Perspective,* and *The Many Costs of Racism,* and has coauthored a number of others, among which are *The First R: How Children Learn Race and Racism, White Men on Race: Power, Privilege, and the Shaping of Cultural Consciousness,* and *Black in Blue: African-American Police Officers and Racism.* His books, including the Pulitzer-nominated *Ghetto Revolts,* have won numerous national and professional association prizes. Feagin has also published more than 180 research articles on racial, gender, and urban issues. He is the 2006 recipient of a Harvard Alumni Association lifetime achievement award and has served as president of the American Sociological Association.

John Hope Franklin was the James B. Duke Professor Emeritus of History and Professor of Legal History in the Law School at Duke University. He held a PhD in history from Harvard University and taught at Fisk University, St. Augustine's College, North Carolina Central University, and Howard University. His publications include *The Emancipation Proclamation, The Militant South, The Free Negro in North Carolina, Reconstruction After the Civil War,* and *A Southern Odyssey: Travelers in the Ante-bellum North.* His best-known work, however, remains *From Slavery to Freedom: A History of African-Americans,* now in its eighth edition. His most recent book was *My Life and an Era: The Autobiography of Buck Colbert Franklin.* His awards included the Jefferson Medal, awarded by the Council for the Advancement and Support of Education (1984); the Clarence L. Holte Literary Prize for the publication of his Jefferson Lecture in the Humanities of 1976 (1985); the Charles Frankel Prize for contributions to the humanities (1993); the first W. E. B. DuBois Award from the Fisk University Alumni Association (1995); the NAACP's Spingarn Medal; and the Presidential Medal of Freedom. Professor Franklin also received honorary degrees from more than one hundred colleges and universities.

Ophelia De Laine Gona is the daughter of the Reverend Joseph Armstrong De Laine. A former U.S. Peace Corps volunteer and high school teacher, she served for twenty-five years as Professor of Anatomy and director of educational outreach programs at the University of Medicine and Dentistry of New Jersey. Her passion for education sparked a forty-four-year career in science and education that affected the lives of both students and teachers, from junior high school through graduate and professional school levels, and has seeded the educational curricula in many schools and communities. After a lifetime of scientific research and writing she turned her attention to writing articles about her father's pivotal civil rights case. In 2004 she and her siblings accepted the Congressional Medal of Honor on behalf of their father, who died in 1974. She is currently working on a book-length account of the *Briggs* case that includes her father's biography.

Lani Guinier is a legal scholar and former civil rights lawyer who specializes in voting rights law, democratic theory and practice, educational access and pedagogy, and social justice, with an emphasis on issues of race, gender, and class. A graduate of Radcliffe and Yale Law School, she taught at the University of Pennsylvania before becoming the Bennett Boskey Professor at Harvard Law School. From 1977 to 1981 she worked in the Civil Rights Division of the U.S. Department of Justice, and in the 1980s she directed the voting rights project at the NAACP Legal Defense Fund. She has authored and coauthored numerous articles and five books, including *The Tyranny of the Majority: Fundamental Fairness and Representative Democracy*, *Becoming Gentlemen: Women, Law School, and Institutional Change* (with Michelle Fine and Jane Balin), and *The Miner's Canary: Enlisting Race, Resisting Power, Transforming Democracy* (with Gerald Torres). Professor Guinier has received many prestigious honors and awards for her teaching, writing, and public service, and is the recipient of eleven honorary degrees.

Richard Herman is Chancellor of the University of Illinois at Urbana-Champaign. A mathematician, Herman came to Illinois in 1998 as provost and vice chancellor for academic affairs. He chairs an initiative called the Science and Mathematics Teacher Imperative, sponsored by the National Association of State Universities and Land-Grant Colleges, to increase the number of middle and high school science and math teachers. Herman also assists the Council on Competitiveness as co-chair of its High Performance Computing Initiative and as a member of the steering committee for the council's Energy, Security, Innovation and Sustainability Initiative. He served as chair of the Council of Presidents of the Universities Research Association Inc., and currently is a member of the Business–Higher Education Forum. He has served as chair of the Joint Policy Board for Mathematics and as a member of the National Science Foundation's Advisory Committee for the Directorate of Mathematical and Physical Sciences. In 2008 Herman was elected to the American Academy of Arts & Sciences.

Darlene Clark Hine is Board of Trustees Professor of African American Studies and History at Northwestern University in Evanston, Illinois. She helped found the field of black women's history and has been a leading scholar in the history of African American experience. Dr. Hine served as president of the Organization of American Historians and the Southern Historical Association and has earned numerous honors, awards, and fellowships from such prestigious institutions as the Rockefeller Foundation, the Ford Foundation, and the National Endowment for the Humanities. She has authored and edited many books, including *Black Victory: The Rise and Fall of the Texas White Primary*, *Hine Sight: Black Women and the Re-Construction of American History*, and *Black Women in White: Ra-*

cial Conflict and Cooperation in the Nursing Profession, 1890–1950. Hine is working on a history of the black professional classes before *Brown v. Board.*

Freeman A. Hrabowski III has served as President of the University of Maryland, Baltimore County, since 1992. He graduated from the Hampton Institute with highest honors in mathematics and finished his PhD in higher education administration and statistics at the University of Illinois at Urbana-Champaign. His research focuses on science and math education, with an emphasis on minority participation and performance. He has coauthored *Beating the Odds* and *Overcoming the Odds,* books that focus on parenting high-achieving African American youth in science. A child-leader in the civil rights movement, his story was featured in Spike Lee's 1997 documentary, *Four Little Girls,* about the 1963 bombing of Birmingham's Sixteenth Street Baptist Church. He chairs the National Academies' Committee on Underrepresented Groups and the Expansion of the Science and Engineering Workforce Pipeline, and serves as consultant to the National Science Foundation and the National Institutes of Health, and universities and school systems nationally. Hrabowski sits on several corporate and foundation boards, and holds numerous honorary degrees, most recently from Princeton and Duke.

John Jennings is Associate Professor of Graphic Design at the University of Illinois, Urbana-Champaign. As a designer and illustrator he experiments with artistic statements that address social and political concerns. He writes and lectures frequently on visual culture, visual literacy, and the use of design for social awareness and justice. His research focuses on utilizing popular culture in design pedagogy, and his own art spans a diverse array of visual arts media, including illustration, graphic design, fashion design, Web-based media, and fine art. Jennings is the coauthor of the graphic novel *The Hole: Consumer Culture* and a cofounder of Eye Trauma Comix, a collective devoted to the recognition of comics as an art form.

Ralph Lemon is Artistic Director and founder of the international touring dance ensemble Cross Performance. He has won numerous awards, including eight Choreographer Fellowships from the National Endowment for the Arts and two BESSIE Awards. Currently dedicated to new forms of presentation, Cross Performance produces cross-cultural and cross-disciplinary projects in films, videos, exhibitions, publications, and workshops through the collaboration of dancers, musicians, media and visual artists, writers, and actors. Since 2005 he has been engaged in *The Walter Project*, a series of works in various art forms developed in collaboration with Walter Carter, a one-hundred-year-old African American man who has lived his entire life in Bentonia, Mississippi. The eventual inclusion of other Bentonia residents in *The Walter Project* has led to creation of the Mississippi Institute, a formal structure through which local residents can participate in the development and production of Ralph's artistic work.

George Lipsitz is Professor of Black Studies and Sociology at the University of California, Santa Barbara. Known as father of American popular culture studies, his work focuses on issues of race, culture, and social identities; twentieth-century U.S. history; and social movements. His seminal essay, "Listening to Learn and Learning to Listen: Popular Culture, Cultural Theory, and American Studies," published in *American Quarterly* (1990), motivated scholars to listen to the popular voices that write, film, photograph, manufacture, dance, sculpt, paint, and thus describe American history, the American story. He is the award-winning author of *The Possessive Investment in Whiteness, Rainbow at Midnight: Labor and Culture in the 1940s, Time Passages: Collective Memory and American Popular Culture, Dangerous Crossroads*, and *A Life in the Struggle: Ivory Perry and the Culture of Opposition.*

James W. Loewen taught race relations for twenty years at the University of Vermont and was on the faculty at Tougaloo College in Mississippi during the years when Brown was implemented (1969–71). Loewen's highly popular book, *Lies My Teacher Told Me: Everything Your High School History Textbook Got Wrong*, was a response to the blind nationalism and plain misinformation he discovered in a two-year survey of high school textbooks conducted at the Smithsonian Institution. He also coauthored the award-winning *Mississippi: Conflict and Change*. This textbook was not approved for use in the Mississippi school system, leading to the pathbreaking First Amendment lawsuit *Loewen et al. v. Turnipseed, et al.* His other publications include *The Mississippi Chinese: Between Black and White, Sundown Towns*, and *Lies Across America: What Our Historic Markers and Monuments Get Wrong.*

Joy Ann Williamson Lott is Associate Professor of Education at the University of Washington in Seattle. Her work has appeared in the *Journal of Negro Education, History of Education Quarterly, History of Higher Edu-*

cation Annual, and several edited volumes. Her first book, *Black Power on Campus: The University of Illinois, 1965–1975,* charts the evolution of black consciousness on predominately white American campuses during the critical period between the mid-1960s and mid-1970s, presenting the black student movement at the University of Illinois as an illuminating microcosm of similar movements across the country. Her text addresses the emergence of Black Power ideology, the impact of black student activism, and notions of self-advancement versus racial solidarity. Lott's most recent book is entitled *Radicalizing the Ebony Tower: Black Colleges and the Black Freedom Struggle in Mississippi.*

Laughlin McDonald has been director of the Voting Rights Project of the American Civil Liberties Union in Atlanta, Georgia, since 1972. He has represented minorities in numerous discrimination cases and specializes in the area of voting rights. He has argued cases before the Supreme Court, testified frequently before Congress on voting rights issues, and written for scholarly and popular publications on a variety of civil liberties issues. His most recent book, *A Voting Rights Odyssey: Black Enfranchisement in Georgia,* is a chronicle of the struggle undertaken by African Americans to achieve their constitutional right to vote in Georgia. In it he illuminates racial discrimination in voting, from slavery to the present, and includes perspectives of both black community leaders and white Georgians. Concentrating on Georgia, one of the biggest offenders of equal voting rights, he spotlights the prominence of race across history in the political process and decision making.

David O'Brien is Associate Professor at the University of Illinois specializing primarily in European art of the eighteenth and nineteenth centuries. His articles have appeared in *Burlington Magazine, French Historical Studies, French History, Contemporary French Civilization,* and in exhibition catalogs. He is the author of *After the Revolution: Antoine-Jean Gros, Painting and Propaganda under Napoleon.* Professor O'Brien has a secondary interest in contemporary art. With David Prochaska he wrote the catalog *Beyond East and West: Seven Transnational Artists.*

James C. Onderdonk is the Associate Director for Education and Outreach for the Institute for Computing in Humanities, Arts, and Social Science and the head of Conferences and Institutes, a division of the Office of Continuing Education at the University of Illinois at Urbana-Champaign. Prior to joining the University of Illinois, he managed continuing education and degree-completion programs for U.S. Navy personnel stationed aboard ships and submarines of the Atlantic Fleet and in the United Kingdom. His research interests include the impact of technology on pedagogy and the future of the textbook.

Harlem-born poet **Sekou Sundiata's** work in print, performance, music, and theater is grounded in African American culture. His work is informed by the Black arts/Black aesthetic movement of the 1960s and 1970s and references the sounds of blues, funk, jazz, Afro-Caribbean percussion and jazz musicians John Coltrane and Miles Davis. Sundiata's poetry lies at the intersection of art, humanities, and public dialogue and involves collaborations with arts presenters, campuses, and communities. His *blessing the boats* responded to his personal experience of heroin addiction, kidney disease, transplantation, and recovery. His last project, *the 51st (dream) state,* performed at the Melbourne Festival and at the Brooklyn Academy of Music in 2006, is a contemplation of a national soul and the meaning of America in personal and public life. The recipient of many fellowships and grants, Sundiata taught as a professor of writing at the New School in New York City for many years. He was featured in *The Language of Life,* the Bill Moyers PBS series on poetry. In 1997 his album *The Blue Oneness of Dreams* was nominated for a Grammy Award. Sundiata died in 2007.

Christopher Teal is a career diplomat with the U.S. State Department and currently serves as head of public affairs for the U.S. Consulate General in Guadalajara, Mexico. Previously, he worked in Washington at the Foreign Press Center in charge of the African portfolio and as the public affairs desk officer for southern Europe and the Caucasus. Before joining the Foreign Service, Teal worked with award-winning journalist Juan Williams on *Thurgood Marshall: American Revolutionary,* his biography of the former Supreme Court justice. Teal recently completed a new biography, *Hero of Hispaniola,* about the first African American diplomat, Ebenezer D. Bassett. He also holds a masters degree in international relations from the George Washington University.

Nicholas Watkins, Ph.D., is HOK's Director of Research and Innovation. He specializes in Environmental Psychology. Among his responsibilities, Watkins creates design solutions for project-specific applications. His research findings can be found in several publications and venues including *The Handbook of Environmental Psychology, Evidence-Based Healthcare Design,* and the *Health Environments Research and Design Journal.* His professional work focuses on interactions between humans and their built environments that reflect excellence in design and contribute to physical and psychological well-being.

Carrie Mae Weems is an award-winning artist who has participated in over a hundred one-person and group shows from San Francisco to South Africa and Germany. Her photography and installations have been featured in exhibitions at the Whitney Museum of American Art, the Museum of Modern Art in New York, the Getty Museum, and numerous other galleries, museums, and universities. Explorations of African American society, culture, and folklore converge powerfully in her art, which addresses the ways in which images, particularly documentary photographs, have shaped our perception of color, gender, and class. Weems has taught courses at Harvard University, Hunter College, and Williams College, and was awarded the 2005–6 Joseph H. Hazen Rome Prize Fellowship.

Juan Williams, one of America's leading political commentators and journalists, is the author of the critically acclaimed biography *Thurgood Marshall: American Revolutionary* and the bestseller *Eyes on the Prize: America's Civil Rights Years, 1954–1965,* companion to the television series. A six-part PBS documentary, aired in 2003, was based on his book *This Far by Faith: Stories from the African American Religious Experience.* As a political analyst Williams has appeared regularly on the television programs *Nightline, Washington Week in Review,* CNN *Crossfire, Capitol Gang Sunday, Fox News Sunday,* and *America's Black Forum,* as well as on National Public Radio. His articles have been published in *Newsweek, Fortune, Atlantic Monthly, Ebony, GQ,* and *The New Republic.* During twenty-three years at the *Washington Post,* he served as editorial writer, columnist, and White House correspondent. Williams's documentaries have won widespread critical praise, and he has received an Emmy Award for television documentary writing.

INDEX

The University of Illinois Press
is a founding member of the
Association of American University Presses.

Composed in 10.5/13 Adobe Minion Pro
with Gill Sans display
by Jim Proefrock
at the University of Illinois Press
Designed by Dennis Roberts
Manufactured by Thomson-Shore, Inc.

University of Illinois Press
1325 South Oak Street
Champaign, IL 61820-6903
www.press.uillinois.edu